BOCA
RATON

LITERARY
SOCIETY

Max M. Kapelman

SPONSORED BY

Northern Trust Bank.
The Private Bank

THE NEWS

NORTHERN TRUST PLAZA • 301 YAMATO ROAD • SUITE 1111 • BOCA RATON, FL 33431-4929

ENTERING
NEW
WORLDS

ENTERING NEW WORLDS

The Memoirs
of a Private Man
in Public Life

AMBASSADOR
MAX M. KAMPELMAN

HarperCollinsPublishers

FIRST EDITION

Designed by Alma Orenstein

Library of Congress Cataloging-in-Publication Data

Kampelman, Max M., 1920–
    Entering new worlds : the memoirs of a private man in public life /
Max M. Kampelman.—1st ed.
        p.   cm.
    Includes index.
    ISBN 0-06-039133-2 (cloth)
    1. Kampelman, Max M., 1920–   . 2. Ambassadors—United States—
Biography.   3. United States—Foreign relations—1945–   I. Title.
E840.8.K26A3   1991
327.2′092—dc20
[B]   90-56381

91 92 93 94 95 AC/HC 10 9 8 7 6 5 4 3 2 1

This Book Is Dedicated to
MAGGIE

who has provided me with a wife's love and
understanding during our more than forty-two years of
married life together. My partner in life, the mother of
our five children (Anne, Jeffrey, Julia, David, and Sarah),
she and they rejoiced with me and anguished with me,
remaining steadfast and caring. Maggie has been my
moral compass and my intellectual inspiration, not
always appreciated but always indispensable.
Without her presence and support, my work would
have been more difficult, my accomplishments
fewer, and my life less fulfilling.

Contents

Illustrations follow page 82.

Winds of Change

Writing a memoir was not something I had ever expected to do. Long ago, I wrote a Ph.D. thesis and then turned it into a book. It was harder work than I could have imagined, more burdensome, looking back, than many more serious tasks I have undertaken since. I could never get out of my mind, as I wrote, that words on paper were permanent and required serious care. One book certainly seemed enough.

Beyond that, I am a fairly private person, even in public life. I welcome compliments, but I have never wanted to preen in public, puffing the sanitized details of my life for readers to admire. I have enjoyed the limelight when I was in it, but leaving my hieroglyphs on the wall for historians to ponder was not especially compelling. Nor did I have an interest in spending my time regurgitating my life. Yet, when several friends and people in the business of book publishing suggested, toward the end of my work in the State Department, that I write about my experiences in negotiating with the Soviets, I began to give it some thought.

The timing was right. I was not quite ready to retire, but I was not going to be as busy as I had been. The Soviet Union was in the midst of significant change, and I had spent a great deal of time teaching and observing the Communist phenomenon and, from 1980 to 1989, dealing with the Soviets on human rights and arms control issues. There were some lessons, I thought, that could be divined from those efforts, although I still wasn't sure they merited a book by me. I knew others with a longer career of dealing with the Soviets and with arms control matters would be offering their views, and I didn't want to be redundant.

What also troubled me was that I never felt fully comfortable in any niche. Studying intensely at the yeshiva, I knew I could never live a life of Jewish orthodoxy. In a college filled with fine middle-class values, I found myself attracted to trade unions and social change. On the eve of a war against evil incarnate, I was a committed pacifist and became a conscientious objector, yet I was a Jew, one of the few in the CO camps. As an adult, my liberalism was permeated with anti-Communism and a commitment to majoritarianism that made me suspect in the eyes of many civil libertarians.

The process continued with my being a Democrat working in a Republican administration, but never able to identify comprehensively with Republican domestic ideology. Finally, even in recent months, with my consistent anti-Soviet record, I found that my belief that the Soviet Union was fast disappearing as "the present danger" to our values and security raised eyebrows.

My comfort comes from the late philosopher Sidney Hook, who wrote: "No one who accepts the sovereignty of truth can be a foot soldier in a party or movement. He will always find himself out of step."

For all that, I decided that my experiences were somewhat different from those of others, in part because I had come to the negotiating table not as a foreign service specialist but after a life that was shaped by early Jewish religious training, a pacifist youth, work with the labor movement, a brief academic career, some years on Capitol Hill as a congressional aide, a longer time as a Washington lawyer, a variety of political and civic activities, and a lifetime concern with democracy as a way of life and a system of government.

I have had a special if not unique window on life in the United States since the end of the Depression and the beginning of World War II. I was, furthermore, born on the third anniversary of the Russian Revolution. My maturing as well as my adult years spanned the period of our country's intense relations with the Soviet Union, with their bobs and weaves, their warmths and frosts. If I could tell those stories as part of telling my own, if I could reflect on a half century of American and world politics as it influenced the scope as well as the minutiae of my life, I believed the story might be worth telling.

There is another reason I decided to tell my story. I recently read that children remember their mothers much more than their fathers. I know I do. The children insisted that they loved their fathers, but that Father worked very hard, generally kept his inner thoughts to himself, and did not talk much. My experience tells me this is true. I write to redress that inadequacy. I want my children to know my story. To that extent, this public book is also a private communication. I also want my children's contemporaries to know the story of this immensely interesting and significant period in which I have lived.

My journey began in an immigrant Jewish family, led me to pacifism and a commitment to nonviolence and brotherhood, and, with evolving experiences, carried me beyond pacifism in a search for peace and freedom. To reflect on this journey and our new relations with a Soviet Union and a Communist bloc undergoing cataclysmic change suddenly made the effort worthwhile.

During my life, I have been privileged to know some historic participants in world affairs. I think particularly of two men, vastly different from one another, who affected my outlook on life and society: one a close and longtime friend, almost like an older brother; the other an acquaintance and a symbol. If I could capture what they meant to me, to the causes they espoused, and to the society of which I was a part, the book would be more than my story. Our interrelationship could provide a context for my own less heroic experiences.

I was blessed early on by meeting Hubert Humphrey, an extraordinary human being and public servant who served with great distinction as mayor of Minneapolis, United States senator from Minnesota, and vice president of the United States, as well as Democratic candidate for president in 1968. He showed me what love of people and the democratic process could accomplish. He led me, as he led thousands of others, into active involvement in the political life of this nation. He was the best teacher I ever had, teaching by word and thrilling example. He was a friend in the fullest meaning of the word for more than thirty years, until his death in 1978.

My negotiations with the Soviets led me to another exceptional person. As I think of the impressive affirmation of human rights that rolled through the Soviet Union and other Communist countries during the period of my negotiating with them, Andrei Sakharov highlighted the process. A brave man, he fought the power of totalitarian government in the Soviet Union at great personal risk and cost. He touched another part of my life. Sakharov kept alive the hope for democratic change in his country when few others had the integrity and courage to do so. He suffered exile, political abuse, isolation. Before he died in his sleep in December 1989, he had been elected to the Soviet parliament and seemed likely to become an ever stronger voice for a new and democratic Soviet Union. To have admired him at a distance, to have known him even slightly, left me feeling that he represented, better than anyone I have even known, the power and the glory of human dignity and the ideals of liberty.

I have in these pages literally told my story. Norman Sherman, a longtime friend since our days at the University of Minnesota, who later became Hubert Humphrey's press assistant, interviewed me for many more than one hundred hours and spent time reviewing my files, personal papers, and voluminous materials at the Minnesota Historical Society. After our taped exchanges and my dictation were transcribed, he edited them into a narrative that I could edit further, shape, and amend. That, plus extracts from speeches and other statements I have made over the years, is the book which follows. Without him, there would not have been a book.

Oddly, I have enjoyed the telling, rediscovering the people who molded my views, recalling the events, some long forgotten, through which I learned something important or played some role in effecting change, and savoring my accomplishments and my public service. It has been quite an unexpected and unpredictable trip and a pretty satisfying life, for which I am eternally grateful.

This is not a history book, although it may shed some additional light on important historical events of my lifetime. This is not a biography in the full sense of the term, in that many details of my life will not be found here. This is also not a primer on arms control or foreign policy, although the political insights and atmosphere provided by this and other books will enhance understanding of the evolution and meaning of disarmament and international relations, beyond their technicalities.

There are a few heroes in the book, but really no villains. This may be a shortcoming. I have not kissed and told; I have not tried to get even with anyone. I have always tried to keep my emotions private, although tears come readily and unexpectedly and quietly to my eyes as I see sadness or joy in myself or in others. I have tried to write a reflection on my times, not a self-indulgent diary of personal pique or praise. There have certainly been people I have not admired during my life, and I say so as gently as I can where it is relevant. There have been people I felt had damaged or hurt me, but I have for the most part ignored or excused them. I have been satisfied in life not to spend much time trying to justify myself, and I didn't think it sensible to do so in this memoir. It is not my personal tendency to go for the jugular, and I trust I can also avoid the tendency to lunge at the capillaries.

Finally, a warning to the reader. My friend Louis J. Halle brought a quotation from William James to my attention that clearly reflected my concerns as I wrote this book and read other autobiographical materials. James said: "The most frequent source of false memory is the accounts we give to others of our experiences. Such acts we almost always make more simple and more interesting than the truth. We quote what we should have said or done rather than what we really said or did; and in the first telling we may be fully aware of the distinction, but ere long, the fiction expels the reality from memory and reigns in its stead alone. We think of what we wish had happened, of possible interpretation of acts, and soon we are unable to distinguish between things that actually happened and our own thoughts about what might have occurred. Our wishes, hopes, and sometimes fears are the controlling factor."

Several people have made this book possible. Jane Dystel was the literary agent who finally convinced me to try my hand again at book writing. Her father, Oscar Dystel, a dean in book publishing, brought us together. Simon Michael Bessie, a talented and highly distinguished editor and warm friend, has, together with his gifted wife, Cornelia, guided us along from the outset. Cynthia Barrett moved in constructively to complete the editing and production of the book. My friend and associate Ambassador Warren Zimmermann made suggestions that have been most helpful. So has my law partner David Birenbaum. My wife, Maggie, with a keen eye for truth as well as grammar, has cleaned up the manuscript in both dimensions. My daughters Julia and Sarah, along with my son Jeff, have shown keen editorial judgment. I don't understand the computer and word processor, so I stand in special awe of Gwen Smith, Nancy Tackett, and Linda Johnson, who have typed and retyped the manuscript in a mysterious way. Sharon Dardine, my secretary and assistant at the State Department, in Geneva, and now again in my law office, has looked after my professional responsibilities and helped shepherd my business life at the same time as she has kept a good editorial eye on this manuscript while it evolved from beginning to end. Finally, I thank my law partners in Fried, Frank, Harris, Shriver and Jacobson for their patience, their understanding, their encouragement, their financial support, and their friendship.

I thank them all for their contributions. I promise them, and myself, that this is my last book.

Walking on Slippery Rocks

There have been many special moments in my public life to remember and cherish. None, however, compares to the balmy June evening in 1988 at Spaso House in Moscow when an agreement to limit nuclear arms was celebrated. Although I did not believe that arms control was as fundamental to the pursuit of peace as many of its advocates asserted, the symbolism and drama of the moment were overwhelming.

The mansion itself, completed in 1914 just before the Russian Revolution, was extraordinary. Built by a rich Siberian merchant family, it had been the official residence of American ambassadors since we established diplomatic relations with the Soviet Union in 1934.* From the outside, with its blue dome and yellow and white painted exterior, it seemed the very essence of Mother Russia. Its elegant interior was worthy of the czarist court and of Count Rostov himself.

But that night it was more than an elegant Russian building from

---

* In January 1934, a very junior foreign service officer, George Kennan, negotiated the lease. Less than twenty years later, President Truman appointed him ambassador to the Soviet Union. Kennan became the author of our Soviet containment policy and was also an eminent scholar and writer. He had served as counselor of the Department of State at the end of his career, as I did. In March 1989, I had the privilege of introducing him to Robert Zoellick, my successor as counselor, at a luncheon I hosted for all living former counselors at the State Department.

an ancient regime; it was an oasis of American spirit and style, open and exuberant. Ronald and Nancy Reagan were hosts at a dinner for Mikhail and Raisa Gorbachev, where a palpable, barely restrained joy overcame formality, and glasses clinked in a celebration of hope. The most routine state dinner is exciting. This was not routine.

That morning, the Intermediate-Range and Shorter-Range Missiles Treaty negotiated in Geneva had been ratified by the two leaders in a historic step that we hoped would lead to a more peaceful world and away from the danger of nuclear holocaust. Both countries agreed to eliminate nuclear weapons that could carry their immense devastation from approximately 500 to 5,500 kilometers in a matter of minutes. Beyond that, and almost more surprising, we agreed on verification procedures that meant observers from each country could be physically present at the manufacturing, storage, and launch sites of the other. For us in an open society, that was a considered concession; for the Soviets and their closed society, an incredible one.

The ironies of American politics were certainly never clearer for me than that night—my being in Moscow as a United States ambassador, a traditional liberal Democrat working enthusiastically and effectively for a conservative Republican president. That I was also a Jew in a country where anti-Semitism had a long, ugly history, and had been almost de facto official policy, made the moment even more ironic.

It was an incredibly long way from the Bronx where I grew up, living for a while in a depressing tenement filled with creepy cockroaches, inhabited by a succession of poor immigrant families, many of whom had come from Russia and its pogroms. They moved in and out, some on their way up in the social and economic world they had adopted, some just muddling through, but all of them free of old-country fears.

In 1985, when President Reagan asked me to head the negotiations on nuclear arms control, few thought we could reach agreement on any of the complex subjects we were assigned. I myself was skeptical and uncertain, although I had helped forge an agreement on human rights and other aspects of European cooperation and security with the Soviets just a year and a half earlier, after three intense years of negotiations in Madrid. That agreement clearly benefited us and enhanced the spread of Western democratic ideals, but I certainly did not trust the Soviets.*

---

* Charles Bohlen, an outstanding American diplomat who served as our ambassador in Moscow, often said that there were two classes of people he knew were lying—people who said whiskey didn't affect them, and people who claimed they knew how to negotiate with the Russians. Interestingly, his daughter, Avis, also a Soviet expert and a career foreign service officer, served as my deputy during our Geneva arms talks.

Soviet leader Konstantin Chernenko, though sick, had been a tough, old-fashioned Marxist head of the Soviet government. He was generally rigid and unyielding, an extension of the Stalin years and of Leonid Brezhnev, whom he had served dutifully. It was hard to believe that the Madrid agreement of 1983 was a foreshadowing of change. But the Soviet Union's attitude, for whatever reasons, appeared to shift in significant ways after Mikhail Gorbachev came to power in 1985 just as our Geneva talks got under way.

Inevitably, there were passing moments during the first year or so of talks when I thought that, in spite of our efforts, the Soviets were not ready to reach an agreement. Ultimately, however, I became convinced that an agreement was not only attainable but would satisfy the interests of both countries and might well serve all humanity.

I often recalled what my friend and mentor Hubert Humphrey* was fond of saying: negotiations are risky. Hubert, who was a great consensus builder no matter where he served, said the process of negotiations was "like crossing a river by walking on slippery rocks. The possibility of disaster is on every side." But, Hubert added, it was often the best way—sometimes the only way—to get to the other side.

We had successfully crossed a raging river in the arms negotiations, walking on slippery rocks. We had found common ground. A meeting that began with an arm's-length "Let's talk" reached a conclusion where we each said, with satisfaction, "Let's act." Now, having agreed on the elimination of intermediate-range missiles, we were continuing, without pause, to talk of ways of drastically reducing the heavier, longer-range strategic weapons of our arsenals, those that reached farther than 5,500 kilometers, that cross the ocean in minutes. The Intermediate Nuclear Force (INF) talks were at an end and the Strategic Arms Reduction Talks (START) were continuing full steam.

I arrived late at the Spaso House dinner because of those continuing negotiations with the Soviets, but I walked slowly from my car to the front door, enjoying the fresh air and gentle wind that had come up. After a long time indoors, it was a moment to savor.

I had been in the residence before, but that night the white columns, the white marble walls, and the circular gallery at the entrance overwhelmed me. It was like a perfect movie set. The ceiling of the main reception room towers eighty-two feet above the floor. An im-

---

* Hubert Humphrey was mayor of Minneapolis from 1945 to 1948, United States senator from 1949 to 1965, vice president of the United States from 1965 to 1969, the Democratic candidate for president in 1968, and then senator again from 1971 until his death in 1978.

mense gold and crystal chandelier, mahogany-framed mirrors, and carved doorframes speak of opulence and artistry.

George Shultz, my boss as secretary of State and a special friend whom I admired immensely, was near the entrance as I came into the reception hall. I moved to his side to describe what had gone on after he had left the discussions that afternoon. He asked several questions and nodded in approval, and though my report was over in a few minutes, we continued to talk. He was exultant and so was I, although neither of us let the feeling show in that public place. The day had been an extraordinary one; we both knew we were witnessing and had contributed to a momentous change in American-Soviet relations from which the fallout would be peaceful, not nuclear.

As we separated, I glanced up and away. There at the room's opposite end was Andrei Sakharov, almost bald, with his distinguishing fringe of white hair, his deep-set eyes searching for some familiar face. The renowned physicist, the Soviet's most visible dissident and winner of the 1975 Nobel Prize for Peace, and his wife, Yelena Bonner, a heroine of the Soviet human rights movement in her own right, caught sight of me. After a moment's hesitation, we headed rapidly toward each other and a warm embrace.

Yelena and I had originally met during her first trip to the United States about a year earlier. She had been as stalwart a dissident as her husband, one of the original Moscow-Helsinki monitors, making the case for human rights in the Soviet Union as consistently and courageously as he. Under world pressure and in their capricious way, the Soviet authorities had finally permitted her to leave Gorky, where Sakharov had been in exile, to come to the United States for medical treatment. We had met for a second time when I joined George Shultz and his cheerful, unassuming, and clearly supportive wife, Obie, in visiting them both in their Moscow apartment after Dr. Sakharov had been released from exile, no longer quite a discard of the Soviet state.

Sakharov had spoken warmly then of my human rights work as the head of the U.S. delegation to the Madrid discussions, part of the Helsinki Final Act review that took place from 1980 to 1983. The words of this gutsy man who had sacrificed a creative and comfortable scientific career to battle for human rights moved me. He said, "You remembered us when others were ready to forget."

Now here he was again, frail but smiling, the guest of the president of the United States in the presence of the highest-ranking Soviets, including those who had exiled him. At that moment, as the three of us greeted one another and embraced with affection, abstract diplomatic talk of human rights took on a powerful personal dimension. The Sakharovs were for me a special manifestation of a changing Soviet society. Their presence was a significant sign of an improving United States–Soviet relationship. That would not have been possible without understanding that America's strength related to its commitment to human values.

Then the moment arrived when the heads of state and their wives appeared. The noise of chatter died quickly, and a receiving line formed. It was a delicious sight to see the Gorbachevs and Reagans standing side by side, animated and obviously pleased with themselves and one another, overcoming, at least for the occasion, stormy rhetoric and intense historic adversarial relationships.

I stood back for a bit and watched as the Sakharovs went through the line. As they approached the Reagans and the Gorbachevs, I found myself staring almost rudely, wondering what would happen. The Reagans behaved as I would have expected: he effusively, she with reserve. Gorbachev himself was almost as welcoming as Reagan, greeting Dr. Sakharov without embarrassment and with some warmth. His wife, Raisa, was much more formal, unsmiling as she acknowledged them. I thought from a distance that I discerned a bit of disapproval showing in her demeanor, but I could not be sure.

In a few moments, I joined the line of guests. When I reached the Reagans, they thanked me for my work in Geneva, he particularly appreciative, aglow in his triumph; she warm and gracious, but more controlled, as she always was. The Gorbachevs then congratulated me with exceptional grace and clear awareness of my role. It was heady stuff, and I went into dinner feeling extraordinarily good. As I looked over the milling guests, I felt even better.

The Sakharovs were not the only Soviet dissidents in the room. When we were seated, there was a refusenik or a religious leader or an intellectual—a Sakharov equivalent, all outsiders or critics of Soviet policy—at every table, talking or smiling or looking tensely across the pink peony centerpieces at Russian and American diplomats and bureaucrats.

At my table, Anatoly Dobrynin, the Soviet ambassador to the United States for twenty years, sat next to me, with Sakharov just a few seats away. In 1975, Soviet authorities had refused Sakharov permission to accept his Nobel Prize in person, but I had often quoted a sentence from the speech his wife delivered for him, and its substance raced through my mind just then.

He had written, "I am convinced that international trust, mutual understanding, disarmament, and international security are inconceivable without an open society with freedom of information, freedom of conscience, the right to publish, and the right to travel and choose the country in which one wishes to live."

I couldn't resist asking Dobrynin whether he had ever imagined being at a formal dinner in Moscow with Sakharov. He began with a diplomat's response, "Sakharov is a Russian patriot—" I interrupted undiplomatically, "Yes, but that didn't stop his exile to Gorky." Dobrynin shrugged and smiled almost imperceptibly, and we moved quickly to other topics, soon including Sakharov, whose English was weak, in our conversation. If Dobrynin was uncomfortable, it never showed. He not only spoke easily with Sakharov, but graciously interpreted for us when Sakharov's English caused him difficulty.

As one course followed another, I thought about my days as a conscientious objector doing alternative service during World War II, a volunteer human guinea pig in a starvation experiment. That spartan life, and its fifteen hundred daily calories, was so far from the opulence I now saw that I mused silently on the different paths I had followed in search of peace and in search of myself.

The pacifism of my youth, my belief in the power of personal witness to change the world, had given way to an acceptance, indeed an appreciation, of force as a deterrent in a nuclear age in keeping the peace, and had made me a tough negotiator. Without that basic shift, I could not have been an effective presence in seeking an arms control agreement. I felt good about where I was, and my feelings were heightened by the day of negotiations and an evening of celebration.

When the toasts were exchanged between President Reagan and Gorbachev, I received a jolt as I heard Reagan speak. It was as if he had read my mind. I did not know it, but his gift to the Soviet leader that night was apparently a copy of a Gary Cooper film of the fifties, *Friendly Persuasion*, dealing with a pacifist Quaker Indiana farm family caught in the dilemmas of the Civil War. Reagan referred to it in his toast, noting the need for "holding out for a better way of settling things." Gorbachev nodded energetically.

There was plenty of glory to go around, and others had claim to the same self-satisfied feelings. I knew I was not the central figure. Certainly without both Reagan's and Gorbachev's desire for agreement, the process resulting in the treaty would never have begun or caught on. It was their triumph first.

George Shultz, an extraordinarily impressive public servant of patriotic fervor, keen intellect, and deep integrity (and the president's loyal friend), had been indispensable to the process, giving me both guidance and negotiating room in the discussions. Without him and his counterpart, Soviet Foreign Minister Eduard Shevardnadze, patiently and steadfastly and endlessly meeting and talking and fashioning the dialogue, the process would have faltered. It was certainly their triumph second.

Without a handful of others, on both sides, who were diligent negotiators day after day, the often tedious and always delicate process would never have survived. Our chief INF negotiator, Ambassador Maynard Glitman, an experienced and persistent career foreign service officer, led the way. It was the negotiators' triumph third.

I looked upon myself as a kind of linchpin in the whole process, holding things together in Geneva, being conciliatory or tough as the situation required, consulting periodically with the president and Shultz, but constantly pushing forward on my own. I was also aware that many in the Congress, particularly but not exclusively the Democrats, doubted the president's sincerity, and looked to me to provide credibility to our negotiating intent. That had made me particularly careful about how I behaved, because without congressional support, all was for naught.

I had listened carefully to the words of the Russians, first in Madrid, where I began negotiating with the Soviets on human rights, and then in Geneva. I had urged the Soviets and my colleagues to understand that two monologues did not make a dialogue.

I had searched behind the words for their true meaning and had tried to fathom their implications as well. Their words often made me angry, particularly during our human rights negotiations in Madrid, disconnected as they frequently were from reality and the truth. As a negotiator, while I controlled my anger, I felt that excessive nonsense had to be labeled for what it was and specious arguments faced down as they were delivered. Slurs against the United States and its honor and truthfulness—against *my* country—demanded quick response. I was an unrepentant chauvinist when appropriate.

In a sense, the negotiations, as process, were more art than science, often more dependent on nuance than on discrete data, on knowing when to respond testily, when to remain silent, when to wait and produce a more formal answer, when to go back to Washington for guidance. But the art required absorbing and balancing a great deal of complicated detail, always aware of the ultimate, omnipresent consideration: could our interests, and those of our allies, be protected and the hope of world peace nurtured at the same time? I became convinced they could.

All of us from Reagan and Shultz on down clearly wanted an

agreement from day one, but as a lawyer, I had learned a long time before that a bad agreement is worse than none. It was a mistake, I thought, for a negotiator to judge success or failure merely by whether talk produces a couple of signatures on the bottom of a page.

Success could only be measured by the content and consequences of the agreement. What appeared above the signatures was not an empty document, agreed to for the sake of having something to sign. It was real. It was important for what it accomplished in arms control, for its service to U.S. national security, for what it meant for future cooperation between the superpowers, and for what it symbolized for the rest of the world.

Not so long ago, our oldest daughter, Anne, presented me with an embroidered pillowcase on which the following 1809 quotation from John Adams was inscribed: "If I had refused to institute a negotiation or had not persevered in it, I should have been degraded in my own estimation as a man of honor." I hope it does not sound pretentious for me to identify with that observation.

Ultimately, the negotiations were my responsibility, my success in some ways, just as they would perhaps have been considered my failure had we not reached agreement. They were, in any case, an appropriate part of a personal quest that had begun long before.

1

Growing Up in the Bronx

Growing up Jewish in the Bronx was a little like growing up Finnish in Helsinki, or German in Berlin. Basically, you met and knew only people like yourself. Until I went to college in 1937 at age sixteen, all my personal friends were Jewish and children of recent immigrants. We were not all precisely alike in our neighborhood, but our similarities far outweighed our differences. We shared common roots and common goals.

Our roots were Jewish and mostly Eastern European. Our parents reminisced about the old countries from which they had recently come, but no one wanted to go back. They might occasionally talk with sadness of family left behind, but there was little yearning for another time or a distant country. They had fled anxious lives in places where fear and deprivation and discrimination were commonplace because they were Jews and outsiders. They had been minorities surrounded by hostility that seemed permanent, certainly beyond their ability to change.

They were happy to be Americans, even when life was frequently tough and sometimes lonely. The reason was simple. In the towns of Poland, Romania, and Russia, in the shtetls of Eastern Europe, survival or escape dominated their thoughts; here they talked of hopes and dreams. If the dreams naturally exceeded reality for many immigrants, if they were still a minority, it was also true that fear was gone, survival seemed certain, and escape was unnecessary. Discrimination existed, but it was almost irrelevant to most of their immediate concerns, and poverty was only a way station soon to be left behind.

"Here is better" was the message I heard from my parents, quietly from their lips but thunderously from their hearts. They believed that here their son (their only child) and their neighbors' children would certainly grow to be successful—businessmen and accountants and teachers and political leaders and doctors and lawyers—and would inevitably thrive in freedom, overcoming any obstacles that might arise. Our common goals were to maintain the essence of our Jewishness even as we grew up to attain important roles in this new world.

We were Americans, democrats with a vengeance, able at last to become not what the state permitted, but what we individually were capable of accomplishing. We might be poor, but we had reached the promised land, and tomorrow would be better. That theme was constant, the variations only slight.

We would learn, we would excel, we would be free men and women and successful Americans. I heard that message from my earliest days: at dinner as I sat quietly among adults, when I walked hand-in-hand with my parents to the synagogue, when we would gather with aunts, uncles, cousins, and friends to celebrate a bar mitzvah or the Passover seder.

We took seriously our ancient religion and the ethical values it taught, but my parents more often conveyed to me with passion an American credo of democracy and justice and freedom. They usually spoke Yiddish to each other in the early days, but they almost always spoke English, albeit not the King's, to me, for that was the language of my future.

All of us, immigrant parents and American children, lived with a single, compelling hope: to find fulfillment in America. I have never lost that feeling. Though our roots were ethnic and religious and distant, we were planted in the nourishing soil of democracy.

I was born on Eagle Avenue on the third anniversary of the Russian Revolution.* But November 7 was simply my birthday; I doubt

---

* In an editorial in the February 1, 1987, issue of *Izvestia*, note is taken of the "cruel irony of fate" which required me, with my "zoological hatred for Communism" (I had been the first president of the Friends of the National Zoo) and my "cheap posturing" (I had been on the board of the Arena Stage) to witness the successes of the Soviet Union being celebrated on every one of my birthdays.

that my family knew or cared that I shared it with that historic event. Their focus was here, and my early years were lived as part of a nurturing family who focused their hopes on me, their only child. (My parents' closest friends and neighbors were Eddie and Bertha Altman. Their eldest child, Eleanor, was two and a half years older than I and my father's favorite before I was born. For years I heard that Eleanor's resentment at my arrival led her one day to lift me from my crib and drag me to the dumbwaiter lift that removed garbage from the apartment. A close call.) Education, of course, was the first step, and public schools were attractive because they were so "American." My parents weren't quite ready for that, however. My parents were not prepared to give up what they knew: the value of the discipline of a yeshiva parochial school education, and their Jewish faith. We were of both worlds.

Though we kept a generally kosher house and went on the high holidays to Rabbi Galant's synagogue on nearby 146th Street, we were clearly not intensely religious in the most fundamentalist sense. I am not sure I understood that then. My parents were believers who were proud of our Jewish faith and its rituals, but faith adjusted itself to their American quest.*

What commanded our attention thoroughly was hard work in this new world. Earning a living was obviously the first serious step away from being a nobody. My father had come to America with his mother and father around 1910 and had, without a formal education, begun to learn the butcher's trade. My mother, whose father was well educated and relatively successful, came alone a little later, grieving for a brother who had been killed in World War I, a conscript in the Austro-Hungarian army.

Though they came from the same small Romanian town, Czernowitz, in the province of Bukovina, they had not known each other in Europe.† They met in a traditional place for young immigrants, one of

---

* I once heard Harry Golden—journalist, humorist, and a lay Jewish philosopher of sorts—say on the radio that when he was young, he said to his father, "If you don't believe in God, why do you go to the synagogue so regularly?" His father answered, "Jews go to the synagogue for all sorts of reasons. My friend Garfinkle who is Orthodox goes to talk to God. I go to talk to Garfinkle."

† My friend and former law partner Richard Schifter, assistant secretary of state for human rights and humanitarian affairs, recently visited Czernowitz, now in the Soviet Union, where he has family roots as well. He told me that the Kampelmacher family was prominently located—reflecting some status in the community—in the old Jewish cemetery, now overgrown and partially destroyed. I had not been aware of that. As a child I had received the impression that it was my mother's family, the Gottliebs, that was held in high esteem.

the self-help social groups based on towns of origin; in their case, it was the Independent Bukoviner Young Men's and Young Ladies' Benevolent Society. My dad borrowed enough money from the society, lent without interest, to start his own butcher shop, although it was not a kosher one.

The meat market was in a mixed neighborhood of many Irish and few Jews about a ten-minute walk from our tenement in the East Bronx. My father's customers were the non-Jews. Our part of the Bronx was poor, but relaxed and quiet, the streets clean, and the only noises the sounds of children playing nearby and the clatter of a trolley car in the distance. A walk to a nearby candy store for an egg cream or to the public library was a trip of friendly interruptions, of waves and smiles, of greetings and talk of new jobs and new residents, of college success and the marriages of children.

My mother and father often left early for the shop while my aunt, my mother's half sister, Tante Shaindel (Aunt Sabina in English, but we used the Yiddish almost exclusively), helped me get ready for the religious school I attended from my first school day until I graduated from high school. Though it is now sixty-five years since I started school, I still remember my first days there and a repeated aggravation. My teacher, a stern lady, had some trouble remembering who I was. She called me Melvin over and over again. It's not a bad name, but it wasn't mine. I suffered in silence, saying to myself, "I am Max," each time she made the mistake. I knew who I was; I was hurt that she did not.

In those early days, Shaindel, who lived with us until she married, shared with my mother the task of taking care of me, sometimes walking me to school, which was not far away, and providing a snack when I reached home or lunch when I had no school. She often read to me before I went to bed, caring for me when my mother was absent or tired from the day's work. Shaindel was devoutly Orthodox and encouraged me greatly toward religious observance, reaffirming what I learned at school. I studied hard and skipped several elementary grades, including the one where they taught proper penmanship, a skill I have never subsequently acquired.

My mother was, I later came to understand, the businessperson in the family, tough and shrewd and determined to succeed. She worked with my father, dealing with the customers, mostly women, while he cut the meat on the block behind the counter, rubbing his messy hands on his white apron. He seemed tall and strong and quite good-looking to me then, although he was clearly a little overweight. His brown felt hat sat securely on his head as he moved purposefully into the walk-in cooler with its huge blocks of ice and slabs of meat, and then out again to the chopping block, and then to the wrapping counter with its great roll of brown shiny paper. He was a quiet, dignified person, warm and kind to everyone and especially loving to me. Above all, I remember him as a proud man, proud of his skill and proud of his success.

When things were busy, my mother sometimes did the wrapping, and she always chatted with the customers, took their money and made change, charged the meat when they could not pay, and listened to their stories. She became each person's friend by listening when the customer wanted to talk. I often sat by her side listening, too.

My day was almost as long as my parents'. While they worked, I was at the yeshiva of the Bronx, learning Hebrew, studying the Old Testament, talking of the ethics and morality of our people even in the early grades. Classes began at nine A.M., and I did not get home until suppertime, around six in the evening. Our mornings were filled with religion, Jewish history, and Hebrew lessons. After their jobs in the public schools, teachers of our secular subjects came to the yeshiva to teach us what we needed to learn so that our schools could be accredited by New York State. Fridays and Sundays were half days, and only Saturday was free of school, although it was assumed or hoped we would spend some of that time at the synagogue.

The signs of change were clear. We moved in my early years from a tenement on the poor east side of the Bronx to an apartment on the west side, then to a duplex, a separate house that was a haven and a symbol of an immigrant's rise from the hovels of Austria-Hungary. It gave us dignity.

Looking back, the weekends were splendid samplers of our lives. In the darkening shadows of sundown in our "American shtetl," Friday nights were special with the chanting of Hebrew prayers and the ritual washing of hands, joyous with tradition and our sense of obligation to God. My parents were not strictly Orthodox observers, but my mother's Friday night lighting of candles to usher in the Sabbath was an essential part of our lives. I liked the mysticism of those nights, and that appreciation has remained with me.

I sat in an adult chair, peering over the newly polished dark wood table that was covered with a lace tablecloth and laden with the Sabbath meal, the intermingled odors of freshly baked bread and chicken soup surrounding us. I looked with a child's love at my father, my mother, and Tante Shaindel as we recited our prayers, my father's voice leading us. As I learned to understand the stories of the Old

Testament, he seemed like Moses at Mount Sinai, powerful, commanding, important in mysterious ways. I recall my child's pride as I recited the simple prayers with them. *"Shema Yisroel, Adonai Elohenu, Adonai Echod*—Hear, O Israel, the Lord is our God, the Lord is One"— may not have been clear to me in all its import, but I liked the sound, and I believed it in my heart. Indeed, it became the central credo of my personal philosophy.

The electric lights were always low, and the candles flickered in the candelabra brought from the old country. It was a pleasant time, an island of respite for my parents in their busy week and a warmly satisfying time for me.

On Saturday mornings, my parents went to work in their small butcher shop. Saturday was the busiest day of the week, and they gave up any pretense of being Sabbath observers. Shaindel went religiously to the synagogue, sitting upstairs where the women were segregated. Downstairs, where I would on occasion join them, Jewish males wore, in comfort and without fear, yarmulkes and tallises, the caps and prayer shawls that had from antiquity set them apart.

After synagogue services, Shaindel would occasionally take me over to our store. Often Buster, our delivery boy, would then walk me across 149th Street to the Hub movie house, where I would watch the weekly Western serial and Disney cartoons, and then he'd pick me up after the show. When I did not go to the store, I would sit quietly doing my homework or reading a book that Shaindel and I had borrowed from the local public library. I was not a driven child, but I was focused and determined even then to learn and get on with my parents' hopes for me. At the end of the day on Saturday or during the summer, I'd sweep up the sawdust scattered on the slippery floor in the store, daring to slide about until my mother told me with a look or a word to stop. There was little time beyond that for play. When I was a little older, about eight years old, I would sit at the cashier's window, replacing my mother as she did the bookkeeping.

For me, the summers were frequently filled by the movies or by the boisterous cries of a stickball game on the street. Summer Saturdays were special, particularly as I reached my teens. Then I savored the excitement of Yankee Stadium, near our home, cheering the Bronx Bombers and especially Babe Ruth, as we exulted alongside our Irish and Italian neighbors. It was in the bleachers that assimilation began, box scores as real for the moment as the Talmudic disquisitions that I began to learn in school.

Sundays were for family. My parents had the day off, and my

father usually drove us all, in our seven-passenger old Buick, to Passaic, New Jersey, where his older brother, Philip, and my Aunt Anna lived with their three children, Harry, Stella, and Mollie.* They were older than I, almost like my siblings, and I looked forward to our visits with great anticipation. Each Sunday was a festive, extended family event that remains indelibly in my mind. My cousins and I played and talked, providing me with a sense of family an only child does not otherwise have. We sat crowded around the table for meals, the closeness a pleasant change from sitting more formally with only three or four of us at home. Birthdays and anniversaries gain from numbers, and those celebrations, while never luxurious, were more fun in Passaic, where I also spent many summers.

These pleasant memories are scarred by only one sad day when I was eight years old. My father's mother, wearing her best wig and with a kerchief around her head in the Orthodox tradition, would generally accompany us to Passaic, together with my uncle Max, her youngest son, a bachelor with whom she lived. At the end of another wonderful Sunday and without warning, our trip home turned into a horror. Grandmother died as we were driving home from our joyful visit. I can see her still, part of the family joy one minute and without life the next.

Our dreams took a beating with the Great Depression in late 1929, but did not crash as much as the economy. By then we had moved up to the Grand Concourse, a fancier Jewish neighborhood, where my father, on the advice of friends, had invested his earnings in some real estate. But the butcher shop fell on hard times, the investments became a drain on a diminished income, and soon we had neither shop nor fine home. We moved from the Grand Concourse to a lower duplex on Findley Avenue. I no longer had my Tante Shaindel as a companion. She had married and moved out. What had been a home virtually without tension or anxiety was now filled with the strains of our tightened situation. Even Friday nights lost some of their charm. It was hard to be Moses when you had failed. Every day was humiliating for my father and difficult for my mother. I sensed it in their moods and words, and I saw it in major events like the loss of the apartment house and the business.

Even little changes robbed us of the pleasures we had earned. My father, though not a very political creature, had become slightly involved

* When Philip arrived at Ellis Island, his name was changed by the authorities from Kampelmacher to Kampelman. My father's spelling was left at Kampelmacher, so we were a close family led by two brothers with different, but similar, names. That led to some confusion, and finally in December 1941, I petitioned to change my name to Kampelman.

in local Democratic politics in the mid-twenties. I loved talking to him about politics. He had met Ed Flynn, the Democratic boss of the Bronx, and, as the result of a small contribution, had received a badge indicating he was an honorary deputy sheriff. It was not much, looking back, but for him it must have been like a diploma indicating his graduation from immigrant status. Now there was no more money for political contributions, no honors to signal the Americanization that he savored.

My first political recollection was that we had cheered Al Smith through the 1928 presidential campaign and were disappointed in his defeat, although I imagine that disappointment was tempered by our approval of New York Governor Franklin Roosevelt. My father's electoral activities were a minor part of my childhood, but they provided at least a glimpse of American politics, and the special excitement stayed with me.

All of that was now set aside, a diversion we could not afford, as my parents started anew in the millinery business, once more with the help and advice of friends and family. My father's younger brother, Uncle Max, managed a ladies' hat shop, one of several owned by another Bukoviner family, Bertha and Eddie Altman. The Altmans were good friends of my folks and convinced them that more money was to be made in hats than at the butcher block and that the endeavor was more dignified. It could not have been easy for my dad to move from his own butcher business to a supporting role among the frills and ribbons of hats, but it was not easy on my mother either as their roles reversed. She was now the expert and the salesperson and buyer, while he was the cashier.

My mother was a strong woman who tried hard to keep the strain from showing. The pain made her more determined. She carried herself with a certain regal quality and had always looked back on her family, the Alter Zvi Gottlieb family, as the most respected one in the Czernowitz Jewish community, certainly more distinguished than my father's.* Almost the only time I remember my

---

* In 1984, my wife, Maggie, and I visited Czernowitz, now across the border in the Soviet Union, but found no trace of the family in either the cemetery or in records. The old synagogue was now a movie house in a university town. The cemetery was so overgrown and destroyed that we could not read the headstone names or even cut through the brush. The visit was arranged by Romanian General Secretary Ceaucescu, whom I met as the result of my work on the Helsinki Final Act. He arranged for us to fly to a town near the border and be driven to a point about fifty yards from it. There a group of Romanian soldiers marched us to the border, where an equally stiff group of Russian soldiers took over and marched us about fifty yards into Russia. There our Intourist escort, a young civilian woman, greeted us. The event had all the warmth and charm of a prisoner exchange.

mother out of control was the day I came home to announce at dinner that I wanted to become a Boy Scout. She asked what it involved, and I described the things I would learn, the merit badges I would earn, the uniform I would wear. Her eyes filled with tears, and her emotions affected her voice, which rose and cracked as she said, "No, Maxie, nó, no, no."

She would not allow it. Her brother, after whom I had received my Jewish name, Moshe Meir, was very special to her, and the thought of my wearing a uniform as he had in World War I before his death was more than she could bear. Her despair was so clear, if a little bewildering to me, that I hugged her and promised I would not become a Boy Scout.

The move from the Grand Concourse was a disappointment, although the new neighborhood had its charms. One family had a son who was a super baseball pitcher, and we were all certain he would make it to the major leagues, thus bringing honor to the Jews. That was important. When he failed, we were devastated, his dreams and our fantasies dying together.

A greater excitement was the periodic arrival of a big car carrying Max Baer, the heavyweight boxing champion of the world, to visit his parents, who lived on our block. Max and his younger brother, Buddy, a lesser fighter but magnificent in our eyes nevertheless, would show up for a Sabbath dinner now and then, and the word would spread through the neighborhood quickly. By the time they left, many of us would have bolted down our boiled chicken and recited a quick final prayer in order to loiter at an admiring distance. When Max lost the crown to Jimmy Braddock in 1935, we were clustered around the radio to hear the fight, anguishing with each punch Baer took.

By the early thirties, I was attending the Talmudical Academy, the Yeshiva College's high school, in Washington Heights, still juggling the two worlds of religion and secular life. It was likely there that I first heard the Talmudic question raised, "Why did God create only one man?" And there that I heard the answer: "In order that all men would have the same ancestor, and no man could claim superiority over another."

But baseball continued to compete with the Talmud for our attention. Though the rabbis who taught us weren't very encouraging, we took over an empty lot across from the school during recess and played baseball with an intensity that exceeded our abilities. I was a classic case of the comic's line, "Although he could not field, he could not hit." My eyesight was not great, but I persisted even when the ball went through my legs or I struck out. We became lawyers and teachers and rabbis, and not professional athletes, but the dream of athletic glory was part of growing up American. If we could not be as good as our neighborhood baseball star or as strong as the Baers, we would not be denied our fantasy of athletic preeminence.

The practical part of the dream was that I occasionally sold programs during summer vacation at Yankee Stadium, made a few cents on each, and got in free, saving the unaffordable fifty-five cents it ordinarily cost to get into the bleachers. Like so many kids, then and now, I memorized batting averages and pitching records, collected a few baseball cards, and on Monday mornings discussed with my yeshiva colleagues Babe Ruth's weekend exploits on the field. Today I wish that I had saved the baseball that he autographed for me. Baseball was an island of joy in increasingly sad surroundings.

The Depression left many of our neighbors jobless, and a pall settled on our dreams. My mother and father struggled on at the hat shop; then, in late 1935, my father had a heart attack. He survived it, but spent much of the next year at home, often weak and unable to carry a full work load. During that summer and on many Saturday mornings, I would take the Third Avenue elevated train from the Tremont Avenue Station in the Bronx, where our store was located, transfer to the Seventh Avenue subway, and get off at Times Square near the millinery manufacturing center of New York. My assigned job was to return or exchange or buy ladies' hats for the store. It required taste and judgment on my part, and my mother came to trust my choices as I returned heavily laden with hats.

My father and I spent more time together than we had before, and our talk had a different dimension from when it was filled with his hopes for himself and for me. Now, though unspoken and never explicit, his hopes were only for me. I would tell him of my studies, and we would talk as if his recovery was inevitable, but we both knew it wasn't. He never did recover. I graduated from high school in February 1937, just a few months after he died of his second heart attack at age fifty-four.* Inevitably our world became more difficult.

After several years of financial struggle, my mother and I moved again, this time seriously down the social scale to a slummy part of the East Bronx, to be near Shaindel and her husband, whom I never called anything other than "Mr. Rothin." He was a bearded older man who owned a small shop where he sold Jewish books and religious articles

---

* I remember my mother sending me to the nearby drugstore for medicine. I ran both ways and got back with it, but later that night my father died. For the next year, I went to the synagogue for the Kaddish (mourner's prayer) every single day as an Orthodox Jew would have. The first prayer service was at seven-thirty in the morning, and there were two later ones, late in the afternoon and immediately following after sundown. The older men deferred to me and let me lead the service most times.

like prayer shawls and phylacteries, the prayer thongs the Orthodox wind around their arms and forehead when they pray.

I remember Mr. Rothin saying to a customer who came in to buy a bar mitzvah present that he would be better off buying an umbrella than the prayer book he had chosen. In mock seriousness, he explained, "An umbrella he'll sometimes open." It must have been an old joke he had told a thousand times, but we all laughed heartily, and the man bought the prayer book.

But there wasn't much laughter in me in those days, or much joy for my mother or Shaindel. Our shabby surroundings were awful and depressing. I hated the sight of the cockroaches that survived every attempt to get rid of them, insolent reminders of our diminished conditions, ugly symbols of our almost dying dreams.

My mother would have liked me to continue my studies after high school at the Yeshiva, possibly ending up a rabbi. It was an idea that persisted despite an earlier evaluation by a rabbi with a reputation as a seer of great wisdom. When I was about twelve years old, Shaindel brought him home, hoping he would confirm her view, and my mother's, that I had "special" gifts qualifying me as a rabbi and leader. The rabbi and I talked long enough for him to decide that he did not share their views of my "calling."

The best evidence confirming he was right came in my quick and untroubled acceptance of his decision. I had not felt I had a religious calling even when I began my secondary education, and that judgment was strengthened during my four years in the yeshiva high school.

What I wanted to become was a lawyer. I am not certain why, but I thought it was a logical profession for me since I didn't want to be a doctor or an accountant, and law related to public affairs, which had become an absorbing interest as I grew up. From time to time, one family member or another would say, "Max, you talk good. You should be a lawyer." That seemed sufficient qualification in their eyes.

There were also some family role models. My mother had a cousin, Birdie Amsterdam, who in 1939 became the first elected woman judge in New York County* and continued on as a respected judge for many years. And my cousin Harry, much like an older brother, had decided to become a lawyer.

* The short-lived liberal newspaper, *PM*, ran a column about her in which she was called a "beauteous barrister" and "Justice Darling." She was, indeed, a lovely woman as well as a very smart lawyer. We all—including Birdie—loved the column. When NYU Law School, her alma mater as well as mine, honored me in 1985, Birdie; her sister, Ruth; and Ruth's husband, Milton Sanders, who was also a judge, came to be with me. Birdie got out of a sickbed to be there. I took special pleasure in their presence.

The first step to emulating them was a college degree. I made the decision on my own to attend the uptown campus of New York University. It was a ten- to fifteen-minute walk from where we lived, and a walk into a new and different world. My mother accepted my decision without complaint,* although the question of how to pay the tuition had no easy answer.

---

* When Yeshiva University gave me an honorary doctorate in 1990, I thought of it as distinct from the other honorary degrees I had received. This one seemed a special fulfillment of my mother's dream, and I knew how pleased she would have been. That thought was ever present with me as I delivered the commencement address.

2

A New World of People and Ideas

New York University was an odd but inevitable choice. I had walked over to the campus during my high school years and watched students come and go. It had seemed formidable and unattainable. I had gone into the bookstore on one or two occasions to browse, listening in on the serious talk of people a few years my senior. They seemed quite wise to a fifteen-year-old. It was a pretty heady atmosphere.

Somehow, as the result of all that, I never really considered City College of New York, even though some of my friends were students there and it fit my pocketbook as a tuition-free school. NYU was not a public school, and tuition was a frightening obstacle. Paying anything was tough because my mother had only a meager income from the store and could not help at all. What little she earned provided for our rent and food, but not much else. My mother also shared with Shaindel, who earned little; her husband had died and she again lived with us.

I knew I would have to earn whatever it took to attend college: money for tuition, books, and food,* no matter which school I chose.

* My usual daily lunch in the university cafeteria was soup that cost a dime and bread that was free. It was not exactly a balanced diet, but somewhat better than the subsequent summer when I sold Fuller Brushes. Then I subsisted on a Hostess cupcake and a pint of milk for lunch.

Where I went to school was, in part, simply a matter of how much I was willing to work. Go to CCNY; work fewer hours. Go to NYU; work more.

I had a lot to learn in college, a lot of growing up to do. This did not distinguish me from other freshmen, but I was younger than most of my fellow students, and my experience was limited. Parochial schools and a totally Jewish neighborhood provided identity and an opportunity to learn (within certain limits), but somehow I wanted more and I knew I needed more.

Until I went to NYU, I had really known only two non-Jewish adults more than casually—Mr. O'Meara, the policeman who walked the beat around my dad's butcher shop, and Miss Nellie McCarthy, who later and for many years helped my mother in the hat store. Now, many of my fellow students and almost all my instructors were not Jewish, but Protestants and Catholics. For the first time, I learned firsthand about different religions and traditions, and that was quite a change.

While the yeshiva schools were very good ones and the teachers of secular subjects worked as public school teachers as well, our surroundings, both emotional and intellectual, were religious. At NYU, it turned out that there was more to Western civilization than I had previously known. I studied a variety of new subjects, including the New Testament as an elective English course. Whether it was conscious or unconscious, NYU uptown was my intellectual escape route from our Bronx shtetl and became a significant part of the Americanization of Max. I had a lot of ground to cover, and I worked intensely.

Fortunately, the discipline of the yeshiva had been good preparation. There was little tolerance there for casual commitment. If you were studying God's word, after all, the obligation for thoroughness was powerful, and the rabbis were not inclined to let you forget it. There is something frightening about the anger emanating from a bearded old rabbi offended to his soul by foolishness and mediocrity, outraged by a lesson unfinished, a text not studied, an interpretation absurd or ad libbed carelessly. Work was not a burden, but as natural as breathing. It was simply an unbreakable habit that was ingrained by then.

I quickly found not one but several part-time jobs, including one as a clerk in the bookstore, where I could work many hours and be a part of the conversation and socializing I had once witnessed only as an outsider. Other students, no wealthier than I, used the store as a place to gather and talk, a social break from the library where they studied for long stretches of time, a substitute for the fraternities they could not afford or had no interest in joining. Mr. Phillips, the store manager, tolerated this "loitering."

Afternoons were particularly active in the store. Students would buy a candy bar or some ice cream and just hang around for the company and discussion. We'd talk politics and philosophy, discuss the great books we were reading, Roosevelt, and the Depression. I learned to listen as well, measuring in silence the merits of each participant, deciding who made sense, who had the better arguments, who seemed to have truth on his side.

One person who made special sense was not a student and not a college graduate, but a full-time clerk in the store who had been denied the chance for advanced formal education by the economics of his life.

He loved books and ideas, and he shared the lessons of his experience humbly. My new friend, Mr. Reagan, was a non-Jew about my father's age, and I learned from him as much as from any teacher the need for intellectual balance and moderation and the value of integrity.

It is interesting, looking back, that I do not recall ever having a serious or prolonged discussion in college about Zionism and Palestine. Like most Jewish children at the time, I grew up with a *pushke*—a little white can about six inches high with a blue Star of David on it—resting on a kitchen cabinet, thereby becoming a structural part of the home and making the act of charity one of its foundations. It was a bank in which we put a few pennies each week and which a rabbi came around to empty every once in a while, sending the money to help build a Jewish homeland in Palestine. We talked about the settlements and felt a bond with those who were there, which, I suppose, is a kind of unspoken Zionism. I was proud that Jews were farmers and that the desert bloomed, that the sands of the desert were being turned into a land of milk and honey. But it was a homeland for other Jews; for us, America was clearly the homeland.

At the yeshiva, a homeland in Palestine was an ever-present part of our religious and historical training, but at NYU, within my circle of friends, it was simply not an issue on the front burner.* We talked

---

* Many Jewish intellectuals were indifferent or even opposed to Zionism and the establishment of a Jewish state. Morris Raphael Cohen, the great American philosopher renowned for inspiring disciples, called it "tribalism" and opposed it for a long time. Sidney Hook, almost twenty years older than I and a student of Cohen's, has written about his own rejection of "nationalism" at the time. Hook noted that it was easy to object to Israel in the abstract, but that Israel, once established, made abstractions irrelevant. Even Cohen shifted ground in facing the reality of its existence.

mostly of social conditions in this country and about how we would make a better society here, solving unemployment, strengthening the labor movement, improving race relations. A just society was our goal, and despite the Depression, we were certain we could create it.

I vividly recall my thought process at the time. It is no great commitment to principle or to democracy, I thought, for a Jew to fight against anti-Semitism or for a Negro to struggle for civil rights. The action is a correct one, but an act of self-interest. How much better and more genuine, I felt, was a Jew's commitment to civil rights for Negroes.* Very early on, I joined the National Association for the Advancement of Colored People (NAACP).

What we on campus did not focus on, certainly to the extent we should have, was the war in Europe. It was distant and, in a peculiar way, almost abstract. While we talked some of Germany and what was going on in Europe, our bible of current events was the *New York Times*, and concentration camps and the Holocaust apparently were not something the paper emphasized or something we knew much about then. Whether it was a kind of protective denial, insensitivity to my fellow Jews, my absorption with other subjects, or my constant activity, I do not know. Certainly, I am not proud of it today.

I stayed busy all the time. When my bookstore work was done, I raced off to other jobs. I sold subscriptions to the *New York Times* on campus. I checked coats during Saturday night campus dances, which were attended mostly by the more affluent students. I don't recall any Gatsby yearning to be part of the scene, and I doubt it was there. I was still a young teenager. I also had bad acne and was, as a result, quite shy. My limited social experience and my lack of self-confidence with girls kept me from learning to dance. Instead I read in the cloakroom to the melodic beat of the big bands booming from the scratchy phonograph in the living room of Lawrence Hall. I was happy just to watch

---

* In this book, I intend to use the terms *Negro*, *black*, and *African American* as closely as possible to the usage preferred by the community at the time under discussion. At one time, until the late 1960s, *black* was considered an insulting reference by many Negroes, and Dr. Martin Luther King, Jr., asserted "Black power . . . falls on the ear as racism in reverse." Jesse Jackson recently announced a preference for emphasizing his "African American heritage." We have learned from experience that it takes time for the elites to persuade the community that it should change its definition and self-image ("From Negro to Black to African American: The Power of Names and Naming," by Ben L. Martin, in *Political Science Quarterly*, no. 1, 1991). What I remember as I write this is a Lillian Smith story I read as a first or second grader, with a little Negro child asking her equally little white classmate: "Did God forget to color you?"

the wire hangers empty of their coats as the evening ended so that I could collect my wages, pick up my tips, and head for home.

In my junior and senior years, I was also the campus representative of Rosenblum's Formal Hire, handling the rental of tuxedos for the proms. Rosenblum's was nearby at 183rd Street and the Grand Concourse, but I took sizes and measurements in the bookstore after three-thirty in the afternoon or through my post office box on campus. The students picked up their outfits at the store and returned them there.

For a while, as the beneficiary of a National Youth Administration grant, I did research work for an English professor studying the writings of Samuel Johnson. I was paid forty cents an hour, worked twenty hours a week, and silently praised Franklin Roosevelt and the federal government for my good fortune.

Even more learning, and earning, took place each summer. I worked off campus to earn a little extra to help my mother, Shaindel, and myself. I spent one summer in a steel factory lugging heavy finished products to the warehouse or the loading dock. I worked as a busboy in a Catskill summer resort restaurant, clearing tables, making salads, hauling those silvery metal rectangles of dirty dishes till my arms ached. I sold magazine subscriptions, Realsilk Hosiery, Fuller Brushes, and Good Humor ice cream, leaving shyness behind as best I could.

Yet, for all the work pressures, my memories of my college days are pleasant ones of new experiences, exciting ideas and idols, and growing up. In those three and a half undergraduate years of emancipation from the strictures and limits of a yeshiva world, I began to enjoy the pleasures of the city and even boy-girl relations.

My first dates were with neighborhood girls, often sisters of my male friends. We might go to the movies, usually as a group, or just to a nearby soda fountain. My closest friend, Jerry Greenstein,* especially loved the theater, so we would save to buy balcony seats for Broadway productions and occasionally, joined by our neighbor and buddy Irving Goldfarb, take our dates there. Clifford Odets was a favorite of ours. At fifty-five cents a seat and subway fare, that was an extravagant evening. More often Jerry, Irv, and I would go to the plays

---

* Jerry and I would talk often about courses we were taking or about teachers we liked. He took a lecture course from Morris Cohen, and I absorbed at secondhand Cohen's positivist attitudes. Years later, I would become a close friend of Morris's son, Felix, a lawyer and philosopher, and an especially wise man, too. Felix had founded the Washington office of the law firm I joined when I left government service in late 1955, after Felix's death.

stag, talking afterward for hours about the playwright's ideas and the actors' performances.

For every hour in the theater, there were many more in the New York Public Library on Forty-second Street. What the bookstore did for me in a superficial way, the library did for me in a more substantial one. I devoured its contents as best I could. When I had finished reading about the specific topic I had come to study, I read more about Western civilization and American history, about government and political philosophy.

With all the jobs and the academic pressures and the sometimes strained family atmosphere, I still found that there were groups to join and things of an extracurricular nature to do. I started writing for our campus newspaper almost as soon as school started. I first did a question and answer column, deciding on the question and interviewing students. The subjects, all handled equally seriously, ranged from whether the library should be opened full days on Saturday and Sunday to whether Hugo Black should be allowed to serve on the Supreme Court even though he had once belonged to the Ku Klux Klan.

I later began to write a column called "As I See It." It had the same range of concern, including one piece criticizing Supreme Court decisions declaring New Deal laws unconstitutional by five votes to four. I wrote, "It is absolutely not wise to have progressive measures, passed by the peoples' representatives, invalidated by the mere margin of one Justice." I thought six to three would do.

I wrote an April Fool's Day column that for some reason didn't get into the paper until April 4, its parodic effect lost by the delay. Since it contended that "the U.S. is not spending enough on armaments," readers expressed a certain amount of outrage, and the paper, at my urging, explained that I was only kidding. It was my first lesson that retractions don't ever catch up to the first story.

Coming from a yeshiva background, I joined the Menorah Society, a kind of fellowship of Jewish students, as a freshman. In my sophomore year, I unexpectedly became its president and, as a result, involved in the association of similar groups at other New York colleges and universities. I ran a fund-raising drive for refugee students, our focus remaining on those who had come to us, more than on those who were left behind. We raised about $85 and thought it was a great success.

Surprising as it may be, Menorah actually helped take me outside the Jewish community. Through it, I became the Jewish co-chairman for several interfaith rallies and events that brought me into contact with people I would not otherwise have known as well, if at all. I found that my new friendships added to my understanding of other religions, helping me to recognize common threads and shared philosophy with my Judaism as I studied the differences.

Through Menorah, I met the faculty adviser at Columbia University, Rabbi Isador Hoffman, a Reform rabbi, who was also president of the Jewish Peace Fellowship, a pacifist group that took its "theology" from the Old Testament I had studied so long in my earlier schooling.

He, more than the traditional rabbis of my yeshiva days, was a melder of religious and secular ideas. It was perhaps through his teaching that I later developed the conviction that democracy was the political expression of our religious ethic. The *Shema Yisroel* of my childhood—"Hear, O Israel, the Lord is our God, the Lord is One"—meant that if there was only one God, then we are all His children, and brothers and sisters to one another. If a government or political system was to be acceptable, it had to honor the individual who was, after all, the child of God created in His image, with godlike qualities that could be developed. That teaching confirmed and strengthened my attitudes and fit snugly into my democratic passion.

Hoffman and other Jewish pacifists pursued the idea of brotherhood and its implications for nonviolence with all the commitment of the Talmudic scholars they were. One of his pacifist colleagues, Rabbi Abraham Cronbach, told the story of the Lord's wrath when the angels rejoiced that the enemies of the Israelites, the Egyptians, had died in the Sea of Reeds, with the result that the Israelites won the battle. The Lord rebuked them, saying, "My children are dying and yet you would rejoice?" The rabbi talked of brotherhood, and I also thought of loving one's enemies.

I joined the John Marshall Law Society on campus and in my junior year ended up as its president. We published a *Pre-Law Review*, and I wrote for it as well as for our campus newspaper.* I let a friend, Burt Cooper, who loved the politicking, yet did not want to run himself, talk me into running for campus office. Neither of us was part of the campus "establishment," and without Burt's organizing skills and glee in the battle, I probably would have lost those valuable experiences. Even with Burt's guidance, I lost an election for class represen-

---

* In our very first issue in the spring of 1939, I wrote a short article entitled "The Lawyer and a Better Society." I said: "The aspiring lawyer of tomorrow . . . will enjoy his work if, instead of asking what society and the law can do for him, he will endeavor to discover what he can do to improve society and the law." I do not accuse Ted Sorenson or John F. Kennedy of plagiarism!

tative, finishing fourth behind the three winners, but taking comfort that I was not last.* As important as all those extracurricular activities were in helping me mature, my teachers helped change my vision of the world around me even more.

Before college, I had never had a teacher who wasn't Jewish. Almost none of the faculty I met at NYU were. One teacher who influenced my outlook greatly, Jack McConnell,† was an intensely socially conscious man who admired the Quakers and introduced me to them. He was tall, thin, and youthful-looking, an odd but splendid mixture of intensity and casualness. As a result, he seemed both a caring friend and a commanding intellectual presence.

Many of the faculty, including McConnell, came from the Midwest, where they had earned their graduate degrees. They were often liberal, particularly as compared to most of the Orthodox teachers of my yeshiva days, but they were not ideologues, not part of the turbulence of Marxism found on other downtown campuses.‡ And that suited me just fine.

Nothing about the Soviet Union persuaded me that it had developed any magical panaceas for social problems. Its advocates were unpersuasive, as best I understood them, their words and Soviet actions quite different from each other. Partly responsible for my attitudes, I suppose, was my deep commitment to the United States, learned from my parents as a child. Partly, I am certain, my religious training made me suspicious of Marxist ideology. Another part was just instinct.

The Soviet Union to me was a dictatorship that denied the brotherhood of man, despite its claims to the contrary. It was anti-religious and, therefore, unacceptable. I had learned in the yeshiva of Russian anti-Semitism, a tradition I knew continued in the Soviet Union, even though the show trials of the Jewish doctors and intellectuals came later. I felt viscerally that Soviet society was an intolerable way of governance, a form of institutional brutality.

* When the time came in my senior year for the senior celebrity poll, I made the list, but not as the "most likely to succeed." My honor: "most ambitious." I accepted it as an accolade, but it is ambiguous.

† Jack later became dean of the Cornell University School of Industrial and Labor Relations and then president of the University of New Hampshire. I think of him as one of the special influences in my life, as both teacher and example.

‡ My obviously different intellectual beginning from that experienced by other young Jewish intellectuals of my day who were at City College of New York or New York University, for example, may account for my failure to travel the Marxist–Leninist–Trotskyite path to neo-conservatism with its stimulating variations.

Domestic Communists were not that attractive either. While I knew none intimately, I met them at conferences and heard them rage against American policies and parrot self-righteously the Soviet line, which even then was clearly false and illogical. I watched their intellectual gyrations, their policy flip-flops, their manipulative badgering of others, and I was repelled.

By 1938 and 1939, I had started to get more interested in social welfare issues and had become increasingly conscious of problems in our country. Yet it never led me to a Marxist point of view, although in 1938, I received some exposure to the Stalinists when I went to Washington as a representative of our campus for a national meeting of the American Student Union (ASU). The session simply confirmed my belief that something had to be done, but within the context of our democratic ways. It was my first trip to Washington, and I stayed at the Harrington Hotel, which, by my standards then, was quite nice, if not elegant. We had little time for casual touring, but I saw the monuments and the Capitol and then, feeling I was a part of history, I heard Mrs. Roosevelt speak to the group at the Department of Labor auditorium.*

I went home to New York certain I would come back to Washington, at least to visit or to work for a while in the future. I went home confirmed in my views that the far left was a threat to what I held dear. I went home to have my youthful values shaped further by my exposure to New York University and its fine faculty.

---

* It was at an ASU meeting that she met Joseph Lash, who became her close friend and her biographer. Joe was a very bright young man and a leader of the student union. Through Hubert Humphrey and the Americans for Democratic Action, I met Mrs. Roosevelt from time to time in later years. I felt the same excitement each time. She was a woman of incredible presence who exuded a sense of powerful humility.

3

Labor and Pacifism: Seeking Social Justice

My professor and friend Jack McConnell's influence was primarily in the area of ideas about social justice and legislation, but he also inadvertently exposed me to the wider pacifist world. I began to read extensively in pacifist literature, from Gandhi and Tolstoy to philosophers of the American Christian pacifist community. What I learned fit easily into my religious views, and particularly, of course, into the Jewish pacifist vision of brotherhood that Rabbis Hoffman and Cronbach enunciated. There seemed to be a spirit of unity among the religions I studied, which provided some direction to my ideas and some strength to my personal commitment and sense of social obligation.

I liked that sense of coherence and common ground, although I never lost my discomfort with the deification of Jesus. Even today, I must admit that pictures of the Crucifixion remind me not of the religious spirit, but of the horrors in Eastern Europe against the Jews. Even though the unifying principle of religion encouraged looking at the human race as brothers and sisters to one another, I came to believe that organized religion ultimately tended to divide rather than unite people, and that was disconcerting.

McConnell introduced me to Frank Olmstead, the adviser to

Christian students at the NYU Washington Square campus, and later a leader of the War Resisters League. Frank fascinated me. He had spent part of the First World War in Russia as a YMCA worker. He was as muscular as an athlete and as gentle as a saint, his smile and spirit exuding goodwill and love. He and his wife, Florence, adopted me into their campus family of students. Through Olmstead and my own related Menorah activities, I also met Dr. Abraham Katsch, his counterpart as adviser to Jewish students. Being a college undergraduate is a special condition of awakening, and Olmstead, Katsch, and McConnell made my time at NYU immensely exciting as they opened my eyes and mind to a broader world.

When McConnell suggested I spend the summer of 1940 at a Quaker work camp, I wrote to the American Friends Service Committee telling them of my interest. In their response accepting me for their Reading, Pennsylvania, camp, they asked for a $5 deposit. I requested a few extra days to arrange for the money. They also provided a scholarship, and I signed up with enthusiasm as quickly as I could raise the $5. It meant I gave up earning money during the summer for law school, but I had already decided that I would go to law school at night and work during the day. Although I had spent some summer weeks in other years as a waiter in the Catskills, this was the first summer I felt really away from home and in quite different surroundings.*

I did not know what to expect in Reading. We were told to bring towels, hangers, bed linen, a blanket, and a "pillow if desired." The town was still economically depressed and had not begun its recovery as other parts of the United States had. It was a railroad center, but as the quantity of freight had diminished during the Depression, it had suffered with that industry. More importantly for me, although most of the mills were shut down, it was a hosiery manufacturing town with a local of the American Federation of Hosiery Workers that unofficially adopted all of us as members of the community. This was my first direct exposure to the labor movement.

Our group was a varied one, including a Smith College debutante from New Jersey (which makes her sound less serious and hardworking than she was) and several refugees from Nazism, one from Germany

---

* When I was about eight years old, someone persuaded my parents to send me to a Jewish summer camp, Camp Mohaph, because it would be good for me as an only child. It still seems odd to me that they did so, although those years were good ones for my parents and they obviously felt they could afford it. I suppose it seemed very American to send a child to camp and was a token of success. During the first week, I cracked my elbow playing baseball and was sent home. No more camps.

and one from Czechoslovakia. Abe Goldstein and I were the only Jews, and only a small number were Quakers.

We lived in a house that had been empty for five years. It had been the Beulah Home for Wayward Girls and was now called the Anchorage. We fixed it up when we could, but our main work was renovating the Reading Iron playground in what was described as a "Polish-Negro neighborhood" and painting slum houses.

When the day's work was done, we read and then talked at length about pacifism, social justice, trade unions, race relations; about the Quaker approach to life; about the Fellowship of Reconciliation, led by A. J. Muste, a Christian pacifist; and about Gandhi and other peace thinkers.

Talk during the day was less with one another and more with our new neighbors. The children would join us in clearing their playgrounds, doing work they would not have done on their own. We got to know both them and their parents well, and the often unemployed adults would bring us water, occasionally lend a hand, and invite us over for neighborhood picnics after work. What little they had they shared.

Our days began at five-twenty each morning, giving us enough time for breakfast and twenty minutes of Quaker meditation before we began work at seven. I found it strange at first to have my fellow campers rise from their seats when they were moved to do so during meditation and recite a line or a stanza of a poem that meant something special to them. On occasion, someone would tell a story of an event that was important in defining how he or she viewed the world. I almost never spoke, but I grew to like the emphasis on introspection and seeking to understand life's mysteries. I liked the personal testimony, the quality of quiet thoughtfulness that pervaded these gatherings. When we prayed, I felt a bit more comfortable with silent prayer than with spoken sectarian or denominational prayers.

It was a splendid summer in many ways. I once more met people from quite different backgrounds. I did manual labor, which I had not often done for long, and I still had lots of time left for reading, meditation, and discussions, particularly about the Quaker nonviolent approach to life that so defined my immediate future.

Possibly the most lasting and important influence of the summer was meeting David Ritchie and his wife, Mary, who were in charge of the camp and were our guides, both literally and spiritually. David was a "full-time Quaker" as the secretary of the Social Order Committee of the Society of Friends. Mary, who had a contagious smile, cleaned and cooked and kept things orderly, but she was a guide as much as David. They listened carefully, questioned with finesse, advocated their beliefs quietly, and became immediate friends. They radiated goodness, but each also had an acerbic streak that showed up when they were faced with what they considered arrant nonsense.

For several years afterward, until I went off on my own service as a conscientious objector, I spent New Year's Eve with them and other camp alumni at Pendle Hill, a Quaker college in Pennsylvania. There were square dances and singing until just before midnight, when we began a silent prayer that covered about ten minutes. The best voice belonged to Bayard Rustin, a new friend, a Quaker and a Negro, whose leadership abilities and spirit of goodwill impressed everyone near him. There was a family kind of joy among us, not the Times Square frenzy and rowdiness, but a quiet reaffirmation of love, and I liked it.*

When the summer was up, I returned to New York to work and attend night law school as planned. Earlier, I had hoped to go to Yale Law School, which had a unique sociological bent to its curriculum, but when I had written seeking a scholarship, they said to get admitted first and then apply for aid for the second year. That was like throwing a ten-foot rope to someone drowning twenty feet away: a nice gesture, but meaningless.

I continued at NYU, this time at the law school on the downtown campus. Olmstead's influence was immense during this time. When he talked of unions, he reflected, unconsciously I suppose, the sense of excitement and mission that existed in the labor movement. That excitement was nowhere greater than in the garment trades in New York. For many people, unions were more than instruments for higher wages. They were like the immigrant societies that helped my folks twenty years earlier—a caring social, economic, and educational presence. There was a passion and intensity that surrounded union activity. People sang union songs as if they were gospel. Organizers worked for a pittance because they saw economic and social salvation for individuals and the country in their efforts. To speak up to the bosses with

---

* Every Christmas, David begins a round robin letter to which all of us camp alumni add in turn. This is now the fiftieth year of the letter. One of those letters was Maggie's introduction to David and Mary, whom she did not meet until later. She enjoyed the letters and was as much taken with the Ritchies when she did meet them as I had been. Three of our children attended weekend work camps with them, and when our daughter Julia was married in 1987, she asked David to speak at the ceremony. While David has remained special in my life, I know he has been disappointed in me as a "fallen-away" pacifist. Mary is now dead, but David continues his good works in the spirit of fifty years ago.

impunity was a special American joy for the mostly immigrant workers.

Olmstead introduced me to Phil Heller, the education director of Knitgoods Local 155 of the International Ladies Garment Workers Union (ILGWU). Through him I found steamer and presser work in sweatshop factories producing sweaters and swimsuits. The machines hissed out steam like venomous snakes. Hauling garments and working the equipment in the heat left me exhausted by day's end, and occasionally even a little faint.

My work was primarily unskilled, but I benefited from the wage structure negotiated by the unions, which rewarded the skilled seamstresses and cutters better than they had been earlier and then trickled down to the bottom rungs in a diminished fashion. I also met Louis Nelson, the local ILGWU union chief and a radical former Lovestonite,* who rejected Stalinism and the Soviet Union as perversions of the socialist dream. He was a true believer in workers' democracy and a great organizer and teacher. He disdained suits and ties as a bourgeois affectation and usually wore a sweater as a protest against what he considered the sartorial pretension of other labor leaders.

Nelson thought the perks of American union leaders excessive and morally wrong. He felt that David Dubinsky's salary as president of the ILGWU was too large for the head of a working class organization.† He fought with Dubinsky but remained loyal to him because the Communists hated Dubinsky as a social democrat undermining the revolution. A common enemy was a powerful bonding force. Since I liked

---

* Jay Lovestone was thrown out of the American Communist party in 1929, unwilling to bend to the dictates and whimsy of Soviet policies. The final argument had to do with cooperation with established trade unions, which made sense to Lovestone and was contrary to the prescribed Communist attitude of the moment, but it really concerned intellectual integrity as well. Lovestone later became a friend of David Dubinsky and through him the international affairs adviser to George Meany and the American Federation of Labor (AFL). He played a major role in keeping the AFL free from Communist influence and a staunchly anti-Soviet force in American life.

† The union was a fascinating clash of ego and ideals, often within the same body. There was such ferment and fervor that division and argument were inevitable and endless. Nelson, who was nonetheless loyal to Dubinsky and a stalwart ally, never hesitated to cry out against what he saw as moral lapses or weakness in pursuing the workers' battles. But the Communists outraged Nelson, and I recall his disdain when the Communists sang their favorite song that went, "The Dubinskys, the Hillquits and the Thomases, they fake the workers with false promises. They make by the workers double crosses. They preach socialism, but they practice fascism to preserve capitalism for the bosses." The words didn't parse and the tune was generally sung off-key, but it echoed with the passion of anger.

them both and shared their view of the enemy, I was pleased that they were allies most of the time.

Dubinsky was an original and a phenomenon, a sort of land-based meteor. He stood about five feet tall, but was diminutive only in physical size. His feet and his tongue moved at supersonic speeds, and so did his mind. When he spoke at a local meeting, members treated him like a brother and a god at the same time. When he spoke at a national convention, he seemed like a prophet of old with a message from on high.* There was a messianic quality to those events. He stirred his audiences with a vision of a workers' world of equity and justice, arms flailing the invisible demons who thwarted their aspirations.

It was a message he had carried for a long time. Dubinsky was born in 1892 in a part of Polish Russia and was sent to Siberia as a teenager after being arrested several times for trying to organize unions in that czarist world. He had been in the United States only since 1911, after escaping from his exile.

Heller and Nelson shared that passion and were more constant and directly influential in my own life. When they asked me to work for the union during my free hours, I did, though there was little time to spare between my full-time jobs and my law studies. A few times each week, I would take the elevated train to the union office in Queens and spend an hour or so on various projects they wanted done, racing at the last minute to my six o'clock classes at Washington Square. My aim was to get to school in time enough to rush into the Chock Full o'Nuts store across the street for a quick glass of milk and their famous date-nut bread and cream cheese sandwich.

My volunteer hours brought me friends for life and filled my free time as well. On weekends, Heller and his education committee of workers would organize picnics, lectures, even small groups going to plays. Union was family, religion, learning all together. There was social solidarity in belonging. When I walked a picket line for Local 155, I felt, in my youthful way, that each step was a move toward a better world. There was a dilemma, however, which I felt perhaps more acutely than others, given my parents' experience. I was often troubled by the confrontation with many small-scale employers who worked very hard themselves and were not amassing significant wealth.

Through our local and my work, I met Elias Lieberman, a heavily accented immigrant who had been one of the early organizers of the

* In later years, when I attended ILGWU conventions with Humphrey, Dubinsky would introduce me to the convention as a member of the union. He found great satisfaction in the cheering that followed, and so did I.

ILGWU, had gone to law school at night, and had become dean of labor lawyers in New York during those tumultuous years of union growth and struggle. I liked watching him work. He was a wise man with a broad crinkly smile who gave his counsel in a quite dispassionate way when asked, although he clearly felt deeply about his role in the labor movement. He and his wife, Dorothy, took a familial interest in my life, and he became another father figure and guide. When he had me analyze the impact of industrial work at home and its relations to wage and hour laws, I charged off with enthusiasm, visiting pieceworkers in their dimly lit tenement hovels.

I watched as men and women sewed buttonhole after buttonhole in mind-numbing concentration, knowing every pause meant less money. I multiplied the number of buttonholes by the piecework rate, and it took no genius to figure out the result. What was clear and what we demonstrated was that the homework institution was an unmistakably greedy method of breaking the wage and hour law.

I timed people, gathered other information, solicited signed affidavits about pay, and ultimately at age twenty-one testified on what I had learned, with Elias, before the Wage and Hour Board in Washington. As a result of that testimony and other work by the union, industrial homework was made illegal on December 1, 1942.* That was a sweet victory made sweeter by the sense of solidarity I felt when our union paper wrote, "Knitgoods workers who know of homework being given out should notify the Union at once." I had, I thought, involved myself in the lives of every family in the union abused by a system of piecework at home.

While law school and its discipline and learning did not have the same emotional satisfaction for me as my work in the labor movement or the same consequence in forming my social outlook, I did enjoy the classes and the friends I made. It may be the nature of the coursework or the result of first exposure to certain social ideas as an undergraduate, but my thoughts return not to what I learned in law school or my teachers there, but to my college teachers Jack McConnell and Frank Olmstead as prime influences on my worldview and social conscience; to Myron W. Watkins, who taught me the danger of economic monopoly; and to Arnold Zurcher, who helped me think about the problems and possibilities of our democratic political philosophy. The students in my night school class consisted primarily of "civilian lawyers," older

* The law was in effect for more than forty years until it fell victim to the Reagan administration's actions that made homework legal again. I found it ironic and irritating and sad that a prized accomplishment of my youth should fall while I was serving that administration.

people who had been lawyers in Europe before the war and now wanted to be American lawyers, which made classroom discussion uniquely interesting. After classes, I usually went to the library from nine P.M. until about eleven P.M., when it closed; then I took the subway home to the Bronx. As citizen and as lawyer, I have never found the law boring, but even in my school days it was always, in large part, simply a passageway to other activities and learning.

One night at law school, I read a posted announcement for a meeting of the American Law Students Association (ALSA). I had found that my shyness disappeared to some extent in a structured social situation, so I eagerly went to the next meeting and joined. We talked less about the law than about political and social conditions and solutions to various national problems. I was struck then by the fact that the focus was much narrower among us "intellectuals" than among Phil Heller's education groups at Local 155, where discussions of current issues were complemented by concern with theater and books.

Like the Menorah Society of my undergraduate years, our NYU chapter of the ALSA joined from time to time with similar groups at other New York law schools, and their leaders met more frequently. Our chapter president, Ben O'Sullivan, was two or three years older than I, liberal, anti-Communist, and pro-labor. When he learned that I worked for the ILGWU, he anointed me a leader and involved me in many meetings and strategy sessions. Those meetings led to a repetition of my undergraduate experience with the American Student Union.

I traveled to Washington as part of the NYU delegation for a national convention of ALSA, where there was a struggle with the Communists for control. The anti-Communist faction lost. The association was divided, as one might expect, into the Communist-Stalinist group and a liberal social democratic group. I was struck once again by the intense energy and vehemence of the Communists. They seemingly knew the "inspired truth" beyond question or challenge, but treated facts casually and their opponents with disdain and ruthlessness.

As instructive as those meetings were, a more lasting influence came from an almost weekly gathering at the Greenwich Village apartment of Estelle Rubin, the girlfriend and future wife of James Ramey, chairman of the Columbia University ALSA chapter.* The apartment, in an old brownstone, had a living room, a bedroom, a kitchen, a

---

* Jim later became staff director of the congressional Joint Committee on Atomic Energy and then a member of the Atomic Energy Commission, appointed by President Kennedy. Estelle became a renowned scientist, a member of the Georgetown University Medical School faculty, and an advocate of women's rights long before feminism was a movement. Their son, James, is my doctor today.

bathroom, and a fireplace that didn't work. It barely held the eight or ten of us, including David Dubinsky's daughter, Jean, who occasionally showed up as Shelley Appleton's date.* It seemed like the subway at rush hour when regulars brought friends and we grew to a dozen or more people.

Estelle had a job teaching chemistry at Queens College while she worked on a Ph.D., and she and her roommate entertained us, paying for the cold cuts and potato salad that we took out from a local delicatessen or for our occasional "gourmet" dinner from an inexpensive Chinese restaurant.

We were all social democrats who worried about the coming war and its effects on American democracy, admired Franklin Roosevelt and Norman Thomas, supported the New Deal with a few reservations, and voiced our incredulity at Communist flip-flops and absurdities. Seriousness gave way after dinner to an oddly boisterous game of charades. I took my turn at being silly and theatrical in ways quite foreign to my ordinary behavior, although I never got over my embarrassment in being the center of attention when my turn came. I still recall my outrageously inept effort to act out Clifford Odets's "There's a drugstore on every corner and you had to get a baby!"

Meanwhile, the more pragmatic task of my legal education needed my attention. I was ready to focus on my future when one of my professors, Paul Kaufman, stopped me after class and asked if I had given any thought to working for a law firm during the day, getting the basic professional experience I needed. He said that Phillips, Nizer, Benjamin, and Krim, a growing firm whose partners were Jewish, needed a clerk, and that he was willing to recommend me for the job. I was delighted. The firm's main practice revolved around the movie industry, about which I knew little, but which held promise of some excitement.

Young Jewish lawyers then did not look for a career with the prestigious Wall Street firms, as they would later. When the investment banking firms did hire Jewish lawyers, they reached for those descended from the old crowd of nineteenth-century German immigrants. I was interested in neither of those worlds anyway. Except for Kaufman's intervention, I would have looked happily ahead to working as a lawyer somewhere within the labor movement.

My work at the law firm proved to be of great value to me. During

---

* Shelley and Jean later married. Shelley became an ILGWU leader in his own right. Ben O'Sullivan and his date, Sonia, sister of Budd Schulberg, the novelist and playwright, also married.

the day, I performed chores, many menial, and did some research. Most mornings, however, I went by subway directly from home to the Foley Square downtown court area. There I learned to file motion papers and answer calendar calls for active litigation cases. At times, I would appear before judges. At other times, I would be in the courtroom available to help Louis Nizer or the firm's other litigators. A year of doing this enabled me to pass the bar exam, including that portion dealing with practical courtroom questions, without taking the courses on the subject.

I had arranged to take the bar examination early under a special ruling of the New York Court of Appeals to assist young men of draft age whose studies were likely to be interrupted by the draft. In April 1943, shy one year's credits of a degree, I was one of 265 people who passed the bar exam out of 478 who took it.

The Nizer firm* (that's how I thought of it) was an exciting place in which to work. Louis Nizer's reputation as an eloquent orator and a brilliant advocate of liberal principles and civil liberties was well known. What I found when I began clerking for the firm was that Nizer was more than a theoretician and much more than the showman I had been told to expect. He cared about people and took an interest in them on a very personal level. When he asked me to do research for some of his speeches, I was thrilled to do it, pleased when he wanted my ideas as well as my research, and delighted when I heard the results of my research delivered by such an artist of the podium.

When the time came for me to face the consequences of my religious objections to war, Nizer and the other partners in the firm were quite supportive, advising me to follow my mind and my conscience, to heed my heart and my instincts. Though Hitler was an unambiguous enemy and the war real and devastating, my pacifism, born many years before, was firmly held, and I do not recall any substantial turmoil or anxiety of "Should I or shouldn't I?" when the time came to register for the draft. The law provided that conscientious objectors would be drafted to perform "work of national importance under civilian direction" in lieu of military service, and I was ready for this.

---

* The firm rose, in large part, as the movie business grew to be an integral part of American life. Louis Phillips, who founded the firm, became involved with Paramount Pictures; Robert Benjamin represented Pathé Pictures; and Arthur Krim, who was close to Lyndon Johnson and a spectacular Democratic party fund-raiser, later became head of United Artists. Both Benjamin and Krim were relatively young when I met them and welcoming to a lowly new arrival. Benjamin was the first chairman of the United Nations Association, and I now serve as chairman of its board of governors.

I wish I could recall more doubts about my decision, for the question has been raised, generally not to my face but whispered, on how I, a Jew, could have been a conscientious objector during the war against Nazi Germany. I am not sure that I have a simple answer even today. I was a pacifist. I did not see how I could kill anyone. How could we ever stop this madness? I knew that many others must have felt this as well. I was convinced that war would not solve the problem of Hitler. Other dictators would rise. Killing could not produce a good end and would produce new problems. I wrote: "War cannot bring peace. Instead, like a weed, it firmly takes root and spreads the seeds for future wars." War, I felt, was the real enemy, with its brutalities and devastation; a greater enemy than the perceived "enemy."

We needed to find alternative ways of resolving the problems of the world. Most of us adopt this credo in our personal lives as we grow; the maturation of nations must involve this process as well. It was time to begin. For me, it began with my pacifism and personal testament as a conscientious objector, an expression of faith that there were alternatives to war. After all, Gandhi, Albert Schweitzer, and Tolstoy were not naive about "evil" and the need to resist it. They were inspiring leaders with a reverence for life and a faith in nonviolent resistance. "Wars will cease when men refuse to fight" was the slogan.

My pacifism grew out of my education and family training and had deep roots in my understanding of the Jewish beliefs that I had been taught, strengthened by my exposure to the Quakers. The news and details of the concentration camps had not yet sunk into my consciousness. I was comfortable with my views, and the law recognized the legitimacy of my position. I felt there was no choice. I talked to my family and friends about my options; they never wavered in their support once I made up my mind. My point of view was not theirs, my chosen course of action not one they personally would have followed. Only my mother fully agreed with me, and that certainly was due to her repugnance toward war and her care for my personal safety. My friends respected my religious convictions, my tolerance of other moral views, and my willingness to accept the consequences of my decision.

As I left the firm, Nizer asked me to keep in touch with him. We not only corresponded during my years of conscientious objector service, but he offered me a job in his law firm at the end of the war.

Had I not had to register for the draft and had I not gone off to a series of assignments as a conscientious objector, I might very well have stayed my entire professional life right there, hoping that some day the firm would be called Phillips, Nizer, Benjamin, Krim, and Kampelman. It was not to be.

4

A CO: From Seedlings to Starvation

By the time of my twenty-first birthday in November 1941, the domestic environment for most conscientious objectors had turned generally difficult, and for some it was overtly hostile. Military preparations had increased at home as the war continued to expand in Europe and official rhetoric took on a more belligerent edge. Hitler's power threatened to overwhelm our friends in Europe and democracy in general, creating a more intense patriotic fervor here.

The Selective Service Act had become law in October 1940, bringing registration and conscription, and leading to felony jail terms for those who would not register, firings of some schoolteachers who registered as conscientious objectors, and occasional social ostracism for those who objected to military service or to helping prepare for war.

Though I was a part of the conscientious objector community in New York and was, obviously, aware of all that, I never felt personally threatened or uncomfortable. The law required "religious training and belief" as a basis for objection and did not accept objection based on political grounds. Unlike some COs who would not register at all for either religious or political reasons, I felt an obligation to follow the law and was intent on serving my country as best I could within the context of my objections.

My draft board accepted my request for CO status without any problem or challenge. I had no question about the validity of what I was doing, and the draft board's action simply confirmed my feelings. I used whatever time I could save from my job and my studies to work with other pacifists.

I had joined the War Resisters' League and the Fellowship of Reconciliation. On occasion, I was chosen to speak at their meetings. I occasionally appeared with Evan Thomas, Norman's brother and a medical doctor. My participation also permitted me to develop my friendship, begun at the Quaker camp in Reading, with Bayard Rustin, himself a Quaker.*

In 1941, I began to work on a newspaper unambiguously named *The Conscientious Objector*. At first, it was produced every couple of months by a consortium of pacifist organizations and later as an independent monthly publication. It sold for three cents an issue and was an all-volunteer effort led by a New York journalist and pacifist, Jay Nelson Tuck, an editor at the *New York World* during the day. I'd write my bit and then go with him and a couple of other volunteers to the print shop to proofread and edit the copy to fit. Jerry Tuck, tall, blond, good-looking, and sheepishly ungainly, was an accomplished writer and editor. A thoroughly independent man, he put out a good paper.

I did not think of myself as a proselytizer but a simple purveyor of information. Yet there is power in the printed word, and you feel it when you are twenty-one and the experience is new. There is something magical about the printing process when you are reproducing words you have written or believe in strongly, words you think may change peoples' attitudes and actions for the better. It is exciting to listen to the click, click of the Linotype machines as lines are reset, to watch the printer tie up the type on the block. Even inadvertently smearing the ink as proof sheets come fresh off the press into your hands has its charm. Finally, of course, the rhythmic thump of the presses as the first pages of the final version pile up brings the satisfaction of a job completed.

---

* Bayard is a virtually unsung hero. His contributions to the labor/civil rights/social welfare politics of our country have never been adequately described, nor has sufficient recognition been given to him. His organizing genius came full flower with the March on Washington in 1963 which he, more than anyone else, conceived and put together as an exercise in nonviolent action. He also had a strong personal commitment to Israel and headed an organization that he called BASIC, Black Americans in Support of Israel Committee. In recent years, he had become chairman of the executive committee of Freedom House and I served as chairman of its board of directors. Our friendship lasted until his death in 1989.

In August 1942, I was listed on the masthead as a member of the editorial staff and began a by-lined column called "Democratic Front." I tried to translate my interests in labor and civil rights, in social and economic liberalism, into short items that might pique the interests of pacifists, having learned that not all pacifists, particularly those from the traditional peace churches, seemed to care as much about those issues as many of us did.

The same month my column began, an advertisement in the paper from the Jewish Peace Fellowship invited interested people to a discussion on the relationship of Judaism and pacifism. My friend from Menorah Society days, Rabbi Hoffman, was one of the signers of the ad, and I felt good to see his name there. My relationship with him was strengthened even as I continued to learn more about other pacifist strains.

I wrote a long piece on the Catholic Worker movement and its origins and founders, Father Peter Maurin and Dorothy Day. I had gone down to their Bowery soup kitchen to visit with them. I also saw and tried to talk to the homeless and hungry discards of that generation, including the shell-shocked veterans of World War I, as they gathered for a hot meal. I had never seen anything quite like it and was moved by the dedication of the volunteers even as I was depressed by the condition of the shuffling beneficiaries of their concern.

The day finally came when I had to leave New York. Saying good-bye to my mother, my family, and my friends; to Phil Heller and Louis Nelson; to Louis Nizer and my lawyer colleagues; and to my fellow pacifists, I headed off on June 1, 1943, to my first assignment as a conscientious objector. I took the bus to Elmira, New York, and hitchhiked to Big Flats, New York. There, 150 men,* from eighteen to forty-five years of age, of twenty-nine different religious or pacifist denominations, lived in an old Civilian Conservation Corps camp left vacant years before and now run by the Quakers as home to a Civilian Public Service (CPS) unit. We continued the soil conservation work begun in the Depression-era CCC program, planting thousands of

---

* There were 7,000 conscientious objectors registered in December 1943, and 2,000 were in prison (mostly for refusing to register). Most of us, I think, were filled with a sense of purpose, a sense that we could thwart evil and change the world. I wrote regular articles for *The Conscientious Objector*, and they reflect my youthful assurance and intensity: "Selective Service prefers to have us plant seeds for fear we may plant thoughts" and "most of us are bucking a social system consciously. We want to help build a better world. We want to serve humanity and rush to the aid of the downtrodden masses in China, India, Africa and wherever else there may be need." The rhetoric is a little embarrassing today, but not all that much.

seedlings in stoop labor. The work left us aching and exhausted each day, but I found it physically exhilarating and satisfying as I would frequently imagine the large trees that these seedlings would grow into.

When that task was interrupted for any reason, often after a snowy winter day, we felled older trees, clearing the forest for new growth. I learned to handle an axe and a saw and took pleasure in growing physically stronger with muscles that may not have bulged, but bespoke physical labor. I was soon at home in these strange surroundings that were spartan but not uncomfortable.

Big Flats was a little like Reading, except that the sounds of the city were replaced by the nocturnal hooting of barred owls or the sound of a distant barracks door shutting. Sounds carried across the darkness with clarity, breaking the quiet of our wooded isolation for a moment before silence overwhelmed the night again.

My compatriots were mostly rural young men, mostly Protestant, ranging in belief from fundamentalist to a broadly liberal religious conviction. There were a few of us from the city, a few Catholics, and fewer Jews. Some were skeptical of the value of what we were doing with our time planting trees, but no one voiced any misgivings about his decision to resist war. We were quite different in education and economic background, but we shared a religious view that elevated the idea of brotherhood under a single God to a Western mantra.

What most of us also shared was a willingness to expose our feelings and ideas. I had come a long way from my reticence during Reading's periods of prayer and testimony. Perhaps because we were so few while millions went to war, we needed to encourage one another. In any case, we all found it easy and important to talk about war and peace, about obligation to conscience and society.

For a few, religious commitment was a personal and bilateral agreement with God that invited little extraneous discussion or anyone else's involvement. They did not join in, but almost all of the rest of us cared deeply about domestic and international events as well as our religious purposes and convictions.

I continued to write for *The Conscientious Objector*. Looking back while writing this chapter, I found a long-forgotten article that gives me pause today. Just before leaving for Big Flats, I had written that about 2 million Jews in Germany were killed by Hitler and about 600,000 more were in jeopardy. I noted that Palestine was the closest haven and should be made a safe place for those German Jews. That, as best I can tell, is the first time I dealt with the Holocaust, and it apparently did not lead me to question my pacifist faith. It may indeed demonstrate, I'm now aware, a certain insensitivity at the least. Certainly, I find an inexplicable lack of outrage. I'm sure I rationalized at the time that my involvement in more killing would solve nothing, that war doesn't solve problems, and that the human race had to develop the power of love and nonviolent resistance as an alternative to war.

All that seems inadequate now. Some wars have solved problems; some problems and threats need more response than passive resistance. In issues of the paper that followed, I wrote no more about it. My concern turned to how peace might come for the whole world; I wrote, "We'll never get anywhere for peace while national sovereignty exists" and "No matter how much force you've got, you can't have community."

Meanwhile, in 1943, someone decided that those of us in CPS units around the country should be organized into the equivalent of a union. We wanted more socially useful work and pressed for new "more significant" projects. A number of us with trade union backgrounds believed that an organization was appropriate, that if the Quakers and the Mennonites and the Brethren who ran the camps had contact with the government, so should we as participants. I was not among the organizers of the union, but joined and participated when I learned about it.

While my writing and reading took up some of my excess time and energy, the sameness of the daily experience grew boring. Planting seedlings and working out-of-doors were not unpleasant experiences and were in their own way fulfilling, but "enjoy" overstates my recollection of those days. I eagerly read the regular notices that arrived listing other CO assignments for which one could volunteer. One day, I read that attendants were needed at a school for "feebleminded" children in Pownal, Maine. It seemed a different, and preferable, kind of service, touching the lives of individuals in a more direct way, so I applied for a transfer and soon received it.

I was able to stop at home to visit my mother, Aunt Shaindel, and my uncle Max and his wife, Rose, on the way from Big Flats to Maine. Life was not financially easy for my mother, and I felt bad that I could not help much. But the visit was filled with warmth and love. It was a moment of calm and family before I faced a scene and a life for which I was little prepared. I took the bus from Portland to an institution that was somewhat better, I think, than most states provided in those days for mentally retarded children, many of whom were unable to walk or talk or feed themselves. Some, mostly very young children, could not control their bodily functions and lived in the hospital section where I was first assigned. We washed them, cleaned them up, cared for them, and carried them when necessary from one place in their stark surroundings to another. A hug, a touch—these were our most effective tools.

The hospital, for all its limitations, was relatively clean, and the attendants were loving and caring. The "do good" inclination is sometimes mistakenly denigrated, but to sense another person, poorly equipped by nature, relax and for a moment feel better from your touch or the soothing sound of your voice is something special. I think conscientious objectors, motivated as we were, who were involved with patients, made a lasting contribution to a change in philosophy in the care of the retarded and ill, demonstrating that love could transcend other limitations. At that time, the attendant-employees in most mental institutions were of the "floater" type. More dependable applicants were not attracted by the low wages and unpleasant tasks associated with the job. Patients were frequently maltreated. The COs, motivated by nonviolence, drastically changed the environment when they appeared. In one hospital alone, it was reported, "accident" rates in the violent ward decreased by 50 percent with the introduction of COs into the staff.

Later, when spring approached, I was asked to move to the school's farm where older and more physically and mentally able patients lived. We took care of animals and gardened and farmed a little in the rocky soil. For the first time in my life, I needed to know how to drive, because there was a tractor for the fields and a car for shopping or for taking a youngster to the doctor if that became necessary. Our Civilian Public Service unit director, Ted Horvath, a CO like the rest of us and a ministerial student who later married Ginny, the camp cook, took on the additional duty of driving instructor. He was surprised to find anyone my age who didn't know how to drive, but I learned quickly on the sparsely traveled roads, and he forgave my subway-induced ignorance. The car was important, but mostly I drove the tractor.

Even in spring and summer, mornings in Maine can be crisp and chilling, but our charges took to the work in good spirits. I climbed aboard the tractor as if tilling the soil was what I had always done, enjoying the feel of the wind and the sun from my high perch.

When the long work day was over, there was little to amuse the patients. Their life was so limited that I asked if I could take several into Pownal on Saturday nights for a movie and an ice cream cone. Ted quickly and enthusiastically agreed, and we received the hospital director's approval. We'd wait at a whistle-stop for a train that came through on Saturday afternoon, or sometimes we'd ride the bus we could flag down on the highway, and on an occasion or two, I had permission to use the car.

I would lead my little group on a welcome break away from their dreary home and out among other people. For virtually all of them, it was the first time away from the grounds of the institution. For the older ones, that meant many years. After the movie, we'd buy our ice cream and then walk along the street, looking into windows, watching cars and lights, an odd caravan of outsiders. For me, my wards became young friends.

Interest in a union of COs, which had begun during my stay at Big Flats, continued. In mid-1944, an organizing committee of delegates from various camps met at the Labor Temple on Fourteenth Street in New York City. Among the other delegates was a new friend of mine, Ben Segal, who came from his assignment in a Philadelphia mental hospital. Ben was a casual friend then, but we became much closer over the years, in part because of his most important contribution at that meeting. He introduced me to his date, Marjorie Buetow.

Maggie was a graduate of Roosevelt University* in Chicago, where she had been born and raised. Her father, who had left school at age thirteen when his own father died, worked for the Victor X-Ray Machine Company as a superintendent in the factory. He loved what he did and often took Maggie to work on Saturdays to expose her to the workplace, hoping to interest her in business. He was successful, although she chose the workers' side and not management's, much to his surprise.

She had gone to work for the labor movement after she left school; when we met she was working for the CIO War Relief Committee. She was a socialist and an anti-Communist, and her work with the trade union movement was clearly more than a job; it was work of the heart. We had much in common, and I quickly arranged to keep in touch with her. We corresponded regularly and saw each other in New York City on the few occasions I could get there.

The organization we began in New York never amounted to much, but my friendship with Maggie flowered into love and a marriage that has lasted a lifetime and produced a family of five children.

After I had spent some months in Maine, a brochure arrived from the Church of the Brethren describing a semi-starvation project in Minnesota for which they were seeking guinea pigs among COs. That seemed more challenging than caring for the retarded and, further-

* When Maggie attended, it was called the Central YMCA College. Later it became Roosevelt College, and ultimately Roosevelt University. The name changed, but a continuing atmosphere of social activism and liberal politics remained.

more, assumed the dimension of a global contribution. I wrote expressing my willingness to be a part of the experiment and was called to
Boston for an interview by several of the University of Minnesota
scientists* who would run the study. During the war, CPS camps with
volunteers were set up to work with a number of medical experiments,
including the testing of drugs for malaria and pneumonia. One experiment required lice to be nurtured in clothing being worn by volunteers
to check for rashes and infections. The COs involved called their
barracks the lyceum.

We were told that very little was known about the permanent
effects of starvation or how best to help starvation victims recover.
They noted too that there was danger, as the result of the experiment,
of temporary or even permanent disability. Knowledge of the field was
so limited, however, that the dangers were imprecise and unclear. The
plan for the project was to near-starve us and then rehabilitate us to
better understand the needs of prisoners of war, concentration camp
victims, and the beleaguered civilians of a ravaged Europe in the postwar period. I was accepted into the program.

The report later issued on the experiment described some of the
problems and purposes:

> Under normal circumstances it might have been impossible to
> secure a sufficient number of acceptable subjects for this study.
> The risks, necessity for surveillance 24 hours a day, undeviat-
> ing adherence to the regimen, withdrawal from ordinary pur-
> suits with drastic changes in most aspects of living, and physical
> discomfort to be expected as an unescapable consequence of
> participation would no doubt have deterred the enlistment of
> most of the candidates.
>
> Several circumstances early in 1944 encouraged and facili-
> tated the institution of an experimental study of human
> semi-starvation and rehabilitation. Reports arriving from the
> occupied areas of Europe and from prison camps indicated that
> starvation was present in many places and that millions of peo-

* The study was headed by Dr. Ancel Keys, a physiologist, who in the early days
of the war designed, tested, and developed nutritionally strong rations to maintain
troops reasonably well fed. The Keys or K-ration was that product. His later work made
cholesterol a household word in the United States. Keys ran the laboratory of physiological hygiene in the School of Public Health. I was interviewed by Dr. Henry
Taylor, a cardiologist; Olaf Mickelsen, a biochemist; and Josef Brozek, a psychologist.
Keys, Dr. Austin Henschel, and the three of them were the chief authors of the
two-volume report on our period as guinea pigs, *The Biology of Human Starvation*,
published by the University of Minnesota Press in 1950.

ple were in grave danger of mass famine. It was recognized that with the liberation of the occupied areas and the cessation of hostilities large-scale relief feeding would be necessary. It was equally well recognized that there was little reliable quantitative information upon which to base an efficacious relief program. The need for a controlled experiment to determine the changes induced by semi-starvation in man and the best type of rehabilitation diet was apparent and úrgent.

I had never been west of Reading, Pennsylvania, when I took the train from New York to Chicago and then to Minneapolis, Minnesota, across farmlands and prairie and up along the Mississippi River. The Minneapolis train station, which would soon see thousands of returning military men in their uniforms being greeted by tearful relatives, was a cavernous, lonely, echoing transfer point for me on my solitary journey.

The cabdriver I hailed thought it a little weird that I wanted to go to the football stadium at the university, since the season had already ended. But underneath the stadium, in a special dormitory and laboratory, I lived from the late fall of 1944 to mid-year 1946, part of a Civilian Public Service unit of fifty-four men—thirty-six volunteers* in the experiment and eighteen who assisted in various tasks related to what we were doing.

We were all relatively young—from twenty to thirty-three years old. We had a twelve-week control period to start, filled with both physiological and psychological tests and preparation for what we were expected to do and experience. Then there was a twenty-four-week period of semi-starvation during which we were on a 1,500-calorie diet of whole wheat, potatoes, cereals, and a lot of turnips and cabbage. The official documents of the study record that "only token amounts of meats and dairy products" were ingested and, in recollection, even that, I think, seems an overstatement.

We ate two meals a day, one at eight-thirty in the morning, the other at five in the afternoon. One basic rule controlled: we couldn't eat more than they gave us, and we had to eat everything on the plate. Each item was weighed on a scale by a dietitian before it reached the plate and measured by calories and amount of protein. Our goal was to lose a quarter of our weight. I went from 161 pounds to under 120 on

---

* Only thirty-two finished. Four found the regimen too strenuous, or the diet impossible to maintain, or broke down under the pressure and asked to be transferred to other service. One of those four cut off a finger working with a saw and was released. The psychologist thought it was done on purpose, although subconsciously, to get out of the experiment and away from its pressures.

the scales before the rehabilitation began; and the weight included significant edema-collected water.

We were expected to put in a forty-eight-hour work week, do our own laundry and housekeeping, help in the laboratory, be tested, and follow the routine set out for us. We were also expected to walk forty-five miles a week.

For most of the experiment, we were under a buddy system. The report says that "no subject was allowed outside the Laboratory or living quarters unless accompanied by one or more of the subjects or another responsible person." I knew, as did the other volunteers, that if I ate anything other than the food provided by the experiment, it would show up in the daily blood and other tests that we were given. I was never tempted to cheat. The regulation did not need to be enforced after a while, with compliance universal.

I attended classes on campus, and, during the control and rehab parts of the program, I remember going to visit friends with a little white container of macaroni measured to weight, like take-outs from a Chinese restaurant. During the semi-starvation phase, I did not visit much. I simply lost the drive to socialize.

We spent a lot of each day on treadmills whose speed could be increased from about three miles an hour to eight, or out-of-doors walking over prescribed routes of three, five, and fifteen miles. Our daily energy output was kept at a minimum of 3,000 calories. We were required to keep daily diaries, including what we dreamed about, our feelings about ourselves and others, and our thoughts about the experiment.

Despite all the duties that made the experiment a full-time job, there was spare time, and I saw a need to occupy my mind with something other than myself, food, and my physical condition.* I still needed a few courses to complete my law school requirements, although I had passed the bar, and I wrote to NYU to ask if they would accept courses from the University of Minnesota Law School. They

---

* The final laboratory report includes a psychological profile of Subject No. 2. That was me. When it appeared in 1950, I was a little embarrassed by it, but today I accept it as probably quite accurate. It reads:

This subject is an example of the men who showed the least psychological deterioration. . . . Neurotic traits in this subject were minimal. . . . He suffered a full share of the consequences of semi-starvation. . . . His psychological symptoms were likewise typical of semi-starvation. He was lethargic, mildly depressed, and somewhat irritable. The latter two symptoms were less marked in this subject than in many. He suffered from hunger pains and was preoccupied with thoughts of food as were all the other subjects, although he seldom talked about it. His sexual interests dropped off severely in the early part of semi-starvation. . . . On the positive side it may be said that he had little or no temptation to break the diet, and that he complained less than the average subject in spite of showing the same amount of physical deterioration . . .

agreed to do that, and Minnesota agreed to let me take those courses I needed.

Their value was more than a question of learning and of completing degree requirements. They successfully took my mind off food and hunger for relatively long periods, and allowed me to be with people who were not involved with or particularly interested in my digestive process.

It is amazing what hunger can do. It dampens sexual appetites, essentially eliminates them. You focus on food. You daydream about it. You read cookbooks and books on nutrition. You go to bed at night thinking of food and wake up in the morning thinking of food. It is boring, if virtually unavoidable. My night dreams, for example, were not of sexual fantasies, but of candy bars. The dullest law course seemed preferable to that. I never see a picture of famine victims without empathizing with the dehumanizing effects on the quality of their lives. It is not just malnutrition I see, but a mind that can think of nothing else. You can feed the body, but I wonder if there is permanent damage to the psyche of those who are not guinea pigs for a while, but victims forever. I wonder, too, if our now ancient experiment may yet be helpful in their rehabilitation, if it comes.

To keep my mind off myself and because I couldn't shake loose from what we were going through, I found that I thought a lot about starvation generally. I became so interested in the subject that I studied it, going back through human history from prehistoric through biblical times and up through World Wars I and II. I later wrote what became the opening chapter in the scientific report. Intellectualizing the experience was a helpful bridge to rehabilitation, almost as much, I suspect, as the few extra calories I began to receive as we entered the rehabilitation phase of the experiment.

The war in Europe ended while I was on the diet. I frankly don't recall much about the day or the news, other than a vague recollection of feeling great relief and happiness. In an odd way, I suspect, the war was less real at that point than the hunger pains. But I do remember the excitement when Dr. Taylor came in to report that the results of our experiment were being sent by cable to European prisoner of war and concentration camps as they were being opened. He felt good about that and wanted the rest of us to share the sense of contribution and involvement the doctors felt. Outsiders visited us from time to time. One visit was described in a newspaper report on July 31, 1945: "Army medical authorities who visited their barracks said their shrunken muscles and swollen joints give the men a striking resemblance to the prisoners freed from German concentration camps."

Not until the atomic bomb explosions of Hiroshima and Nagasaki did I begin to be jarred loose from my pacifism and my faith in the power of nonviolence. If simply pushing a button can produce massive destruction and loss of life, how can passive resistance prevail? What hope is there of persuading an enemy with love, with words, or with reasoning if he can fire without ever seeing your face, your emotions, your love for him, or the cruelty of the damage he is inflicting? My confidence in the capacity of nonviolence to prevail was ruptured. It was a traumatic time for me as I read, talked, and thought. I concluded that it was a greater evil to permit evil to win by acquiescing in it than to control and defeat it by violence or the credible threat to use violence if necessary. It was appropriate and helpful that I was at the University of Minnesota during this period of introspection.

Ultimately, an immensely valuable part of the experiment for me was simply being in Minnesota. It is a special place with special people who are open and welcoming in a way I have rarely found equaled elsewhere in the country. Generosity of spirit seems to come with the clear water, legislative innovation from the fecund soil.

I came as a stranger without a person to locate, without a phone number to call. I could easily have remained one, isolated, surrounded only by my CO colleagues and thoughts of food and myself. But kindly people would not let that happen. Our doctors at the university looked on us as more than guinea pigs, and Joseph Brozek and his wife, Eunice, introduced me to a friend of theirs, Betty Mae Aldrich. She insisted on going along on my obligatory long walks so that I would not be alone. Her own good spirits made life less onerous.

I met a young woman, Betty Joseph, who was dating a law school friend of mine, Howard Sachs, and she took me home to meet her parents, Annie and I. S. Joseph. He was a Jewish grain trader in a conspicuously Yankee domain and a leader of the Jewish community. In addition to Betty, there were two sons—Roger, who became a practicing attorney although later paralyzed by polio and needing an old-fashioned iron lung to help him breathe, and Burton, who became one of my first clients and a dear friend when I went into law practice and he took over the family firm.* The Josephs provided an emotionally comfortable place for me to feel part of a family as I certainly had not for a long while.

* Burton's wife, Geri, who had been an award-winning newspaper reporter for the *Minneapolis Tribune* before they married, later became Minnesota Democratic–Farmer–Labor–party chairwoman, national committeewoman, and, in 1968, the highest-ranking woman in the Humphrey campaign. Geri, like Eugenie Anderson, brought the DFL a distinctive combination of intellect, beauty, and regal carriage. Geri was appointed by President Carter to be our ambassador to the Netherlands. She and Burton remain dear friends of ours.

When I needed permission to sign up for my law courses at Minnesota, I thought it might be denied. The school was crowded with returning veterans, and it would have been easy for the school to say no to someone from out of state who wanted only a few courses. But Minnesotans are inclined to work things out. Dean Everett Fraser, a native of Prince Edward Island who seemed a rather dour and forbidding presence to me and, therefore, an unlikely ally, listened to my request and did not hesitate to approve it.*

What all these people shared was a genuine and kindly attitude, a sincere but unhurried concern with their community, and a candid gaze at the world. You simply could not remain a stranger in their midst for long.

Even the difficult Minnesota winters have their charms. They are interminable and cold, giving validity to the local joke that there are two seasons in Minnesota: winter and the Fourth of July. But when I watched a gentle snowfall fill the empty stadium, the cold didn't matter. There was peace there. When the snows ended and the wind subsided, I would sometimes stand and look out over the flat field, brilliantly white in the sunshine, and count the rows of seats in the stadium piled high with snow in undulating parallels from the field to the top.

Only the weather was cold. The faculty and people I met were not. When I had finished my law courses, I continued with courses in political science and soon had enough credits for a master's degree and ultimately started on a Ph.D.

Two young faculty members, not much older than I, took a special interest in me and became mentors and good friends. Herbert McCloskey was from New Jersey, Jewish, and a former Trotskyite who had forsaken that ideology, but still carried deep animosity toward the Stalinist Communists and the Soviet Union. Carroll Hawkins was a nondoctrinaire socialist and a self-proclaimed radical. I took courses from both of them, and although they were not particularly sympathetic to the pacifist movement, they were at least understanding of my beliefs and intrigued by the starvation experiment.

They shared one other important trait. They were students and disciples of Evron "Kirk" Kirkpatrick. Kirk was an Indiana farm boy

---

* Dean Fraser's son, Don, was a stalwart part of the anti-Communist movement in Minnesota: in the American Veterans Committee, the Americans for Democratic Action, and the early efforts to build the Minnesota Democratic–Farmer–Labor party. He later served in the Minnesota State Senate from 1955 to 1963, in the U.S. Congress for sixteen years after that, and now as mayor of Minneapolis, elected first in 1979.

with a Yale Ph.D. turned political scientist and government servant. He was in Washington much of the time, but his wife and family were in Minneapolis, and teaching assignments brought him home regularly. I met him, latched my academic star to his, and began a learning experience and friendship that has lasted with increasing closeness to this day. Another of his students, Hubert Humphrey, had become mayor of Minneapolis, and through Kirk, McCloskey, Hawkins, and another Kirkpatrick student, Arthur Naftalin, I soon met the mayor and became involved in the infant political party they and others had created, the Democratic–Farmer–Labor Party of Minnesota.

When I finished my law courses in Minnesota and was awarded my degree at NYU, I was ready to be admitted to the New York bar. I ran into immediate trouble; my admission, which should have been automatic, was held up. I had anticipated that my service as a conscientious objector might cause some minor question to be raised, but when the delay suggested that some people in the New York bar believed that my being a CO morally disqualified me from being a lawyer, I had to deal with it. I pointed out that there was a distinction between serving in a civilian unit authorized by law and being sentenced to jail for not registering, a felony that takes away the right to vote and at least temporarily any claim to join the bar. That did not seem fully to persuade the chairman of the Committee on Character, and the delay continued. Finally, through Louis Nizer, the New York chapter of the American Civil Liberties Union took an interest in the principle.

The president of the ACLU at the time was Whitney North Seymour, the epitome of an establishment figure, and he convinced the committee not to delay my entrance to the bar. I was admitted, but, for the moment, it was irrelevant. I had found a new excitement, a new mission in Minnesota. I began to teach, and I began to work in politics. I loved both.

5

Minnesota: Meet Hizzoner the Mayor

The University of Minnesota after the war was vibrant with returning veterans, an exceptional faculty,* and a heightened spirit of innovation and social activism. It was an illustrious example of a land grant college, the grand American experiment in higher public education begun in 1862 when the Congress donated public lands to states with the understanding that the proceeds from the sale of those lands would be used to establish colleges. The university had for years educated most of the young people of Minnesota who received college educations. It had influence that reached beyond education into the economic, social, and political life of the state.

There was a constant flow of information from the university on agriculture, tax policy, social services, economics, and public administration. Medical care was exceptional in the state because doctors and nurses received an extraordinary education. Even the livestock was better for the veterinary medicine learned there. Well-trained teachers

* Robert Penn Warren and Saul Bellow were in the English department and James T. Farrell joined in the summer; Al Nier, a physicist who isolated the U-235 atom, was in the physics department; Walter Heller and George Stigler (who later went to the University of Chicago) were in economics. Minnesota was considered one of the leading public universities in the nation, and every part of it seemed filled with intellectual excitement.

went back to school districts far from the cities, filled with new ideas and old values. Simply, ideas flew from the ivory tower into every aspect of life in the state; they reached every hamlet, and the people there listened and responded to what they had heard and learned.*

If a state could be sensitive, this one was, and nowhere more so than in its political life. Prairie agrarianism and an active trade union movement stirred the pot constantly, and political discourse seemed part of the soil and air and water. Minnesota was a state in search of change, always looking for answers, always willing to try something new, rarely accepting problems as beyond solution.

The influence of the university affected politics in form as well as content. The Democratic–Farmer–Labor party was not entirely the creation of university folks, but their influence was substantial. A good share of the political inspiration and initial direction in the early to mid-forties came from Evron Kirkpatrick and was carried to fruition by the energy, intellect, and persuasive spirit of a young politician named Hubert Humphrey.

They had first met when Humphrey returned to the university from South Dakota in 1937. Humphrey had been there earlier for two years, but the Depression and Dust Bowl, which dealt so harshly with the farmers who patronized his father's drugstore in South Dakota, dealt him a blow, too. Without money for tuition, he left the university, headed home to help his near-bankrupt father in the store, took a quick course in pharmacy, and settled in behind the counter as though he would never leave.

But life in the dust, deprivation, and poverty of the plains was oppressive, and the drugstore life insufficient to sustain his intellectual interests. He soon left Huron with little money, but with a new wife and the determination to learn more and become involved in politics and government service.† By the time he returned, Kirkpatrick had

* One measure of Minnesota's quality may be its exceptional record on rejection of draftees by the military on mental and medical grounds. It was the lowest (with Nebraska) during World War II and in 1962 was still the lowest at 2.7 percent rejection. That year, New York had a failure rate of 34.2 and South Carolina of 51.8.

† Humphrey describes this part of his life in fascinating detail in his autobiography, *The Education of a Public Man*, published by Doubleday in 1976. Indeed, the entire book captures a special time in the history of our nation and his own involvement in it. On a visit to Washington in 1935, he wrote to Muriel, his soon-to-be wife: "Maybe I seem foolish to have such vain hopes and plans, but . . . I can see how someday, if you and I just apply ourselves and make up our minds to work for bigger things, how we can someday live here in Washington and probably be in government politics or service. I intend to set my aim at Congress."

joined the faculty and had become a quiet force running with the liberal and against the radical tide.

There had been a great deal of radical activity on the Minnesota campus in the thirties, and the state had more than its share of Communist party members among the trade unions, in some of the farm organizations, and around the university. Many people were sympathetic to the Soviet Union's ostensible purposes, not a surprising condition considering Minnesota's economic and political history of prairie radicalism and agrarian protest.

But both Kirk and Humphrey were adamantly opposed to the Soviet system and to its advocates in Minnesota and in the rest of the United States. By the time Humphrey returned in 1940 from Louisiana, where Kirk had arranged for him to study under Charles Hyneman for a master's degree, Minnesota liberal politics was dominated by the far left, including people quite comfortable with every switch and twitch of the Communist party line.

The Farmer-Labor party, an amalgam of more radical as well as liberal voices in the farm community and the labor movement, was essentially the second party in Minnesota after the Republicans, and, indeed, during the Depression in the thirties, had been the dominant one. It had helped elect Floyd Olson governor in 1930 and again in 1932 and 1934. Olson was an eloquent and charismatic leader who gave voice to the dispossessed during the Depression and who was gaining an influential national voice. After he died of cancer in 1935, he was succeeded by his lieutenant governor, Hjalmar Petersen. Petersen, a decent man and editor of a small-town weekly newspaper, was not strong enough to keep the radical wing from taking over the party and the gubernatorial nomination in 1936.

Elmer Benson, a small-town banker and radical, was elected and led a coterie of Communist party members into the state capitol.* They were too much even for Minnesotans, who historically tolerated, indeed encouraged, third parties and nonconventional wisdom and candidates. Benson lost the governorship to Republican candidate Harold Stassen in 1938, but the Farmer-Labor party remained in control of its radical wing, in large part because there was little opposition, and what opposition existed was weak and unfocused.

The Democratic party, through all those years, was the third and

* In 1947, the Communist party claimed only 74,000 members nationwide. Locally, the Communists said there were fifteen clubs in Minneapolis with a total membership of 280. It was not their numbers that were noteworthy, but their influence in labor unions, farm groups, and politics.

by far the weaker party in Minnesota. Its leaders inspired few follow-
ers, presented no distinctive program beyond support for Franklin
Roosevelt, and rarely elected anyone to office in the state. The party
had little appeal outside Minneapolis and St. Paul and existed mainly
for the patronage function of a party in national power. They could
nominate rural mail carriers, federal attorneys, IRS commissioners, and
census workers.

Kirk and Humphrey became the prime movers in bringing together the Democratic and Farmer-Labor parties. They had an immediate and practical objective: make sure the state and its electoral votes
went for Franklin Roosevelt in 1944. They knew that only a single
strong party could successfully challenge the Republicans and win.

In addition to trying to put the party together, Humphrey's interest in public office began with an unsuccessful but surprisingly effective run for mayor in 1943. He decided to run less than a month before
the election, with almost no staff or money. What he lacked in those,
he made up in energy and oratory, racing from church basement to
union hall to service club to speak to a handful of people or a roomful,
shaking hands at plant gates in the morning and in bars at night.

In 1945, at the age of thirty-four, after successfully creating the
DFL party and leading the state into the Roosevelt column, he was
elected mayor of Minneapolis. By charter, the election was a nonpartisan one, but Humphrey emerged as the unquestioned new leader of
liberal forces in the state. He had been ridiculed by some, before the
election, as leader of the "diaper brigade," but the ridicule stopped
and the cheers began as he moved quickly and forcefully to change the
face and character of Minneapolis by driving the gamblers out, closing
down the brothels, and ending police corruption.

I arrived on the political scene at just the time that an expanded
group around Humphrey was beginning to reach out for more political
power within the DFL, looking to overturn radical wing dominance
and seize the leadership for the center. I had stayed on at Ancel Keys's
stadium laboratory as director of a small unit that remained for further
testing and sorting out of data growing from the starvation experiment.
At the same time, I continued my work and study in the political
science department.

Humphrey had been elected mayor in June, and soon after that I
met him at Herb and Mitzi McCloskey's apartment near Dinkytown, a
neighborhood of student hangouts, bookstores, restaurants, grocery
stores, other shops, and housing near the campus. Later, we would
gather at the McCloskey home in Prospect Park, an enclave filled with

faculty families not far from the university campus. On many Saturday nights, a group of political scientists, their spouses, and a few friends would join for talk and snacks at the McCloskeys or some other junior faculty member's house. Popcorn, Cokes, potato chips, and beer or inexpensive wine were the mainstays of social sustenance—although not of mine at the beginning since I was still under the starvation diet control—but talk and politics were what brought us all together.

In addition to the McCloskeys and Carroll Hawkins, Arthur and Frances Naftalin were almost always there and occasionally hosted the gathering themselves. Art had been a reporter on the *Minneapolis Tribune,* and that gave him an aura of worldliness in our eyes. He had all but completed his Ph.D. in political science before he joined Humphrey in the mayor's office as his chief aide. I had become friends with a fellow political science student, George Demetriou, and he was a regular, too. George had come to Minnesota from Long Island to study Japanese as part of an army program and stayed on to take a Ph.D. in political science. (Later, George succeeded Naftalin as Humphrey's secretary in the mayor's office.) Saul Bellow, who was a good friend of the McCloskeys, was occasionally there, adding a little different perspective by contributing a keen literary sensibility to the discussions.*

Humphrey was a frequent visitor and an electrifying one. He was unable to come quietly into a room. He arrived with a smile and with delight crackling from his voice and sparking from his eyes. He burst in like a human generator on wheels. He would arrive late, often not until midnight, usually after a speech at a dinner and an appearance at another place or two. No wedding, no wake, no union dance, no public gathering was off limits to him. His energy seemed infinite; his interest in people unbounded. He inhaled experience as others inhaled oxygen.

With his arrival, the talk and arguments that had started earlier would continue with a new passion. Herb and Carroll, arguing from a socialist position, would bait Humphrey, sometimes in jest, most often seriously. Carroll, who identified Democrats with New York's Tammany Hall, would go through an elaborate bowing-and-scraping routine as he addressed "Hizzoner the Mayor" and would proceed to complain regularly about streetlights that were out and not replaced quickly, blaming the inefficiency on Humphrey and city government, asserting that socialism would never permit such neglect.

* Saul and his wife, Anita, rented me a room when we became closer friends. I got good conversation as well as a roof over my head. I would babysit with their young son, Gregory, and usually talk politics, not literature, with Saul.

Humphrey, who was so often accused by his opponents of being a socialist, or even, absurdly enough, a Communist, always took a free enterprise, nonsocialist position. He would taunt Hawkins with the suggestion that all public utilities be sold to private companies whose profit-making purpose would make them more efficient than government control.

These arguments were real and useful in refining Humphrey's ideas. Humphrey learned by talking and by argument. He was often criticized, then and later, for talking too long (and he did), but it was not so much a compulsion or lack of discipline as a pleasurable habit. He contemplated with the sound on. He thought out loud. He was a teacher always, interested not simply in asserting but in explaining and persuading. His theory of teaching and speechmaking was quite simple: "You tell them what you're going to tell them; then you tell them; then you tell them what you told them." It worked, but it took time.

What we agreed on always was the need to deal with social and economic disparities and inequities by some government action, particularly when the private sector could not deal with them. For Humphrey, however, government meant the city and the state, and not just Washington. His commitment to local government was basic and yet frequently overlooked in later years by both his allies and his opponents. He understood that services were delivered at the local level and, as a result, probably more sensitively and efficiently. For the most part, only when the states or localities failed to acknowledge responsibility or acted in constitutionally irresponsible ways did he urge federal action.

We talked a lot about the treatment of Negroes and the need for legislation guaranteeing fair employment practices. Our involvement with the trade union movement meant that we spent time talking about the need to organize workers, the role of unions in the social life of the country, and the necessity to make unions more democratic and more effective. We all had theories on education to propound. Humphrey had worked as a Works Progress Administration (WPA) instructor of union members and unemployed teachers. As a result of this experience, he became a strong advocate of adult and continuing education. He gave out little certificates to his students, feeling their Depression-burdened lives had so few visible signs of success that even a bit of paper signed by him meant something. In later years, he often met people who told him that the "diploma" was framed and hanging on a wall at home.

We talked about farm cooperatives and how the cooperative techniques could also provide medical care for everyone at reasonable cost. We argued about Palestine and a homeland for Jews, Humphrey staunchly for it from the beginning, others questioning how it could be done, some simply opposed in principle to any form of increased nationalism.

Our talk was important, but we were an interlude in Humphrey's daily life of getting things done. As mayor, he was a doer. The city had been run for years by corrupt elected officials and been "protected" by a corrupt police department. City councilmen were on the take, lords of their wards. Illegal gambling and after-hours clubs were routine fare. Houses of prostitution ran openly, customary little red lights shining in the night.

Humphrey moved virtually overnight to change the face of the city. There were a lot of surprised people. The changes had been promised before, but had never been carried out.

While the city charter defined the office as a "weak mayor" form of government, with most of the power resting with an independent city council, Humphrey transformed it into something quite different. In large part, that success came as a result of his ability to energize community and group support virtually for whatever he sought for the city.

One effort in which I was involved did not accomplish all we had hoped for, but it is useful as an example of the direction in which he was headed. Humphrey appointed me vice chairman of the mayor's Commission on Charter Reform, with the hope that we could convince the city council to accept certain changes that would have made city government more responsible and efficient. The charter was not changed, but Humphrey, with the publicity we attracted, was able to improve both law enforcement and efficiency in providing services to the city.

He worked his secular miracles by gentle and sensitive persuasion. One day, I walked into city hall to discover him talking to tavern owners and their spouses in a conference room just outside his office. He had somehow cajoled them into coming, although I didn't know how. There was an awkwardness in the room, filled with uncomfortable men, mostly Jewish and Irish, and their overdressed wives. They depended on the city for their licenses, felt threatened by this young idealist, and feared for their livelihood if he continued to do what he had promised in the campaign.

Humphrey explained that he knew they had often been set up by the police sending in underage males who looked old enough to buy drinks. The cops, ready to arrest the bartender, were at the bar before the first sip of whiskey hit the lips of these minors. The result was a choice for the owner: pay off the cops to lose the arrest papers, or lose the liquor license for violating the law. They had all made the same business decision when necessary: pay off.

Humphrey's pitch was a simple one: provide the city with more money from liquor licenses so that police salaries could be raised. He promised to fire the dishonest shakedown artists in the police department and to make the force honest. But, he said, the tavern owners influenced the aldermen more than he did, so they had to convince the aldermen to raise their license fees. It was a pitch met with silent, wary suspicion, and it clearly was not winning the day.

Then, with that proposal before the group, Humphrey spoke softly and directly to the wives, saying in effect, "Don't you want your husbands involved in a legitimate business where policemen aren't bribed and you and your children never have to fear being shamed by dishonor and dishonesty?" No words were required for their answer. There was suddenly common interest where they had anticipated nastiness. There was dignity where they had expected discomfort.

He created, from that day on, allies who never left him. The tavern owners went to the city council requesting that their license fees be raised so that in turn police salaries could be raised, mystifying aldermen, reporters, and business leaders with their freshly gained sense of civic improvement. Humphrey quickly delivered on his promise. He had found and installed an honest and strong police chief, Ed Ryan, who cleaned up his department. Salaries went up, the shakedowns stopped, and only legitimate arrests took place.

This emphasis on group and community involvement was a hallmark of Humphrey's philosophy of government. His style was a combination of candor, persuasion, and then conciliation. It was inclusion and involvement. Civility and decency did not mean skipping over disagreement, but finding a common ground. What I saw in that room, working with people often considered on the fringe of respectability, was effective with the establishment, in boardrooms and in country clubs, as well. It was in those places that basic social problems had to be solved.

Bribery in some ways was easier to deal with than the anti-Semitism and racism that were pervasive in the city. Although there were few Negroes or Jews in Minneapolis, there were some, and they were the ultimate outsiders no matter how legitimate, successful, and law-abiding they were.

Jews were not even permitted to join the AAA, the automobile club that changed flat tires and jump-started cars on frigid mornings, much less the private clubs in town. Minneapolis earned the description given to it by Carey McWilliams in the *Nation* magazine as "the capital of anti-Semitism in America."

Negroes who had the nerve to enter certain restaurants or bars were subjected to the humiliation of seeing glasses they had sipped from broken ostentatiously. Neither Negroes nor Jews were easily hired in the management of establishments they didn't own. Humphrey vowed to change that environment.

He learned of a self-survey technique developed by Fisk University social scientists, and he soon had appointed scores of community-wide citizen groups to hold a civic mirror up to themselves and the city. A number of us from the university were included in the project, but many of the insights came from others. Bankers were asked to look at their internal practices; realtors and merchants and teachers and union officials, among many others, at theirs.*

Perfection did not immediately follow, bigotry did not disappear, but major changes did take place, and Minneapolis became a city where brotherhood seemed more real. It became the first U.S. city to establish a Fair Employment Practices Commission. By 1948, three years later, the atmosphere of the city had changed so much that the National Conference of Christians and Jews gave the city its brotherhood award.

I learned a great deal then from Humphrey. He had an instinct for resolving or diminishing differences, for helping people become allies for a time, for making change unthreatening and compromise tolerable. His talent for bringing people together grew out of an infinite reservoir of goodwill and delight in people of all sorts. He saw individuals, not crowds.

This was a time when historians and others spoke of the melting-pot America with approval, and Humphrey liked the idea. He and George Demetriou, his friend and aide in the mayor's office, frequently stopped after working late or after meetings to get a beer or hamburger at neighborhood cafes, sometimes at the East Hennepin Cafe, an ordinary sort of place of dark booths in a back room and a long bar up in

---

* Humphrey's talk of holding a mirror up to the city was not original. It may have come from the Fisk study. It was a concept suggested by Gunnar Myrdal, the Swedish scholar who studied the American treatment of blacks saying in effect about our society, "If they like what they see in the mirror when they compare it to their American ideals, fine. If not, they will want to bring about a change." I used Myrdal's *American Dilemma* as a textbook in a class I taught then.

front. Humphrey soon knew the regulars by name and he became Hubert to them, as he did to thousands of Minnesotans who never met him. It was melting-pot democracy at work. He was a Midwest Ellis Island, providing those who came near him confirmation that they were truly Americans who, by God, could talk to their mayor, whatever their accents.

His success as mayor permitted our university crowd to talk with excitement of Humphrey's future. I know that there are politicians all over America in every generation who think that they can become president of the United States. I know that they have many friends who agree with and encourage this idea. In most cases, of course, the goal of the presidency is a fantasy.

But Humphrey was an astonishing human being and a natural political leader. He was a uniquely gifted orator,* a popular political figure in Minnesota almost immediately and without equal. His special qualities seemed beyond containment on a minor stage.

The advice in those days was that he should run for governor next, since the political wisdom then was that no one went from the Senate to the presidency. The stepping-stone to the White House began in the state house. We all cited Wilson, Coolidge, the Roosevelts, convincing only ourselves. Humphrey wanted to run for the Senate, and responded to our "logic" with the silencing observation that "you fellows also told me that no one ever moved any place after being mayor except to jail or oblivion."

More than anything else, we talked about how to gain control of and strengthen the Democratic–Farmer–Labor party that Kirkpatrick, Humphrey, Naftalin, and their allies had put together in 1944. To defeat the Communists and eliminate their influence became our purpose, our passion, our pleasure.

The DFL state party conventions in Minnesota began in late winter with precinct caucuses during which delegates were elected to county and congressional district conventions and then to the state convention. At the 1946 state convention held in St. Paul, we thought we could win. But, as it turned out, we had not done an adequate job

---

* Humphrey could go on too long in his speeches. Muriel once said to him, "Hubert, a speech does not need to be eternal to be immortal." One source of his problem was that he knew a great deal about a lot of subjects. He collected information all day long, seeing things, registering new stimuli, thinking about what he saw, interpreting and assimilating. He grew up admiring the Chautauqua tradition of long speeches and followed it even though he knew it bored some and aggravated others. For the most part, however, his Minnesota audiences were thrilled, inspired, and educated by his words.

of getting our people elected at the grass roots, and we did not count noses accurately.

The radical wing outwitted and outorganized us and took over, electing virtually all the party officers.* They were hard, and though Humphrey was the top elected DFL officeholder in the state and thought he could persuade them to moderate their views, they simply ignored him. At one meeting, a couple from the other side rudely shoved Muriel Humphrey, an act that an outraged Hubert never forgot.

I was on the floor when Humphrey addressed the convention, although I wasn't a delegate. When I was asked in a needless confrontation to leave the floor, I refused. There was no vote going on, I was doing nothing but listening, but Frank Puglisi, a burly fellow who was about four times my size, picked me up and helped me out of the hall. Humphrey's verbal remonstrations from the podium were about as useful as my nonviolent, passive physical resistance.

Beaten at every turn, angry at the roughhouse treatment, we were a whipped bunch as we left the hall. When we got over our distress and sense of humiliation, we had time to think about the political injunction, "Don't get angry, get even." We decided we could overcome our adversaries, who figured we were politically dead, and began immediately to prepare for the 1948 conventions, to take back the party in the presidential election year. The effort began in late 1946 and continued with greater intensity throughout 1947 and into 1948.

Art Naftalin became the chief organizer of that effort and managed it brilliantly, even while running the mayor's office. My own role was limited but taught me about grass roots democracy in a special way, exposing me to a whole different stratum of American life than I had known before.

When I started teaching in 1946, I managed to confine my lecturing obligations to morning hours so that I could be free in the afternoons. My original plan was to use the afternoons and evenings to complete my doctoral degree work. But politics took over. I would eat a sandwich at my desk, visit with a student or two, think briefly about the next day's lecture that I had generally planned ahead of time, and

---

* They only gave us Orville Freeman for secretary of the party as a sop to Humphrey. It was a mistake for them. Orv was a Marine veteran who had been shot through the mouth at Bougainville, had spent a year in therapy to recover his speech, and was as tough as they come. They could not bully him at the convention or later. Their sop became our strength. In 1954, he was elected governor and then was appointed secretary of agriculture by President Kennedy in 1961. He and his wife, Jane, good friends of ours, continue to work on how best to alleviate world hunger.

then head for the curb outside Nicholson Hall, a classic campus building with pretentious Greek columns, where the political science offices were housed.

A car would soon show up to take us to meetings with DFLers all around the state. Some days, Humphrey would be in the car; most days he would not be, although he was clearly the most persuasive voice we had, the most magnetic personality. Our other most able advocate was Eugenie Anderson.

Unlike most of us, she came from a family of means and a background of traditional civic gentility. Eugenie was well educated, intelligent, and immensely effective, a woman of great dignity, beauty, and commanding presence. She provided an aura of respectability in a way that no one else among us could. She was from Red Wing, a small and prosperous town just south of the Twin Cities, had a Scandinavian last name, and had been the president of the Minnesota League of Women Voters. The league was nonpartisan and the symbol of the quest for good government that "respectable" forces in the state embraced. But she also brought a wise and independent and tough political instinct to our struggle. Her gentle demeanor, which was real, cloaked an equally real spirit that was determined and unyielding.*

Generally, we would end up with a driver and four or five other people. The regulars were Dorothy Jacobson, a political science professor at Macalester College who had arrived there from a farm in western Minnesota via Columbia University; her husband, George, a farm cooperative leader who created one of the first prepaid health clinics in the United States; Jack Jorgensen, a Teamsters Union leader; and Barney Allen, a rural and agricultural leader who had come up from Iowa a few years earlier. Eugene McCarthy, then a professor at St. Thomas College in St. Paul, occasionally joined us.†

Though the trips were part of Art Naftalin's master plan they were quite ad hoc for the rest of us. My first question after I got into the car was often, "Where are we going today?" or "Whose house are we going

---

* Eugenie became the Minnesota Democratic national committeewoman until President Truman appointed her U.S. ambassador to Denmark in 1949, the first woman to serve at that level in the foreign service.

† McCarthy, a handsome and articulate man, ran for Congress in 1948, and I was among those who urged him to do so. One of his closest friends and a fellow faculty member at St. Thomas, Marshall Smelser, was also a friend of mine. Marshall wanted Gene to run and asked me, as a Humphrey surrogate, to talk to Gene about it. I did, as much in my own voice as in Humphrey's. Gene, of course, was elected to Congress and to the U.S. Senate, and ran for president in 1968. His inexplicable public reticence after the nomination possibly cost Humphrey the election.

to?" It didn't make a whole lot of difference where we went since our message was essentially the same everywhere: we were first and most strenuously for Humphrey for the Senate nomination in 1948 because he could provide the leadership progressive forces needed to make change possible.

We waved a patriotic flag—our battle cry was that we could not let the Communists extend their control of the DFL because it would hurt our country, bring political defeat, and shove the liberal spirit of the state in the wrong direction. We believed what we said, we were convincing in describing our mission, and because of that we were able to create a powerful statewide precinct organization where none had existed before.

Most of our meetings, since Humphrey himself was concentrating on the cities, were two or three, occasionally four, hours away in a small rural town or in a solitary farmhouse. Some local person would have gathered a few friends and neighbors, perhaps as many as twenty, and we would explain what we were about and why it was important to regain party control from the left. It was certainly no secret after our first meeting what we were up to, and occasionally there were people waiting for us with hostile questions. We were young, intense, and a challenge not only to the radicals, but to the status quo in the party.

In the dairy sections of the state, farmers would often come directly to the meetings from their milking, strong men in blue bib overalls, Sears Roebuck boots recently scraped of mud or manure. Some came from the fields, dusty and sweaty. Their wives, if they came at all, were at first silent in the background, but sooner or later one or two of them would speak out, often those who had some leadership experience in the Farmers Union or other cooperatives. These women often became officers in our county leadership, doubly valuable for their roles in local or farm organizations. This was all a new life for me, with new people and different cultures. I recall once accompanying Hubert to a rural meeting in a Norwegian community about a two-hour drive from Minneapolis. I had become accustomed to roaring applause during a Humphrey stemwinder, and I knew that with his mother's Norwegian heritage, the crowd would be friendly. I sat in the rear of the hall. Humphrey gave it all he had—but very little applause, mostly silence, no fever. What was wrong? It puzzled me. At the end of the meeting, Humphrey was surrounded by dignified well-wishers. As the crowd emerged from the hall, I heard: "Dat vas gut!" I had a great deal to learn about Norwegians.

The Progressive party presidential candidacy of Henry Wallace, when it came, both helped and hurt us. Wallace had many supporters in Minnesota. His family magazine, *Wallace's Farmer*, published in Iowa, was like a secular bible to many rural people. He understood the family farm and the work and problems of rural America. People saw themselves in him and respected him. We had to try to wean his supporters away from the left leadership in the DFL.

The Communists among Wallace's supporters tried to hide their allegiance to Soviet foreign policy behind isolationist rhetoric, but their strident attacks on Truman's Marshall Plan (attacks required by the Soviet line) made it difficult for them to do so. We appealed to the state's sense of patriotism, loyalty to Roosevelt and Truman, and opposition to aggression. Farmers, for both humanitarian and economic reasons, took kindly to the idea of providing food for the hungry and the needy. We were able to focus on support for President Truman as an important part of what we were doing.

Our task was not an easy one. The Soviets had benefited from the wartime propaganda that proclaimed their value as allies and from the fact that their heroism in facing the Nazis could not be denied. They profited from the old adage that the enemies of my enemies are my friends.

On a much crasser level, people liked to be with those in power. Since the left controlled the DFL party, just as it controlled a number of international unions, going along with radical leaders brought certain perks and status. But we succeeded often enough in winning people to our side to make the effort well worth the incessant travel that frequently brought us home at midnight or later.

Our battles were part of a national confrontation. In January 1947 the left Progressive Citizens of America and the centrist Americans for Democratic Action (ADA) wee both formed. The Progressive party was largely the creation of the left, including the Soviet sympathizers in the United States, and they were able to use Wallace as their front man. Wallace disliked and mistrusted Truman for good reason. He had served as vice president for four years, and had he not been dumped by Roosevelt before the 1944 election, he, not Truman, would have become president at Roosevelt's death. Wallace, decent man that he was, acknowledged in his memoirs that he had been used.

The ADA was organized by New Dealers-in-exile, trade unionists, young liberals, and social Democrats. Eleanor Roosevelt was one of the original members and became a symbol of the movement. The primary emphasis of the ADA was less on ideology in the narrow sense and more on anti-totalitarianism, anti-Communism, and the need to elect dedicated liberals to public office so they could enact liberal legislation at the state and federal levels. Humphrey was one of the national leaders, and I, with my university and labor colleagues, was among the organizers in Minnesota.*

During all this political activity, something that was of great importance to me in later years took place. Israel became a sovereign nation. It was not then a central concern of mine. I was proud to be Jewish and certainly never hid from it, but I had not been an active Zionist. I was pleased by Israel's birth and felt deeply about its importance to Jews everywhere, but the Middle East and a Jewish homeland had not been an area of special concentration for me.

Humphrey was ecstatic. He was in some ways more of a Zionist than many Jews. He saw in Israel's spirit and values the triumph of democracy in an area where there wasn't much that came close to those ideals. In later years, people sometimes suggested that Humphrey's support of Israel resulted from the political support he, in turn, received from many Jews in the United States. He did have many Jewish friends even in those Minnesota days and many more, of course, who supported his campaigns later, but his support for Israel was more basic and predated any significant political gain. There was then no political benefit, no political compulsion to support Israel.

During all of this, I kept working for my Ph.D., taught courses, wrote a scholarly article or two, and continued my work with the labor movement as part of my values and my political commitment to Humphrey. The CIO itself was in the midst of a battle to rid its own international unions of Communist leadership and control and, thus, understood and supported our mission. Humphrey had traveled east to meet with Phil Murray, the head of both the Steelworkers Union and the CIO, and with Jim Carey, secretary-treasurer of the CIO and head of the United Electrical Workers union, to secure their help, and they were forthcoming. Both unions were important in Minnesota. The Steelworkers were particularly powerful on the Iron Range, where they had organized the miners.

Murray sent us George Weaver, an articulate union organizer from the Railroad Dining Car Workers and a perceptive student of American politics. George was a Negro. Minnesota was a state where a mixed marriage, it was said, was one between a Norwegian Lutheran and a

---

* It is strange the way labels are attached to movements. We were often called "cold war liberals" as though that were a sin or impure. Considering the alternative was a hot war or abdication of the nation's responsibility as democratic leader, that did not seem so horrendous to me.

Swedish Lutheran. There was not much of a Negro population in the state, much less a Negro political or union presence. I don't suppose many of my students had known a Negro person where they lived. There were few Negro students and there was only one Negro faculty member during these years at the university.

One evening on George's first visit to Minnesota, after he suggested we have breakfast together, I asked him, on the spur of the moment, if he wanted to attend my class the next morning. I taught three successive classes beginning at nine A.M. on Monday, Wednesday, and Friday. George came to the earliest one, a freshman class on American government. I introduced him, and he spoke well and effectively on the American labor movement and its role in American social and political life. He suggested coffee at the end of that class, but I dragooned him into my ten A.M. class on American political thought for upperclassmen, where he spoke about the role of minority or third parties in America; and then into the third class, a graduate seminar on problems of democracy. He finished up his morning with a lecture on the reasons that Marxism had never had a lasting or very deep appeal to American labor. Each class listened attentively, and they later expressed their appreciation of his visit. I thought then that his three lectures on three different subjects without time to prepare was a brilliant tour de force and a tribute to the democratic labor movement. I still think so.

George shortly thereafter arranged for me to be hired as a political adviser to the Twin City Joint Board of the Textile Workers Union. I ran educational programs and helped the union work with other unions in battling Communist influence in the Minnesota CIO. I then arranged for our American Federation of Teachers (AFT) local on campus to select me as a delegate to the Central Labor Union of the AFL.*

I now had better access to both the AFL and the CIO leadership, and when I wasn't traveling out of state, I was often working in the Twin Cities to secure their cooperation in the Humphrey-led efforts. As a result of this activity, my earlier ILGWU experience, and George's friendship, I also began a summer routine of teaching at the School for Workers at the University of Wisconsin.

Maggie was there, too, and I began to court her seriously. I found that beyond our common interests in social issues we shared other

* Kirkpatrick was the AFT president, and the vice president was a young economist named Walter Heller. Walter later was named by John Kennedy to be chairman of the Council of Economic Advisers and was a preeminent presence in the economic life of the United States until his death in 1989.

values and dreams that brought us together. (In going through my files recently, I found a 1948 one-inch ad in Norman Thomas's *Socialist Call* on May Day that said, "Greetings Marjorie Buetow, Milwaukee, Max Kampelman, Minneapolis.")

As we walked around the lake in Madison, watching the students frolicking and boating and shouting to one another, our own romantic feelings flourished. Since she was now working full-time in Wisconsin as the education director for the ILGWU and I was not far away in Minnesota, we were able to see each other regularly with relative ease.

DFL prospects brightened as a result of all our activity. In 1946, the DFL had elected one person, John Blatnik, to major public office. He was easily elected to Congress from the northeastern Minnesota congressional district, filled with ethnic workers in the mines of the Mesabi Iron Range and on the docks of Duluth. In 1948, with Humphrey on the ticket, it appeared that much greater success was possible. I felt close to Humphrey, but I was not an essential cog in his campaign. Nor did I think my professional future was tied to his. I did not want to be part of a staff, having learned from both Art Naftalin and George Demetriou that it was not as satisfying as it might seem. I began to consider my own options—teaching or practicing law.

Both Louis Nizer and Elias Lieberman wrote to invite me to join their law firms. I considered their offers seriously, but I quickly realized I was not ready to leave teaching, which I had found so fulfilling. The law would have to wait. I began to look for a full-time academic appointment.

William Anderson, the respected chairman of the Minnesota political science department, had, in 1946, when my name was proposed as an instructor in the department, only reluctantly agreed because, he said, I had no political science specialty. He pointed to my interests in the law, labor, American government, legislation, politics, political theory, and international affairs as evidence of a lack of focus or discipline. By 1948, he had come to accept my varied interests and to be pleased at the reports he was receiving of my success and popularity as a teacher. He encouraged me to keep in the profession, but pointed out what I knew: universities don't ordinarily like to hire their own Ph.D.s because it leads to intellectual inbreeding. Bill urged me to start elsewhere and think about coming back later, a more seasoned political scientist.

He told me that there was an opening at the London School of Economics for an Americanist and that the job was not a permanent one, but would last two or three years. That seemed perfect. I applied for the job, and after some rapid negotiations, it was offered. Pay, housing, date of arrival were all set in a letter that also noted that one of their faculty, Harold Laski, was teaching for a semester just then at the University of Chicago. I was encouraged to take the opportunity to get acquainted with him.

That, as it turned out, meant I was faced with a dilemma. I admired Laski for much of his earlier work and thought his reputation as a creative and thoughtful scholar well deserved, but he had fallen, it seemed to me, into a benign view of Stalinism. As a result, I had just written a piece for the *Journal of Politics* that was very critical of him.

I wondered if I should write to him without mentioning the article, but I decided that I really could not ignore it, so I wrote that I was soon to join the faculty at the London School, and would like to visit him. Then, in a postscript, I noted that I had recently written about him and suggested that if he had not yet read my article, he should not do so until after we had met. That seemed an artful way of being honest. I hoped he had a sense of humor and balance about himself that would survive my visit and my article.

My letter seemed to work. I received a gracious response from him saying that he and his wife would be delighted to meet me for tea in their apartment. I went down to Chicago on the same train line that brought me to Minneapolis when I was about to begin the starvation experiment, and spent several hours with them. Neither of us mentioned my article, and I thought I had done wonderfully and that the conversation was only the first of many we would have.

Soon after, I received a letter from the London School that said there had been a terrible mistake and there was no vacancy. So much for Laski's graciousness. So much for my charm and brilliance. I began to look elsewhere.

I visited Roosevelt College in Chicago and was invited to join their faculty. But the college had no campus and was really lost in the midst of the city, so I hesitated to accept the offer. Then I heard of a job at Bennington College in Vermont. When I visited there, I knew I had found a perfect professional home. The campus rests in the hills just outside a charming New England town, and seemed itself like a self-contained little village in a bucolic setting. When I talked to students and faculty, I found them bright, alert, liberal, creative, and open. Bennington's only immediately obvious liability was that the student body was entirely female. That gave me pause since I liked the chemistry of teaching mixed-gender classes. But I did not hesitate long. I accepted and made plans to leave in the fall before the election, feeling much as I had when I left the Bronx for my first assignment at Big Flats, filled with excitement, anticipation, a little fear of what might be in the new surroundings, but certain of my choice and my direction.

I also put an end to my bachelorhood. In September, Maggie and I were married by a rabbi at the University of Wisconsin* and also at her parents' home in Hale's Corners, Wisconsin, by Bill Anderson, a classmate of Maggie's.† We set out to live the life of an academic couple, fortunate enough to begin in the Bennington environment. Maggie would give up her union job and miss it. I would miss Minnesota, Hubert Humphrey, and the special politics of the DFL, but it was time to get on with my career and our lives.

---

* Maggie had many Jewish friends and was attracted to what she knew of Jewish culture and history, even though she considered herself an agnostic about formal religion. Not long after our wedding, primarily to satisfy my mother, she became a convert to Judaism. My old friend, Rabbi Isadore Hoffman, performed a small ceremony in the presence of my mother.

Jews seem to be ambivalent about conversion. There is a rabbinic strain that goes to great lengths to discourage people from becoming Jews and places many obstacles in their path. On the other hand, a more prevalent historic strain emphasizes that Abraham, the first Jew, was a convert and quotes the Hebrew Bible to the effect that the Messiah will be a descendent of Ruth, a convert. The Talmud, they continue, states that Israel was exiled among the nations "in order to increase their numbers with the addition of converts" (*Pesachim* 87b). Rabbi Akiva, one of the great sages and heroes of Jewish history, was reportedly the son of a convert.

† When our daughter, Julia, married Andrew Stevenson in September 1987, she requested Bill Anderson to join the officiating rabbi and be a part of the ceremony.

6

Bennington: Teaching the Girls

Bennington College was very different from the University of Minnesota. The school I left was an exceptional example of American higher public education. The University of Minnesota in the late forties had about 15,000 students on its two Twin City campuses, which were connected by a clanking trolley line that looped back and forth all day through Minneapolis and St. Paul.

Many of the students when I was there were World War II veterans. They were mostly male, many with wives and young families, all on the GI Bill. That act, which provided books and tuition, made college education possible for millions of veterans who could not have considered college before the war because of the cost. Their opportunity for advanced learning had profound effects on American education and society. They were serious students with broad experience; teaching them was exciting and stimulating.

The University of Minnesota had hundreds of faculty members, a campus spread over several thousand acres, a Big Ten football team of national renown that drew 60,000 roaring fans (including me) on a good Saturday, and large numbers of commuters who quickly disappeared to work and home when their classes were over. For all the fraternities and sororities, the university was a working-class school, too.

On its "farm" campus, a herd of cattle was cared for and studied in the dairy science curriculum; pigs, sheep, and horses were kept for animal husbandry students; and oats, barley, and corn grew on an experimental farm where tractors chugged powerfully not just to till the soil, but to teach. The children of poor farm families, as well as those from more affluent families, learned what was new and practical in agricultural science.

At the main campus, the Mississippi River, filled with huge barges of grain moving slowly downstream and coal coming up, flowed past grain elevators and flour mills and switching yards of track and freight cars, not far from major manufacturing companies. The whole area vibrated with the energy of the postwar world of America's economic dominance and free enterprise success.

The university was a successful example of a land grant college, part of a program that had transformed American education since it was enacted in 1862. Not only had it trained the state's young people, it had functioned as a cohesive social force, involving business, labor, and the professions in a special way. In part because of the university, Minneapolis had become a regional capital of trade and commerce.

What I came to in Bennington was a tiny jewel of private education, part of a community, but separate from it. Bennington had no more than 300 students, all female, nestled in rural southern Vermont, where, if you took the time, you would notice that the day began with bird song and ended with bright stars. In between, there was quiet. Even the sound of a shouted greeting or the laughter of the students was moderated by the trees and hills. Often, the single sound intruding on contemplation or reading was the gentle warning bell of a bicycle being slowly pedaled along a walk. There were virtually no sounds of the city to break the scene.

Quiet or not—and Maggie always appreciated nature more than I—my wife would rather have been in Chicago. It was her home. Roosevelt College, where I could have taught, was her alma mater, and Chicago was an industrial area filled with the activity of labor unions and their members. But since I had made my decision, I felt the die was cast.

It is significant and revealing, looking back, that I simply never considered Maggie's desire to pursue an independent career, even though I knew how much she loved her work with the union membership. I suppose, to the extent that I thought of it at all, that I blithely felt that if she wanted to work, she could find something wherever she was. I suspect that such a unilateral process would be unacceptable today to any of our children, male or female, and they would be right.

I thought only of my career and the opportunity I had to begin teaching in the special place that was Bennington. In this tiny college with its small but talented and creative faculty, there was an intensity that fed on itself, creating additional intellectual energy. You knew everybody almost immediately.

Fred Burkhart, the president, was a philosopher-historian, and Erich Fromm, a psychiatrist whose books I had read and admired, had recently published what was to become a classic, *Escape from Freedom*. I had used the book as a text in my classes at Minnesota, and now to be his colleague was satisfying.

Literary critic Stanley Hyman and his wife, the writer Shirley Jackson, were at the beginning of exceptional careers. A young poet, Howard Nemerov, later became poet laureate at the Library of Congress, as did Stanley Kunitz. Ben Belitt was another talented poet. The music and dance faculties seemed to keep to themselves, but they were gifted and highly esteemed.

I shared political science teaching with Oliver Garceau, a distinguished New Englander who was everyone's stereotype of a reserved, stiff native of Maine. Peter Drucker, not a political scientist but a social scientist just beginning to establish an international reputation as a sociological commentator on American business life and management, also taught some in our area. Edward and Mildred Hall,* cultural anthropologists, and Tom Brockway, a historian, taught me new ideas simply by sharing small talk. June and Jane Hanks, both distinguished anthropologists, lived in North Bennington in a rambling old house, and were particularly friendly to Maggie and me. Phil Sperling, a psychologist, later, with his wife Shirley, joined us in Washington. He and June Hanks died while I was writing this manuscript.†

---

* The Halls later came to Washington, where Ned served as a consultant to the State Department, advising diplomats on how cultural characteristics in countries to which they were assigned had to be understood. Their book, *The Silent Language*, proved very helpful.

† The person who has had more impact on my understanding of international affairs than any other I met at Bennington was not on the faculty, but had come there because of a friend who was. Bernard Taurer was an Austrian refugee invited to settle in Vermont by Horst Mendershausen, who taught economics at the college. Taurer had spent some time in the anti-Nazi underground in Norway with Willy Brandt, but, by the time we met, had focused all his intellectual energies on studying the Communist world. His wife, Bertha, worked in a local Vermont factory so that Bernard could spend his time reading and thinking about the Soviet Union, China, and the

I'd heard many of these names; I knew their books; I'd read their letters to the *New York Times* and their articles in scholarly journals and popular magazines. To be a beginner among them was, I felt, a great honor. To be accepted as a peer by some of them was even better. It was a wonderful place to start an academic career and indeed not a bad place to end one.

The faculty welcomed us warmly, and Maggie and I quickly grew to feel comfortable in Bennington. While they respected one another's privacy, the faculty were collegial and basically had only one another for intellectual discourse and stimulation, denied as they were the casual cultural opportunities that an urban surrounding provided so readily. It was a new world for me, and an exciting one.

I taught two classes, which I scheduled for Tuesdays and Thursdays so that my weekends began Thursday evening and ended on Tuesday morning. I certainly anticipated plenty of time to finish my Ph.D. thesis. Classes were small, never more than ten students and frequently fewer. The student body was mostly Eastern and affluent, with a strong bent toward art, dance, and music. For the most part, they were bright and eager to learn. Life for them was still a seminar to seek new experience and to probe its limits, although I found that the campus atmosphere made it possible for too many students to escape the realities of life.

My first day on campus, several of the students invited me to their rooms after class for a drink.* An innocent gesture, I know, but strange after Minnesota, which still had single-sex dormitories, no visiting privileges by the opposite sex, and certainly no alcohol or visits in the rooms by professors of the opposite sex.

For all the joys at Bennington, campus-centered politics in a Republican state, with no substantial or visible trade union presence,

---

Communist movement. Bernard taught an occasional class but was a compulsive free spirit who did not like regular teaching. I once arranged for him to do some work for Humphrey on a Senate committee, but he didn't like that either. He now lives in San Diego and still reads extensively about the Communist world. After forty years, we still correspond. Over those years, his analyses of the Soviet Union and China have been of greater value to me than the works of any other expert.

* One of those students, Sally Lieberman Smith, later came to Washington and started a school, as a pioneer in the field, for teaching children and adults with learning disabilities. Sally and her roommates were bright and serious students who took my course, Problems of Democracy. We began by studying the anti-democrats and, as a teaching technique, I would defend them against the challenges of the class. Years later, Sally told me that she and her classmates had decided I was a fascist and were ready to turn me in to the administration. When we began reading the pro-democracy writers as the course progressed, I was saved from their wrath.

seemed a little less real than the politics of the DFL, the career of Hubert Humphrey, and workers' education. But my political glands kept working, and I found minor ways to be active.

In late September, the *Bennington Banner* announced that "Norman Thomas . . . will be introduced by his personal friend, Professor Max Kampelman." I did present the Socialist party leader at a small meeting attended almost entirely, but not quite exclusively, by members of the college community, some of whom could vote.*

An irony of the evening was that though Maggie was still a member of the Socialist party and devoted to the Thomas candidacy, I had never joined. Indeed, as I introduced Norman, I felt it necessary to point out that I was not a member of the Socialist party, even as I spoke of my great affection for him and what he stood for in American life; I intended to vote for him.

Norman knew I was a social democrat and didn't expect a different kind of introduction. His friendship and affection invested me with a kind of distinction among the faculty and students, and I liked that. For Maggie, it was a more special evening, since she had not previously met Thomas. She followed up with a letter to the Bennington paper praising him and then, of course, voted for him in the fall presidential election.

It was a short autumn. We arrived in September and school broke for vacation in December, so I had little time to put down either geographic or academic roots.† I contacted the local Democratic party and its leaders, the Goodall Huttons, who became friends immediately. As soon as Goodall learned that I had worked with Humphrey, he had visions of my rising to a special role in state politics under his patronage and guidance. But the party was neither very active nor influential, and I had been spoiled by the DFL. As a result, although I planned to become more active in Vermont politics with time, my doctoral dissertation had to be completed and sent to Minnesota for approval. That would be my first priority after teaching.

---

* Thomas did not understand why I later left Bennington to work for Humphrey. He was skeptical of all politicians, including Humphrey, whom he had not yet met, and thought I was a good teacher and should remain one. In 1950, when Thomas was in Washington, I arranged for the two of them to get together. Humphrey's admiration for Thomas's integrity and leadership came through during the meeting. They hit it off well enough so that when Thomas left, he indicated that he understood my choice.

† During the preparation of this book, I received a telephone call and then a visit from Dr. Elizabeth Coleman, Bennington's current president, asking me to visit the college this autumn and spend some time with the students and faculty. I was very pleased to accept. I no longer think of returning to the campus to teach during my retirement from public life, but for many years I did.

7

Washington, Here I Come

The national political scene in 1948 was not, I thought, very attractive or compelling. The presidential campaign offered an unexciting set of candidates, none of whom captured my enthusiasm, none capable of articulating an inspiring vision for the postwar world.

Tom Dewey, the Republican candidate for president, was considered the inevitable winner. For Maggie and me, that seemed a dismal result, electing a man who represented so much we found unappealing in our society, a leader of the status quo of inequity and insensitivity.

Conditions on the left were even more difficult. The Henry Wallace candidacy had become an excursion into nonsense led by the Communists and their fellow travelers; and, of course, Norman Thomas and the socialists had not a glimmer of a chance, as much as I liked and deeply admired him. Harry Truman should have been an easy choice for me, but I viewed him with very little positive feeling. The fact that he was a "common" man without the aristocratic and commanding style of Roosevelt did not trouble me, but I thought of him as an undistinguished product of the Pendergast political machine in Missouri, with inadequate qualifications to be president. His Senate record did convey a healthy commitment to public service and his straight talk during the campaign was appealing, but, on balance, I remained skeptical about him. In retrospect, of course, I was very wrong about Truman.

He had been the victim of three years of political assault and invidious comparison. Roosevelt's death and the end of the war had changed the political climate in the United States. Differences between conservatives and liberals had been muted during the war. Roosevelt, for all the right-wing criticism, had been too popular to be damaged by even sustained attack, much less sporadic outcries. His personality and power overwhelmed his opponents.

Truman was another matter. He was relatively unknown when he became president and functioned without the charisma that would have deflected conservative criticism or attracted strong liberal support. From the moment he was sworn in, the contentious issues and problems of the postwar world, at home and abroad, were debated, often bitterly and divisively. In my youthful impatience, I missed his strengths and solidity. I was not alone.

Even the Americans for Democratic Action had toyed in 1947 with seeking an alternative to Truman, for a while thinking about drafting Dwight Eisenhower as the Democratic nominee. That failed, of course, but it further damaged Truman's credentials with many liberals and left him with reservations about ADA leaders, including Humphrey.

Truman and Humphrey resolved those differences quickly after the convention and campaigned well together in Minnesota. Humphrey, with his normal enthusiasm, became an ardent Truman advocate and friend. I, at a distance, was much more reserved. Though Truman said the right things during the campaign and developed his feisty "give 'em hell, Harry," persona, it was his opposition from both left and right that made him the best real choice for the country in my eyes. That was not a lot of inspiration. It made paying attention to my teaching career easy, with my political thoughts, such as they were, essentially on Minnesota and Humphrey's Senate election.

With each passing day, Humphrey's election seemed more likely. As a result, I looked to Minnesota on election night with special anticipation. Bennington was an hour ahead of Minnesota. Paper ballots took a long time to count and results were reported slowly, particularly from rural areas, so I patiently waited until late to make a call "home" to Minneapolis, since long-distance phone calls were an extravagance even on an election day. It would be close to midnight before enough results were in to be definitive, but even earlier the returns were encouraging.

I talked to Eugenie Anderson and others who confirmed Humphrey's impending victory. "We're going to win. We're going to win" was the repeated refrain, a mixture of surprise that it was actually happening and excitement about what it meant. Alone with Maggie in Bennington, I nevertheless felt a part of the celebration as we savored Hubert's victory in our little apartment a thousand miles away from the celebrants.

Then, as we continued to listen to the radio, the news about Truman unexpectedly carrying states he wasn't supposed to win served to increase our excitement. We listened, first with skepticism, then with more and more wonder. In those days before television and exit polls, when only the radio brought the results as they were available, there was a different quality to your attention. You stayed close to the radio set and listened more attentively, more quietly somehow since there were no visuals to provide further information. If someone talked at the wrong moment, the information was gone; there was no switching channels to grab what had been lost. While you could move from radio station to radio station (and did), not much of that was done.

By morning, the fact of a Truman triumph over Wallace and Dewey made up for the campaign. From Humphrey's point of view, that victory was certainly important. He had campaigned hard for Truman, invited him into Minnesota, and helped carry the state for him. That was more than electoral votes; that was political bonding. For a freshman senator, being tight with an incumbent president is not an insignificant advantage.* For many of us, part of the Humphrey circle, there was immense satisfaction in knowing that Humphrey's leadership and our work in the previous several years had paid off. There were many mayors, but only ninety-six senators. "Senator Humphrey" had an impressive ring to it.

On that crisp Vermont morning after the election, although I was tired from lack of sleep, my smile was particularly wide as I greeted friends and students. I had expected Hubert to win, but the reality was breathtaking even at a distance. Getting good things done was what democracy was all about, and now Senator Humphrey could lead the way in promoting liberal programs nationally.

* That was never clearer than the morning in 1952 when the *Washington Post* carried the obituary of a federal district judge. Minnesota Governor Luther Youngdahl, a politically attractive Republican who would have been the logical and the most formidable candidate against Humphrey in 1954, had told Humphrey that he would consider leaving elective politics for a seat on the federal bench. As I finished the obituary, I reached for the telephone to call Humphrey. When he answered, I asked if he had read the morning paper. He laughed and said he had already called the White House and had an appointment with the president that morning. Truman remembered that Youngdahl had been the most prominent Republican to support him when he fired General MacArthur and soon appointed Youngdahl to the bench, where he served with distinction. Humphrey's most dangerous potential opponent was now removed from the race.

In my father's arms behind my grandmother in her babushka. My mother is to her left and in front of my Uncle Max. At the top right are Bertha and Eddie Altman, with Eleanor between them.

At age three—I have been resisting black-tie functions ever since.

With my parents at summer camp, 1935.

With my Aunt Shaindel in front of her Jewish bookstore in the Bronx, 1938.

With my mother at my graduation from college, New York University, 1940.

Our Quaker work campers, Reading, Pennsylvania, 1940.

Taking a Sunday break at CPS Camp, Big Flats, New York, 1943. To my right are Gunnar Peterson and Marvin Penner.

The day we were married,
August 21, 1948, Milwaukee.

With labor lawyer Ben Sigal and Humphrey aide Bill Shore at our small
Washington apartment, 1949.

Celebrating Hubert's birthday at the Humphrey home on Coquelin Terrace, Chevy Chase. Muriel receives her piece of cake with Mondale looking on. Daughter Nancy next to Hubert; Cyril King at far left; Bill Shore back of Muriel; staff wait their turn. 1949.

With President Harry S. Truman and some Minnesota friends, 1951.

With Maggie and the children, Ensenada, Mexico, 1961.

The Happy Warrior, Hubert Humphrey, with some of his spellbound supporters—Julie, Anne, and Jeff, 1964. (*City News Bureau, Washington, D.C.*)

"Washington Week in Review" during the early days with *Time*'s Neil MacNeil's back, Peter Lisagor of the *Chicago Daily News* next to him, Charles Corddry of the *Baltimore Sun*, and Hedrick Smith of the *New York Times* to my right, 1968.

A conversation with Israel's President Ephraim Katzir, Jerusalem, 1974.

With President Gerald Ford, 1976. (*Wagner International Photos*)

A tour of the Old City of Jerusalem with Mayor Teddy Kollek, former Secretary of State Henry Kissinger, and former U.S. Senator from Connecticut Abraham Ribicoff, 1978.

A handshake with Egyptian President Anwar Sadat. Witnesses are Ted Mann and Egyptian Ambassador Ghorbal, 1978.

With Secretary of State George Shultz, closing session of Madrid CSCE meeting, 1983.

The Geneva Nuclear Arms Reduction Talks open as I greet Soviet Ambassador Victor Karpov at the U.S. Mission in Geneva, 1985.

A final briefing and sendoff for the Geneva negotiations, the White House, March 1985. Moving from the president (*bottom right*) to the vice president (*bottom left*): Secretary of State George Shultz; Arms Control and Disarmament Agency head Kenneth Adelman; presidential adviser Paul Nitze; the three negotiators; National Security Adviser Robert McFarlane; his deputy Ron Lehman (*next to him*); presidential adviser General Edward Ronny; Chairman of the Joint Chiefs of Staff, General John Vessey; Secretary of Defense Caspar Weinberger. (*Official White House photograph*)

Greeting Vice President and Mrs. George Bush at dinner in Geneva, 1985.

The president is a good listener, 1986. (*Official White House photograph*)

With my Soviet colleague, USSR Head of Delegation and Deputy Foreign Minister Yuri Vorontsov, Geneva, 1987.

With Yuri Vorontsov and U.S. Senators Moynihan, Johnston, and Pell, Geneva, 1987. (*Photo D. Stampfli, © Associated Press, Zurich*)

Greeting Israel's President Chaim Herzog at White House state dinner in his honor, 1987. (*Official White House photograph*)

Greeting Raisa Gorbachev at the official state dinner in honor of her husband, the White House, 1987. (*Official White House photograph*)

At my desk in the Department of State, 1988.

Toasting our oldest, Anne, and Dennis at their wedding at our home, June 1984.

Some of the family visit the State Department. Sarah next to Maggie, Jeff and Nina to the back, Julie and Andy to the right, 1989.

Greeting an Ethiopian Jewish family, Jerusalem, 1991.

Greeting President Mauno Koivisto of Finland, Finnish Embassy, Washington, D.C., 1991.

With Speaker of the House of Representatives Tom Foley, 1991.

Since we took seriously his prospects for being president of the United States, the election was also a giant step in that direction, and that was good for Hubert and the country. My participation was of no importance. I would cheer him from a distance, help him only as an extracurricular activity. I had been there in a special way early, and that made me feel good. I would not be far away, no matter where I taught, in the future.

Almost immediately, I began to hear from mutual friends, particularly Eugenie Anderson, George Demetriou, and Art Naftalin, about Humphrey's plans. They contained no surprises. He would pursue the civil rights fight he had defined so well and dramatically at the Democratic convention that summer; he would work closely with the labor movement on issues it cared about—labor legislation including Taft-Hartley repeal and minimum wage, education and health, and taxation. All that seemed logical and settled.

The staff was another question. Neither Art nor Eugenie wanted to leave Minnesota, and George was never comfortable as a staff aide. Art liked teaching, writing, being part of the university community, and, in short, being his own man. He had tried the staff role in the mayor's office and didn't really care for it.

Eugenie had a young family and substantial wealth and was a leader in her own right. She was not interested in working on anyone's staff and I am sure that neither Hubert nor she gave even momentary, much less serious, thought to the possibility. Her prestige and skills were vital to a strong DFL, and she certainly had more to contribute in Minnesota than she would have had on a Washington staff.

But Eugenie and Art, like so many close Humphrey associates, worried about who would be on his staff, who would invite their involvement, who would not reject their advice. I thought about that, too. Each of us felt we had a special relationship with Humphrey that would survive any staff, but we knew how powerful a staff can be.

I now know that the concerns were not unique to the Humphrey entourage. Friends, family, and staff invariably compete for the attention of elected officials, too often becoming turf warriors in a battle that does not help anyone. The term "palace guard" comes quickly to the lips of those at a distance. Within the palace, there is often a gatekeeper who protects the king from the courtiers. Some officials take silent pleasure in the infighting; others just suffer silently. Few ever do anything about it.

I assume that Eugenie and Art thought I would be good for Humphrey while remaining a close friend of theirs. Their prime concern was his success and the advancement of our liberal ideals, since patronage, power, and celebrity were not their motivations.

I told them that I was not interested in leaving my new home and my new career, that I had a doctoral thesis to complete, a family to begin, a career to continue. My ambition did not carry me toward staff status, any more than theirs did. But none of that took into account my interest in Humphrey, his distinctive warmth and appeal, or my curiosity about new political experiences.

Soon after the election, Bill Shore, a friend and Humphrey's bright young aide, called, filled with talk of the future, and said Humphrey would like Maggie and me to meet him in New York City while he and Muriel were there for a League for Industrial Democracy (LID) dinner where he was to be the main speaker. The league's leaders included our friend Norman Thomas and Harry Laidler, LID's executive director since its beginning, a kindly and courtly socialist activist and thinker. Humphrey was close to the labor leaders from the needle trades and to A. Phillip Randolph of the Brotherhood of Sleeping Car Porters, the leading Negro trade unionist in America, who supported the league and was important in defining its activities.

The league was more than a letterhead committee, even though it had limited membership beyond its New York–based officers and board. Its youth activities found a ready audience on college campuses, and its published studies were widely distributed. It had been created and financed by our friends in the unions, functioning as an educational and advocacy force encouraging stronger trade unions, among other things. The league had a strong democratic socialist emphasis mingled with traditional American liberalism.

All of that appealed to Maggie, who did not know Humphrey well and Muriel almost not at all. I thought that she would enjoy Humphrey in that setting and that the trip would give us our first break from Bennington. Among friends, Humphrey was likely to turn in an exciting performance.

While Humphrey was a great conciliator and persuader of those who did not agree with him, he was even better at raising to new heights the spirits of those with whom he shared liberal goals. If preaching to the choir was an art, he was as good as Michelangelo. He excited not only his audiences but himself, and it was fun to watch.

He arrived at the podium with sparkling eyes and a smile that gave people a good feeling before he even opened his mouth. His body language explained, "I am really glad to be here. I have an important message." He almost never worked off a prepared text but began with a few notes, often not knowing precisely what his paramount message would be. Laughter was always part of his repertoire, not from canned jokes, but from jollying someone on the dais, making fun of himself, deflating some "enemy" of the group.

That introduction behind him, he would take off into a description of the better world that was possible if only we all worked together. His voice was not a deep one, but he gathered in his audience, whether they were college professors or workers, enveloping them in his vision of the good society of justice and liberty that was not only possible but inevitable if we had the will to make it real.

He preached a gospel of love, though he almost never used that word. People sometimes cried as he described social sins and deprivation. They cheered when he offered hope and urged change. Humphrey thought there was a correlation between perspiration and inspiration, and he worked hard at the podium. He often talked too long, but it was a rare audience that didn't go away feeling better about themselves and their country.

Humphrey loitered after his speeches, shaking hands, signing autographs, chatting with friends. He had phenomenal recall of names and faces, of children in college, of mothers and fathers and their health. He not only *seemed* to care; he *did* care, and people sensed it and responded to him with affection. He found the process refreshing.

We had a wonderful, chatty weekend, visiting with old labor friends and new ones, sharing the edge of the spotlight on Humphrey. We talked of his future, of his goals in the Senate, of how the liberal forces might be led nationally, as they had been in Minnesota, and coalesced into a more powerful presence. It was heady stuff, but I still thought only of helping from a distance as I pursued my academic career. The question of my becoming part of his staff never came up.

Indeed, Humphrey asked me to join him as he interviewed Milton Stewart, chief aide to Congressman Franklin D. Roosevelt, Jr., to be his legislative director. I strongly recommended Milton, whom I knew and liked as an experienced Washington hand. Milton would balance Bill Simms, Humphrey's mayoral aide, who was coming from Minnesota to handle the management of the office and politics back home. I returned to Bennington assuming that would be the outcome.

I heard no more from Humphrey until just before Christmas. Bill Shore found Maggie and me in Chicago. He called to say that Milton Stewart had not been hired and that Humphrey wanted me to come to Washington to help Bill Simms set up the policy side of the office.

I explained that Maggie and I were spending the holidays with her family and would return to Vermont after that so I could work on my thesis. Part of the appeal Bennington offered had been the three-month winter break while the students were on a unique work-study program. I hated having my thesis unfinished and hoped to complete it during this break.

Humphrey followed up, first with a telegram early in January that read: "Can you come help us for your three-month break. Wire collect." Then he reached me by phone, humorously chiding me for my soft life with few classes and long vacations. He said, and truly believed, that it was sinful for anyone to have five months of vacation a year. Humphrey barely approved of vacations at all and certainly not of long ones. His Protestant ethic was offended by it. As Bill Shore had warned and the telegram indicated, he wanted me to help get his office started.

Despite our wonderful reunion in New York at the league dinner, I was momentarily reluctant, but the hesitancy faded almost immediately. I told myself that two or three months was not forever, that it would be a nice change of pace from academic work that had begun in Minnesota and continued in Bennington, and that Maggie and I had many friends to visit in Washington.

I did worry that working for Humphrey would affect my personal friendship with him. Being a staff member is by its nature a subservient relationship in almost all cases. I didn't want that. On the other hand, being a colleague was clearly impossible since he was the senator and I was not. I liked the relationship as it was. I did not like being someone's camp follower or sidekick, even someone for whom I had great respect and affection. A short trial run made sense. If it didn't work out, I would have lost nothing, and our relationship probably would not suffer. If it did, I could look forward to both teaching at Bennington and having a periodic presence in Washington as well.

There were other potential problems. People before and after me complained that working for Humphrey was sometimes disconcerting. They fretted aloud that he was into a thousand different subjects, since everything interested him. His staff sometimes, and his critics always, said he could never say no to supplicants and was moved by the last person who saw him. There was no question about the former and some truth to the latter.

Strangely, both criticisms seemed reasons for me to join the Humphrey staff, to try to deal with those problems whenever they were real. There was a role for me, I decided, because my own interests were broad and I could put in context the advice he got. I did not see myself as his alter ego, but I did not see myself as a clerk, either.

There was a remaining problem. Maggie had just found a large union in Albany, New York, that was interested in hiring her to do educational work. Albany was about forty miles away from Bennington, which was a long commute, but she was prepared to do that to continue her career. Thus she was dismayed when I told her I was considering our moving to Washington. Since she was still a socialist and looked on the major parties with some skepticism, she didn't share my involvement in Democratic party politics, or, since she hardly knew him, my intense admiration for Hubert. I was selfishly convinced, however—and I am probably part of the last male generation for which this was true—that we simply could not afford to permit Maggie's preferences to prevail, given the opportunity we had. I expected, and was prepared, to support our family while she raised the children. But in return I had to be free to make the necessary decisions pertaining to my career. I remember telling Maggie that she should cultivate a more flexible attitude. She answered rather testily, I thought, that it was easier to be flexible when you were the one making the decisions.

I said to Maggie, in a rationalization that changed my life, "I can always teach, but this is the opportunity of a lifetime—to see Washington and American government up close. What could be better for a political scientist?" I agreed to put off finishing my thesis and to move to Washington for three months. That is all I intended to do.

They were three fascinating and fulfilling months. I discovered that I could be Humphrey's friend and that our relationship would not be less for my serving on the staff. Humphrey took me around with him to caucuses and meetings, if not as a colleague, at least as a close friend and associate. He took pleasure in introducing me as Professor Kampelman or Dr. Kampelman, at that point an honorary degree awarded unilaterally by him. The introduction began as a kind of joke, but there weren't many Ph.D.s on congressional staffs at the time, and he seriously thought it added a certain prestige to both of us, particularly as members of a tiny liberal group seeking some respectability on the road to legislative success and social change.

Humphrey, of course, had special problems with many of his colleagues, who saw him as a wild firebrand of liberalism, brash and aggressive. He was younger by far than almost all of them. They knew him only from his civil rights speech at the 1948 Democratic party convention, which led many Southern delegates to walk out, and they did not like or trust him.

When he made the cover of *Time* with a background depiction of a tornado out of the west, the metaphor confirmed their antagonistic feelings. Tornadoes were mostly wind, destructive, and unpredictable. They were to be avoided at all costs. Those early months were a strain on a man who liked to be liked by everyone, frustrating because there seemed no immediate solution.

The solution arrived by indirection. He was asked to become the national chairman of the Americans for Democratic Action. At first blush, becoming spokesman for the most liberal non-Communist organization in the United States seemed the wrong thing to do, inevitably inviting more wrath and anger. Both Humphrey and I felt he ought to do it anyway because there was an obligation to lend the stature of his new office to what he believed in. Further, the role meant recognition as a national leader.

Instead of thinking of himself only as a discomfited young liberal freshman senator from Minnesota, he could now think of himself as a national liberal power of a vital and growing force in American politics. One clear and almost immediate sign of his power came when he was able to convince the Steelworkers and other unions to join the Textile Workers, the ILGWU, and the United Auto Workers in making monthly contributions to keep the ADA strong enough to present its views and influence the social agenda in the United States.

Self-esteem grew out of that change fairly quickly and somehow translated into a begrudging respect from the other senators. As he struggled less directly to be liked, he set about doing what came naturally to him, working conscientiously at his job, learning the rules so that he could respect them and use them, and cultivating friendship in the normal course of his work and without feeling that the Senate was the only place to shine.

He did, of course, quickly shine there. His tongue, which often got him into trouble outside the Senate as it became identified with loquaciousness, soon became an asset in the Senate. The criticism that he spoke on too many subjects disappeared, to some extent, as it became clear that he spoke not just with sincerity, but also with a command of the subject matter.*

With his ability to express spontaneously and vividly what he had to say, he was entertaining. To listen to Humphrey in debate was to hear the Senate in frequent laughter and enjoyment. He was always courteous to his opponents, although his keen mind and quick tongue could deflate the pompous and expose specious arguments with ease. His responses could hurt, particularly where the opposition itself had been sharp or unkind, but Humphrey usually resisted the impulse to nail an opponent meanly.

* His critics, including some liberal ones, thought his intense glibness was demagogic. It is true that he could rouse an audience when he chose to inveigh against the bankers, the rich, or the utilities, but he seemed to be aware of this danger, as he would inject balancing notes into his speeches before ending them.

One day, extolling British life under the Labour party policies and direction, Humphrey was challenged by Senator Homer Capehart of Indiana to "tell us one thing that Britain has that we do not." Without missing a beat, Humphrey responded with wonderful irrelevance, "Westminster Abbey." The laughter bewildered Capehart, and Humphrey flew blithely on.

My adjustment was easier than Humphrey's. I came in as an unknown and worked quietly to get along with conservatives as well as liberals. The Senate was a far different place then.* Each staff was small, and working relationships with the principal were often intimate and sharing. Basically, all substantive matters were my domain. I was the legislative assistant; there was no other. When Humphrey pursued an idea or program, I was the crew behind him, or the scout moving on ahead. His fertile mind would have kept a small army busy, and it surely kept me busy.

Our office rarely closed before eleven P.M. or midnight. We behaved as though there were no clock or lifestyle or family that had equal priority. The scene was the same every night: a secretary or two would be typing letters to constituents, getting ready to cart the letters to the nearby post office as a final stop on the way home. When Humphrey was out somewhere making a speech or entertaining a constituent, he might well show up still filled with energy at ten or eleven o'clock, ready to dictate or sign letters or talk about the next day's schedule. If you didn't get out before he arrived, the day could go on for several additional hours.

The mail had a compulsive hold on Humphrey, who thought of fast response as a form of social work. He said, "There are a lot of lonely people out there who don't get mail every day. The least they deserve from me is an answer if they write." So we wrote. Periodically, we would have "form letter night," during which we would spend from two to four hours sealing and addressing form letters done in response to some issue that had evoked a lot of letters, many of them form inquiries or comments. We worked at least half days on Saturdays to clean up the week's leftovers.

Others—staff, volunteers, or friends—would be there pursuing all sorts of policy dreams, day and night, weekday and weekend. We worked in three narrow, high-ceilinged rooms cluttered with boxes of

---

* The growth of congressional staff has been phenomenal. There were 31,000 professional staff members in 1989, at least eight to ten times the number in 1949 when I joined the Senate staff. The congressional budget in 1990 is an estimated $2.7 billion, or about $5 million per member.

stationery and newsletters and documents and lined with file cabinets. The wastebaskets were smudged with traces of the crumpled, worn-out carbon paper that was testimony to the prodigious amount of constituent correspondence that flowed into and out of the office. Minnesota newspapers piled up for the moments when someone could read them not so much for the news, but to clip notes of anniversaries and events so that Humphrey could send out congratulatory or condolence letters.

Humphrey's personal office had the standard Senate furniture: dark wooden bookcases filled with *U.S. Codes* that he would never read and *Congressional Records* he would scan and file. He still smoked and would go through one Lucky Strike after another as he sat behind his desk or moved frenetically around the room. Late at night, when all of us should have been home, Bill Simms and I would sit in the heavy brown leather chairs in front of him, going over the day's events, talking about programs and ideas that needed to be presented, about speeches to be made, about people he needed to see. While Humphrey and I disagreed on some things and argued occasionally, it was eerie how often our approach, our interests, and our reactions were similar or identical.

Our discussions throughout the day and into those evenings were about matters before the Senate and the nation. The country seemed polarized between Republican isolationism and Truman-advocated involvement in the reconstruction of a war-devastated Europe. The battle had been going on since Truman's swearing in, and the Senate became the battleground where many issues were fought out and the ideological battle lines drawn. They were not easy times for Humphrey's ideas or for the Truman program.

In theory, liberals then never had the votes to pass anything. In fact, Truman's election scared some of those who might oppose him and a liberal program into a begrudging support, at least part of the time. The logic was simple: if he had the support of the people, he had clout with Congress. We were prepared to focus on persuasion, tactic, and incremental advance, and to be satisfied with almost imperceptible gain. Carrying Truman's program or pushing his own ideas, Humphrey, and thus the rest of us, was inspired to move more aggressively and purposefully.

We were liberal on domestic policy and strong on defense issues, as Truman was, as the Democratic party was, and as Franklin Roosevelt had been.* But working for Humphrey meant working toward those ends in his distinct way. We rarely dealt with opposition in anger, preferring conciliation. We meant to carry the day through persuasion,

---

* This historic Democratic party support for a strong defense program has been too often forgotten or ignored in more recent decades at great political cost to the party.

whelming those with whom we disagreed with kindness, not meanness, forgiving rather than hating. This was instinctive with Humphrey, a deeply religious man, and compatible with my personal pacifism and personality.

Even as we focused on the office and the Senate itself, I was also the main contact with the labor movement, with the ADA and other liberal groups, and with the national Democratic party. Since we had no press secretary, I dealt with the national press as well. Both necessity and inclination kept my door open to everybody—press, politicians, academics, lobbyists, and constituents. It was instant and total immersion in a world of real power with the means to change society. I was not yet thirty years old and Humphrey himself only thirty-seven. The future could be ours.

It was an interesting time for Maggie as well. She was among people she knew and liked. We stayed at first with our union friend John Edelman, who was then the legislative director of the Textile Workers Union. John and his wife, Kate, were older than we and had a big rambling house in Virginia, now empty of children. They welcomed us like their own children, but treated us like colleagues.

Their daughter, Anne, had married Ben Stephansky, a friend of ours who taught at Sarah Lawrence, where Anne was a student. We had all been involved in the workers' education programs at the University of Wisconsin. Ben and Anne had been at our wedding in Wisconsin, and we all drove to New York together soon after the ceremony.

When it became clear that we would stay in Washington more than a few weeks, we rented an apartment of our own. That apartment on Connecticut Avenue was a sterile place and confirmed Maggie's belief that only a house was a home.* But, again, of course, it was to be only a temporary place before our return to Bennington.

The three months raced by in a spasm of sixteen-hour days and seven-day weeks. They were not fatiguing but exhilarating, not a drain but an inspiration. I was not ready to leave Washington, and Hum-

---

* Humphrey grew up in small towns where virtually everyone, no matter how poor, lived in a house, since there were no real apartments. When it later appeared we might stay in Washington, he and Maggie teamed up to weaken my fears about taking on a mortgage for a house. I remembered my father. I resisted for a while, but finally caved in. About a dozen years later, when the Humphrey children were off on their own, Muriel decided she wanted to move from their suburban home, with its mortgage paid off, to a more compact but elegant apartment near the Capitol. Humphrey wanted to stay put, but the move made sense to me. I helped Muriel arrange the condo purchase, and we presented the papers to Hubert for his signature, a virtual fait accompli. He accused me of finally "getting even," but grew to love the apartment, even as I had grown comfortable living in our house.

phrey did not want me to leave. Instead of hiring a legislative aide, I hired myself. Maggie once again went along, although I knew her feelings were mixed as I plunged into a second new career in the first six months of our marriage.

Since the new semester at Bennington was soon to begin, President Fred Burkhart and I talked about what I intended to do. I was teaching two courses at Bennington, two ninety-minute sessions per week for each course. Burkhart suggested that, as I was undecided, I put the question to the students: would they like a different professor, would they like to drop the courses, or would they prefer a four-hour session for each course led by me every other weekend?

There was a certain exotic quality in my flying up from Washington, and they chose that option. For the rest of the year, I taught on every other Friday night from seven to eleven P.M. and on Saturday morning from eight A.M. until noon, staying over Saturday night to socialize with the faculty. It was a doubly rewarding but exhausting arrangement. I wanted to continue to do both, but it hardly seemed possible as it became clear to me that Humphrey needed my full attention and energy, and I wanted to focus on legislation and politics. We both wanted our newly defined relationship to continue.

I turned to my old mentor, Evron Kirkpatrick, who had helped welcome Maggie and me to Washington, introducing us to academics and government officials he knew. He had himself done a similar double duty earlier, commuting to Minnesota from time to time to teach even as he worked in Washington. He confirmed my decision.

By June, I decided it was fairer to everyone if I simply took a leave of absence from Bennington in the fall.* A leave that never ends was not fair either. When the three months stretched into years, I ultimately simply resigned my teaching post at Bennington.

Dreams came true during those early years in the Senate. Humphrey became more and more a national leader and spokesman for liberal and progressive causes. He went from pariah to respected peer long before his reelection in 1954. His apprenticeship as a senator was clearly a successful one, and we knew he would soon be not just a journeyman, but a master.

I worked with him, and I learned with him. It was a time of immense satisfaction. My earlier concerns that a staff role would di-

---

* I decided earlier that my parting effort of the year would be to have Humphrey give the commencement address, sharing with my colleagues and the students the warmth and wisdom of this special friend. He was invited and accepted and then gave a truly awful speech, wandering, repetitious, and uninspiring. It may be that he was still the nervous country boy faced with the sophisticated and affluent East.

minish our friendship totally disappeared. He went out of his way to make me feel we were partners in a liberal mission.

As a result, every day felt like a triumphant one for me, bringing some small accomplishment, filled with little acts that helped him on his way and occasionally defined new ideas for the liberal caucus. Every day made us more confident that we were moving the country closer to a just and decent society for everyone. I woke each morning excited by what I might get done that day or that week. I went to bed each night exhausted, but satisfied that the democratic process worked to the peoples' benefit and that I had contributed some little bit to that process.

This life seemed right to me, more socially productive than either my wartime civilian public service or my brief teaching experience, as much as I had felt comfortable with both. It was fulfilling. I could see change, and I liked it. I dealt with people of ideas and commitment who turned to Humphrey as a voice and a vote who could make things happen. I could watch an idea of mine, or one I had gleaned from others, catch Humphrey's imagination, be elevated and expanded by his mind, and blossom as it attracted support among liberal and labor leaders who looked to Humphrey for direction. If it worked its way into policy, either as a directive of an executive agency or as part of legislation and became law, I enjoyed a real sense of accomplishment.

I have never gotten over the thrill, even to this day more than forty years later, when I approach the Capitol dome, sit in either the Senate or the House chamber, or walk the historic congressional corridors.

Our small staff followed Humphrey's fertile mind and unlimited interests into civil and human rights issues—getting the American Bowling Congress to allow Negroes to bowl where they had been kept out; helping the ethnic groups from the Baltics and Eastern Europe in their quest for identity here; providing wheat to the starving in India;* protesting Soviet anti-Semitism.

---

* Some time during 1950 or 1951, I was visited by an elderly refugee from Germany whose severe lameness required him to use a cane. He identified himself as Dr. Francis Joseph Weiss, a biochemist with a degree in economics as well. He had heard Hubert speak at an ADA meeting. He appreciated our Wheat for India campaign, but we should know, he said, that most of the wheat shipped would rot by virtue of the weather and vermin and would barely help those who were starving. He talked to me of an ancient biblical food, bulgur, a form of parboiled wheat, which could also be substituted for the less nutritious rice and was immune from rot. He gave me some of his articles to read. I introduced him to Humphrey, and we employed him to write a report for us on the subject.

It took years for us to overcome bureaucratic resistance, but with the later help of Orville Freeman, when he became secretary of agriculture under Kennedy, and George McGovern, Kennedy's Food for Peace director, bulgur became one of the commodities we sent overseas under our relief programs. It also remains a staple in the Kampelman household diet.

We worked on expanding Social Security to include medical care for the elderly and incurred the wrath of the American Medical Association. Humphrey looked for ways to use American agricultural surpluses to feed the world's hungry, and he pursued labor's goals, which transcended their prime interests in labor legislation into broader education and social agendas. Humphrey, remembering his life as a pharmacist and family drugstore employee, became the champion of small business to the surprise and chagrin of some and the delight of others.

There was quite literally nothing that he would not take on legislatively if he thought a distressing condition could be improved, or a problem could be solved. I was student and teacher every day, working on old issues and new ones, hoping to mold them into a progressive direction. I reached out beyond our office to strengthen relations with other liberal senatorial offices and with the liberal establishment in Washington.

With the decision to remain, Maggie began to look for a job in the labor movement and soon, after a brief stint working for the government, which she disliked, began what she liked so much—working with union members who came to Washington for mini-institutes on political education and congressional relations. It was an exciting time in our lives.

8

The National Political Arena Opens Its Doors

One of Humphrey's first appointments to his Senate staff was Cyril King, a resident of the U.S. Virgin Islands, who was pursuing graduate studies in public administration and political science at American University. With a wife, Agnes, and a newborn baby, Lillia, he needed a job and was brought to Humphrey's attention by his secretary, Charlotte Orton. Cyril, a dignified, effervescent, and energetic young man, started as an office runner and very quickly became, in effect, the office manager, expediting the large number of tasks required for the development of constituent relationships.

Early on, Humphrey invited Cyril to join him for lunch in the Capitol's Senate dining room so that they could become better acquainted. I was with them and witnessed the tension and subdued excitement in that private room as Cyril and Hubert entered. The headwaiter told me that he believed Cyril was the first Negro to be served in that room since the Reconstruction days following the Civil War. Senator Russell Long of Louisiana, a former classmate of Hubert's at Louisiana State University, soon followed in Hubert's footsteps.

Maggie and I became good friends with Cyril and Agnes, who constantly urged us to vacation in the Virgin Islands. At the time, I wasn't even quite certain where the islands were located. When Cyril received his degree in 1954, he became increasingly active in the politics of his home. Shortly thereafter, Maggie and I purchased an apartment in the Virgin Islands on one of its beaches. We and our children thoroughly enjoyed that beautiful island, and through Cyril's recommendation, I helped organize the College of the Virgin Islands.

When Jack Kennedy was elected president in 1960, he appointed Ralph Paiewonsky, a highly respected St. Thomas community leader and businessman from a noted family, as governor of the U.S. Virgin Islands. Humphrey persuaded the president to appoint Cyril as government secretary, the equivalent of lieutenant governor. The Kennedy administration later introduced full democracy into the islands by providing for the two top government positions to be elected rather than appointed. Paiewonsky and King were then elected to their respective positions. Cyril in 1974 ran for governor and won, becoming the first elected native-born black governor of the Virgin Islands. He asked me to become the attorney for the islands in dealing with their Washington relationships. This fortunately required us to make frequent trips there. We derived a great deal of satisfaction as we watched Cyril mature and stubbornly insist on high standards of integrity and efficiency in government. With Cyril's death in January 1978 from cancer while still in office, an era ended in the life of the Virgin Islands, and our family's interest and participation in its affairs waned.

One day, while Paiewonsky, an extremely capable and innovative public official, was governor, he told me of conversations he had with the governor and leading officials of the British Virgin Islands who indicated the timeliness of discussing merger with the U.S. Virgin Islands through acquisition by the United States. Ralph favored the approach, as did I, but he could not get anyone's serious attention in the Kennedy White House. I interested Hubert in the idea; he told me some days later that he found no opposition but little interest in either the White House or the Department of the Interior. I do not know how seriously Hubert pushed the idea, but I vividly recall thinking that I hoped the country and some future president would not regret our shortsightedness of the moment.

My main concern was the Senate itself. As wonderful as those times were, I had my own adjustments to make. As a political scientist, I had read and taught about the Congress and understood, I thought, the tensions between it and the executive branch. I favored a strong political party system that could facilitate the enactment of needed legislation. I had thought of the Senate, with its conservative coalition of southern Democrats and northern Republicans, as a swamp of nay-sayers. That certainly was the conventional wisdom held at the time by the liberal forces in the United States and particularly by academics who wrote about the Congress.*

Yet, once I was a part of the Senate, my feelings began to change. The ambiance as well as the experience contributed to that change. The Senate wing of the Capitol was about a block from our office. If you walked the block outside, you saw the Supreme Court and the Library of Congress at the edge of the greensward facing the dome. At the dome's peak, the statue Freedom, a truly American goddess, stood alone in the sky, silent sentinel over the city as she had been since the days of the Civil War.

If it was cold or rainy, you went underground from the Senate Office Building to the Capitol. The rattling little subway, four open cars with benches for three people facing each other, had its own charm. When a senator got on board, the train immediately took off, the operator waving aside tourists and staff alike, shouting, "Watch the doors."

Marble stairs or tiny elevators delivered you outside a magnificent, overdone reception room next to the Senate chamber. It was decorated in the nineteenth-century style with gilded arches and intricate designs on the walls. Crystal chandeliers hung down from the high and ornate ceiling, and the floor was tiled in an elaborate and colorful mosaic. Dark benches framed the room, and a large table filled one end of it. People and furniture were reflected in the large wall mirrors. For all the busy quality of the decor and the numbers of constituents and lobbyists waiting for a senator, it was a quiet room.

Through a large entryway, you made your way to the chamber or to the cloakroom area behind the chamber, and that's where awe be-gan. I never stepped into the Capitol without being overtaken by a sense of history, feeling both proud and humble. It seems to be an intimate place where you instinctively whisper and move slowly.

When the Senate was not in session and the lights were dim, if you stood alone in the silence, as I sometimes did, you could touch the desks where heroes of democracy, like schoolboys, had written their names and their years of service on the inside of the drawers. You could savor the memory of momentous debates and significant votes. And you realized how lucky you were to be there.

* The story was told of a question addressed to Dr. Edward Everitt when he was chaplain of the Senate: "Is it your job to pray for the Senate?" "No," Dr. Everitt was reported to have replied. "My job is to look at the Senate and pray for the country."

When the Senate was in session, even a quorum call had importance. When senators assembled for close votes on historic issues, and the clerk called out, "Mr. Humphrey," or "Mr. Taft," you waited for each aye or no with anticipation. When debates took place and I stood at the rear of the room or close to Humphrey, with notes in hand, I felt myself a part of American history, American life, and the American future. It is an easy place to love and certainly one to respect.

Even in our office, surrounded by paper, besieged by phone calls, interrupted by constituents, the sense of working at democracy was intense. On the floor it was even greater. The Senate in 1949 and during the years I worked there was filled with many individuals of intellectual depth, a sense of history, and a love for the institution. It is true that some were mean-spirited and petty, and a handful found partisanship their highest calling. A few, without any question, were racists reflecting their roots and ugly prejudices—cleaned-up representatives of a lynch-mob mentality.

For all that, most senators, by far, were essentially decent and honorable. Senators like Walter George, Richard Russell, Eugene Milliken, Everett Dirksen, Claude Pepper, James Murray, and Robert Taft (they said of Taft that he had the best mind in the Senate until he made it up), whether you agreed with all or any of their positions or not, were quite special. Most were well educated, some even brilliant men who were superb debaters, hard workers, and master politicians, filled with the skills gained through years of political apprenticeship at home and in Washington. They loved the Senate and had an overriding loyalty to it.

I sometimes think that, as much as I admire some senators today, the number of giants is significantly fewer. I don't believe that this is born simply of nostalgia, the self-delusion of an old hand looking back. Television, campaign costs, and the changing quality of political parties has made a difference in who gets elected. The Senate, however, continues to demonstrate even today that the institution matters to its members, almost to a point of reverence. Willful and capricious actions are still likely to bring disapproval and censure. If some sins of personal behavior were tolerated or ignored, affronts to the integrity of the Senate were not. I believe that is still the case.

We liberals often criticized the atmosphere of a "club" that tended to keep real power in the hands of the most senior senators, usually Southerners and conservatives, beyond their formal titles and exceeding their numbers. That "clubbiness," in its positive effects, helped keep people in line to the ultimate benefit of the Senate and, in most instances, the democratic process.

The negative power was, of course, substantial. It permitted civil rights legislation to be bottled up for years. It permitted all kinds of social legislation to be killed in silence in committee. It too often kept organized labor without the tools it needed to protect the rights of workers. For whatever its value and its merits, the club had to change.

What Humphrey from the liberal side, and ultimately Lyndon Johnson from a more conservative position, did was to affect the chemistry of the body and bring change within the traditions of the Senate. They were able to do that with very different personalities and techniques because they worked together shared an understanding of the vanities and needs of their colleagues. They helped open up the club. Ideology and suspicion gave way to some extent to understanding and trust.

Several years after I arrived, I had a glimmer of why that change was coming. Staff were not ordinarily welcome in the cloakroom, the inner sanctum of the club, where senators sat around socializing with one another, some drinking a bit, all savoring the uniqueness of their positions. In the days when travel was not easy and people were not jetting off for speaking engagements, the cloakroom was the ideal place for senatorial camaraderie and for senators to measure the mood and commitments of their colleagues.

A few of us on the staff were granted phone privileges there. We did not sit around as though we were senators. We were in and out. We did not drink with the senators who were there. We were deferential, but we were recognized and to some extent were directly involved there in legislative matters when it pleased the senators.

I went into the cloakroom one day to use the phone and inadvertently overheard some of the Southerners talking about Humphrey. Walter George had a deep booming voice; it was hard not to hear his puzzled exclamation, "Why, that young fellow, he really means that stuff."*

That exclamation crystallized for me the fact that the Southerners looked upon Northern liberals as being strongly pro–civil rights for political reasons. We liberals, of course, disdained the Southerners as demagogues on civil rights for political reasons. Neither side could believe that the other really believed what was said as a matter of principle or conviction. This insight, which Humphrey early appreciated, made accommodation and progress possible.

What Humphrey was able to do, because of his ebullient nature and friendly style, was to help change the perceptions conservatives

---

* I have seen similar stories attributed to others. I heard this myself.

held about liberals. The onus of his 1948 civil rights speech, which was such a burden at first, ultimately became, in a sense, testimony to his integrity, which led some Southerners to believe that he was serious and not a liberal showboat taunting them for political self-gain.*

The mutual respect that evolved between Humphrey and Walter George had its origin in one of the few Senate debates in modern times that was in the tradition of the nineteenth-century Senate. When Maggie and I came to Washington, we had been introduced by mutual friends to Joe and Sylvia Pechman. Joe was an economist in the Treasury Department, specializing in taxation. We visited with one another frequently, and Joe rarely missed the occasion to point out that liberalism was meaningless in American politics unless it came to grips with how tax monies are raised, an issue fundamental to the economic and social structure of the country. I decided to bring Joe and Humphrey together. The result was a decision made in early 1950 that Joe would assemble a group of outstanding tax experts to work with Humphrey in preparing a legislative program for closing tax loopholes and thereby introducing greater equity into the process. I was to be the go-between.

Joe's team was an impressive one. He persuaded Charles Davis, then counsel to the House Ways and Means Committee, to play a quiet but leading role in the group. He also brought in two or three lawyers from the private sector whose everyday talents were directed to creating and then using tax loopholes for their clients. One of these lawyers was Lou Oberdorfer, now an outstanding U.S. district court judge in Washington, D.C. Secrecy was indispensable. The members of the House would not have been pleased had they known of Davis's activities helping Humphrey. The lawyers did not want their clients to know.

Joe forged a team of experts, and they began teaching Humphrey the tax system. They were demanding, and Humphrey was a superb student, spending many evenings reading and studying. He persuaded Senator Paul Douglas of Illinois to join him in the effort. The formula was a simple one. Our experts would describe the loopholes to be corrected, and Humphrey would then decide whether it was an issue he felt comfortable raising. For each loophole that they agreed to work on, they prepared a full explanation of how it functioned, why it constituted an inequity, and how defenders of that loophole should be answered.

---

* Walter George so liked Humphrey that he volunteered to come to Minnesota to speak for him in 1954 and wrote letters supporting Hubert to a number of Minnesota bankers. It shocked some of Humphrey's friends to have this symbol of the Old South in Minnesota, but it represented a significant breakthrough for Humphrey.

The work was enormously painstaking and detailed. Humphrey knew that his proposal would not be popular on the floor of the Senate. The power of the Senate was located in the Senate Finance Committee, headed by Walter George of Georgia and Eugene Milliken of Colorado, the deans of the Senate in both parties.

Humphrey went to Walter George before the debate began on the tax bill and explained what he intended to do. George, forewarned, graciously encouraged him to express himself honestly on the floor. The regular Senate chamber was being renovated, so the debate took place in the nineteenth-century Senate chamber, which had also been used for a time by the Supreme Court. It was a much smaller room, the same one in which Daniel Webster and Henry Clay had debated.

The debate was extraordinary. It lasted a full week. I sat next to Humphrey with a case full of notes indexed for ready access. Our experts sat in the visitors' section. It took at least a couple of days for Humphrey's efforts to be recognized and appreciated, but the longer the debate continued, the larger our audience of senators grew as they witnessed a learned, effective, and respectful debate in the best traditions of that body. Hubert had mastered his subject, and that astounded and impressed the Senate, particularly the leaders of the Senate Finance Committee. Soon, ridicule gave way to respect.

We lost the amendments, as expected, but the Senate would never again be the same. No longer were tax bills enacted automatically or the judgments of the Senate Finance Committee considered final. When the debate was over, the elderly Walter George and his equally elderly and distinguished colleague Gene Milliken came over to the young Humphrey and congratulated him on the quality of the debate and the responsible and constructive way Humphrey and Douglas had performed. Their gesture was not lost on the rest of the Senate. It remains indelibly and emotionally fixed in my mind as a moment of historic change.

The Senate was process, but it ultimately was people as well. My favorite senators during my early days were Paul Douglas of Illinois, Herbert Lehman of New York, and Wayne Morse of Oregon. What they had in common was an uncommon integrity and an unfailingly progressive view of social change and possibilities. Beyond that they were quite different. Herbert Lehman was a patrician Jew of great wealth from New York, a former governor of that state, already old and somewhat physically fragile. He carried himself with dignity and had a strong commitment to liberalism. Humphrey admired and loved him.

One day, attacking the depreciation allowance of oil companies,

Lehman garbled his words, combining depletion and depreciation into "depletiation." Bob Kerr of Oklahoma, as capable and as mean-tongued a man as I saw in the Senate, a powerful spokesman for the oil industry from which his own fortune grew, ridiculed Lehman, mimicking his mispronunciation. It was not the normal behavior of senators toward one another, but Kerr had an ugly streak in him that surfaced out of control in this instance.

Humphrey bounded to his feet and defended Lehman as he soundly chastised Kerr for his personal attack. It was shocking enough for Kerr to have done what he did; it was astounding that so junior a senator as Humphrey should take on one of the titans of the Senate. But he was defending the mores of the Senate, the civility that was expected, and he gained, rather than lost, the esteem of Kerr's friends.

Paul Douglas was a University of Chicago economist whose books I had read as an undergraduate at NYU. He was a Quaker and a pacifist who had also been a Marine during World War II, signing up as an enlisted man when he was forty-six years old. He was deeply fascinated by my CO service in the starvation experiment, and we became quite good friends. Indeed, it was he who steered me to the Marine Corps reserves in 1955 when he learned I was no longer a pacifist and was looking for a way to demonstrate this important change of conviction.

I also learned something significant from him about integrity in public office. After the 1948 election, a liberal Minneapolis businessman who manufactured shirts sent Humphrey a box of them and asked him to determine Douglas's shirt size. The businessman had never met Douglas, and didn't ask to, but was merely delighted at his election to the Senate. Hubert asked me to follow up on the request, and I called Frank McCulloch, my counterpart in the Douglas office, explaining what I needed and why. Frank said he was sorry, but Douglas would not accept any gift of that nature.

I said, "Look, the man doesn't do any work for the government; he doesn't want anything from Paul. He has never asked Humphrey for a thing. All he wants to do is express his admiration in a way that makes sense to him. He manufactures shirts. Paul wears them. This is just an expression of appreciation, and we don't want to offend him."

Frank said, "Sorry, absolute rule—no exceptions. No gifts worth more than five dollars. *No shirts*." That seemed rigid and silly to me at the time. I saw no compromise of integrity, no conflict of interest in the innocent offer. Ultimately, I have come to believe that the rigid Douglas standard is the proper one. Strict standards do not leave room for any ambiguity, any empty pleas that "I didn't know."*

Humphrey and Paul Douglas were a close couple ideologically, but they had very different personalities. They both supported an interventionist foreign policy, voted for the funds requested for a strong defense force, and agreed on liberal tax policy and social issue questions. Humphrey used his friendship with Lyndon Johnson, Senate majority leader, to get Douglas a seat on the Finance Committee, a place generally reserved for conservatives of both parties. Johnson wanted Douglas on that committee, and I recall him berating the sincerity of liberal senators who preferred to be on the "meaningless" Labor Committee where they could grandstand for labor votes rather than on the "tough," hard-working Finance Committee where the real economic power structure of the country was affected. Breaking the ideological line on Finance changed the nature of the club, too. As the power centers became less monolithic, additional points of view had to be taken more seriously, since power came with position.

Wayne Morse was a wonderful maverick. A Republican turned independent and then Democrat, he curried no one's favor, sometimes it seemed even that of the constituents who elected him. He could be cantankerous and difficult in going his independent way. He frequently stayed late in the Senate making speeches to an empty chamber so that his views on whatever interested him at the moment would be on the record. He had been a professor of law and was an expert on the Constitution, but he seemed almost as interested in raising Black Angus cattle on his farm in northern Virginia. Yet he applied his fine mind to whatever issue was before the Senate or the country, made it up without much concern about the consequences on his political life, and treated the Constitution with the respect it deserved.

Douglas and Lehman had assistants with as close a relationship to them as I had to Humphrey, and the three of us soon became a liberal troika serving all the liberal members, through our peers generally, but directly with the senators when they chose.

Frank McCulloch, Douglas's assistant, moved with a certain ease that may have come from his affluence. He was thin and graceful and, with his intellect, was altogether an impressive man. He had been on

---

* There is the old story about the farm woman who one evening finds a newborn calf so attractive that she decides to carry it into her home to look after it. It becomes a habit. Each night she lifts it and moves it inside. At some point she realizes that she is struggling to carry a cow. Ethical compromise in public office is like carrying a calf. It imperceptibly grows into a burden that cannot be borne.

the faculty at Roosevelt College teaching labor relations before coming to Washington with Douglas. Maggie and I were drawn to him for what he taught and thought and where he had taught. He was a distinguished person who attracted instant respect.

Julius Edelstein, Lehman's assistant, had been a naval commander during the war and was a bright, dedicated, and hard-working public servant. As Lehman got older and physically fragile, more and more people thought that Julius, with his great energy and organizational skills, ran not only the office, but Lehman. I think that was generally erroneous. Lehman was no one's pawn even in his declining years, although there is no question that he depended on Julius to an extraordinary extent. The Lehman staff, incidentally, was the largest in the Senate, with many fine young staff people on the personal payroll of the senator.

McCulloch, Edelstein, and I, working with other senatorial assistants,* were able to develop legislative programs and present the ideas coherently to our principals, other staff, and liberal senators who wanted to be briefed. Because staffs were small, we were all required to be generalists, not advocates for one program or one interest. We were, in fact, surrogate senators to some extent, balancing issues and political considerations, but although we were close and had the confidence of our principals, we knew we had not been elected to their jobs. Our senators, furthermore, were able to keep close tabs on what their small staffs were doing.

For years, the liberal view was that additional congressional staff would mean equity with the executive branch, that more information would guarantee better legislation. I am no longer sure we were right. Some changes have had good results, but some have made things worse. The Congress today too frequently appears to be paralyzed through preoccupation with detail, excessive oversight functions, and the mass of issues on their platter. The size of congressional staffs today is particularly appalling and stultifying. In addition to more than 20,000 congressional employees, there are at least 250 subcommittees dealing with micro-management. On an ordinary day, as many as fifty

---

* Senator William Benton of Connecticut, for a time had my friend, Dr. Steve Bailey, one of the country's outstanding political scientists and later president of Wesleyan University, as his administrative assistant. Wayne Morse's legislative aide, until he was appointed to the National Labor Relations Board, was Pete Peterson. Senator Mathew Neely of West Virginia, seeing the need to make his contribution to the process, persuaded the distinguished New Deal lawyer David Ginsberg, who had been born and raised in his state, to join us, but Dave did not find that wonderfully incorrigible old man easy to work for.

hearings might take place, with more staff than members usually attending.

Other changes we advocated also had unforeseen consequences. When the "markups" of bills—the process of compromising and rationalizing differences—was ordered out of the back rooms and into open committee meetings, we invited grandstanding. Unfortunately, taking an extreme position for the publicity of it, to enhance a more "liberal (or conservative) than thou" posture is ruinous to mediating and reaching consensus. Important public policy questions are simply more difficult to resolve at crucial moments in that process. Secrecy is seductive and easily leads to abuse, but compulsory openness can lead nowhere.

McCulloch, Edelstein, and I became the focal point for labor and liberal lobbyists and advocates trying to move legislation ahead in a variety of fields from tax policy to labor legislation and all the social welfare issues that were important then. Senators turned to us frequently, using us as well as their own staffs and, in some cases, inviting us virtually to enter as personal a relationship as we had with our own senators.

One of those who sought me out was Texas Senator Lyndon Johnson, in part, I suppose, because he and Hubert got along so well from the very first. They were much different in temperament and style, but found a common ground on certain issues—education particularly—and in certain roots. They both revered Franklin Roosevelt and found in him an example of principled but pragmatic political method.

When Johnson wanted to be elected majority leader in 1952 so soon after being elected to the Senate, liberal suspicion of him was great. The more liberal Senators—including Lehman and Douglas—simply could not swallow voting for him for leader although they knew that he would be elected. Humphrey somewhat uncomfortably took charge and attempted to rally the liberal votes behind James Murray of Montana, a fine man everyone knew to be too old and weak and not equipped to be leader. What was instructive for me was that many of the liberals who let Humphrey believe that they would vote for Murray simply did not do so. Johnson had their commitments. This did not surprise Humphrey, who had much earlier been told by Johnson that he had firm promises in hand. The not-so-funny joke at the time was that Murray himself supported Johnson and may even have voted for him. Johnson had offered certain favors to the liberals if he could receive unanimous support. When it was clear that Johnson had a majority vote for leader at the Democratic caucus, Humphrey arranged for the vote to be made unanimous and warned Johnson he intended to collect on his promise.

Johnson was not a lovable man even when he sought support and needed approval, but he was immensely smart and even more immensely competent in matters of the Senate. He understood others' vanities, needs, and weaknesses, and he was prepared to exploit them all as needed to pass legislation. He was an artist at manipulation. Indeed, in spite of the fact that I did not particularly like Johnson personally and seriously questioned his frequent crudeness as a reflection of character, I came to respect him as the best Senate leader of our century. He understood the legislative process and the need to modify Senate habits in the interest of all the people.

Not only did Johnson break the rigid control by the conservatives of the Senate Finance Committee but, after he became majority leader of the Democrats, he established a rule under which every United States senator could have one seat on a major committee. He thereby broke the back of the seniority rule. It meant that a new senator could achieve one major committee assignment even if that meant bumping somebody with higher seniority. That was an immense change which seems simple but had profound effects.

Johnson once said to me in exasperation: "Humphrey and all your famous liberals go out making speeches while I stay here in Washington and do their dirty work for them. I'm the real liberal." There was some truth to it. Johnson enjoyed wielding his power, whipping his adversaries, showing them up if they behaved in ways he found unsenatorial. Once, Johnson was angry that the Republicans, without having alerted him, were meeting at lunch and ignoring the session. He took a piece of wage and hour legislation that the Republicans didn't like and moved it off the calendar onto the floor for a vote. With only Democrats on the floor, it passed. With an additional parliamentary maneuver preventing reconsideration, the liberal proposal became law when the president signed it. The Republicans, of course, were livid. The organized labor movement and the Senate liberals loved it.

When senators whose votes he needed were returning to Washington, he would telephone the Federal Aviation Administration to make certain that the airplanes carrying them would receive speedy landing privileges. On one occasion, a commercial plane carrying Humphrey was caught in a snowstorm and could not land in time for a vote on a housing measure. It seemed pretty certain that the Democrats would lose that vote, but Johnson, seemingly as a courtesy to Humphrey, said he wanted to protect Humphrey's right to be present for the vote and to be counted. He talked to the Republican leadership and they, believing they had the votes in any event, agreed to put off the vote from two P.M. to four P.M. In agreeing to the request, the Republican leader deliberately put on the record that Humphrey was out making a speech. Johnson either feigned or felt real indignation at the personal nature of this unseemly jab at Humphrey. He went around the floor storming about this lack of senatorial courtesy, and when four P.M. came, with Humphrey present, the vote was taken and the Democrats won narrowly by one or two votes, the margin of victory coming not on the merits, but more on the question of courtesy.

Working with Hubert Humphrey was exciting. He was infectiously energetic and spontaneous. Moments were not given the chance to be dull. As I write about it now, I recall a particularly tense and hair-raising afternoon for me on Washington's Birthday, February 22, early in the 1950s. Humphrey, who was out of town, called me shortly after noontime. I believe he was in Minneapolis or Detroit. His plane had been held up by bad weather, and he would arrive later than planned. I did not think it mattered because it was a holiday and the Senate was not in session, but he said he had a talk to make that afternoon in Washington that I was not aware of. He usually spoke without a text, unless somebody on the outside prepared it, because he and I were both too busy. In any event, I heard the words: "I'd like you to take this speech for me, Max." This was not an unusual request, and I agreed.

After learning, as I suspected, that there was no text and he had intended to make some notes on the airplane ride back, I asked for the subject and the auspices. I was astounded to learn that the talk was to be at an Ash Wednesday service in the Episcopalian Washington Cathedral. There were two speakers, Hubert and Senator Henry Cabot Lodge of Massachusetts. It was now close to one P.M. The service was scheduled for three P.M. The subject was "God, Man, and The Hydrogen Bomb." My protestations to Hubert that there was no time to prepare, that I was neither theologically nor culturally nor ethically nor religiously qualified to take the assignment—all these were to no avail. "You can do it," he said. I did.

Hubert was a grand and passionate speaker. He spoke the language of democracy, the language, George Will recently said, "of Jefferson, Madison, Washington, Lincoln, Thoreau, Emerson and Thomas Paine." Hubert knew that democracy is about speech and the accompanying respect for the mind. He talked about the joy of politics. He had matured before television, and that proved to be a political handicap. He unabashedly practiced and mastered oratory and rhetoric. He sought to instill a sense of public purpose. Sound bites were alien to him. Politics was his life. Democracy was his political religion. These qualities strengthened him. They also made him a leader of America's liberal forces and then of the Senate itself. His relationship with Lyndon Johnson helped that process.

In the middle of Humphrey's first term, I found myself involved in presidential politics in a way I had not anticipated. Suddenly what had been only a theoretical and distant possibility turned real. When Harry Truman announced that he would not run for reelection in 1952, a number of liberal and labor leaders asked me if I thought Hubert could be persuaded to run for president.

That anyone, much less significant leaders of the Democratic party, should raise the question seemed to both Humphrey and me a clear political vindication of his actions at the Democratic convention in 1948. To me, it was also totally unrealistic, albeit a good omen for the future. People not only thought he should be president but believed that he could be nominated by the party he had divided at the last convention. For Humphrey, who wanted, more than most, to be liked, who was by instinct a healer and conciliator, not a polarizer, the expressions of serious interest were themselves a not so minor triumph.

Senator Brien McMahon of Connecticut and John Bailey, then Connecticut state Democratic chairman and later a formidable force for John Kennedy's nomination and election, urged that Humphrey run. Sal Hoffman of the Upholsterers Union and Emil Rieve of the Textile Workers both wanted to help organize support for Humphrey, and many ADA leaders, including some who joined the Kennedys in 1959– 60, wanted Humphrey to carry their banner. Humphrey was barely over forty. He told them without equivocation that he would not consider running, that he was too young, too new on the national scene, and that his best contribution to the liberal cause was to worry about the 1952 platform and focus on his 1954 reelection campaign, which he expected to be a tough one.

I thought that was a realistic and sensible view of his situation and tried to turn off any pressure on him to change his mind. Fortunately, many of our friends, particularly in the ADA, soon had a new hero to support in Adlai Stevenson. President Truman clearly favored Averell Harriman, a close associate of Franklin Roosevelt and one of our country's most distinguished diplomats, but an aristocrat who had not demonstrated any political appeal. Vice President Alben Barkley was also very much interested in the nomination.

Estes Kefauver, the senator from Tennessee whom Harry Truman detested, and who was anathema to the big city–machine politicians, began seriously to emerge on the national scene at this time. Estes did have a liberal voting record and, just then, great public appeal as the man who had taken on the "rackets" and racketeers in the United States.

Kefauver was not a giant of the Senate and, because he kept his own counsel and liked to fly solo on legislative matters, was not particularly well liked. He was certainly bright and well educated at Yale University, but few of his peers considered him a heavyweight, a hard worker, or of presidential caliber. Kefauver was also a heavy drinker, occasionally a boisterous one in the days when the press said virtually nothing about a man's private behavior, but the facts were clear to his colleagues and party leaders.

His public popularity did not surprise me, and, as a matter of fact, I knew him as a kind and courteous man who treated me like a friend. He was folksy and comfortable in his role as a man of the people, above political machines and corruption. It was a calculated definition of himself, but it worked.

What surprised me was the change in Humphrey's view of Kefauver, who was clearly no match for Humphrey in intellect or legislative artistry. He took Kefauver more seriously as a leader as soon as Kefauver became a candidate. Whatever his limitations, he might be president. Humphrey, like the rest of Washington, dealt with people differently once they had a chance of becoming president. This is a phenomenon of political life. A candidate, whether self-selected or chosen by the "Great Mentioner,"* is immediately lionized and quickly surrounded by a coterie dazzled by the instant fantasies of newspaper stories declaiming their insider status immediately, with a White House job later looming on the horizon.

Stevenson was the most attractive candidate to the party leaders and their constituency. Humphrey and most of the Minnesota DFL leaders were attracted by his charm, wit, and style. Humphrey did not know Stevenson well, but proved to be a central figure in the selection of Senator John Sparkman of Alabama as Stevenson's 1952 vice presidential candidate, something not immediately popular with all our liberal friends.

Sparkman was a decent man with liberal instincts who represented

---

* Quadrennially, names of prospective candidates for the presidency are "mentioned" in the media, generally in some formulation like, "Sources within the party say (*fill in the blank*) is being thought of as a potential candidate for president." The anonymous sources, sometimes the candidate himself, have become the generic "Great Mentioner." I believe Russell Baker of the *New York Times* coined the term.

the state of Alabama and could, of course, hardly survive politically if he sounded and voted exactly like Humphrey. It was enough for us that he showed consistent courage and pushed to the limits of his constituency, particularly in labor and social legislation.

Sparkman and his Alabama colleague, Senator Lister Hill, had also been helpful to us in a tactical change of language before the convention. Humphrey had decided that the term "fair employment practices," or the FEPC, had become a needlessly divisive symbolic description of what liberals sought. FEPC was a symbol of Northerners standing in judgment of the South, which turned off many Democrats we needed.

Humphrey, with Sparkman's help in the Senate, relabeled the concept "equal opportunity in employment," something that was consistent with the American ethic. The Southerners who wanted to do so could accept it without raising the ire of their own communities. It was another lesson for me in how words themselves can impede or encourage reaching political harmony.

In those years, political harmony seemed to be a national party necessity and a convention imperative. Humphrey was comfortable in that search as long as there was no retreat from the 1948 civil rights platform. The party sought a candidate who could bring together as many of the factions as possible. That required some judgment about qualifications as well as a judgment about the candidate's ability to win the election.*

After the 1952 convention, Humphrey asked me to stop in Springfield, Illinois, to have lunch with Stevenson as Maggie and I drove back to Washington. He was concerned about his own role in the national campaign and wanted to help Stevenson with those liberals who were somewhat suspicious of the candidate, in part because they didn't know him and in part because they did. While Humphrey had already told Stevenson of his interest and willingness to travel on the ticket's

---

* This process was criticized as decision making in "smoke-filled rooms," and yet I believe it was more effective and more responsive to public opinion than what has replaced it today. Every candidate had to survive a process that looked for candidates with the ability to forge a broad consensus and win. We Democrats have lost that in recent decades, too frequently nominating people who win primary elections by appealing to narrow factions and special interests, thereby undermining their ability to attract consensus. Jesse Jackson's Rainbow Coalition, for example, is ultimately divisive and correctly perceived as the gathering in of various fringe or special interest groups and not a real coalition as I understand the word. To win a primary, candidates try to avoid offending Jackson and his supporters, and that process tends to identify the candidate with the far left of the nation's political spectrum, thereby losing broad political support.

behalf, he thought my visit would confirm his offer. I called Bill Blair, Stevenson's able aide, and arranged to have lunch with them on the first day of August at the governor's mansion in Springfield, where Stevenson lived.

Lunch was delicious, the setting lovely, Stevenson, Blair, and their younger brilliant partner, Newton Minow, gracious hosts. For me, it was also a disappointment. I found Stevenson to be indecisive or unclear on issues, tentative on plans, and lukewarm about Humphrey, whom he did not fundamentally know and certainly did not understand. I ultimately worked for his election and voted for him, of course, but as much as I admired his rhetoric, I did not feel he would be a great president if elected. I understood but did not share the frenzy of Stevenson-love that swept through the academic world then and continued through later elections.*

My reactions at lunch were mild compared to Maggie's. She was not overawed by politicians in general and found the luncheon atmosphere more than a little too high-hat for her taste. She compared Adlai Stevenson unfavorably to Paul Douglas, who was also gracious, but warm and solidly liberal, terms she would not apply to Stevenson. We were not, as the campaign signs later read, "Madly for Adlai." I later learned that Stevenson had been asked by a reporter from the *Chicago Tribune* about the luncheon with me and whether this was arranged by the ADA to move him to the left.

Our reactions did not deter Humphrey from leaping into the campaign with all the energy he could muster. He went wherever they asked him to go, but worked where he was strong and Stevenson was not—in the agricultural Midwest and in labor areas in California and the urban East. He never held back, and Stevenson clearly appreciated his efforts and grew to like and respect him. When the Eisenhower landslide had taken place, Stevenson was a national figure as he had not been before and clearly the leading candidate for 1956.

Eisenhower's election helped drain some right-wing intensity from our political system, but the issue of Communism and Communists was real in those days. The ultra-right conservatives saw them everywhere, applying the label quite carelessly to a wide spectrum of people.

Even the club atmosphere of the Senate did not prevent this

---

* Stevenson had a literary touch that Eisenhower did not, and that alone seemed important to many. A story went around Washington that when a gushing supporter said to Stevenson that all thinking people supported him, he replied: "Yes, but I need to win a majority." FDR or Truman would not have expressed or had such a thought.

irresponsibility from manifesting itself. In a radio debate originating in the Senate recording studio in the spring of 1951, Homer Capehart of Indiana accused Humphrey and Herbert Lehman of being Communist sympathizers and supporters of Red China, ranting on in a theme developed by conservatives over the next few years. Humphrey kept cool during the broadcast, but when it was over, he moved up to Capehart in a rare display of anger, snapping, "I resent your vilification and character assassination. I'm tired of your malicious statements." Capehart grabbed Humphrey and started to push him back when Lehman, not much over five feet tall and already in his seventies, leapt on Capehart's back to help the surprised Humphrey. Finally, we separated the three of them, and calm returned for the moment.

The indiscriminate charges permitted the real Communists to hide themselves in the cloak of peace and justice, giving them an aura and power they did not deserve. At the same time, many in the far right seemed willing to destroy what was legitimate and democratic on the non-Communist left.

The American Communist party was never strong in numbers, but it had influence far beyond its size. That had been true in Minnesota politics, which I knew firsthand; in the American labor movement, where I was close enough to see the Communists' insidious role (and wrote about it in my doctoral dissertation); and in my several student experiences, where disciplined minorities exercised more power than their numbers merited.*

For me, Stalinists who knowingly gave their allegiance to the Soviet line and the Stalinoids who followed them were not reformers dreaming of democratic institutions at work. They were totalitarians pretending to be democrats. They were people who had given up intellectual and social integrity to follow a line of thought and action dictated from far away.

The fight against American Communists had to be made. I felt it had to be led by liberal social democrats and socialists who were inevitably the first victims of Communists in search of power and thus knew

---

* I wrote in my Ph.D. thesis on the Communists and the CIO, "The Communists have never been a significant numerical factor in American life or within our unions. The largest number of members which the Communist Party has had during the last 10 years was probably 70,000. Assuming that of this number one-half belong to unions—and that would probably be an exaggerated figure—they would have a maximum numerical strength of 0.002–0.0023 of the 15,000,000 labor union members. Yet at the height of this power drive within the CIO, they dominated 12 to 15 of the 40 international CIO unions." In 1946, Communist-controlled unions amounted to 15 percent of union membership.

their enemies best. Furthermore, it would then take place within the boundaries of civil liberties. The battle began in the trade union movement, where infiltration had been going on for many years.

The American Communist party position was quite clear:

> It goes without saying that it is in the trade unions that we in the United States must show our greatest activity. This must be done through organized and well disciplined fractions. Without any exceptions whatever all Communist fractions must work under the immediate leadership and control of the party committees . . . doing all possible to carry out the party policy in all organizations wherein they function. The party's instructions and decisions are obligatory in fraction work, and no member of the fraction, once a decision is made and a policy laid down, can in any way take a stand against such a decision or policy, no matter what his opinion may be regarding the correctness of the policy.*

Fortunately, the CIO leadership, after John L. Lewis left office, was tough and principled and not about to be bullied by the Communists. Philip Murray, its president, was a devout Catholic, a democrat of personal integrity, and a devoted battler for a free trade union movement. The secretary-treasurer was Jim Carey, who had seen the Communists at work within the United Electrical Workers, and Arthur Goldberg, the CIO general counsel, who was a close adviser to both.

Together they developed an internal union trial system to decide whether loyalty to the union or loyalty to the Communist party controlled decision making. The process was a union judicial proceeding. Witnesses were called; those charged could defend themselves. If the "jury" of other union leaders determined that the prime allegiance of those before them was not to the union, but to the Communist party, the person or the union, as appropriate, was expelled.†

This tended to strengthen the anti-Communist elements within

---

* I also quoted this passage in my thesis. It came from M. Jenkins, *The Communist Nucleus*, published in 1928 by the Communist Party's Workers' Library Publishers.

† Mike Quill, flamboyant leader of the Transport Workers Union in New York, had been part of the left caucus at CIO conventions. He ultimately became disillusioned with the Communists, and later testified about meetings he had attended: "Whether they were members of the Communist Party or not I don't know. But they got their instructions at these meetings from John Williamson, the secretary of the Communist Party."

all the unions because they no longer required as much courage to face down the pretenders. There was explicit support from the top of the unions, and certainly implicit support from President Truman and his administration as well.

As early as 1950, Humphrey looked for some way to bring Communist party members into the open. He pursued the question of a legislative step toward that end with friends, looking for some solution that was both constitutional and effective. If there was to be "truth in advertising," as we later used the phrase, under our laws; if financial investors are protected by Securities and Exchange Commission requirements of full disclosure, why not protect the American voter with full disclosure requirements about political affiliations? Humphrey had discussed the idea long before with his teachers and friends, Evron Kirkpatrick and Benjamin Lippincott. Ben was not quite as close to Humphrey as Kirk in the early days, but important nonetheless in guiding Humphrey through democratic political philosophy. He was a thoroughgoing democratic political theorist of note who thought the goal constitutional and admirable.

A decision involving a Communist case by Learned Hand, the highly respected liberal judge of the United States Court of Appeals, provided Humphrey with additional support for his belief that he was on the right track. A democracy, he would repeat as the essence of what he had learned, has a right to defend itself against enemies from within who would destroy it.

Humphrey had first considered introducing legislation on the subject in 1950. He felt that the Truman administration should come up with an anti-Communist security protection program of its own, with proper democratic safeguards, to meet the threat of internal subversion that the Congress felt should be met. His recommendation was not accepted by the Truman administration, even though it was for a time seriously considered by the president. Humphrey felt he was too new to the Senate at that time to assert his own judgment without administration support.

McCarthyism was growing in influence. Whether by accident or design or both, Senator Joseph McCarthy of Wisconsin had begun a dangerous and irresponsible campaign of intimidation against political liberals, recklessly and loosely accusing them of being Communists and traitors. Many innocent people were attacked, reputations tarnished, jobs lost. Politicians were afraid to challenge the cloud of intimidation that corrupted the political climate of America. Their fear was based on the fact that McCarthyism tapped a vein of great public concern about Communist subversion. Liberals, who should have led the political struggle against the anti-democrats of both the right and the left, seemed to relinquish the fight against the Communists and permitted the McCarthyites to gain public credit for that effort. Regrettably, the McCarthyites, with their lack of sympathy or understanding for civil liberties, were unqualified for the task. Because of McCarthy's character assassination broadsides, actual security risks could more easily escape detection, losing identity in the crowd of innocents who were accused.

Humphrey, who had successfully worked to undermine and defeat Communist influence in Minnesota and within the American labor movement, was appalled and outraged by McCarthy, who for his part, it appeared to me, went out of his way not to offend Hubert. On a number of occasions, when either Humphrey or I heard of people we knew on the Hill staff or elsewhere who were being unjustly threatened or intimidated, Hubert usually successfully went to bat for them, either directly with McCarthy, or on the Senate floor, or with the appropriate government agencies.

In Humphrey's judgment, a proposal to declare the Communist party part of an international conspiracy designed to overthrow the government of the United States by force and violence would be the proper approach to deal with the problem of subversion and the political need to be perceived as dealing with it. A "knowing" member of the Communist party would by that fact alone be considered part of that conspiracy, but a judicial proceeding, with the accused having the right to provide a legal defense against the charges and with a presumption of innocence, would be mandated. Party membership had to be proved. If it were not, the false accusation of Communist allegiance, a criminal act, would subject the accuser to libel and slander claims.

In 1954, he and I began drafting the Communist Control Act. The fact that right-wing conservatives grabbed the mantle of anti-Communism and patriotism irked him. The Humphrey bill we prepared never became law in the form we proposed, but a statute by the same title, the Communist Control Act of 1954, was enacted. The residual controversy within the liberal movement became sharp and intolerant, turning into an angry confrontation early in Humphrey's political life. Though Humphrey was clearly the inspiration of the bill, I, as the principal drafter of the legislation, became a secondary target for much of the anger, including anger from many of his good friends who did not approve of the bill and could not believe Humphrey would support what they considered "McCarthyite" legislation. Joseph Rauh,

an old ADA Humphrey supporter and friend, became, I thought, ir-
rationally hysterical at what he considered this "treason" to liberalism
and began an effective national campaign of attack and character assassination. I was distressed by the hostility and found some of it, from
people who should have known better, hard to understand.

One friend, Tom Harris, the assistant general counsel of the CIO,
severely criticized the legislation. I considered his opposition strange.
He had helped us analyze the problem and draft the legislation, but
later wrote, "Max practically wrote the statute, while I observed his
activities with pain and mortification." His pain was not visible at the
time of writing the proposed legislation, but revisionism, I learned,
doesn't necessarily take decades. Indeed, my recollection is that we
asked Tom to check with the labor movement and that he reported
support for the introduction of the bill.

The bill was not my writing alone, nor only of Humphrey's spon-
sorship. There were sixteen sponsors, including Jack Kennedy, Paul
Douglas, and, more importantly, Wayne Morse. Senator Morse was not
only a law professor but an expert on the Constitution, as well as an
uncompromising liberal, whatever party he was in. He shared our concerns about the Communists and about protecting the civil liberties of
Americans. He took a back seat to no one on those matters.

Humphrey and he had talked about our approach, and when a
final draft was ready, Morse took it home for quiet and careful study.
The next day, he came back to Humphrey with his lawyerly evaluation: the bill was constitutional, protected those who should be protected, attacked those who should be attacked, and should be passed.
We might have moved without his approval, but I doubt it. With it,
Humphrey proceeded.

Many friends within liberal organizations were far more distressed
than our friends in the labor movement were. Arthur Goldberg, who
was quite supportive during this period, arranged for me to participate
in a conference of CIO lawyers from around the country, where I
explained and justified our position. Labor had faced the Communist
challenge and, for the most part, understood the need for what we
proposed.

Mulford Sibley, a pacifist socialist professor of political science at
the University of Minnesota, who had also ended up as my thesis
adviser, wrote us in that tone. I answered:

> . . . Hubert has felt for a long time that the liberal movement
> unnecessarily abandoned "anti-communism" to the reactionar-

ies . . . the result of this abandonment was the fact that the reactionaries were able to grab hold of the issue and not only gain politically but also perpetrate on the American society a whole series of legislative proposals that tended to injure the innocent as well as the guilty people . . . It was, therefore, not a question of compromising his principles in order to be "anti-communist."

The criticisms were many, ardent, and often quite personal. On the other hand, the articulate support of friends was especially precious at the time, and a balance to the critics. I took special pleasure in reading a *University of Chicago Law Review* (Winter 1956) article written by Carl Auerbach, a stalwart member of the ADA and a friend of Joe Rauh's, as well as a law professor at the University of Wisconsin (and later dean of the University of Minnesota Law School). The article strongly supported, with careful legal argument, the constitutionality and desirability of the bill. The proposal, he pointed out, did not aim at "ideas and beliefs" or "utterances," but rather at an organized movement, whose capital is Moscow, with organizational ties to the Soviet machinery for war, espionage, and terror. Auerbach concluded that the Humphrey amendment "does not represent an abandonment of the liberal tradition."

The debate over the bill diminished nationally, but did not disappear. In Minnesota, although it was an issue, it seemed to have no negative influence on the election itself. All those letters and all the steps Humphrey had taken for agriculture, for the labor movement, for education and health seemed far more important. In that election, the DFL, with Humphrey leading the way, carried the governorship and all other elective state offices, and for the first time in many years, the state House of Representatives and five of nine U.S. representatives.

Washington was a city of more than politics, of course. It was home to all kinds of people in a transitional period in race relations, a time of social and demographic change. Maggie and I sensed it and occasionally experienced it.

One night soon after we arrived in Washington, we were invited by Adam Clayton Powell, a congressman and minister from Harlem, to sit with him at a piano concert his wife, Hazel Scott, was giving. We joined Powell and his other guests, who included the manager of a movie theater in downtown Washington. I had recently driven past the theater and noticed picket signs that indicated Negroes were excluded.

I said, "Mr. Wagner, explain something to me. You are here as a guest of Adam Clayton Powell and Hazel Scott, but you would not permit them to get into your theater. I do not understand how you can do this." He said, obviously embarrassed, "I don't own the theater. I just manage it." He paused and said, "If they really wanted to come in, I would find a way to get them in."

I persisted, "It is not a question of them, but what about others? What about my friends? If they are Negroes, I can't go to your movie house with them. It's the principle of the thing." He responded, "Any time you want to attend a movie at the Playhouse with any of your Negro friends, you let me know."

A few months later, George Weaver called to say his wife, Mary, was away, and he wondered if Maggie and I were free that night. I told him that we were planning on going to dinner and a movie and that he should join us. When Maggie and I spoke later, she asked where we would go. I thought about it and called George back and told him about my conversation at the Scott concert. I said, "George, if you're game, let's see what happens." George said, "Let's try it."

I called Mr. Wagner and explained that a Negro friend of ours would be joining us for a movie and that I would like to take him up on his earlier offer. There was silence. Then he said, "The movie is about racial discrimination. He won't like it."

I told him we knew what the movie was about and I thought George would like it, but, in any case, we would take that chance. We arranged to see the late movie after our dinner in Union Station, about the only place in town where mixed groups could dine. When we arrived, an usher was watching for us. We were obvious, of course; the usher approached and said that Mr. Wagner had a previous engagement, but that he would take us in. Maggie quickly figured out that we were headed for the balcony and said, "Max, I see some seats down here. I'd rather sit on the first floor." With that, she moved away from our guide and down the aisle to some empty seats. We followed. When our eyes adjusted to the darkness, we saw that the balcony had been emptied, obviously in our honor.

Washington was a city divided, more Southern than Northern, but we liked it and felt it was home. It was time to move on professionally and to put down roots in other ways. I had decided before the 1954 election, this time with Maggie's assent, that it was time either to return to teaching or to begin the practice of law in Washington. It had been a great six years with Humphrey. I loved Humphrey and the Senate and my job. That was hard to set aside, but at thirty-five, with a wife, a house, and a family, I was ready for something different.

9

The Law: Private Practice and Public Policy

I had thought of leaving the Humphrey staff earlier, but after the Eisenhower landslide in 1952, Humphrey seemed nervous about the 1954 reelection campaign, unnecessarily fearful that he might be beaten. I decided not to think about the future or discuss my options with him. I had become a political security blanket, and change in the office so close to the election would have been too disconcerting for him. Hubert knew that I would one day move on, but neither of us was ready to talk about the timing.

On election night 1954, with Humphrey an easy victor, I could look forward to a life with ease and without guilt. I told Humphrey that, with a resounding victory behind him, I would soon be leaving his office. It was not desertion so much as a rite of passage. It seemed an easy, unemotional, and logical part of a celebration. Neither of us felt uncomfortable with the topic or the decision. Our friendship had not only survived, but grown stronger during my years on the staff. I was leaving because it was time to leave.

He asked what I was going to do, and I told him honestly that I was not sure, except that I wanted very much to be in charge of my own life, to be "my own man," to practice law. I wanted to make money to take care of my growing family and to avoid the pain that my father endured when he fell on hard times. I wanted to work in Washington surrounded by policy debate and public affairs. I wanted to remain in as free a position as possible to help Hubert and his aspirations as they evolved. All of this led to the law rather than to teaching.

Humphrey said, "Why don't you stay through the next session of the Senate, find someone to replace yourself, and use the time to decide precisely what you will do." That made good sense, serving both of our needs.

I set my departure time for the end of the first session of the next Congress and left in the fall of 1955 when it was over. I had found my replacement quickly. About two years earlier I had hired Tom Hughes, a University of Minnesota Phi Beta Kappa student, a Yale law graduate, and a Rhodes scholar, to be counsel of a subcommittee of the Senate Labor Committee. Tom was young but mature, balanced, and wise. Extraordinarily bright and an excellent writer, he was from a small town in southern Minnesota.* While foreign policy was his main interest, he had an inquiring mind and broad knowledge of domestic issues. With Herb Waters already on the staff to handle politics, the press, and agriculture, the transition went smoothly.

Finding a legal home was a little more difficult, although I intended to practice by myself and needed only an office and possibly someone to work with and share the rent. In the previous year, I had hired another young lawyer, Harold Green, for a temporary assignment on a subcommittee that Humphrey chaired. Harold had been at the Atomic Energy Commission working primarily on security matters, and we had needed someone knowledgeable about national security loyalty requirements.

Harold and I got along well and soon became friends. Since his assignment was a short-term one, I asked one day what he intended to do when he was done, and he said he thought he would go into private practice. We agreed then to share office space, although not as partners but as independent cooperating practitioners.

At that point, I had never talked to anyone about retaining me as lawyer. I didn't feel comfortable with prospecting while still on the Humphrey staff. I am not a great risk taker, but I felt confident that I could find clients. I had decided that I would be a traditional professional lawyer, doing government-related law as well, but that I would

---

* Tom left Humphrey to work for his old Connecticut friend Governor Chester Bowles, who had been elected to Congress in 1958. With the Kennedy election, he moved into the State Department as director of intelligence and research. In 1969, he became the president of the Carnegie Endowment for International Peace.

not lobby the Congress. I did not want my success dependent on Humphrey, and even though I consider lobbying a proper and necessary vocation, I also believed it was somewhat undignified and wanted to avoid it. My success, I vowed, would rest entirely on what I had learned and how I was able to put that knowledge to work on my own. Contrary to the fact, many people apparently thought I did lobby in the Congress, particularly as I became more financially comfortable. Frankly, when I saw people I knew on the Hill, I wanted them to think: "I haven't seen Max in a long while," rather than: "I wonder what he wants now."*

My plans, as tenuous as they were, were changed by several coincidences and friendships. Felix Cohen, who practiced law in the

---

* To engage in legislative lobbying is to perform a constructive role in the legislative process. That conclusion, however, is not widely shared in the community, where lobbying is identified with selfish pursuit in behalf of special interest groups at the expense of the national welfare. It is identified in the public mind with wealth and the efforts of narrow business interests to gain special advantage by making large campaign contributions to legislators. Much in this belief is borne out by fact, but successful efforts over the years by Ralph Nader, for example, in support of his views of the consumer interest, and by labor and church organizations in support of various social legislative objectives, demonstrate another side to the picture.

One of the most effective lobbyists I met during my days in the U.S. Senate was Clarence Mitchell, Jr., the Washington bureau director of the National Association for the Advancement of Colored People, who held that position for nearly thirty years. Mr. Mitchell, with whom I worked very closely and whom I respected immensely, usually worked away from glaring lights and television cameras, but he was a master political strategist and highly effective in the corridors of national power. Without him, the civil rights laws of the 1960s would not have been enacted. His power did not come from the votes he could garner on election day, which were then relatively insignificant. He had a unique way of identifying himself with America's highest values and aspirations. He was clearly a man of faith and communicated fairness, honesty, and integrity. That was his strength.

Another important spiritual figure among the lobbyists I worked with was E. Raymond Wilson of the Friends Committee on National Legislation. A dedicated pacifist, he worked relentlessly in support of his vision of peace. He had an extraordinary influence on congressional foreign policy decision making. He worked the corridors steadily and was respected by all who knew him. Access to the Congress was always available to him, and legislators listened to him because he too combined a sense of realism with a deep spiritual idealism that was a part of his religious faith. He consistently opposed totalitarianism of the right and left and was a great exponent of democratic values.

Perhaps the most professional lobbyist I knew was a U.S. Marine Corps colonel, J. D. Hittle, who efficiently protected and advanced the interests of the corps without fuss, money, or publicity. In 1953, he successfully kept newly elected President Eisenhower's reorganization plan for the Defense Department from being approved by Congress because it reduced the influence of the Marine Corps. When White House strategist Bryce Harlow identified the source of his difficulty, Hittle was temporarily transferred to Europe. Shortly thereafter the plan was approved and Hittle returned to the Pentagon.

Department of the Interior, where he became a passionate advocate for American Indian rights, frequently came to our office for legislative assistance. We had many mutual friends, and he and his wife, Lucy, and Maggie and I soon became friends. He and I had met during my law school days, when I came to Washington for the American Law Students Association convention, and that joint experience served to strengthen our relationship. When he left Interior, he had started in private practice on his own, but soon was recruited by Strasser, Spiegelberg, Fried, and Frank, a New York law firm interested in having a Washington office. Felix had two other young lawyers associated with him, Arthur Lazarus and Richard Schifter, both Yale Law School graduates.

I had once dated Arthur Lazarus's sister in earlier years. His mother had been a pacifist, active in the conscientious objector movement in New York, and a warm personal friend of mine. Richard Schifter had come to Washington to work for Felix. He carried a letter to Humphrey from Chester Bowles, saying that Dick had worked for him and could be a valuable resource for Humphrey.

Then, in 1955, Felix suddenly died. Arthur and Dick came to me shortly thereafter with a problem and a suggestion. To replace Felix and head the Washington office, the New York partners had decided to engage a retired diplomat of the society world. Arthur and Dick objected, feeling the man did not have a sufficiently liberal spirit, and asked if they could recommend me to the New York office as an alternative.

I did not like the idea at all. Even though I thought I would enjoy working with them, I did not know anyone in the New York office and I just didn't want to be a partner of strangers. Harold and I moved ahead with our plans, renting space in a new building in the heart of downtown Washington, just a few blocks from the White House.

Dick and Arthur persisted. To introduce me to the New York office, Dick and his wife, Lilo, invited Maggie and me to dinner at their home. Hans Frank, one of the New York senior partners, was there. The evening went badly. We started off by disagreeing and continued to do so throughout the evening. I liked him, but I found him opinionated and inflexible. My own steadfastness grew as a counterpoint to his stubbornness. We argued about civil rights and civil liberties. He took a pure libertarian viewpoint that I found excessive and unrealistic. I said so. It was a contentious evening.

When Maggie and I got into our car, I said, "There goes Dick's dream of my becoming a partner." I was certain that I had offended

Frank beyond reconciliation, and I didn't care about the consequences. As it turned out, I had misjudged Frank. To my surprise, the invitation to join the office came soon. It was too good an offer to refuse. We would have a year's trial period, during which their office would be next to mine, but we would have separate entrances. They guaranteed me support. A young attorney practicing law for the first time could not turn that down. While I joined a large New York law firm, I was, in fact, very much my own man in Washington, and that was important to me. The wisdom of the move was readily obvious when I found, during the first week we were together, that I had to be in two places at the same time. On that occasion as well as others, Arthur and Dick filled the breach along with Harold Green.*

Even as practicing law took up most of my time and energy, Maggie and I felt that we needed to be active in the political and cultural life of our community, so we moved into the District of Columbia from suburban Maryland, and I dropped my Minnesota voting registration.

We had been living just over the District line, about a half mile into Maryland along Connecticut Avenue. The neighborhood was lovely, but our house was too small for our growing family. We put it up for sale just before I took off for Wilmington, Delaware, to meet with a client. In the midst of a meeting there, I was called to the phone to speak to Maggie. That was not her style, and I expected an emergency that involved a child or illness. Instead, Maggie said that she had a buyer for our house who wanted to make the arrangement right then. I agreed to speak to the buyer, but she put on the phone not the purchaser, but his brother-in-law. That seemed odd, but the gentleman was obviously a take-charge sort of person. He was also a popular band leader and singer, Mitch Miller, who had made a career of getting people to sing along with him.

He explained that he, his sister, and his brother-in-law, Lear Grimmer, all loved the house. Grimmer, who was an expert on snakes

---

* The intimacy of a little office and the need to cooperate was a bonding influence. The experienced secretary I hired, Irene Oppenheimer, remained with me for nearly thirty years. Arthur is still a partner in the firm; Dick left to become the assistant secretary of State for humanitarian and human rights affairs under Reagan and still holds that job, performing splendidly. Harold is now a law professor at George Washington University Law School. Today the Washington office of Fried, Frank has 110 attorneys and a total of 300 employees. I rejoined the firm in 1989, and it has been extremely comfortable, but I miss those early days when law seemed more a profession and less a business. I think something special has gone out of the law and that this generation of highly paid young lawyers is being cheated.

and other reptiles, had just taken the number two job at the National Zoo. We agreed to the sale on the phone. By selling the house to the Grimmers, I inadvertently became involved in my first major civic activity in Washington.

Not long after, when Maggie and I had moved into a grand but run-down old house, Lear Grimmer came to visit us. He was worried. A group of people in the area wanted to organize a citizens' advisory committee, and the zoo professionals were concerned. A similar effort in New York had left the zoo there in the hands of citizens rather than the directors and experts, bringing needless conflict between volunteers and professionals, he explained.

Lear and his boss, the zoo director, Theodore Reed, wanted my advice on what to do. I explained that my knowledge of the zoo was limited to visits with my children, but that I thought a citizens' group might be made helpful and obviously could not be avoided. I urged them not to appear hostile, thus making enemies they didn't need, but to get their own people on the board. I said I assumed that potential board members were well-motivated people or they would not be asking to be involved.

My legal work took me to Wilmington again not long after that meeting. When I arrived home, Maggie asked, "Why did you agree to become president of the Friends of the National Zoo?" I said that I hadn't. She explained that Grimmer and Reed had recommended me to the citizens' group as president. In the face of no opposition, I had been elected. It was not something I chose, but it was also not something I felt I should avoid after the fact.

Within a week or so, zoo news was all over the papers. Tuberculosis was rampant among the animals; a two-and-a-half-year-old child lifted up by her grandfather to better see the lions was mangled when one lion reached out with a paw and pulled the child's arm between the bars into the cage. It was a frightening and ugly incident that Grimmer and Reed told the papers could easily be repeated.

Clearly, there were extensive safety problems in addition to the health problems. I found they reflected financial conditions and the zoo's place in the governmental structure. The zoo was included in the District of Columbia budget, which meant it competed directly with schools, social welfare programs, motor vehicle registration, and a myriad of other services. It invariably came up last. Unless the zoo found a better organizational home, nothing else could be solved, so I threw myself into bringing order out of structural chaos.

I decided that the zoo needed a different financial sponsor. The task was to persuade Congress to move it fully under the jurisdiction of the Smithsonian Institution. There, at least, it competed for money with dinosaurs and old airplanes, not with living and needy children.

I also raised some private money so that a master plan, sorely lacking, could be developed.* With that as a base, there was the wherewithal to begin to solve the health and safety problems.

Later, I got involved in another matter that had direct impact on some of the zoo's animals. Animal rights activists objected to the carnivorous animals being fed live creatures. Yet some snakes, I was told, won't eat anything already dead. They needed to fulfill their hunting instincts by seizing live prey. My friends at the zoo asked if I could resolve the crisis and bring the warring factions together.

Our compromise was to experiment with a device that could shake humanely killed rodents in a manner that made them appear alive enough to attract the reptiles being fed. That seemed to satisfy the animal rights activists as well as the snakes. This was not what I had envisioned as a hobby when I left the Humphrey office, but it was strangely challenging and interesting.

Despite the distraction of the zoo, most of my time was spent on my practice. My first clients came from Minnesota corporations. In addition to Burton Joseph, I was retained by Max Rappaport, who owned Northwest Auto Parts Company (NAPCO). Soon, Minnesota law firms, including that of my law school friend Milton Altman, began to use me for their clients' Washington needs. People I had met over the years began to call on me.

Very early on, I initiated a business venture of my own, which proved helpful to my career even though it never matured. The Washington transit system was based on trolley cars and had been publicly criticized as inadequate and under absentee ownership. The prevailing view was that a modern bus system was required. No local businessmen were coming forward with ideas. I knew nothing about the business, but public transit was an essential part of a community. I talked to Nathan Shapiro, an old Minneapolis friend of Humphrey and me, about the presumably well-run Minneapolis bus system. He introduced me to one of his friends, a major investor in that system who worked closely with General Motors and was prepared to assemble a group of investors. I persuaded the Washington Board of Trade to join me, the Minneapolis group, and the General Motors bus manufacturing divi-

---

* The Friends of the National Zoo (FONZ) now has more than 50,000 members. Through donations and profits from the concessions it runs at the zoo, FONZ now raises almost $1 million each year for the zoo.

sion in a venture to obtain a franchise to create an absolutely new system for Washington. Local businessmen would control policy.

On the eve of what I thought would be a favorable local government decision, I began to hear ugly rumors about the reputation of our Minnesota associates. I called Nate, who understood the seriousness of the problem and the reasons for my deep concern. He confirmed the rumors. I immediately shared the information with my Board of Trade associates and pulled the group out of the running. In the short term, this was a disappointment. In the long run, my exposure to the Washington business community and my directness in pulling out of the competition when it looked like we would be granted the franchise proved very helpful to me.

Another entrepreneurial experience attracted my attention at about this period. Maggie and I had met Marie and Sam Cohen through mutual friends. Sam, an executive at the Hecht Company, Washington's largest department store, was enthusiastically creative and imaginative. Fully persuaded that atomic energy would be the world's primary source of energy and that uranium would be a prime mineral of the future, he had read extensively on the subject. He wanted to go to Colorado and find a uranium source that could be mined. He knew where to go, and I was a sympathetic listener. But we needed partners ready to invest money in our project so we could stake a claim, hire some people, and start a surface mine.

I brought my friend Eugene Feinblatt, a highly respected young Baltimore attorney, into our group, and he in turn brought with him his friends Jerold (Chuck) Hoffberger and Irving Blum, also from Baltimore, who owned the National Brewing Company and later the Baltimore Orioles baseball team. We spent hours reading, talking, and planning. Sam flew to Colorado, found an experienced, available miner, and identified a uranium source that he promptly claimed for us. We shortly heard that we had, indeed, discovered uranium, and we began mining. In excitement, we all flew to Grand Junction to see our mine and to be photographed with our miners' caps. We even began making a little money until, finally, we received an offer from a larger company to buy us out. By now, we were each off on other tangents, saw that we would not become rich from uranium, and sold out at a modest but welcome profit.

In the midst of this excitement, I received a visit from a member of the uranium mine owners' trade association. Uranium had the benefit, as I recall, of a 10 percent tax depletion rate while oil had 27 percent. Would I help them enlist Humphrey and my other congressional friends in support of a 20 percent rate for uranium? After all, I was now an owner. He seemed incredulous at my response that I opposed depletion allowances as unfair tax loopholes. I concluded that I was not cut out to be a mining mogul.

The next challenging question was whether I was cut out to be a banker. My dentist and friend, Irving Lichtman, decided to leave dentistry to become a real estate investor. He invited me to join. I did, along with a few other friends and associates.

One day, as we discussed our plans, Irving noted that while most of our investors and partners were Jewish, there were no more than one or two Jewish bank directors in the whole city, and no bank, except a small industrial bank, had any Negro directors at all. Why not, he asked, explore creating a new bank in Washington and stir up competition?

My law firm was commissioned to proceed. We learned that no new national bank charters had been granted in Washington in four decades. We thought that the comptroller of the currency, James Saxon, might be receptive to encouraging increased competition in banking. We studied the laws and regulations and gathered commitments for the $3 million capital fund we needed to open the bank. I helped gather an interracial board of men and women—people of substance and reputation in the community. The pace was slow; the objections from the existing banks were intense. Out of the effort came the District of Columbia National Bank.

We found the New York banks ready to work with us, but increasingly felt opposition from the largest of the Washington banks, Riggs National Bank. Nevertheless, we survived criticism, mistakes, inexperience, and false charges. I was asked to chair the bank's executive committee. I found the challenge as exciting as I found the subject matter boring. We made our mark. Other groups followed our lead and obtained charters of their own. Competition was injected into the Washington banking structure. In a few years, Leo Bernstein, a successful savings and loan banker, asked me whether we would be prepared to sell our stock to him. I was certainly ready, if the price was right. Others joined me. The price was right, and we sold.

My life as an entrepreneur took another turn, from the boardroom to the locker room. Joe Robbie, Hubert's old friend from South Dakota, came to see me. After losing a race as the Democratic gubernatorial candidate in his state, Joe moved to Minneapolis to practice law and unsuccessfully ran for mayor. He was one of the most energetic, determined, and voluble men I knew—as well as the most rapid talker.

Disappointed in politics, but with no diminution of ambition, he decided to put his powerful mind and legal talent to work in a business that provided excitement and personal notoriety and attention. He had learned that professional football would grant a franchise to a responsible group ready to operate in Miami, Florida.

Joe told me that one of his partners was the actor Danny Thomas, a fellow Christian Lebanese and friend, who was also a strong supporter of Hubert's. Could I help him? By coincidence, one of the stockholders in our bank had told me of his desire to purchase a baseball franchise in Philadelphia. I told him of Joe's plans, and he quickly offered to be part of the franchise group, suggesting that I could have a small part of his interest. Joe succeeded, and the Miami Dolphins were born.

The new investor soon came onto hard times and was unable to fulfill his continuous financial obligation to finance the team. Joe came to me for help, and I agreed to step into the breach for a short time, thus owning more of the franchise than I expected or wished, and for a longer time.

I recall the first play of the first game opening the first season of play for the team in Miami. My son Jeff and I were in the stands just behind the home team bench. On that first play, the Dolphins received the ball and ran the length of the field, scoring a touchdown. I no longer remember the team we played or the name of the player who made the touchdown, but it was clear to all of us who invested in the team that the fates had spoken. It was a good omen.

My interest in football continued, but my interest in investing in football quickly disappeared. The following year, Danny Thomas telephoned me to say that he would be selling his interest to another group brought in by Robbie. Since Danny and I had talked about our mutual desire to get out at a profit, he invited me to join him in the sale; I did. I still am a nostalgic rooter for the Dolphins, but only when they are not playing the Washington Redskins.

In my law practice, I handled a few divorce cases, although I did not like the work and spent as much time trying to reconcile estranged couples as I did litigating their differences. During one case involving a very rich wife-beater, the victim's vindictive mother-in-law caused me such time-consuming misery that I told Irene Oppenheimer, who kept track of my hours, that we would bill for legal time and aggravation time. We did. In the final agreement the husband was required to pay the bill.

Most of our practice was simply routine corporate work, mergers, acquisitions, wills and estates, tax questions, contracts, and some real estate. We handled contracts with government agencies and some representation with regulatory agencies. We did almost no legislative lobbying, except in behalf of a number of American Indian tribes, clients inherited by Arthur and Dick from Felix Cohen, and clients for whom we were already working on other matters.

During those early years, it was hard to turn down clients, but I did. On two occasions, for example, a good friend, Leslie Biffle, a Truman crony whom I had gotten to know when he was secretary of the Senate, sent me prospective clients. The first was the National Tax Equality Association (NTEA), whose mission was to get cooperatives taxed differently than they were.

What the association obviously wanted to use was not my legal expertise but my friendship with Humphrey, who was deeply committed to agricultural cooperatives and opposed to the NTEA program. I agreed with Humphrey on this matter and could not find it in my heart to represent them in any fashion.

Les Biffle later sent another person to see me. This man did not care about domestic policy matters. He explained that he represented Trujillo, the dictator of the Dominican Republic. He was interested in engaging my services at an attractive annual retainer. As I tried to learn what my duties would be, he wondered aloud, "By the way, could you persuade your good friend, Senator Humphrey, to visit the Dominican Republic to see for himself that the charges of dictatorship are highly exaggerated and even irrelevant." To be Trujillo's attorney was an honor I would not accept at any price, and I certainly did not want to put a price on my friendship with Humphrey. I politely turned the offer down. I was disappointed when Franklin Roosevelt, Jr., took on that representation.*

On only one occasion did I find myself involved in a serious criminal case. Once was enough. Judge David Bazelon, of the United States Court of Appeals for the District of Columbia, gave me a *pro*

---

* There are several kinds of lawyers, and you have to choose where you wish to belong. Alexis de Tocqueville, over a century ago, said that in "all free governments, of whatsoever form they may be, members of the legal profession will be found at the head of all parties." He knew that of the fifty-six signers of the Declaration of Independence, thirty-three were lawyers. In contrast, a nineteenth-century dictionary explained that the "lake-lawyer" fish got its name from its "ferocious look and voracious habits." The Illinois Grange in 1872 accepted anyone as a member, except actors, gamblers, and lawyers. I once heard Golda Meir, Israel's prime minister, tell an audience that Israeli lawyers made good front-line soldiers. The general would order "Charge!" and, Golda added, "Let me tell you. They know how to charge!"

bono assignment involving the murder of the son of a prominent Washington attorney, not far from where I lived. After I talked to him, I felt the accused man was guilty beyond a shadow of doubt and clearly seemed to have no remorse. I asked Bazelon to take me off the case, an appeal from a trial conviction, and find me some other assignment. He refused, saying it was the obligation of the "respectable" bar to represent those who needed counsel, even if their alleged crime was repugnant. I did the best I could, appealing the original conviction on narrow legal grounds, believing that was my client's only hope. The appeal was correctly rejected and confirmed that I was not cut out for criminal work.

Another case, that first year, taught me quite a different lesson. A New York lawyer called to ask me if I would represent the Revlon Corporation, which was being investigated by a committee of Congress. Revlon then sponsored a TV game show, "The $64,000 Question," on which the answers and contestants were manipulated; the results were fixed. Had the show been less popular, public wrath at this show business fraud might have been less, but as it was, congressional interest was inevitable.

I met with Charles Revson who, with his brother, Martin, ran Revlon. I was convinced, after a full examination of their files, that he and the company had nothing to do with the deception. Indeed, Charles Revson himself watched each weekly show, cheering for one contestant or the other, believing the show was totally honest. He was among the duped—disappointed when his favorite lost.

After I came to know him and had reviewed the files, I urged Revson not to testify before Congressman Oren Harris's committee. Revson seemed relieved and agreed. Revson looked slick on his good days, slippery on his bad ones, and I felt he would add nothing to the inquiry. Beyond that, he was not well liked in the business community and was seen as an early version of a corporate raider before that was an acceptable activity. He did not communicate stability or integrity, or inspire confidence. I said that if we opened up all the files to the committee staff, they would probably be satisfied. I convinced the committee staff person, Richard Goodwin, later of Kennedy White House speechwriting fame, that Revson had no knowledge or information to offer and should not be made to testify. I thought I had accomplished a great deal.

Revson called shortly after to reverse our understanding, saying that his public relations firm thought he should testify and help clear the name of the company. When I could not convince him of the appalling error of that advice, I said he had to understand that he now needed his own personal attorney to represent him since I represented the company. This puzzled and upset him, but his New York lawyers agreed. When he asked me to recommend someone I could work with, I suggested Clark Clifford, already well on his way to mythic proportions as a super-lawyer. I shared the results of my committee discussion and intensive review of the files with Clifford. Subsequently, Revson appeared before the committee with Clifford at his side. My concerns were justified; Revson embarrassed himself needlessly.

When the hearing was over, Clifford called to ask what I thought he should charge. I was surprised to be asked and said, "I don't have the slightest idea. Charge whatever you think you should." He then stated a number that was close to what I hoped to make in my entire first year of practice, far more than I was intending to charge for my work over a much longer period of time.

I whistled in disbelief, thinking of the relatively few hours he had put into the case. Clifford responded to the whistle and said, "Max, let me tell you something. Revson will be unhappy with my bill, and he's going to yell that it's highway robbery. But he'll pay it, and next winter when he's playing pinochle with his cronies in Miami, he'll talk about his Washington lawyer, Clark Clifford. At that moment, it will be worth every dime to him." Name dropping as well as aggravation time seemed billable. I increased my own bill.

Occasional opportunities arose for helping clients beyond their business interests. One day, one of our New York senior partners, Sam Harris, called to say I could be helpful on a project he and one of our clients, Joseph Hirshhorn, were working on. I had met Joe before I had any relationship with the firm when our mutual friend, Chicago labor lawyer Leon Despres, had introduced us in 1950 while I was working in the Senate. At that time, Joe persuaded me to invest a few hundred precious dollars to purchase shares of stock in Canadian uranium development companies he had formed.* Filled with exuberance and malapropisms, Joe was then a hustler par excellence. He was now, about five years later, a multimillionaire with one of the world's outstanding art and sculpture collections.

Joe was ready to contribute his collection to a museum that would carry his name. Governor Nelson Rockefeller was pressing hard for a New York City or Albany location. Israel wanted it. The Canadian government was urging that it be located where Joe had made his

* My small investment in those penny stocks enabled Maggie and me to purchase our first home three years later.

money. The United Kingdom made its appeal. Dillon Ripley was pushing for the Smithsonian Institution in Washington, D.C.

Joe wanted my judgment. What did I think? It seemed simple to me. Washington was the capital of the world and the collection belonged here. I talked to Humphrey, who eagerly grasped the idea. Both he and Abe Fortas, together with Ripley, talked to President Johnson. Joe was wined and dined at the White House. But the Smithsonian could not match what others proposed unless Johnson could persuade Congress to match the offers. The Congress reluctantly acquiesced. Today the Hirshhorn Museum stands proudly on the mall as if it could be in no other place as appropriately.

Our law firm functioned without a formal plan, but grew substantially each year. I led by instinct, making decisions on the available evidence, neither anguishing too long over failures nor gloating too much over our many successes. I did not have a long-range plan. When any of my partners insisted we have "retreats" to make such a plan, I would agree, then not know where or how to begin. We were not an old, established law firm with a stable of blue-chip clients and the luxury of strategic planning. We took the clients who came through the door and worked hard to serve them well and build a reputation. It worked, it seemed to me, quite well and without a lot of planning activity.

I continued to see Humphrey and help out where I could on his political needs. That led, however, to one of the more disappointing political events of my life and certainly of Humphrey's. By 1956, many of us were thinking of Humphrey as a vice presidential candidate on a Stevenson ticket. So was Stevenson. That spring at a Washington political dinner, both Humphrey and Stevenson spoke. They were seated at the head table, of course, and I saw them speak to each other several times. As the dinner ended, Humphrey caught my eye and signaled to me to join him. As I moved close, he turned to exclude those near him and said softly, "Adlai would like to see us."

I knew that Adlai wanted to see Humphrey, not me, but I also understood that Humphrey clearly didn't want to see Adlai alone. In retrospect, Humphrey may have had a sense of what might take place and wanted a witness. In any case, the two of us worked our way through the crowd and to the elevators as quickly as we could. When we were admitted to the Stevenson suite, the governor was already in his pajamas and clearly tired, finding the politicking as exhausting as Humphrey found it energizing. Bill Blair was there as well as Jim Finnegan, the secretary of state of Pennsylvania and Stevenson's campaign manager. Finnegan was a very bright urban, big-city, industrial-state "pol."

Stevenson, feeling confident of the presidential nomination, began to talk about potential vice presidential candidates, including dark horses, long shots, and those who seemed more likely. He asked for Humphrey's appraisal of each name, but this was mostly an exercise so that Stevenson could present his own views for confirmation. He sniffily dismissed Kefauver as unqualified to be vice president, much less president.

He liked Jack Kennedy, but said firmly that he was too young and too inexperienced. He then concluded with what was probably in his mind from the beginning. In effect, he said, "You know, Hubert, there's only one man left. That's you. I want you to be the vice president, but we have a problem. I need the South. I can't have someone who is looked upon as an enemy of the South."* Stevenson continued, "I need two or three important Southerners to say to me that they want you. That's all I need."

Humphrey and I looked at each other for a split second, our eyes saying to each other, "We can get the South." Stevenson then turned to Jim Finnegan and asked him and Blair to work with us. Humphrey and I could barely control our excitement, but we did, getting up to leave almost immediately, since Stevenson's fatigue was clear and his agenda completed.

He said as a parting blessing, "Keep in touch with Bill and Jim and let's go to work." There was nothing ambiguous about the offer, although we knew there was also nothing certain if we could not meet his Southern needs and strategy.

Hubert immediately asked Walter George and Richard Russell,† the senators from Georgia, two men who had initially disliked and distrusted Humphrey's views and style, but who had grown to have great respect for him, to speak in his behalf to Stevenson. They agreed. We heard they did. Hubert also asked Lyndon Johnson, by then ma-

---

* Possibly I have forgotten a word or two, or changed a phrase, but Humphrey and I repeated them again and again as soon as we could do so without embarrassment in order to make sure we understood Stevenson precisely. If a word is wrong after all these years, the essence is not.

† This was not easy for Russell. He had desperately wanted to become president of the United States in 1952, and certainly felt he was more competent, dedicated, and experienced than others whose names kept surfacing. But he was not acceptable to Northern party leaders, liberals generally, and Truman specifically. He was now being asked to support someone whose friends had rejected him, unfairly he thought. But his respect for Humphrey had grown and, out of that, friendship, too.

jority leader, to speak to Stevenson, and Johnson soon reported back enthusiastically that he had spoken to Stevenson and had told him that the South would not be a problem. The list of Southern leaders ready to announce for Humphrey was impressive.

We approached the national convention confident the next major step in Humphrey's career was about to take place. We encouraged some news stories. In July, Humphrey told Allen Drury of the *New York Times* that he had indicated to friends that they could "work actively in my behalf." The *Minneapolis Tribune* ran an article that said, "Southern Opposition to Humphrey Eases."

Humphrey considered it inappropriate to run for the nomination in any public and high-pressured manner. There was no tradition of running for vice president, no political pattern to follow. Except for the contact with the few Southern senators, we did not reach out, possibly because we did not really know how to organize nationally, but certainly because we did not think it necessary.

Neither the Kefauver nor Kennedy camps shared our ingenuous attitude. They campaigned hard. Ted Sorenson carefully and ably prepared an analysis of the Catholic vote in American politics, and John Bailey managed a precise distribution of the story to overcome what they believed to be Kennedy's chief problem—his religion—and turn it into an asset.

Once in Chicago, we found it difficult to reach Stevenson, Finnegan, or Blair.* Their silence was unnerving, particularly when talk of Kefauver and Kennedy increased. We did not, once again, do anything about either one, since we knew that Stevenson had been disdainful of Kefauver and thought Kennedy not ready. We waited for a call from Stevenson, but none came. Then we heard on television that he was throwing the convention open so that the delegates themselves could decide who should get the vice presidential nomination.

Hubert was crushed. He had received no word or warning that Stevenson had changed signals. I was furious. Stevenson's grace and charm had disappeared for me, replaced by unforgivable rudeness. We were embarrassed and humiliated, even though almost no one had been told of Stevenson's commitment, except for the Southerners we needed and the few insiders around Humphrey.

* Jim Rowe, a neighbor and one of Washington's political sages going back to his service as FDR's first administrative assistant, wrote me several years later: "In my opinion, Bill Blair knows the details of the centers of power in each State better than any other human being. . . . He is tough and his heart belongs to Adlai . . . I think he is the most underestimated politician I know, probably because of the Groton manner and the fact that he was the self-appointed conscious 'no' man and cold SOB of the Stevenson group."

When Stevenson finally reached Humphrey by phone the following day to explain that he had been under great pressure and had chosen the only way he could find to resolve the problem, Humphrey, in a response that was uncharacteristic, remained cold and virtually monosyllabic.

By the time Humphrey was asked a few weeks later to campaign for Stevenson and Kefauver, he was ready again, jumping into the fray with his normal enthusiasm.

Almost immediately after Stevenson lost in 1956, Humphrey's friends began to talk of him as the liberal candidate in 1960. It seemed a logical idea. By late 1957, Humphrey had essentially made up his mind to run. He had the experience he had lacked in 1952 and the self-confidence that came with a successful political and legislative career. While his Senate term also ended in 1960, he knew that he could probably hold on to the DFL nomination or the Senate seat if he were eliminated from the presidential race. He felt it was worthwhile for him politically even if he won the nomination and lost the general election. It would give him a leg up on 1964.

We started slowly. Herb Waters, a solid and wise political operative, was a little possessive and protective of Humphrey and inclined to exclude other advisers. I tried to be the bridge to others.

I invited in my neighbor Jim Rowe, a youthful Roosevelt brain-truster and a close friend of Lyndon Johnson. Jim was a Montana boy with a Harvard education and great political instincts and experience. He was helpful, but out of loyalty to Johnson kept a certain distance from us. Jim's involvement drove Joe Rauh wild. Joe was a dedicated and effective civil rights leader, but he was also a rigidly self-righteous "liberal" whom I came to believe was illiberal in judging others. The unraveling of his close friendship with Humphrey began with Humphrey's support of the Communist Control Act in 1954 and was hastened by Rowe's arrival in the inner circle.

In 1958, Humphrey set out on his first major political excursion probing the presidential waters on a trip to the West Coast. It was well and carefully planned. California, Oregon, and Washington all had strongly liberal Democratic voters. They were our kind of states and necessary as a base for Humphrey if he was to be successful. But the first day out, a labor matter considered in the Senate lost by a single vote. Labor was angry. For all practical and symbolic purposes, the election was over when Humphrey canceled the trip, got on an airplane, and returned to try to salvage the vote.

He told us that while he wanted to run for president, he would not ignore his responsibilities as a senator to satisfy his ambition and desire to be president. That made long-range commitments impossible, made all of us tentative in our work, and made him a virtual prisoner to Washington legislative caprice. Nevertheless, Humphrey traveled widely, albeit with inadequate planning; appeared on network interview shows more than anyone else; and made the cover of *Life* magazine after an eight-hour interview with Khrushchev. The press at the time voted him "best" senator and most qualified to be president.

His major opposition seemed likely to come from Kennedy and Lyndon Johnson, although others, including Averell Harriman and Stuart Symington, were eager to run. Kennedy still seemed ill-defined and had not yet paid his liberal dues. Johnson, for all his immense competence and basic populism, was unacceptable to most of the labor and liberal leaders. He carried a Texas stigma related to style, accent, frontier politics, and the petroleum industries.

I came to feel I was the proverbial skunk at the garden party when our small group of Washington Humphrey supporters would assemble. It appeared obvious to me that Humphrey would lose in Wisconsin unless he committed more time there than he seemed willing to do. In the winter of 1958, Maggie and I had visited her folks in Wisconsin. I drove around the state visiting friends, talking politics, taking the political temperature, and trying to evaluate, rather than only persuade. I came back believing we would lose; I therefore urged Humphrey not to run. We had neither money nor organization; the Kennedys were all over the state with both.

I had begun to worry, particularly when I talked to Bill Proxmire. He acknowledged that he would not ever have been elected to the United States Senate without Humphrey's persistent help and would not have received the committee assignments he had without Humphrey's intervention with Johnson, but he refused, albeit gently, to make a commitment to Humphrey. I knew then we were in trouble. If we couldn't depend on "Prox," I wondered aloud to Maggie, whom could we depend on?

There were worse troubles. The labor movement, which should have been solidly for Humphrey, was not. Many union members were Catholic and attracted to Kennedy. Humphrey expected Walter Reuther and the United Auto Workers (UAW) to support him, but Reuther was frequently not for Humphrey when the political crunch came. Since Humphrey was Reuther's most stalwart ally in the Senate and the ADA, his actions were difficult to understand or accept. They were alike in a number of ways—charismatic, fine speakers, deeply committed to liberal programs, natural leaders. There was, I thought at the time, an element of jealousy in Walter that made him want to see Humphrey thwarted at crucial moments.

Most often at our meetings, we talked not about people, strategy, or schedule, but about money. We were not great money raisers, although Humphrey's old friend, Marvin Rosenberg, a New York curtain manufacturer and a solid liberal, worked the New York community with great energy. Dwayne Andreas, a brilliant agro-businessman and one of Humphrey's closest friends, and a few other generous wealthy friends were also extraordinarily encouraging with their money.

We learned as we went along and got better in many ways, but we were frequently outplanned and outorganized by the Kennedy forces. Certainly the press, attracted by the monarchical qualities of this super-rich family, seemed to magnify our sins and their virtues.

In the heavily Catholic districts, Kennedy and his family were immediate star attractions. No Catholic had ever been elected president, and the emotional importance of his candidacy was undeniable. When anti-Catholic pamphlets were mailed to Catholic households, as if by mistake, there was reason to believe that someone in the Kennedy campaign itself had done so deliberately to enhance the religious fervor for him. We could do nothing about it, except deplore anti-Catholicism.

I was walking alone with Humphrey after one of our meetings in Washington and, in response to his questioning, said, "You are probably going to lose in Wisconsin, and I don't think you can get the nomination without winning there. Our friends are now Kennedy's friends. The family has spread out across the state, and people we need now see themselves as intimate friends of Eunice or Bobby or Teddy. Beyond that, the Catholic pride in Kennedy's campaign is widespread and deep, and the primary law makes it possible for Republican Catholics to cross over and vote for Kennedy."

My words did not fall on ears that were totally deaf, but close to it. In his typical fashion, he remained hopeful, worked harder, and received contrary evaluation and counsel from others. For all our problems in Wisconsin, Humphrey and most of our advising group felt certain he could win there. I hoped I was wrong, but the evidence I could discern prevented me from changing my mind. I worked harder, too, moving to Milwaukee during the closing weeks of the campaign to put in my full time and energy. But we were outspent, outmaneuvered, outcampaigned, outclassed.

Even as the Wisconsin election wound down, we had to look ahead. West Virginia loomed next on the primary horizon. In our earlier strategy, we had eagerly wanted to match up against Kennedy there. West Virginia, after all, was a workingman's state, a union strong-hold, and 97 percent Protestant—all pluses for Humphrey. We had been pleased when Kennedy entered the West Virginia primary. There would be a match-up.

The Wisconsin election came, and while we did reasonably well, we clearly lost. On the way back from a television appearance on election night, Hubert was pleased that one additional marginal congressional district had just gone for him. It was not enough to sway me. I said, "Hubert, you have a decision to make tonight and tomorrow. Do you get out now with some dignity or do you go to West Virginia?"

He knew where I was headed. I continued, "I think we are going to lose there." I had not been to West Virginia, but I knew that Kennedy had the momentum and that we were broke. That was a devastating combination. Cash was especially important in West Virginia in those days, cash for a sheriff, cash for a minister, cash for party officials—what was euphemistically known as walking-around money. I also knew that we did not have the skilled team in adequate numbers to win. Our maximum effort had already met its match in Wisconsin.

People like to go with a winner. The bandwagon effect is real and powerful, as Humphrey himself had noted earlier. While we were later critical of the Kennedy forces for "buying" the state of West Virginia,* we were ourselves prepared to put up our money. Our problem was that we did not have enough to compete with them.

The Kennedy forces outsmarted us, moreover, by making a failure to vote for Jack Kennedy appear almost an act of bigotry, no matter what the basis for the decision. We also did not anticipate the intense campaigning by the Kennedy forces. In West Virginia, Franklin Roosevelt, Jr., used his honorable name to peddle a dishonorable story about Humphrey's lack of military service in the Second World War. The label "draft dodger" was applied by Roosevelt, who knew it was not accurate. He persisted even after both Jack and Bobby Kennedy had promised Humphrey that they would rein him in.

I said again to Humphrey, "I think you will lose and that you will risk being humiliated. You could end up tarred as an anti-Catholic, which is not good for you or your position in seeking reelection in

* Richard Cardinal Cushing once described to Humphrey how he and Joe Kennedy sat in the cardinal's library deciding how much each minister who would take a donation would get. In 1968, John Bailey recounted to a group how he sat in Washington National Airport with a suitcase full of cash, headed for West Virginia when an innocent Teddy Kennedy, on his way to a different plane, came up; he was rudely shooed away by Bailey, who was fearful the suitcase would somehow pop open and spill its contents in a Kennedy's presence for all to see.

Minnesota in November. Inevitably, some of our supporters in the state are going to move around with anti-Catholic arguments because they want to win, and they will sense they are behind."

Kennedy overcame the conventional wisdom about West Virginia, devastated us, and took a giant step toward the presidency. Humphrey turned his attention to his Senate reelection campaign and to the 1960 national convention, no longer as a presidential candidate.

As the 1960 convention approached, Stevenson, with characteristic indecisiveness, belatedly indicated his availability for the nomination. I urged Humphrey to support Kennedy. I thought he had grown tremendously. I also knew how to count; Kennedy had the convention votes. Also, Orville Freeman, as a Protestant Midwestern governor, had a chance to get the vice presidential nomination to balance Kennedy's Eastern Catholic roots. Humphrey chose to support Stevenson, in part because Mrs. Roosevelt urged him, in part because there was some residual anger at Kennedy and some residual affection for Stevenson. I thought neither the nation nor Humphrey's own career was well served by this gesture, and a gesture was all it could be.

The convention began on an interesting note for Humphrey. After the West Virginia primary and Humphrey's withdrawal from the race, Arthur Goldberg, Dave Dubinsky, Walter Reuther, and Alex Rose, head of the Liberal party in New York and a prominent labor leader, had called on me to say they knew Hubert was hurt, but they believed that he should be the vice presidential candidate and that the ticket could win. They felt they could get a commitment from Jack Kennedy that he would choose Hubert if Humphrey agreed. I took them to see Humphrey, who was cold to the idea. They persevered and arranged a "chance meeting" between Humphrey and Kennedy on the Senate floor, which led to a long private talk of reconciliation between the two. Humphrey then asked me to keep in touch with the labor leaders, without any commitments on his part, since he remained skeptical about their plan.

Their reports to me were frequent and optimistic. They were convinced they had a Kennedy commitment. On the eve of the Los Angeles convention, when, at his request, I met Humphrey on his arrival at the airport, he asked me to tell "our friends" that there was no deal, and he would not run for vice president. He turned them down in large part because of his own feelings and his unwillingness to give up his Senate seat for a tight race, but also because Muriel had been particularly annoyed at the Kennedy family by the campaigns in Wisconsin and West Virginia. Goldberg, Rose, Reuther, and Dubinsky insisted on seeing Humphrey as soon as I gave them my report, but their assertion that the deal was set had no effect.

The convention was a bittersweet one that marked, for me, what I felt would be the end of Hubert's quest for the presidency. I thought that Kennedy would win against Nixon and that Humphrey's timing would not be right for another run. Johnson would succeed to the nomination after two Kennedy terms and, whether he won or lost, another generation of candidates would likely then come forth.

I also found that I was no longer as interested in presidential politics and campaigning as I had been in advancing Humphrey's career and possible service in higher office. His intellect, interests, and qualities were special. I did not see them matched in others. Furthermore, I became skeptical about the process—not about its importance or its indispensable role in a democratic society, but what it too often did to people involved in it. I had watched personal ambition devour good intentions. I did not see myself as a generic "braintruster" for campaigns, coming into political heat every four years as a presidential campaign approached.

Now, at the age of forty, I was ready for new worlds, without, however, cutting my ties with the old. I eagerly looked forward to new opportunities in my professional life as a lawyer and my personal life as husband and father to a growing family.

10

Humphrey for President at Last

Leaving the Hill and beginning private law practice provided me the distance and detachment to watch and observe the political process even as I remained close to Humphrey. I watched novices come to the House of Representatives, devote themselves to a committee and subject, and become wise in their area of responsibility. Every laggard of inconsequence, I learned, is more than balanced by someone who studies the issues and thinks of the future with care and concern for the commonwealth.

I have watched congressmen rise above mediocrity, innocence, or ignorance and develop into thoughtful public servants. I have watched others without the capacity for growth, except perhaps in their own self-esteem. Nowhere, however, do people have a greater chance for growing than in the presidency. On-the-job training is inevitable. It cannot be otherwise, since there is no other job like president of the United States. Many people can claim that their prior experience has prepared them for the presidency. No one really knows. The test comes when the responsibility is real.

Eric Goldman, an eminent American historian who served briefly and uncomfortably in the Johnson White House as the house academician, once wrote that every society has certain values that it considers essential to survival. Each society seeks to find in one human being the symbol and ultimate guardian of those values, one who communicates the strength and stability required for that role.

The president obviously is the one to whom the American people look as the personification of those values. Most Americans seek in their national leader a combination of patriotism, broad religious principles, and commitment to the preservation of the republic and the strengthening of democracy. That leadership depends not only on those values but on personal growth as well. A receptivity to stimuli from new sources is fundamental. A president, who does not ever come to the office perfect, must be a listener as well as a talker to become at least better.* A president must be willing to consider other views and all options.

Accommodation to realities obviously cannot come from an unyielding, intellectually arrogant, closed approach. It must begin in the heart and in sensitivity. Change does not mean inconsistency run rampant, but a balance of old ideas and views tempered by a realistic evaluation of available options. Without that, a president can mouth the correct words, but be, in fact, empty of real leadership.

A good president has the flexibility to permit internal adjustments to evolve and the intuitive ability to absorb external experience. A president must be open not only to new ideas but also to new events and new people. Without that openness, a president soon runs out of people and falls victim to cronyism.

The weaknesses of those elected to the presidency obviously do not disappear, but their strengths have a chance to flourish on a broader stage, and that is what we generally remember. Sometimes, of course, character flaws overcome their strengths and damage their ability to serve. Lyndon Johnson and Richard Nixon come to mind, their extraordinary qualities and talents victims of personal quirks.

In more than forty years of observing presidential aspirants and the presidents themselves, I have misjudged them almost as often as I have been right about them. I was wrong about Harry Truman, who developed into a first-rate and courageous president. He, more than any other president, set the tone of firm moral leadership for our country's postwar international role. Observers have emphasized his decisiveness, energy, and optimism; and Dean Acheson, his able secretary of state, characterized him as an inspirational and inexhaustible leader. He was accused of cronyism but, in fact, he found exceptionally tal-

---

* Would anyone have believed, as he took office, that Dwight Eisenhower would depart warning, right or wrong, about the power of a "military-industrial complex"?

ented people, among old and new friends, to help and advise him. Charles Murphy, for example, was a nonspectacular, yet experienced and wise Washington lawyer. He was also a person of great decency, high moral standards, and good political instincts, who served well as Truman's right hand in the White House. Richard Neustadt was a very young man in the Truman years, bright and brash, with no particular previous public record of accomplishment by which to be judged. Truman and Murphy simply recognized his talent and potential. He became an outstanding scholar of the presidency, teaching at Columbia and Harvard, writing books of special insight. These men represented the qualities wise presidents, if they are willing to be open, can find to expand their abilities: competence, loyalty, ideas, creativity, and integrity among people they know as well as among those they do not.

I was also, in some measure, wrong about John Kennedy but right about Dwight Eisenhower. In spite of Ike's apparent inability to utter a spontaneous whole sentence or paragraph without endless "uhs" and errors of syntax and grammar, I recognized a professional, in the best sense of that word. I did not accept the prevailing notion of the time that he was only a symbol through which others functioned.* He obviously carefully nurtured an image of ease. He deliberately wanted to give the appearance of reigning rather than ruling.

John Kennedy as president made the political world and the country vibrate with his youthful exuberance and charm. He was a fine example of the truth that the presidency has frequently stretched its occupants to become much more than they were when they took office. There had been no question, during Kennedy's career on the Hill, about his intelligence, only about his character, seriousness, and willingness to work. Would he be a perpetual playboy, a dilettante at life? My early impression was that playboy was a permanent condition, lazy and frivolous the most likely dominant traits. But Kennedy was not a captive of his own economic and privileged past. Clearly, he was not lazy, and he was serious as president, reaching out to a wide variety of people of talent, skill, and enthusiasm to join him and help him. It was the spirit he brought to the country that makes him memorable.

I was not particularly close to the Kennedy White House, but I marveled at the aura that Kennedy created and the speed with which he transcended the mediocrity of his congressional service to become a truly national treasure. He created excitement merely by his presence.

* The recent writings of Berkeley's Aaron Wildavsky and Princeton's Fred Greenstein, two of our most distinguished political scientists, demonstrate Eisenhower's mastery over the instruments of government and policy.

The family glamour was from time to time excessively trumpeted by the media, but even in a democracy, citizens like to see their "first" family exhibit some distinctive taste and style.* Rank has its privileges, and those perks, displayed with discretion, do not seem offensive to most citizens.

What Kennedy had communicated in West Virginia to the impoverished people there seemed to have captivated a good share of the nation, rich and poor, as well. It was valuable in transfusing the society with new vigor and civic pride. Democratic government is not merely a matter of cold reason and the analytical development of public policies. Color, flair, and symbolism are indispensable parts of effective power and, for the most part, the Kennedys displayed those attributes admirably and used them with the necessary restraint.

Some people will find it strange, I know, but I think Jack Kennedy and Ronald Reagan had some qualities in common. Despite Reagan's frequent clutching at automatic ideology, he was, in fact, open, and did grow in office. While he remained loyal to his old California cronies, he also accepted and even welcomed newcomers who did not fit their mold. I certainly found in my conversations with him on human rights and arms control that he would listen and absorb what I, and others, had to say. Furthermore, and perhaps most important, he, too, instilled a new sense of confidence in the American people, strengthened the country's faith in its own potential, and stimulated a strong sense of civic pride. Reagan's unauthorized biographer Lou Cannon pointed out that just as Charles de Gaulle was great not because he was in France but because France was in him, so is the greatness of Reagan due to the fact that he carries a vision of America's strength in him.

It is too early to anticipate the judgment of history, but historians will have to take into account that it was under Ronald Reagan's stewardship that the cold war with the Soviets began to come to an end. Also under his leadership, the seven-year period from 1982 to 1989 was, in the words of the distinguished economist Herbert Stein, "the longest and strongest non-inflationary expansion in our history," creating 18.7 million new jobs and some $30 million worth of goods and services, with inflation dropping from 12.5 percent to 4.4 percent, unemployment from 7.1 percent to 5.5 percent, and prime interest rates from 15.3 percent to 9.3 percent. I am aware that skeptics claim

* Interestingly, the terms "first family" and "first lady" did not appear early on in American history—not until about the middle of the nineteenth century, in the "gilded age." Indeed, the terms were first used sarcastically by critics of pretension and posturing.

that we are now paying a high price for that record, but I suspect that Reagan has carefully nurtured and relishes the role of being an underestimated politician, content that history will have the last word. Critics found him "inattentive, unfocused, and incurious," but Berkeley political scientist Aaron Wildavsky noted that he was able to move the nation powerfully in the direction he wanted it to go.

Jimmy Carter, whom I grew to respect, was much more closed as president and suffered for it. He gave the impression of rejecting new people and new ideas, although I doubt that he did so consciously. His self-righteousness was caused, I think, more by his sense of being an outsider than by his deeply held religious convictions. In any case, an ineffectual saint is not admired, certainly not as president of the United States.

"Call me Jimmy" may have been intended to be friendly, but it is ultimately demeaning for a president. Early in the administration, I wrote a memorandum to my friend Stu Eizenstat, Carter's close associate, strongly urging that the "Jimmy" was bad politics and not the symbolism that the country needed in its president at that point. What the country needed, I felt, was what the Romans called "gravitas" in their leader. Out of office, however, Carter has grown and become what the people respect in their ex-presidents. He has risen in public estimation with his dignity, good works, humility, and compassion.

To return to Kennedy, soon after the inauguration I received a call from Newton Minow, a former Stevenson aide and law partner who had been recently appointed chairman of the Federal Communications Commission by Kennedy. Newt, who later accurately described commercial television as a "vast wasteland," asked me to be his lawyer, checking the contract on a house he intended to buy and changing his will to reflect his new job. When he called one day after all that had been taken care of, I assumed it was again a private legal matter, but he said unexpectedly that he wanted me to become the chairman of channel 26, WETA-TV, the struggling, impoverished educational television station in Washington. I was surprised and said, "Newton, I've never watched channel 26 in my life. It's UHF and we don't get UHF in our house. I don't know anything about it."

I thought that would settle the question, but he persisted, insisting that I at least have lunch with him and Willard Kiplinger, the founder of the *Kiplinger Newsletter*, who was then chairman of the board of the station. We had lunch, and I reluctantly agreed to become vice chairman of the board, assuming it would be just as interesting, not as time consuming, and still useful to Newt. Soon thereafter, Kip resigned, feeling his age and health required conservation of his energy. I found myself as chairman overseeing a public television station with a weak signal, no real professional staff, and problems with the lease for its inadequate studio in a high school in northern Virginia. The station had one exceptionally good engineer and a flock of volunteers, including an unusually gifted and saintly woman, Elizabeth Campbell, who volunteered full-time on classroom television programming. She and the other volunteers kept the station alive and functioning in those infant days of educational television.

I worked out an arrangement with Howard University by which they provided better studio facilities in exchange for the services of our staff in teaching and training students. I hired a first-rate manager, Bill McCarter, who attracted other quality people and moved the station toward professional levels.

In addition, I set out to raise money for the station, which had only a shoestring budget. John Kluge, the wealthy owner of Metromedia, a small independent network, came through with a generous donation of $100,000 that lifted WETA-TV from its misery and set it on a course toward excellence and innovation. I asked Newt Minow and the other FCC commissioners to attend a small reception at which John handed over his check. He received good press and the chance to impress the commissioners.

In my approach to Kluge and others, I maintained that the commercial sector had a community responsibility to support educational television, but beyond that our failure would lead to someone in the private sector taking over our license and someday, when UHF was more generally available, becoming a competitor of the private stations. Those arguments apparently made sense to Kluge as well as to NBC, which generously made a similar grant. With their money in hand, I was also able to convince the Ford Foundation to take an interest in our station. Learning and working in this new field was interesting, particularly in the context of the energy and optimistic atmosphere that the Kennedy administration brought to Washington and the country.

Kennedy's success seemed to confine Humphrey's future, but it did not restrain his enthusiasm for Kennedy. He became an intimate of that White House and those who worked in it. He developed a close relationship with Larry O'Brien and Ken O'Donnell, the two young Massachusetts political craftsmen of the presidential campaign who played key roles in the White House and spent a great deal of time with the president. One day, Myer Feldman, a counsel to the president, called me to say that Hubert had just left the White House after talking to Kennedy about a judgeship for a Minnesota attorney. "The president asked me when Hubert will be coming in with your name for a judicial appointment," he said. I was moved by Mike Feldman's thoughtfulness in calling, but both the life of a judge and the nature of the work were, at the time, unappealing, and the timing seemed off.

The horror and anguish of Kennedy's assassination shook all of our lives. The days after Kennedy was shot were a whiplash of emotion. The nation wept, and Washington was in shock as we watched the instant replays of murder. Disbelief and despair were unshakable companions in our thoughts.

For Humphrey, who had developed great affection for Kennedy, the event was devastating, partly, I suppose, because he knew that no one in public life is invulnerable to the same act of insanity. It was a time of mourning for him and not a time to contemplate old dreams resurrected.

Within a day after President Kennedy had been shot in Dallas, I had taken a dozen calls about Hubert seeking the vice presidential nomination on a Johnson ticket in 1964. I had similar thoughts myself and made similar calls. None of us apologized for our calls or thoughts. We were looking to tomorrow and the next year. Mourning diminishes rapidly when the republic must be run. It virtually disappears when elections are not far off, choices must be made, and plans cannot wait. Neither does ambition wait. The grieving comes and goes in almost schizoid episodes, replaced with a political plethora of plans that contain old dreams not easily buried or hidden. Resurrection is a handmaiden of political life.

The night of the Kennedy funeral, Humphrey asked Maggie and me to join him and Muriel for dinner at their home. When we arrived, we found that Adlai Stevenson, who was then ambassador to the United Nations, had also been invited.* The Humphreys still lived in the house they had moved into when they arrived in Washington—a modest colonial in a postwar development of similar houses, on a suburban corner just off a busy street, next door to George McGovern and up the block from Russell Long.

We sat in a tidy living room like so many others in America, a small

---

* When Kennedy was considering appointments to his cabinet, Humphrey urged him to appoint Stevenson as secretary of State, a position Stevenson wanted and others advocated as well. Kennedy would not hear of it at all. It was then that Humphrey persuaded him to appoint Stevenson to the United Nations and provide him with the added rank of cabinet status. Hubert later told me, "It wasn't easy."

rectangular room where the Humphrey children had crawled and learned to walk, had listened to their music and entertained friends. The TV played in the background and impelled us to its side regularly.

Much of the evening was spent discussing what Kennedy had accomplished, what might have been had he lived, how the country and the world might react, and then in expressing our cautious hopes about what would happen under Lyndon Johnson. Hubert had spent part of the afternoon with Johnson.

At one point I joined Humphrey in the kitchen as he washed the dishes. He quietly told me that Lyndon Johnson wanted me to join the White House staff as counsel to the president. He either did not speak as softly as he might have, or Maggie sensed something was up. In any case, she joined us and expressed her dismay at the idea, saying, as I recall, "Hubert, you can't do that to Max!"

Stevenson left. Humphrey moved from the kitchen chores to vacuuming the rugs, and we talked over the noise about why it was a bad idea for me to join the Johnson staff. Johnson and I had a good relationship. Indeed, when I left Humphrey's office for private life in September 1955, the *Washington Post* ran a story by its political and legislative reporter, Robert Albright, commenting that I had "played an important role" in bridging the gap between right and left and asking what would happen to the Johnson-Humphrey alliance in the Senate now that I was leaving. Yet I certainly could not serve Johnson and still be an advocate for Hubert as the vice presidential nominee and do what had to be done to make that possible. Furthermore, although I had independent evidence of Johnson's respect and even affection for me, I knew that he had a well-earned reputation for eating up his staff, which is what worried Maggie, and I did not want that.

The Humphrey campaign for the vice presidential nomination was under way shortly after John Kennedy was laid to rest. Hesitation would have been unwise. Political people like to be asked early to be part of a campaign. On the one hand, there is a sense of being in the innermost circle, and that is important. On the other hand, when people are not asked, they believe they are being left out while others are being included. Political paranoia sets in. It is almost better to ask and be turned down then not to ask at all.

Unlike 1956, there were things we knew should be done. We understood that, and with only passing deference to the idea that one shouldn't, in good taste, run for the vice presidency, we were off.

Humphrey's immediate efforts were not dictated by politics, but by friendship for Lyndon and the need to heal the country's pain. His first desire was to serve Johnson, the new president, and he was there reaching out to liberals who remained suspicious of Johnson or just didn't like him. Beginning on Saturday, less than twenty-four hours after the assassination, still drained by the emotion of the event, he had begun to do what he could to help. He called Reuther, I. W. Abel of the Steelworkers, and other labor friends to solicit their advice and to urge them to express their confidence in Johnson. He counseled Johnson, and before Johnson delivered his first speech to Congress as president of the United States, Humphrey suggested the theme, "Let us continue."

Continuity was what Johnson sought. For Humphrey, now Senate whip—a formal leadership role—that meant carrying the Kennedy program forward, picking up the social legislation that Johnson himself liked, creating and pushing the War on Poverty, moving on education, and defining and leading the civil rights battle.

While Humphrey did that, the rest of us, and others, began our political work one-on-one with labor leaders, Democratic party officials, state officeholders, and the press, including not only reporters and columnists, but publishers when we could reach them.

Bill Connell, a highly capable communication expert and former speechwriter from Minnesota, was now Humphrey's administrative assistant, and we began to meet regularly, at least weekly at times, with Jim Rowe; Gus Tyler, an intellectual labor leader who worked in New York as a leader of the ILGWU; Dick Maguire,* a Kennedy "pol" who had served at the Democratic National Committee; and Al Barkan, an old Textile Workers organizer and now head of the AFL-CIO Committee on Political Education (COPE), as the regular participants. Others joined us sporadically, including Joe Rauh, who energetically helped with the ADA wing of the party.

Although each of us had some political base to work, Barkan was particularly valuable. COPE was the political arm of the unions, spread across the country into every state, and therefore immensely powerful in the Democratic delegate selection process.

Our job, we quickly agreed, was to box in Johnson so that Humphrey's selection was inevitable. Humphrey did not need to spend much time thinking about the vice presidency, even if it was never far from his mind. Others did it for him. And that is typical of Washington,

---

* Dick was part of the John Kennedy "Irish Mafia" as they were called, but did not like Robert Kennedy. He became a stalwart Humphrey supporter and a bridge to other Kennedy people like Ken O'Donnell who had grown to like Humphrey and respect him for his contributions to the Kennedy administration.

too. The spear carriers are advancing even as their leader rests or is otherwise occupied.

Our goal was not so much to win a competition with other people, but to elevate Humphrey beyond competition. Our purpose was not to make him first among equals, but without an equal, and thus the only possible choice for Johnson. We began with a helpful advantage.

Humphrey and Johnson were quite different kinds of men but shared so much in goals, commitments, and mutual respect that differences seemed irrelevant. For more than a decade, they had depended on each other for support in times of legislative need. They did not often socialize together outside the Senate, but that didn't make much difference, since both of them spent most of their lives in the Senate or its political environs. There was a bond that would not easily be unraveled, though the capricious part of Johnson's nature made it impossible for Humphrey ever to relax about the relationship.

Ultimately, the decision had to be made by one man, Lyndon Johnson, and not by political forces in the abstract. He had to be the focus of our attention, and Jim Rowe was closer to Johnson than almost anyone, certainly more than any of the rest of us in the Humphrey camp. He talked to the president often and brought back to us valuable knowledge of Johnson's thoughts. He was like a magnifying glass on Johnson's mind. It was more than instinct and understanding that made Jim valuable. Johnson fed Rowe information, intending that it would get back to Hubert. Once Rowe reported to Humphrey in a memo that Clare Booth Luce had met with Johnson and "told him he should take Hubert Humphrey as Vice President and that a Catholic was not necessary." Jim was probably the source of a story that in December 1963, at a lunch with Dwight Eisenhower, Richard Nixon said that Johnson should select Humphrey as his vice presidential candidate because Humphrey was the most qualified. Why that pleased us so much I do not recall, but if Johnson thought it worth repeating, that was certainly enough for us.

In the meantime, Humphrey was busy reaching for his legislative epiphany—the passage of the Civil Rights Act of 1964.

America was ready. A powerful consensus was created and grew in strength. Traditional advocates of civil rights—blacks, unions, Jewish leaders, liberal politicians—were joined by the white establishment churches, college students, housewives, businessmen, and unlikely politicians. Even in the South, where bigotry and hatred remained deep-rooted and relatively widespread, there were enough heroic souls to make a difference. For the most part, there was a joyous uprising of brotherhood. What Humphrey had worked for as mayor, spoken for in 1948 at the Democratic convention, and pursued as a party position in 1952, was finally more than an elusive dream, but a real possibility.*

His heart and mind were there as a matter of principle and long-time commitment, and would have been there no matter what Johnson wanted. Fortunately, Johnson desperately wanted the bill passed, and when it did pass with wide bipartisan support in spite of a Southern filibuster and other delaying tactics, Humphrey had succeeded in doing what was right for the country and its moral center. It also proved quite essential for his own reputation and his claim on Johnson's allegiance.

While that was going on, our political strategy seemed to be working. As we approached convention time, the choice, we thought, had to be Humphrey, even though Gene McCarthy's name was occasionally mentioned as the "other" candidate. He was Catholic, he was not Bobby Kennedy, and Johnson liked him. I did not take McCarthy seriously as a candidate, although Lady Bird Johnson and Walter Jenkins, probably Johnson's most influential aide, seemed to be for him. Johnson also toyed with other potential candidates, perhaps seeking to maintain drama and doubt.

At the very last minute, in a bewildering episode, Johnson had both Senator Tom Dodd of Connecticut and Humphrey come to Washington from the Atlantic City convention on a small chartered plane. When the call had come from the White House directing Humphrey to the Atlantic City airport for a flight to Washington, we were exuberant. We were certain then that our efforts had, indeed, paid off. I did not take the Dodd gambit seriously because I knew Johnson was aware the convention would have exploded into a political revolution if Humphrey had been unceremoniously rejected. Furthermore, I was convinced the president had quietly helped arrange the inevitability of the choice. That had been confirmed to my satisfaction when Jim Rowe, the previous evening, had called and asked to have dinner with Hubert, Muriel, and me. He came with a message. We could relax. The nomination was Humphrey's. We all understood, however, that a typ-

---

* Humphrey's chief legislative aide then was a young political scientist, John Stewart, who had been an American Political Science Association fellow on the Hill and later directed the fellowship program for the APSA. John was crucial in the long battle for the bill, drafting language, orchestrating compromise, constantly informing Humphrey and following his direction. Watching John made me yearn, if only for a moment, to be on the Hill once again for that historic effort. It was the only time I had ever felt that way since I left, and I satisfied myself with frequent counseling with John and others, including Humphrey.

ical Johnson idiosyncrasy could lead to difficulty should the fact of the dinner conversation leak to anyone outside the room.

The talk of the presidency, which had begun for me in Herb McCloskey's apartment at least sixteen years earlier, and probably among others before that, came one step closer with a thunderous convention ovation: Humphrey was going to be vice president of the United States.

The election itself was anticlimactic. Once the nomination was behind us, we could only look ahead with optimism. Soon Hubert Humphrey was vice president, heir apparent, and a spokesman for the Johnson program, including Vietnam.

The night of the election, Johnson invited Humphrey to visit his Texas ranch the next day. I went along. They spent most of the day together in private conversation, but the president did find the occasion to pull me aside. Would I join Hubert's staff? I said I would not, but could help. He spoke to me about finding an official residence for the vice president and asked me to investigate the possibilities for such a home. Finally, he asked me to help Hubert organize his office.

On the flight back from Texas to Washington late that evening, Humphrey asked me to sit next to him. He quietly confided to me that Johnson had told him he would not run for reelection in 1968, and he wanted Humphrey to prepare himself to move into the presidency. He asked what I thought of this development. My response was that the president was serious, that we should take his statement seriously, never whisper a word of it to anybody, but understand that presidents can change their minds.

I studied the available houses for a vice presidential residence and finally recommended Tregaron, the old estate of Joseph Davies, a former U.S. ambassador to the Soviet Union and a wealthy political contributor. Johnson rejected that advice and selected the house of the chief of naval operations on the Naval Observatory grounds. Ultimately, Johnson postponed his decision about providing any residence, fearful that it would look extravagant to renovate the CNO's house when the war in Vietnam was going on.

It was a delicate balancing act to organize and strengthen the vice presidential staff on one hand, but not do it so well or so openly that it fed Johnson's political paranoia about a government-in-waiting being assembled. I liked and respected Bill Connell, who had energy, ability, and good judgment. I concluded it was his task to find the balance. I could not do it from the outside and did not want to be on the inside.

The vice presidency was a mixed blessing in some people's eyes, but not in mine. Historically, the vice presidency has for some time been treated as an object of humor, if not derision. The legendary Mr. Dooley, for example, described it as "not a crime exactly . . . but it is kind iv a disgrace." That has changed with the knowledge that nine vice presidents, more than one-fifth of those who have held the office, have succeeded to the presidency upon the death or resignation of the president. Four others have gone on to become elected presidents. A vice president who chooses to run for president today has a presumptive claim to the party nomination; and six of the eight most recent vice presidents received that nomination.

It has not been easy for most vice presidents to find their niche. When, in 1967, the Twenty-fifth Amendment to the Constitution was adopted, the vice president was assigned new roles in cases of presidential disability, and a mechanism was established to provide that the office would never remain vacant for long. The vice president has a specific legislative responsibility under the Constitution to preside over the Senate, but no specific executive responsibilities are assigned. Presidents now habitually assign special tasks to their vice presidents, usually as diplomatic and political representatives. Whether a vice president becomes a senior confidential adviser to the president, however, is frequently a matter of the chemistry between the two individuals. Insecure White House staff sometimes feel threatened by the vice president's intrusion into their daily business lives, which can potentially undermine the relationship.

The problem of how the vice president should be selected remains a matter of concern to students of our government. Indeed, I am a member of a task force commissioned by the University of Virginia to study and recommend how best to select the vice presidential candidate. At the beginning, the Electoral College chose the runner-up in the presidential election to serve as vice president. Today, the national party convention selects the presidential and vice presidential candidates, and they run as a team. When the convention rules required a two-thirds majority vote for a presidential candidate to be selected, the vice presidential nomination frequently was a pawn used to gather that extraordinary majority. With the presidential nomination being determined by a majority vote at the convention, as it is today, there has been a growing tendency to select a candidate who will help heal the wounds of the party following a bruising contest. In any event, the presidential candidate designates a running mate for convention approval.

Clearly, the national interest requires the selection of a vice president who is a capable political leader, qualified to govern, and able to grow in office while fulfilling specific assigned responsibilities and witnessing the complexity of presidential duties and responsibilities. Obviously, the vice president must be compatible with the president and must appreciate that there is only one president who serves the country at any one time. Political reality also requires that the selection of a vice presidential candidate and performance in office inure to the political advantage of the president.

Our present system, under which the president announces a preference and the convention automatically reaffirms its support by accepting that preference, seems to work fairly well. Our vice presidents have, in the main, been people of stature, who have met the expectations of the American people. Spiro Agnew was certainly an exception, and his selection proved embarrassing and a discredit to Richard Nixon. The selection of Dan Quayle by George Bush did not, I believe, meet the prevailing standards essential for the system to function properly. I met Dan Quayle in connection with my Geneva responsibilities, and my experience with him has led me to have a much higher regard and respect for him than one would expect from the intense criticism that his selection met in the press and the political community. He is intelligent, a quick study, a serious public servant, and a man who has grown during his period of service as a senator. He has, however, shown no sign of being presidential in any reasonable sense of the word, an inadequacy unfortunately and inexplicably exacerbated by his occasional inarticulateness. There is an understandable unease on the part of large numbers of Americans about the prospects of his assuming the presidency in the event of an emergency. A result of the poor response to his selection has been a renewed focus on how best to select vice presidents.

Perhaps the present method is the best and should not be changed. I frequently tend to that view. A recent Twentieth Century Fund study concludes that the vice presidency, on balance, is a healthy institution. But does a person running for president have enough time and opportunity conscientiously to consider a vice presidential choice in the midst of a campaign for the nomination or the hurly-burly of an active political convention? Since public opinion surveys tell us that, with rare exceptions, the vice presidential candidate does not affect voter choice in a presidential election, the question can logically be raised whether it is necessary to make the vice presidential selection at the time of the convention. Why not wait until after the election and build on the Twenty-fifth Amendment to our Constitution, which states that in the event of a vacancy in the office, the president will send up a name to the Congress for approval? Why not provide that the president, prior to inauguration but after election, designate a vice president and send that individual's name to the Congress for speedy approval by both houses? This approach has been suggested by some scholars and journalists and is worth serious consideration.

Humphrey grew as vice president in every dimension of his public character, establishing himself even more as a national presence, gaining an inestimable amount of knowledge and experience in meeting foreign leaders, probing more deeply into economic and other policy matters, and developing political contacts and support more widely than ever before. Humphrey used to say that five minutes inside the White House was more valuable than five weeks outside picketing it. I never doubted that he also believed it was more valuable than five days on the Hill.

Then, one day in 1965, President Johnson's secretary called, asking me to come over immediately because the president wanted to see me. I couldn't imagine why, and no hint was given, but a request from the president, even through an intermediary, was a command to be obeyed.

When I reached the White House, the president greeted me warmly, made passing reference to our good days in the Senate, and then said that he intended in a few minutes to announce my appointment as chairman of the city council of the District of Columbia, with Walter Washington as mayor. There had previously been a three-member board of commissioners appointed to run the District, but as a step toward home rule, the law had been changed to permit a mayor and a city council, although they were still not elected.

I wondered at first whether Humphrey had been somehow involved, but quickly learned that this was entirely Johnson's doing. Humphrey was out of town and only learned of the appointment later that day. My guess is that Johnson had given the job little thought until that day, suddenly thought of me as a lawyer who had been active in the community, and indulged himself in his penchant for surprise. It had happened before. The previous year, Humphrey had called one morning at ten A.M. The president wanted to announce that afternoon my appointment as a judge in the United States Court of Claims. He had plans to appoint me in two years as a judge in the United States Court of Appeals for the District of Columbia to fill a vacancy he knew would open. Hubert added that the next step could well be the United States Supreme Court. But, Hubert said, Johnson needed my decision by two P.M. that day. I phoned Maggie and Arthur Goldberg, both of whom were pleased. But it was up to me. I gave it intense thought and then asked Hubert to report my appreciation to the president, along with a no. The decision was too important to rush, and I had doubts whether I wanted to be a judge and greater doubts about the prospects for the Supreme Court down the line.

The city council chairmanship was another matter. There was some hesitation derived in large part from my conviction that I had a lot of mouths to feed, not just in my own family, but in the law firm. I felt the firm still required my presence. Johnson, anticipating my concern, assured me the job was only a part-time responsibility and, according to the attorney general, would not require my leaving my law firm. I don't remember whether I was ever given the opportunity to agree or decline. Within a half hour of my arrival, my appointment was announced and photographs were taken. I barely had time to call Maggie before she would have heard it from the media.

I returned to my office to a startled but generally pleased group of people. In a power town, a presidential appointment of whatever rank is heady material, and everyone seemed quite excited at the honor. Despite my own excitement, I asked that the law governing my appointment as chairman of the city council be checked immediately. A few days later, my partners Harold Green and Dan Singer told me the law was clear, but clearly not what I had been told. Even though the council chairman had little to do with the work of federal agencies, if I worked at the job for more than 129 days a year and remained a partner in my practice, the law firm could not represent our clients in their dealings with the federal government. That meant, for example, no work on SEC matters, on tax questions, or on antitrust problems. That would have essentially wiped out the firm's existence.

I turned to Senator Alan Bible, who was head of the District Committee and author of the revised statute. He, like Johnson, had been a longtime friend, and when we spoke, he expressed his delight with my appointment. When I explained the problem, he said that had not been the intent of the law and he would quickly move to amend it, exempting the job from the normal conflict of interest restraints, in what he saw as a technical and noncontroversial action. He agreed there was no way to serve responsibly as chairman and work fewer than 129 days.

But controversy was soon available on other grounds. NAPCO, my early client and a continuing one, had arranged in the sixties to sell a Detroit truck factory it owned, the Federal Motor Truck Company. Essentially, the factory consisted of tooling and truck manufacturing equipment. The purchaser was a company formed by NAPCO and its Indian partners in Delhi, India. An Agency for International Development (AID) loan had been secured and, when the papers were ready, I signed the agreement as NAPCO's attorney and a member of its board, since I was in Washington and its officers were not. When the loan was slow in receiving approval, Max Rappaport, NAPCO's president, and a financial contributor, suggested I enlist Humphrey's help in trying to expedite it. I did not want to ask Hubert, and I recommended that Rappaport not involve Humphrey, since it was unnecessary. But when they met one evening in Minneapolis, Rappaport raised the question, and Humphrey in typical fashion responded on his constituent's behalf by sending letters to AID requesting the decision be expedited. His intercession, however routine from his point of view, turned out to be my albatross.

When the equipment arrived in Delhi, NAPCO's Indian partners claimed that the tools were not what they had expected or what had been described for the AID loan. NAPCO claimed the equipment had rusted on the docks because of malfeasance on the Indian partners' part and their inability to get their act together in a timely fashion. Lawsuits followed, and ultimately NAPCO was exonerated of any fraud or misrepresentation, but the case became grist for a journalistic vendetta engineered by *Des Moines Register and Tribune* reporter Clark Mollenhoff. Mollenhoff had previously told colleagues, I was informed, that he was going "to get" Humphrey, and I became the convenient tool.

Mollenhoff used as his mouthpiece Republican Congressman H. R. Gross of Iowa, a self-styled "conscience" of the House who was in fact generally viewed as a reactionary, angry little man with a reputation for wild and irresponsible partisanship. Mollenhoff wrote Gross's statements, a suspect act for a journalist that so offended his colleagues that they told me what he was doing.* With the immunity of the House as his shield, Gross was able to make a stream of accusatory statements, unrestrained by fact or fairness. In his dirty work, he was aided by Senator Carl Curtis of Nebraska and Congressman Burt Talcott of California, Republicans, who tried to portray me as a draft

---

* Mollenhoff won a Pulitzer Prize for his reporting on Jimmy Hoffa and the Teamsters Union, but was held in such low esteem by many of his colleagues that they opposed his membership in the Cosmos Club, a prestigious club of accomplished academics and authors. I had not known of Mollenhoff's application for membership until another journalist telephoned me to say he and others had vetoed the proposal. I later also learned that when Mollenhoff was in line to become president of the National Press Club after rising up the ladder to first vice president, his colleagues, for the first time in their history, broke precedent and elected someone else as president.

dodger and criminal. The depths of their partisan poison and depravity were astounding.

Mollenhoff would then call my office and Humphrey's for response to the Gross statements and other congressional statements, write a story for the next morning's paper reporting on what the congressmen, under congressional immunity from libel action, had said, and then have Gross introduce the articles into the *Congressional Record* with further accusations. Gross's position was simple: the commitments made by NAPCO were never intended to be met by them; I, as signatory to the agreement with AID, was guilty of fraud against the United States government; and therefore I was not fit for presidential appointment.

It was an embarrassing and distressing time. Other journalists and papers, particularly the *Washington Post,** picked up the story. I felt wounded and demeaned. As angry and depressed as I was by it all, Maggie suffered even more, sensing coolness and suspicion from "friends," and curiosity in stores from clerks who recognized her name. She was concerned about what our children were hearing. We became overnight pariahs.

I went back to see Alan Bible to discuss the situation. He said, "Look, Max, everybody knows H. R. Gross for what he is. Sure, the press is awful, but we have the votes to amend the law and see you in the job." That was enough for me, but not for Lyndon Johnson. His feet grew cold, his resolve weak. I did not hear from him directly, but Joe Califano, who worked for him in the White House, and Ramsey Clark, his attorney general, both wondered aloud to me if it was worth the bother to change the law so that I could take a part-time job. I learned later that Califano, who had always seemed cold toward me, had contributed to Johnson's wariness. No one directly asked me to withdraw, but the message was clear. The damage to my reputation lingered, with people willing, I found, to believe the worst of you and repeat what they remember, like a child's game of "telephone" extended over years. Alan Bible, may God bless his soul, would not let the matter rest with my withdrawal and placed in the *Congressional Record* what he considered a full and detailed exoneration. There will

* Newspapers often invite people in the news to meet with their editorial and news staffs. This time I asked to meet with *Washington Post* executives, including Katharine Graham, publisher; Ben Bradlee, the executive editor; and Walter Pincus, a reporter who, along with Richard Harwood, reported extensively on Gross's accusations. The NAPCO flap inevitably came up. Years later, Walter told me that he had been excluded from similar meetings for a time because his aggressive behavior toward me apparently offended Graham and Bradlee as much as it did me.

always be a warm spot in my heart for my old friend George McGovern, Congressman Sid Yates of Illinois, and Senators Charles Mathias of Maryland and Wayne Morse of Oregon, all of whom attacked my attackers and spoke in my behalf without my having asked them. Maggie and I will also always remember and appreciate a strong unsolicited letter of support written by our friend, Hyman Bookbinder, and published in the *Washington Post*.

I ended up bitter about Mollenhoff, the power of the press, and the lack of their accountability. The job meant relatively nothing, my reputation everything. To lose the job was of no consequence, but to have my reputation damaged by a highly praised, prizewinning, but irresponsible reporter and by ventriloquist's congressmen was considerably more than I felt I deserved.*

I have remained sensitive to the plight of people who are paraded across the pages of newspapers for all sorts of reasons, who are demeaned by the press. I tend to give the victims of journalistic self-righteousness and wrath the benefit of the doubt, unless and until I see very hard, incontrovertible evidence of their guilt.

That view was confirmed by my own experience, but as early as my teaching days at Minnesota, I had lectured in my Problems of Democracy classes about the need in a democracy not only for a free press but for a responsible one. I pointed out that there are restraints on power in the United States, restraints on the president and the executive branch, on the Congress, the Supreme Court, on corporations and labor unions, on state and local governments, but really none on the press.

Certainly the First Amendment is sacrosanct, but other democracies take a much more restricted view of what is permissible, and I sympathize with those, like me in the NAPCO instance, who became sitting ducks in the public shooting gallery. Journalists are not professionals in the same sense that doctors, dentists, lawyers, and accountants are. There are no credentials to be given, no statistics to be measured by, no agreed-upon enforceable code of ethics, no withdrawal of approval by peers that means professional exile. They are self-appointed, self-governed, self-sanctioned.

* I decided to write about my experience and what I considered press irresponsibility in an article in the prestigious *Columbia Journalism Review*, called "When Press Bites Man" (*Columbia Journalism Review* 7:1 [Spring 1968], pp. 43–46). Later, I wrote a long article on the power of the press in our society that was widely circulated and used in some college classrooms. Two people who bought bulk quantities of the article were Frank Sinatra and Howard Cosell. See "The Power of the Press: A Problem of Democracy," in *Policy Review* 6 (Fall 1978), pp. 7–39.

It has been said that reporters are like birds on a wire. When one flies, they all fly. To change the metaphor, there is a feeding frenzy that takes place when blood appears in the public waters. I don't think reporters write to sell newspapers, although some editors and publishers may encourage them to do so. Something deeper is involved. Bullies know that their victims cannot fight back, and there is some of that at work with investigative reporting. Having bylines and getting your words in print are ego inflating, and that surely is important. The awards that journalists bestow on one another are generally related to investigations. Prizes and notoriety are exciting and satisfying, too. I don't know even now what precisely is the ultimate motivation, but I've seen the process at work over and over again, and I must admit I don't like it any better when I am not the target than I did when I was.*

Saying my piece in the *Columbia Journalism Review* provided me a catharsis, and I then turned my attention again to Hubert Humphrey. We talked often about things that troubled him. Vietnam, of course, was one of them. My advice was to support the president. I hardly needed to recommend that. It was his inclination because of the office he held and because of the war itself. We did not view the conflict in Vietnam simply as a civil war, but as a further intrusion of the Communist world on others. Both of us saw our reaction as consistent with the Roosevelt-Truman tradition, as a logical extension of our anti-Communist commitment and well within the post–World War II position of standing up to the Communists around the world.

Many Americans, in growing numbers, did not agree with that

---

* In searching for background material for this chapter, I came across a memorandum I had prepared for the board of trustees of channel 26 in Washington on December 8, 1970. As chairman of the station, I now had an opportunity to have some influence on its sense of responsibility in covering public affairs. I urged a "clear distinction . . . between those presentations on the air which are strictly 'news' and those which are an analysis of the news." The personal opinion of the broadcaster, I urged, should not show, either by word, reflections, or facial expression, in the presentation of straight news. I expected that our employees would be intelligent and sensitive, which meant that they had views. It was essential, however, that they not permit those views to be injected into the news process, and one way to refine that sensitivity was to be aware of one's bias. I pointed out that "since air time belongs to the public and is scarce, there is no justification for using public broadcasting to disseminate the personal views of a broadcaster unless the individual is particularly qualified and well informed or unless we have reason to believe that he has a viewpoint that the public is interested in learning about." I recognized that there are only two ways to be quite unprejudiced and impartial—one is to be completely ignorant and the other is to be completely indifferent. I did not feel that our reporters and commentators should be either. They should be aware of their views as they try to present matters objectively and impartially.

view, and Humphrey increasingly became the man out front for Johnson's policies and thus the target of hate and anger and protest. My sadness at the treatment he got grew as it included more and more academics and students, more and more of our liberal allies.

Yet the only path, it seemed to me, was to stick it out, and simultaneously to explore every opportunity for a constructive peace. In terms of his political career, I was convinced Johnson would, in spite of his early feelings to the contrary, now run again with Humphrey on the ticket, and that the Democrats would win.

The deep emotions and intense division that characterized the Vietnam debate also touched me. Many liberals remembered my identification with the 1954 Communist Control Act and were prepared to believe the worst whenever new rumors or reports emerged. One such problem developed in the 1966–68 period and related to the CIA. My old professor Evron Kirkpatrick and I worked together in the American Political Science Association (APSA), where he served as executive director, and I was the attorney and treasurer for many years. Kirk asked me at one time to set up a nonprofit foundation, Operations and Policy Research (OPR), that would assist the United States Information Agency (USIA) by enlisting social science professors to review books, thereby providing the agency with guidance as to which books it should purchase and distribute to libraries around the world. It was important that the process be professional and free from partisan politics. This was a public service, and Kirk received no income from it.

Kirk then helped develop a program to foster free elections in Latin America. This was somehow tied in with public opinion polling. Shortly thereafter, the CIA found itself under attack from liberals in the Congress. Among the materials that emerged was information that two of the foundations supporting OPR were, in turn, receiving CIA funds. Robert G. Sherrill, who had written a critical biography of Humphrey, editorialized on the subject in the *Nation*. The left in the APSA began to attack Kirk and me for being officers of OPR. I decided to issue a statement that I distributed widely, expressing my pride in being associated with the good work of OPR and APSA. "To the extent that they or I cooperate or are associated with any agency of the United States in carrying out our bona fide purposes, I am proud of that association," I said. "Ours is a free and democratic government and people who have an opportunity to serve it are indeed privileged," I concluded. To a reporter's question as to whether that included the CIA, I said: "It certainly does." I still feel that way.

Kirk and I weathered the storm as our friends mobilized majority support in the association. I then decided that twelve years as an APSA officer without compensation was enough. The APSA was in excellent financial condition. I did not run for reelection in 1968.

While all of that went on, in 1967 I had found a new "career" in television. My role at WETA had been primarily organizational, financial, and advisory, but I soon began to appear on camera as well. I was being pressed by Hartford Gunn of Boston's WGBH, the best and richest educational television station in the country, to provide a good Washington news analysis show. Gunn indicated that WGBH would go its own way in producing one if we didn't.

We had enough problems without facing competition in Washington from our own family of stations, so I began to think seriously about such a program. I knew that television covered the Congress inadequately, and turned to an expert on the institution. As a teacher, I had used a book on the Congress by Neil McNeil, a *Time* correspondent. We had met when I first came to the Senate, and he was as good in person as his book suggested he might be. I asked him to develop a fifteen-minute weekly report on the Congress.

I then decided to expand on Neil's program by analyzing those events of the week that historians would consider significant when they looked at our times five years or more down the line. We turned to a format of three or four exceptional journalists and a moderator talking about the events of the week during a half-hour program. The idea, expertly refined by Bill McCarter, evolved into "Washington Week in Review." The station found a moderator, and the program went on the air. Almost immediately, McCarter and other station personnel decided the moderator was not right and the program seemed too much like commercial television. In desperation, I have always thought, they turned to me, believing that I could not possibly be confused with a commercial television talent.

Neil McNeil remained a centerpiece of the program, talking about the Congress. Dick Frykland of the *Washington Star*, my former student at Minnesota who had become a recognized expert, became our military affairs analyst, until he was attracted to work at the Pentagon. He was succeeded by the serious, studious, and urbane Charles Corddry of the *Baltimore Sun*, who is still on the program. Peter Lisagor of the *Chicago Daily News* joined us shortly thereafter and became the real star of the show. Bright, entertaining, insightful, forthright, and charming, he may well have been the best journalist of his time in Washington. I served as moderator for nearly four years, enjoying the challenge and the chemistry with the journalists. The Emmy certificate we earned for our accomplishments is still in my office.

While I was occupied with my old law practice and my new television work, Lyndon Johnson once again disrupted my life. On the March night that Lyndon Johnson withdrew from the 1968 presidential race, Maggie and I were returning home from an early evening out. Driving slowly, we listened to his speech carefully on the car radio, hardly passing a word between us, until he came to the end and suddenly announced that he would not run again. The recurring Humphrey dream that had disappeared from time to time had come back with startling quickness.

I drove home much more quickly and ran up the walk to our front door and to the telephone. Humphrey was in Mexico, and I did not try to reach him, but Bill Connell had already done so. Bill and I talked at length about what must be done immediately to secure the presidential nomination for Humphrey. We divided up the political players and began to call them.

Humphrey arrived home two nights later to a cheering crowd at the airport, including cabinet members Orville Freeman, Willard Wirtz, and Dean Rusk. A few of us gathered at his home to discuss what we had learned during the two days that he had been gone, where his support was, where his problems might lie, and how we would proceed. Humphrey was tired from the flight, emotionally drained, and strangely, most of the exuberance for the presidential race came from us, not from him.

We were already on the presidential road again, but he put up an unexpected "do not enter" sign. We had a reluctant candidate, who, recalling Wisconsin and West Virginia, did not want the public humiliation of another loss to a Kennedy, and Robert was running. His affection for John did not at that point extend to Robert Kennedy, and Humphrey assumed that Bobby could not be stopped. He simply didn't have the heart to try. We said, "Go fast." He said, "Go slow."

This was an uncharacteristically cautious Humphrey, and his hesitation seemed only a way station on the road to a bad final decision not to run. The evening ended ambiguously. I left wondering if, ironically, his dream was to be denied when it was finally within his grasp, and denied by no one other than Humphrey himself. I could only think, "The brass ring is coming around, and Hubert may not even reach for it." I suspected we could find the reason in how deeply the 1960 primaries had hurt him, and how silently he had suffered his humiliation, letting loyalty to the president become a superficial balm for his injury.

If it had not been for George Meany, the burly, principled, veteran AFL-CIO labor leader, the wavering might have continued until it was too late. Al Barkan arranged for Meany to visit privately with Humphrey. Meany turned him around: he pledged labor support, and he told Humphrey that he owed it to the party and liberal forces in America, that he couldn't at that point in his career back away from the challenge. He could not, said Meany, abdicate to Bobby Kennedy.

Meany was a gruff old plumber, but, in that meeting, he was also an eloquent labor statesman. Humphrey came out of the meeting convinced that with solid labor support he had a good shot, and he would take it. He gave us free rein to raise money, organize a staff, and begin the campaign.

We began the rollercoaster ride of a tumultuous year. The assassinations of Bobby Kennedy and Martin Luther King, Jr., the racial uproar, the continuing protests on Vietnam have been chronicled in detail elsewhere, and were a devastating time for our country. The violence took the good flavor out of the democratic process and left Humphrey dispirited. Humphrey announced for the presidency in April and had sewed up the necessary votes for nomination well before the convention. One of the continuing fictions of that year and since was that Bobby Kennedy would have received the nomination if he had lived, and that Humphrey was, therefore, the usurper of a tarnished prize. That was nonsense presented by instant revisionists, including some very bright writers like Theodore White. Before Bobby's death, Larry O'Brien and Kenny O'Donnell, who were excellent vote counters, told Humphrey he would win and that they could not. At a breakfast with Humphrey, Kenny said that Bobby would withdraw after the California primary if he lost either Oregon or California. Bobby himself had indicated to Humphrey that he would support Humphrey after the convention.

Humphrey decided early that the campaign needed a young face, or as it turned out, two young faces. He had asked Senator Fred Harris of Oklahoma, a Kennedy family friend and an outspoken liberal, and Walter "Fritz" Mondale, his own replacement in the Senate, to become co-chairmen of the Humphrey effort when he announced he would run. En route to a short Easter holiday in the Virgin Islands with Maggie and our children, I had stopped in Miami to see Humphrey and his friend and financial supporter Dwayne Andreas when Humphrey made the decision final, and no one I knew had any objection; indeed, we thought it was a good idea. I looked forward to working with them. That proved harder to do than I expected.

It became clear to those of us who had carried the campaign to this point that Mondale and Harris preferred to talk over the campaign with their own people, doing it their own way. They did not seem interested in what Bill Connell, Dick Maguire, Al Barkan, and I, along with many others, had built. This was a mistake, but I felt it was theirs to make.

One day soon after I returned from the Caribbean, I walked into the campaign headquarters and was told, much to my surprise, that there was a campaign meeting going on. As I approached the door of the room where the meeting was in progress, I heard Fritz Mondale announce that he did not want anyone to look to me or Bill Connell for direction, that he and Fred were running the campaign, and that their authority would not be shared with me or Bill. I did not expect to share in their authority, but the personal attack infuriated me. I was hurt and more than a little surprised at what I considered an act of personal disloyalty by Fritz. It was the NAPCO case again. Since Max Rappaport had been a major contributor of Fritz's and since Fritz had frequently thanked me for supporting his appointment to the Senate, I thought it particularly unfair for him to believe the worst about me and to speak about me as he did.

I subsequently told Humphrey what had transpired and that I would not force my presence on the campaign managers. I was simply too proud to indulge in turf battles, and I had never expected or wanted to run the campaign before or after Mondale.

I did not ask for Humphrey's intervention in changing their minds or in finding me a more visible position.

Humphrey and I agreed that we would continue to talk often as we long had, that my most important role was to be there when he needed me and to react honestly to whatever he shared with me. There were things on his mind that were important to him and that he entrusted to me. Later, after the convention and when the campaign began to look better, he had me develop a potential cabinet and top official list, knowing that after the year of discontent that was 1968 he would need to start fast and strong if he became president. It was both encouraging and relaxing for him to play the cabinet game when we spoke. He would send me memos about people who impressed him when he traveled around the country. Interestingly enough, I became convinced from our talks that Humphrey had two and only two candidates in mind for his national security adviser: Henry Kissinger and Zbigniew Brzezinski, both of whom came to assume that role without his help.

One of my first tasks before the convention was to evaluate and check out the potential vice presidential candidates—Senator Ed

Muskie of Maine, whom he favored from early on, Mayor Joseph Alioto of San Francisco, Governors Richard Hughes of New Jersey and Terry Sanford of North Carolina, Senators John Pastore of Rhode Island and Fred Harris of Oklahoma. I first learned of Humphrey's strong preference for Muskie on the night of Martin Luther King, Jr.'s assassination. I was broadcasting my "Washington Week in Review" show when the news of the death came over the wires. A large Democratic National Committee fund-raising event was being held that night at the Washington Hilton Hotel. At the conclusion of my broadcast, I rushed there to talk to Humphrey, who was to be the leading speaker that evening. When I got there, I found the dinner proceeding as if nothing had happened. I went to the dais and told Humphrey that he must end the meeting immediately. He stepped up to the podium and did so. As he was suggesting that I join him and Muriel at their apartment, Ed and Jane Muskie walked by. Humphrey said, "There's my vice presidential candidate." I responded: "Then why do you want to spend the evening with me? I think you should spend the evening with Ed and Jane." He took my advice.

Humphrey wanted to feel certain that whomever he chose would have no embarassing skeletons popping out of closets. He remembered the stiff questioning he had received from Jim Rowe at Johnson's request before the 1964 convention. Humphrey asked me to talk to most of the potential candidates, and I studied them intensely. I particularly looked at Joe Alioto and John Pastore, since Richard Scammon, the noted election analyst and former director of the Census Bureau, had told Humphrey that the Italians were a voting bloc of immense importance in California and northern industrial states and could mean substantial, and crucial electoral votes. Many Italians had drifted away from their fathers' allegiance to the Democratic party and now as suburban men and women of a new generation found respectability with the Republican party.

I liked Alioto as Humphrey did, but Alioto said he thought his earlier client list would open him up to questions that might handicap the ticket. He suggested, however, that keeping his name alive would be politically useful to him as well as to Humphrey. We did that. Pastore, an extremely capable and efficient legislator, whom Hubert liked very much, wouldn't consider it at all.

I had another candidate. Muskie was clearly the choice, but we did not know what might come up, and we needed to explore. I felt we needed to do something to heal the social wounds and national divisiveness. I knew that Humphrey got along reasonably well with Nelson

Rockefeller, that Rockefeller would be bitter if Nixon received the Republican nomination, and that some dramatic gesture was necessary to salvage hope for the American people out of the turbulent political scene.

I urged Humphrey to break new ground and dramatically announce at the convention that Nelson Rockefeller was his choice for vice president. I thought that would create chaos in the Republican party and help us. I also thought that, with some last-minute artful efforts, it could be sold to our own convention and that the bipartisanship would be appealing to the country.

Humphrey was skeptical that it would work, but he was intrigued by the idea of making a healing gesture to the nation. He talked to Dwayne Andreas, a close friend of Nelson's as he was of Hubert's, about the idea, hoping, I think, that Dwayne might discover whether Rockefeller found the possibility attractive.

Humphrey told me to talk to Endicott "Chub" Peabody, the former governor of Massachusetts and a friend of the Rockefellers, who had made the same suggestion and had, Humphrey thought, pursued some discussions with the Rockefeller family.

Chub and I agreed that he would talk to David Rockefeller. When no immediate rejection was forthcoming, I became hopeful that it might work out. Hubert simply said, "Let's not close the door. Let's just see." As no word came, we put the possibility aside until the convention was about to begin.

Just before the convention, Chub came back, saying the Rockefellers "wanted to know whether Hubert is serious." Humphrey was serious, but ultimately neither Humphrey nor Rockefeller was willing to take the chance. Rockefeller finally said no, and Humphrey never had to make the decision. After the election, Nelson's wife, Happy Rockefeller, at a small Rockefeller family dinner I attended at Pocantico, indicated that she had voted for Humphrey. Nelson smiled, but gave no indication how he had voted, although he told me quietly how much he appreciated my confidence in him in the period before the convention. Indeed, he then invited me to work with him on his Commission on the Critical Choices Facing America.

Kenneth O'Donnell also passed word along to Humphrey, as the convention was beginning, that Ted Kennedy was not available for the vice presidency and that the family would consider it an unfriendly act were Humphrey to select Sargent Shriver as his vice presidential running mate. So much for the suggestion that the Humphrey ticket include a Kennedy. There had been many rumors about the family strain between Shriver, who had married Ted Kennedy's sister, Eunice, and other members of the family. This may have had to do with Shriver's friendship with Lyndon Johnson. Hubert was very fond of Sarge, whose genial and charming exterior hid a strong sense of principle, personal integrity, and stubborn independence. I learned a great deal about those strong assets a few years later when Sarge and I became law partners.

The convention itself, which had been scheduled to open in late August to coincide with President Johnson's birthday, was an exercise in ugliness, hate, and anger, in violence and events out of control. I spent some time mingling with the young and not-so-young people called "liberals" by the press, who assembled on the Chicago streets in front of the hotels, attracting national television attention with their "Dump the Hump" placards and vitriolic shouting. We would see them during the campaign as well. To me, they seemed to be more fascist than liberal in their style and behavior. The Secret Service brought us solid reports from their undercover informants of discussions of assassination plans, with Mrs. Humphrey as the target. There were other scenarios of lesser disruptions that put us all on edge. In that year, no one was able to reject any of that information as impossible, since there were indigenous terrorists afield, and not just decent people searching for peace.

A serious effort was made before the opening of the convention to defuse the Vietnam issue by finding language that supported the Kennedy-Johnson program of the past, but in looking ahead called for a decisive peace effort to end the war. Humphrey and Johnson both authorized the effort, and the president had a number of representatives in Chicago who could negotiate for him. As the convention opened, we were told a deal had been struck, only to be informed a few hours later that the president insisted on unequivocal support for his policies and no deal. The Soviet invasion of Czechoslovakia had persuaded him that he dared not show any weakness through accommodation with his critics.

During the convention, the question of changing the party rules to "open up" the presidential selection process gathered force. Humphrey was attracted by the changes, and in his misplaced hope that the young and the liberals who had excoriated him before and during the convention could be mollified, he supported those changes with his customary optimism. It was an action that brought the Democratic party a misery that has not yet ended. More participation did not inevitably mean more democracy or wiser choices.

Humphrey, who wanted to be loved and who was filled with love, who was a conciliator and a compassionate public servant, found his moment of triumph tainted by the bitterness and divisiveness of the convention. He left Chicago with a greater sense of sadness than euphoria.

The campaign floundered, gasping in fits and starts, seriously lacking money and coherence. Our errors were compounded by our inability to formulate a consistent Vietnam policy, and by the merciless questioning from the press about when Humphrey "would be his own man." What the press and the critics really wanted to see was a break between Humphrey and Johnson, and Hubert refused to provide that. Johnson remained an ominous, hovering presence, like a thundercloud at a picnic, a presence that might drift away without harm, but too threatening to ignore. Finally, both issues, so intertwined as they were, were met in a single speech in Salt Lake City on October 31.

Humphrey's speech on Vietnam distanced him only ever so slightly from Johnson, more in emphasis than in substance, but managed to satisfy some of the critics who were beginning to realize that by their actions they were in effect helping to elect Nixon to be their president. As I read the speech carefully before it was delivered, I thought of the advice I had given Humphrey during the first night of the convention, that in his acceptance speech he resign as vice president while praising LBJ as president and supporting our Vietnam objectives.* This, I felt, would give him the freedom he needed to formulate his own Vietnam policy and explicate it without the psychological and tactical restraints of remaining Johnson's vice president. He could justify his resignation by his need to put all his energies into the task of defeating Nixon.

Johnson's role during the campaign has been a matter of controversy, with some believing that Johnson secretly preferred Nixon as president. I do not agree. Johnson was a sad figure during the last year of his presidency. A crushing blow was the advice of many, including some of his close friends, not to show up at the Chicago convention of his own political party for his own birthday celebration because of the negative reaction it might produce. He then found his old friend Hum-

---

* Others did, too. Averell Harriman was possibly the most eminent, but many of our old friends—Herb McCloskey, Evron Kirkpatrick, and John Hoving, among others—felt it was the best path to election. Humphrey simply would not consider it seriously. Resigning from an appointed office was one thing; resigning from an elected one like the vice presidency, he thought was dishonorable. When I raised it with him in Chicago, pointing out that a new amendment to the Constitution had just been adopted permitting the president, with Senate approval, to appoint a new vice president in the event of a vacancy, he dismissed the idea without hesitation.

phrey, according to the press, surrounded by people who wanted Hubert to break away from him and renounce his policies in Vietnam, policies Hubert had supported. He could not understand why Hubert simply didn't renounce those advisers. He had, therefore, frequent doubt about Humphrey, occasional anger, and some bitterness.

Johnson did raise money for Humphrey, who could not have won Texas in the general election without Johnson's active support and energizing force. We must also remember that during all of this time, Johnson was energetically trying to move toward a peaceful settlement of Vietnam through the Paris Conference. He was aware that such a peace settlement before election day would inure to Humphrey's benefit. He would have pulled it off had it not been for Madame Chennault's interference during the last weekend of the campaign.

On the Saturday evening prior to the election, November 2, I received a telephone call from Louis Harris, the pollster, saying he had been trying to reach Humphrey by phone. Could I pass on a message? He had been keeping Humphrey regularly informed about current poll developments, which showed that Humphrey was rapidly catching up with Nixon. He wanted Humphrey to know as soon as possible that the most recent polling data of that day showed Humphrey had surpassed Nixon—43 percent to 40 percent—and he expected that the victory on Tuesday would be comfortable, since the trend lines were clear. This was exhilarating news. I located Humphrey and passed the message to him.

Why, then, did we lose? Theodore White, in his splendid narrative history of the 1968 campaign,* publicly recorded the incredulous developments of the weekend involving Anna Chan Chennault, the beautiful Chinese widow of General Claire Chennault.

The month of October was filled with intensive back-door negotiations designed to bring the war in Vietnam to an end. The talks had begun in the spring and summer with Averell Harriman serving as chief negotiator for Johnson, with Cyrus Vance as his deputy. The objective was to end the bombing in North Vietnam as part of an overall approach that would bring South Vietnam and North Vietnam into direct negotiations. By October, both sides were proceeding seriously, and a breakthrough was apparently at hand with General Thieu, the South Vietnamese president, supporting Johnson's willingness to arrange a bombing halt. Humphrey had been kept fully informed of these talks.

* *The Making of the President 1968*, by Theodore White (New York: Atheneum, 1969).

His reluctance to be flexible about Vietnam during the campaign was clearly due to his desire not to interfere with what he knew to be a serious negotiating process quietly under way.

By October 26, reports were coming out of Asia. By October 27, Harriman and Vance informed Johnson that an understanding had been reached. On October 28, President Thieu of South Vietnam gave his agreement. By October 29, the press informed the American public that the preliminary talks had been successful and a serious negotiation would soon get under way in Paris. On Thursday evening, October 31, Lyndon Johnson made a public announcement ordering a cessation in the bombardment of North Vietnam and asserting that this action could lead to a peaceful settlement of the war. He expected "prompt, productive, serious and intensive negotiations in an atmosphere that is conducive to progress."

This was the context in which Lou Harris telephoned me with the good news of his poll results.

At this point, Madame Chennault became very busy. She was chairman of several Nixon committees, raised money for the Nixon campaign, and apparently decided that she had to sabotage the October negotiations. Using cable and telephone, she communicated the impression to important people in the South Vietnamese government that she spoke for Nixon. Her communications with Asia were tapped by the American government and brought directly to the attention of President Johnson. Within a matter of hours, a group of South Vietnamese legislators publicly announced that they opposed the agreement and that the South Vietnamese government had not agreed to it in spite of press reports. They said that General Thieu had spoken only for himself and not for the national assembly or for the country's vice president, General Nguyen Cao Ky. Under pressure, on Saturday, November 2, President Thieu announced: "The Government of South Vietnam deeply regrets not to be able to participate in the present exploratory talks."

Johnson telephoned Humphrey. He was furious. The Republicans were now saying that Johnson had rushed and manipulated the announcement for political reasons without having a basis of fact behind his announcement. He wanted to blast Nixon publicly because he was convinced that Nixon was behind the Chennault activity. Humphrey was reluctant to turn the promising peace effort into a bitter political fight. He urged Johnson to call Nixon before deciding on any public announcement. I was aware of Humphrey's advice, and even though I felt Johnson and Humphrey should openly attack Mrs. Chennault's sabotaging efforts, I marveled at Hubert's patriotic and selfless instinct. Nixon said he had not known of Madame Chennault's activities and, when they talked by phone on Sunday, persuaded Johnson that he was not a part of the sabotage plan.

Apparently, on Friday and Saturday, Americans were convinced that peace was at hand. Lou Harris caught that in his polling, which indicated a lead for Humphrey. By Monday, following the weekend reports, Americans were upset by the conflicting news from Saigon. Over the weekend, according to a Gallup Poll, Nixon was again ahead by the narrow margin of 42 percent to 40 percent. With all of this polling, there was, of course, a three-point margin of error. The election results on Tuesday showed a one-point Nixon victory margin in the popular vote.

It was not unreasonable to conclude that if the election had taken place on Saturday, November 2, or on Thursday, November 7, Humphrey would have won the popular vote. Theodore White, in referring to this incident, said that he knew "of no more essentially decent story in American politics than Humphrey's refusal" to make political capital out of Mrs. Chennault's sabotage. Humphrey refused to air the story and persuaded the president to be similarly restrained. I was proud of my friend and my candidate. A number of months ago, during a dinner, Richard Nixon obviously referred to this incident when he talked to me about "Hubert's patriotism."

I was convinced at the time and remain convinced today that had Johnson run for president in 1968, he would have been reelected.*

A disappointment of the campaign was Gene McCarthy's apparent indifference to Humphrey's need for his vigorous support. With a hatful of rationalizations, he clutched one and then another to avoid any clear gesture or word that might have made a timely and real difference, particularly in California. This most eloquent of men was mute when it counted. George McGovern, no less committed than McCarthy to ending the Vietnam war, helped as much as he could from the start. I often thought of how much differently Humphrey would have behaved had the situation been in some way reversed, and McCarthy the candidate.

The fact that Humphrey, by dint of his personality and perseverance alone, came so close to the victory was, I think, testimony to what

---

* I believe the verdict of history is still out on the Vietnam war and our involvement in it. Since North Vietnam "won" the war, millions of Vietnamese have been killed, persecuted, and degraded, regrettably justifying the concerns of Kennedy and Johnson that a Vietcong "victory" could produce an appalling human tragedy. The story of the boat people and their tears and anguish never seems to end.

we had always seen in him and loved: an optimism that soared over obstacles, an ability to communicate his humanity and his vision. As sad as I was after the election, I did not think it was the end of the road for Humphrey, the man or the public servant.*

I was more worried about the emergence in our country of new and uncivil voices following the assassinations of Martin Luther King, Jr., and Bobby Kennedy. Many voices in the peace movement became hoarse with the sounds of hate. Their spirit became tinged by violence as they belligerently rampaged through the campuses. Amid the legitimate anger and fear and distress, the civil rights battle took a disastrous turn. Civil rights—brotherhood—had been part of my education from my earliest days, and part of my experience from college on. I felt a bond with men like Walter White, Clarence Mitchell, and Roy Wilkins of the NAACP; Lester Granger and Whitney Young of the Urban League; Bayard Rustin, George Weaver, and A. Philip Randolph. We talked a common language and shared common goals. Many of my Jewish friends and I were devoted to overcoming the de facto apartheid that existed in so much of American life.

Indeed, the American civil rights movement from its beginnings had a substantial Jewish element in it, intellectual and moral on the one hand and financial on the other. It also always had a substantial reservoir of non-Jewish white support. Clearly, the vision of the Civil Rights Act of 1964 found its greatest spokesman in Martin Luther King, Jr., but the act would not have become law without a medley of support from whites, church leaders, labor union officials, and members of the Jewish community, from politicians as liberal as Humphrey and as crusty and conservative as Everett Dirksen.

America moves forward in consensus, not in separation and division. Social problems are solved and incremental gains made by working together. That spirit died in 1968, the victim of Martin Luther King, Jr.'s assassination, the misdirected extremism arising from black pride and power, and a new black leadership. That was understandable, but debilitating nonetheless.

Hostility and anger can be explained, the need for blacks to chart

* Nixon made a serious effort to enlist Humphrey in his administration by designating their mutual friend, Dwayne Andreas, to offer him the ambassadorship to the United Nations, which Hubert declined. Humphrey and Nixon then met face to face at the Opalocka Airport in Florida to discuss the offer and Nixon's promise to clear all Democratic appointments with Hubert. Nixon had been told by Johnson that Humphrey had declined in the final two days of the campaign to yell "foul" at Mrs. Chennault's successful effort to thwart the Vietnam peace talks.

their own future can be understood, but the idea that a multiracial, egalitarian society can be created by one race alone is absurd, unrealistic, and truly un-American. The historic strength of the black family and church needs to be supplemented by the commitment and friendship of those whites who are either eager or at least willing to cooperate.

It is not paternalism on the part of whites or Uncle Tomism on the part of blacks when dialogue, not two monologues, takes place. It is easy to say that bigotry exists and, therefore, that one must go it alone, but that merely leads to further schism, not to brotherhood. It is the road back, not forward. We follow separatist shibboleths at our social and national risk. I despair today at the young blacks who do not learn because it is "white" to do so. I gag at the corruption or ineptitude that is excused because "whitey" is ostensibly out to get black leadership. When former D.C. mayor Marion Barry's deep corruption with drugs and Illinois Congressman Gus Savage's rabble-rousing diatribes about "Jewish money" and a "white media plot," designed to excuse his sexual aggression against a Peace Corps volunteer, produce a reaction from Benjamin Hooks, head of the NAACP, that there is a "vicious assault on black leaders," rather than a moral condemnation of those outrageous actions, we are witnessing a bankruptcy of leadership. That is the siren song that draws us to the shoals of racial disharmony and keeps us from the safe harbor of brotherhood.

We are on a path that leads nowhere, dominated not by voices of reason but voices of division. Louis Farrakhan, an active, effective black preacher with a disciplined following, is not only a negative force in American life because he is anti-Semitic, but because he delays a real and lasting solution for blacks with his hate, factionalism, and scapegoating. Jesse Jackson speaks of a coalition, but really operates on his own personally ambitious third-world program of the moment. He makes good sounds, although I am inclined when I hear him to think that poetry comes from truth, not rhyme, and that he cannot tell them apart.

There is a new generation of blacks coming forth, and I hope they can, once again, help move all Americans into a common effort to defeat racism. The chief victims of our twenty-year wanderings into the racial wilderness are blacks themselves, victimized by leaders and rhetoric that impede their moving up in social, educational, and economic terms. But we all, black and white, are victims.

It was ironic, I thought, that some black students at Macalester College, where Humphrey went to teach after his 1968 electoral defeat, staged a protest in his office, ignoring his record and commitment in their own adolescent posturing. Humphrey had turned to teaching there and at the University of Minnesota to refresh himself and to use the time to decide what he wanted to do.

It was by no means certain that he would run again for the presidency and I was among those who urged him to run again for the Senate in 1970, whether Gene McCarthy withdrew, as he suggested he might, or not. Humphrey belonged in public office, not in a classroom.* The Senate was a comfortable place and provided the opportunity for him to be an involved, working elder statesman.

Whenever he came back to Washington after the 1968 election, I arranged for him to lunch at the Madison Hotel with small groups of influential Washingtonians, journalists, academicians, politicians, office holders, contributors. There was no plan, but the gatherings permitted him to maintain a presence in Washington and to discuss current issues with those responsible for defining the national agenda. He liked it, they liked it, and no political commitments of any sort were asked.

When he ran successfully for the Senate in 1970, he came back to a Senate role that was different from before. He worked as diligently, but at a somewhat different pace and not as an official leader. We had many moments to talk about the 1972 presidential election. He was once again a reluctant candidate and simply said he would wait and see if his 1968 running mate and friend, Ed Muskie, could make it.

When Muskie failed, George McGovern had already begun to run. I had been a friend of George's for years,† and Humphrey had helped McGovern from the beginning, virtually discovering him and encouraging his transformation from college professor into a party activist and public servant. South Dakota, of course, was special to Humphrey since he was born and grew up there; and, liberals in that state, like those in Wisconsin, regarded him as their third senator. McGovern shared many of Humphrey's attitudes and aspirations for the country, and they were good friends. Indeed, they were close enough that

* When Malcolm Moos, the president of the University of Minnesota, announced that he had negotiated with Humphrey for his return to the campus, one political scientist opposed Humphrey's appointment within the department because "he was out of touch with the field."

† I had once been George's attorney. We brought a libel action in his behalf against a newspaper that scurrilously attacked him. We won. When he lost his 1960 South Dakota Senate bid, we provided him an office at the law firm while he waited for a presidential appointment as Food for Peace director. Maggie and I liked and respected both Eleanor and George McGovern, but I regrettably felt that his foreign policy views disqualified him from being president.

McGovern once wanted to nominate Humphrey for a Nobel Peace Prize.

The Minnesota State DFL convention in the spring of 1972 reflected the continued polarization within the Democratic party. Eugenie Anderson presciently wrote Humphrey:

> I am sure you are more acutely aware than I that Minnesota's DFL Convention is only a microcosm of what the National Convention in Miami will be, and all on national TV networks. I seriously doubt whether you, or anyone else who might be able to wrest the nomination from McGovern, would find that it would be worth much, after such an explosion as would occur. The Coalition delegates are for the most part so irrational, emotional and aggression-bent that their rage, if they lose, would wreck not only the Convention, but all chances for the Democrats in November. They probably will damage McGovern's chances, too, for that matter, if they comport themselves in Miami as they did in Rochester. I doubt if even McGovern will be able to control them unless they got *everything* that they want, and then they will be controlling him, not vice versa.

The 1972 race for the nomination became a bitter one with the June 6 California primary. It became clear to both the Humphrey and McGovern forces that the nomination would be decided by that primary. Humphrey quietly asked Muskie if he would run with him on the same ticket in California; a Humphrey-Muskie ticket would have revived the spirits of many Democrats in the state and nation. But Muskie, dispirited and disappointed at the unfairness of his earlier need to drop out of the presidential race, was too exhausted to consider the matter seriously. California was the only one of the fifty states that refused to abide by a rule of the Democratic National Committee that decided the delegates to the national convention were to be chosen on a basis proportionate to the number of votes each candidate received in the state's primary. California insisted on "winner take all." We attempted to persuade the national Democratic party to insist on its own rules, but to no avail.

Eugene Wyman, a close personal friend, was in charge of the Humphrey effort in California. A successful lawyer and highly respected businessman, he raised in California what he considered adequate funds for the California primary campaign. About two weeks before the primary, he asked me to spend as much time in California as I could. I arrived at the Beverly Hilton Hotel the next evening and found a troubled Gene waiting for me. The Washington campaign office had issued some checks that they were in no position to cover at the banks. They wanted Wyman to transfer funds from his California account to Washington. We agreed to wait for Humphrey's return to Los Angeles late that night. Humphrey heard Wyman explain that he had budgeted California carefully and that if any significant portion of what he raised could no longer be spent in California, it could very well mean defeat in the primary. He had allocated the funds in question for expenditure by Phil Burton, the congressman from the Bay Area, and Mervin Dymally, then a powerful state legislator and now a congressman from Los Angeles. Both were considered pivotal in bringing out the black vote in the San Francisco and Los Angeles areas, a vote that should naturally go to Humphrey in light of his civil rights record. McGovern, however, according to the press, had budgeted $2 million for California and was spending large sums of money in those areas. Wyman felt that we would be at risk if we withdrew what he called "walking-around money" from the campaign. Humphrey insisted that he would not tolerate bounced checks, and after complaining energetically about the inefficiency of the Washington campaign office, he asked Wyman to transfer the funds.

McGovern narrowly won the primary race and claimed all the 271 delegates attributed to California. The press expressed surprise that Humphrey did not win overwhelmingly in the black neighborhoods, and we went to the Miami convention of the Democratic party without California.

We decided to challenge the right of California to send a slate of delegates chosen on a "winner take all" basis and pressed hard for a decision that would permit enough Humphrey delegates to be selected to reflect the percentage of Humphrey's votes in that primary. The Credentials Committee of the convention agreed with us and recommended that only 120 delegates be authorized for McGovern. The issue would be presented on the convention floor as a challenge by McGovern to the report of the Credentials Committee. We proposed that since the composition of the California delegation was at stake, they abstain and not have an opportunity to vote on a question of their own qualification.

We had reason to believe that, if California were not permitted to vote, a majority of the convention would side with us and require a proportional vote identical to that in effect for the other forty-nine states. With a California vote divided proportionately, we and others felt that there would be more Humphrey than McGovern votes at the convention and that Humphrey would be the nominee. Humphrey asked me to be in charge of this effort. We failed because Lawrence O'Brien, our friend who was the chairman of the convention, ruled that the 120 McGovern delegates could vote on the issue while the 151 non-McGovern California delegates could not vote on the Credentials Committee report.

I could never understand that development because I felt O'Brien had accepted the logic of my position when I presented our case to him. Later, O'Brien explained to me that the intensity of feeling on the part of the McGovern delegates was so strong that, had he ruled for us, he feared a riot at the convention. His ruling was obviously not based on the correctness of the position. This contributed significantly to my decision to reduce my involvement in Democratic party politics.

That year after the convention, Arthur Goldberg and Arthur Krim, a movie mogul and major Democratic party fund-raiser, sent a form letter to a number of people, including me, who were reluctant to support McGovern. I was accustomed to political hyperbole and had certainly used it myself, but their descriptive words were far beyond what I could accept as accurate, or even tolerably close. I wrote them my objections to both their letter and McGovern's policies.

> I am not happy with the statement . . . to the effect that George would bring the war to an end and bring home our POWs. This is an oversimplification that I don't like to be associated with, particularly since I believe that the President has not done badly in this area.
>
> . . . I don't want to be associated in any way as a supporter of George McGovern's publicly announced defense [policies] . . . I do not now believe that George McGovern is of the same mind as I in this vital area. Nor . . . would I want to claim that Democrats who refuse to support McGovern (including some of my closest friends) are "profoundly" wrong. Furthermore, I would not favor including a sentence referring to "sunshine soldiers or summer patriots."

Needless to say, my suggestions were not accepted and my party continued on a path away from what I understood to be Democratic party principles and purposes.

The nation went through Watergate, the presidential resignation, and the political dyspepsia that followed. It was hard not to look back to 1968 and think what might have been had we been successful. But politics is tomorrow, not yesterday; and as 1976 approached, Humphrey measured whether he should run for the nomination one more time. He had ended the 1968 campaign defeated, but with dignity, a come-from-behind hero. His tentative campaign for the nomination in 1972 had done him no political harm. His stature as a national leader had increased, and no one better or more logical had come to the public's attention. Humphrey wanted to be president, but he was not sure he wanted to run for it again.

While he delayed, Senator Henry "Scoop" Jackson had become a candidate for president, and I felt comfortable supporting him. We were friends and I liked him. I found his views on defense and foreign policy compatible with my own. His campaign never took off, unable to present Scoop as the man he was. As the deadline to enter the New Jersey primary approached, the Jackson campaign had faltered, particularly in Pennsylvania, and Scoop urged Humphrey to enter and pledged his support. He told me he would help raise campaign funds.

Humphrey by then saw the Carter selection as almost inevitable, though not very appealing. I encouraged him once again to consider seeking the presidency. His years in the Senate after his return were not always easy ones, but he had a national forum for his ideas. He was like the old Humphrey when he pursued every new idea with excitement, and demonstrated again that he was an eminently effective legislator.

A small group of us gathered in Humphrey's Senate office the night before the filing deadline for the New Jersey primary. We talked that night about his earlier losses, whether he was too old, whether he had gone to the well too often, whether it was time to step aside for younger men. I did not think his age or his losses were relevant.

By the time I left, he had made his decision: he would run. I talked later that night to Muriel, who had been hesitant, and she was satisfied with the decision; any reservations she might have had were now set aside. The next day, the final day to enter the New Jersey primary, Humphrey would announce, and Bob Barrie would fly by charter to Trenton to file the papers in a dramatic last-minute gesture. That was the plan. The polls in the state were showing Humphrey significantly in front of Carter, and the New Jersey AFL-CIO was promising strong support.

When ten A.M. came, while Barrie waited at the charter terminal at Washington National Airport, I stood in the Senate caucus room, which was packed with Humphrey supporters and the press, and heard him say, to my disbelief, that he had decided not to run, that he would not let his name be entered in New Jersey or anywhere else, and that his running for president was something of the past. (In retrospect, I am convinced that Hubert, whose bladder problems had presumably been successfully treated, had a sense that his illness was too serious to permit him to serve, but we never talked about it.)*

Carter locked up the nomination, after ungraciously declaring he would have licked Humphrey, and again I dismissed presidential politics from my mind. Actually, when my friend Stu Eizenstat, a Carter aide, telephoned me before the convention for a Mondale appraisal, I gave him high marks. When he selected Fritz Mondale as his running mate, I cheered. Fritz and I had not seen much of each other since our tensions of 1968, but I was pleased, in part because of his personal good qualities, but in even larger part because it pleased Hubert, and I knew that Mondale drew his strength from the wellspring of DFL politics. A handwritten note from Mondale to me read, "I have forgotten 1968 and I *hope* you have too. Let's go."

I had met Carter at a meeting in Atlanta set up so that some of us could present our views on the Middle East. He impressed me more than his campaign did. I had seen an uptight, narrow human being, arrogant, petty, and unlikely to rally the nation to a reaffirmation of its values. I began to question my judgment after a few hours with him in Atlanta.

I knew and liked Gerald Ford. When he was a young congressman from Grand Rapids, Michigan, I was the chairman of an American Political Science Association Committee that presented him a public service award for his services to the Congress. I watched his constructive leadership with approval. When he became president, I thought he worked effectively and successfully to help heal the nation's Nixon wounds.

The election of Carter and Mondale provided me with new opportunities to be active with public issues. A few weeks after the election, Walter Wriston, head of Citibank, called me to ask if I would meet in his New York office with him and Hans Angermueller, the

---

* Hubert did say to others that he thought it lucky that he had not been the Democratic candidate since his health had deteriorated so. He had some good periods in 1976 and 1977, but not many. He went to the best clinics available, saw doctors, underwent surgery and chemotherapy, but nothing helped. When he died of bladder cancer in January 1978, I was saddened beyond description. When he was honored in the Capitol rotunda with a final Washington service, I stood crying far back from the luminaries, knowing that our country was the less for his death and the fact that he had never become president.

bank's senior vice president and general counsel. They told me that ARAMCO, which was deeply involved in Saudi Arabian oil, had come to Wriston for advice. Saudi Arabia was eager to improve relations with the United States. Could I advise them how to proceed?

I suggested that the Saudis may well have been motivated by Carter's pledge during the campaign to support a strong legislative move against the Arab boycott of companies doing business with Israel. I also suggested the ARAMCO official meet with Dr. Zbigniew Brzezinski, who would undoubtedly serve as Carter's national security adviser. I then proceeded to set up the meeting for them.

A few days later, Angermueller called to discuss the Arab boycott. What could be done to heal the breach that had developed the previous year between the business community and the Jewish community on the boycott issue? The breach had led to an impasse on legislation that was highlighted in the presidential debate between Carter and Ford. Angermueller had discussed the question with Irving Shapiro, chairman of Dupont, head of the Business Roundtable, and active in the Jewish community. Did I think that Burton Joseph of Minneapolis, head of the Anti-Defamation League (ADL), could help, and did I know him? My answer to both questions was yes.

The result of these discussions was an unusual meeting in New York between the leading lights of the Anti-Defamation League and the leadership of the Business Roundtable. When I entered the boardroom on the morning of January 28, 1977, not long after Jimmy Carter had been sworn in as president, I was introduced not only to Mr. Shapiro by Walter Wriston and Hans Angermueller but to H. Brewster Atwater, president of General Mills; C. C. Garvin, chairman of Exxon Corporation; Reginald Jones, chairman of General Electric; Thomas Murphy, chairman of General Motors; David Rockefeller, chairman of Chase Manhattan; George Shultz, chairman of Bechtel; and senior officials from the Mobil Corporation and other large companies. I had never been with such a small group of men who embodied so much business power and influence.

The meeting was a moving one. Ben Epstein and Arnold Forster of ADL, with eloquence and emotion, presented the case against the boycott and in favor of a strong United States–Israel relationship. The business leaders expressed their concerns. The result was a request to Hans Angermueller and me to find a formula to resolve our differences. We each were backed by other members of a committee.

I persuaded the ADL to turn our committee into a broader one by adding representatives of the American Jewish Committee and the

American Jewish Congress to it. This brought in two exceptional Washington lawyers, Paul Berger of Arnold and Porter, and Alfred Moses of Covington and Burling. The three of us became a team. We negotiated with the business representatives diligently and argumentatively from early February until May. We informed the White House of our activities and found the president and his staff eagerly encouraging. Appropriate members of Congress were kept informed. We had ups and downs. At one point when I went to the Virgin Islands with my family during Easter, thinking that we had resolved the most important issues, I received a frantic call from Shapiro and Angermueller telling me that the deal had fallen apart. We put it back together again.

We did agree on a piece of legislation that in 1977 overwhelmingly passed both the Senate and the House. The White House enthusiastically accepted our results and invited us to the bill-signing ceremony. The legislation remains on the books. It makes it illegal for American companies to comply or cooperate with the Arab boycott of companies that do business with Israel. It is working. It has not been altered.

The successful resolution of the problem led to Carter's grateful appreciation and possibly his subsequent appointment of me as ambassador and head of the U.S. delegation to the Madrid Review Meeting of the Conference on Security and Cooperation in Europe under the Helsinki Final Act. Later, President Reagan continued me in that post and ultimately, because of Shultz's interest, named me to head the arms control talks in Geneva.

For the moment, however, I took great pleasure in being able as an American Jew to help resolve a problem that involved Israel and the United States, as well as the Arabs, and the responsible American business community.

11

There But for the Grace of God Go I

To be born a Jew in the United States is a special blessing. From our nation's earliest days, Jews, with good reason, have had a unique romance with America. There have been problems of anti-Semitism, of discrimination, of rejection, but that behavior has never been the tool of the majority or the national policy of government. There have been times and places and incidents of vicious acts against Jews, and they continue even now, but we have had the opportunity and the support to fight back. For every enemy today in the United States, Jews have a multitude of friends. We are a minority, but we have rarely in this country been a beleaguered one for very long.

It had been quite different for Jews born in this century in other lands. I recall vividly conversations with my parents, their friends, and my teachers about pogroms when people were brutalized and killed just because they were Jewish. Immigrants brought with them haunting and unshakable memories that made them that much more intense about their new country. This impression has remained with me since childhood, and I could never escape the thought that "there but for the grace of God go I."

The Holocaust, of course, dwarfed the pogroms by comparison. Many Americans, including Jews, were slow to see the dimensions of

183

the devastation, cruelty, and degradation. We had all grown up inured to what we considered the propaganda that accompanied war. The tales coming from within the bowels of Europe seemed unbelievable until we saw the photographs and heard from the eyewitnesses. Numbness then gave way to outrage, to care, and then to the outpouring of gifts to Israel, in a frenzy of giving never before experienced in philanthropy.

In the post-Holocaust era, Jews have been spared that dimension of violence, although anti-Semitism lives on with a particular virulence in the Soviet Union and other countries of Eastern Europe despite the diminished numbers of Jews and the recent surge of favorable conditions for democratic government. Ironically, as totalitarian regimes have toppled, the restraints on the anti-Semites and extreme nationalists have diminished, too. Public expressions of anti-Semitism seem to be an ugly consequence of positive political changes. It is worrisome to consider the turbulent political and economic times ahead for these countries and what they may mean for the few Jews who remain.

Part of the reason for the very different American experience is, I think, the way religion took hold in the Colonies. The Puritans spoke Hebrew as the language of their prayer; they cherished the Holy Land as the home of Christianity; they spoke of brotherhood and quoted the Old Testament prophet Micah, who asked, "Have we not all one Father? Hath not God created us?"

They believed with the Talmudic scholars that God had created only Adam and Eve so that each of us had the same ancestors and that no one could thus claim superiority over another. This is not to say, of course, that they all followed those views all the time, or that our society was always fair to Jews or blacks or other minorities. But the Judaeo-Christian heritage is not meaningless rhetorical display devoid of resonance. It could be invoked without hypocrisy and with conviction here as in virtually no place else in the world.

Jews actually arrived quite early in American history. One of Columbus's crew was Jewish and reportedly among the first to set foot on our soil. As early as September 1654, twenty-three Jewish refugees fleeing from Brazil—where they thought the newly arrived Portuguese would reintroduce the Inquisition—landed at New Amsterdam, intending to settle there. Peter Stuyvesant, the Dutch governor, was unhappy with their arrival, protesting to the Dutch West Indies Company, "Giving them liberty, we cannot refuse the Lutherans and Papists." Despite that, they were permitted to settle, and subsequently they asked to join the militia guarding the colony. The governor refused that, too, but ultimately the Jews prevailed and served their adopted country. By 1775, there were about 2,000 Jews in the Colonies. With the Revolution of 1848 in Europe, and reaction to it, hundreds of thousands of Jews, including 150,000 from Germany, came to America.

Beyond religion in colonial days, there was geography. It made a difference, too. There was a vast and empty land to fill. Early on, the frontier spirit of openness permitted people to wander as the spirit moved them, to set down roots where they wished, and to undertake trades that had been forbidden them elsewhere. Jews were simply not regulated and restricted as they had been for centuries in other places. Peddlers of needles and notions walked the dirt roads from farmhouse to village to little town until wanderlust departed or fatigue set in. Then they settled down and became part of a community. They might become haberdashers or butter-and-egg men or buyers of hides and furs. No one denied them a place in the sun, and they gathered their families around them and attracted other Jews to join them.

Later, the cities, in an underpopulated country, absorbed millions of people, some Jews, many more not, in a patchwork of ethnic cohesiveness within a national tendency toward assimilation. Even there, where prejudice might be felt and bigotry was real, Jews maintained their culture and their religion with minimal interference. With the assassination of Russian Czar Alexander II in 1881 and the resultant pogroms, two million additional Jews fled to America. This flow did not stop until the mid-1920s when the United States enacted strict quota legislation and virtually closed its gates.

Jews thrived not just because of religious tolerance and an open land and society. It was a question also of a free market economy, of little businesses started on a shoestring, where growth came from energy and skill. Even as robber barons exploited others and industrial titans created empires, there was within the American culture a fear of monopoly power, a love-hate relationship with bigness. Suspicions of economic power were deep in our secular soul.

Somewhere, somehow within that economic structure, a Jewish businessman could find a niche to fill, even as my father did as a simple butcher. Increasingly, Jews found a way to become professionals, as I did. My father and I were not exceptions, just part of the democratic socialization of America in a wide-open economic system.

That we Jews should thrive here, then, is no accident. The unique character of American democracy made it possible. Today, more than 40 percent of all the Jews in the world live in the United States. History is likely to judge that this American period is the grandest one yet for Jewry; that this is truly a golden age of Jewish history. Our primal concern as Jews with justice and equity and the law has been encouraged by our Constitution and our American traditions. Arts and science flourish in the United States with inspired Jewish contributions. The greatest libraries for Jewish learning in the world are here. There is a significant Jewish presence in academia, politics and government, journalism and the media.

As a result, within this encouraging open environment, our beliefs, as both Americans and Jews, in human brotherhood and in human dignity have been harmoniously interrelated and enlarged. That not only makes us better Americans but reinforces our interest in things Jewish. Thus it is from the values reinforced by two cultures that the inspiration for a special relationship between the United States and Israel came into being. Our early presidents, from the time of John Adams, motivated by their Christian learning, proclaimed Palestine as the land of Israel. In more modern times, a political friendship for a fellow democracy has added an ingredient to the alliance. A special feeling of most American Jews for Israel has grown because the common values of the two cultures and societies led to loyalties that were not in conflict with one another. Furthermore, for most American Jews and others in the diaspora, when Israel's security, or the Holocaust, or Soviet Jews come to mind, there is the stark realization: "There but for the grace of God go I."

The idea of a Jewish homeland—Israel—has been a part of my life for as long as I can remember. That little white box with a blue six-pointed star, the Star of David, sat in our apartment all the time I was growing up. It was a flimsy collection box of thin cardboard sides and tin top and bottom, about six inches high and half as wide, but it proclaimed a hardy message as it reminded us of our fellow Jews in Palestine. Every week I put coins in it, nickels in good times and pennies in bad, but something every week. Even penny-bank philanthropy can help build a nation and teach the joy and responsibility of sharing.

From time to time a rabbi would drop by to pick up the box, replace it with another, and talk briefly to my mother and father about Palestine and Jewish life there. He spoke with a Zionist passion and proselytizing zeal they did not entirely share. We made our contribution, we cared about the people who had gone to those barren lands to create a Jewish nation, but as recent immigrants to the United States, my parents never expressed any interest in moving to Palestine or in doing more than contributing what they could. For them the United States was, in fact, the Promised Land.

Within that ambivalence, the idea of a homeland had a certain mystical attraction. Anthropologists tell us that there is such a thing as "folk memory" deriving from strong cultural, ethnic, and national feelings that become an integral part of a community's thought processes. Deep in the Jewish folk memory, the presence of a homeland—of Israel—persists ineradicably, and we cannot contemplate the future without it.

But I never thought of moving there any more than my parents did, although some of my classmates talked of it and a few ultimately went to Israel. For many years, my own identification with a homeland varied in intensity, remaining in my emotional background, never able to overcome or compete with the pressure of education and jobs, or with my drive to succeed here. But no one who grew up studying in yeshiva schools could escape knowledge of the Zionist movement.

In 1918, just before I was born, the Hebrew University of Jerusalem was founded on Mount Scopus. Many thought it was absurd and questioned the wisdom of establishing a university in the midst of shooting when there was no state to support and protect it.* They asked what sense it made to create a university in a barren land with a sparse population in the midst of struggle in a hostile environment. The answer came from Chaim Weizmann, a visionary, modern prophet and the founding president of Israel, who explained that anyone with the "soul of a Jew" would understand that the symbol of learning as the justification for a Jewish state had to precede its creation. That was a little arcane for most, but they accepted more easily the idea that the "people of the book" must have the book and a place to study it.

In later years, I learned in school of other justifications that seemed more powerful to me. I learned that justice and law and learning were fundamental Jewish values and that the ancient scholars of Judaism felt that the development of godlike qualities in the human personality required a just society based on order and equity.

That was an important lesson, a prophetic instruction I believed then as I do now. I also learned that godlike attributes did not come easily because there is in each of us a moral duality, something that is good and noble and godlike, and something that is evil and mean-

---

* The university grew in the new part of Jerusalem when Mount Scopus fell from Jewish control in 1948. After the Six-Day War in 1967, Mount Scopus became Israeli territory and the campus was moved back there. It was a cherished moment for me when I was later invited to serve on the university's board of governors.

spirited as well. Reinhold Niebuhr, Humphrey's colleague in founding the Americans for Democratic Action and a preeminent American Protestant theologian, noted this dichotomy in his book, *The Children of Light and the Children of Darkness*. I made the book required reading when I taught the freshman course in politics at Minnesota. This was consistent with what I learned as a youngster at the yeshiva that in each of us there was a *Yaitzer Hatov* and a *Yaitzer Harah*, that in the soul which was noble and that in the soul which was evil.

What existed in individuals was also reflected in the societies they created. So it was that a country as special as ours still had strains of darkness, of hate not love, impulses that denied justice and equality. But those qualities of moral ugliness did not live easily in a democracy. They thrived more readily where totalitarianism existed, an expression of the destructive drive. A lot of my friends among intellectuals, academics, politicians, and journalists found Ronald Reagan's use of the term "evil empire" in referring to the Soviet Union offensive and absurd. It may have been tactically wrong for a president to say so (although I am not even sure of that), but I thought it was factually correct. The Soviet Union disdained justice, defiled the law, and strangled unfettered learning. That was darkness. That was evil. Putting people in psychiatric hospitals to punish them for political statements is evil, too. We ignore the dark side of people, and nations, only at our peril.

When Israel came into existence as a nation in 1948, I was proud and pleased, but Israel was not then a compelling interest of mine. Perhaps it should have been, but putting pennies in the *pushke* years before had not made me an ardent Zionist so much as it had made me take the existence of a Jewish homeland rather for granted.

What did excite me was that this Jewish homeland was a democracy in a part of the world with few democracies, indeed in an entire world with few true democracies. I had written in *The Conscientious Objector* in 1943 that Palestine should be the home for Jews who wished to settle there, a haven for victims of the war. Israel was more than a haven, more than a homeland; it was the triumph of the spirit and the commitment to values that the United States and the Jewish faith shared. Making the desert bloom was not an idle dream, nor only one of vegetation. It was more.

If I was excited, Hubert Humphrey was transported. His enthusiasm was unbounded and he exulted in Israel's creation, feeling both a secular and a Christian religious fulfillment. His commitment was of the heart. He went as mayor to his friend I. S. Joseph's synagogue to celebrate Israel's recognition, and he spoke in countless church basements about the importance of Israel.

Once in the Senate, he was soon recognized nationally and internationally as a stalwart friend of the new nation. Both American Jews who cared as much as he about Israel and Israeli diplomats in Washington sought his counsel. As a non-Jew, he was an especially effective advocate for Israel in the Senate, with the media, and in meetings around the country, where he inspired Jewish philanthropy and educated both Jews and Christians about the Middle East. He championed Israel with a passion and commitment and eloquence that few matched anywhere. He seemed to be a Christian-American Theodore Herzl, Chaim Weizmann, and David Ben-Gurion rolled into a single prairie politician, more a Zionist, if that was possible, than the rabbi who gathered the coins. If his tongue never could handle a Hebrew word comfortably, his heart still beat with joy when he spoke of the land of milk and honey.

All of that meant that I, in turn, became more involved with Israel each year, meeting more and more of its diplomats who came to Washington to serve. The first ambassador, Eliyahu Eilat, left in 1950* and neither Humphrey nor I got to know him well then, although I met him later at the Hebrew University.

Abba Eban, his successor, was a distinguished scholar and political leader whom Humphrey liked immensely. He seemed to me more British of the old school than Jewish of the new nation, but Eban was charming, erudite, visionary, and inspiring to be with. He preferred to deal with senators and not staff, and because of that and because he was shy and reserved, we never established a close or warm relationship.

Golda Meir was the first prime minister I knew, and she remains even now my favorite among all Israeli leaders. She was foreign minister after an assignment in the Soviet Union, where one of her concerns was for the lives and conditions of Soviet Jews. In 1971, she sent an Israeli foreign service officer, Nechemia Levanon, to see me after she learned that Humphrey was to visit the Soviet Union and meet with Aleksei Kosygin, its premier.

* We did meet that year the Irish-born Israeli military attaché, Chaim Herzog, and his wife, Aura. We have remained friends ever since. Several years ago I visited him in Israel, after he had been elected to the largely ceremonial but important post of president. I learned from him that no Israeli president had ever been invited to the United States for an official state visit. When I returned home, I urged that the visit take place, and it came to pass. I take some credit for that gesture, although I think others were recommending it at the time, too.

Levanon had been born in the Soviet Union, spoke Russian fluently, and had been responsible, as a civil servant, for Soviet Jewry concerns in Israel. He explained to me that Jews in Soviet Georgia were not being permitted to emigrate. They were not, for the most part, the educated professionals and intellectuals the Soviets said could not leave because the state had invested so much in their education. They were rather people in skilled or semiskilled jobs, such as carpenters, painters, or electricians.

Nechemia was accompanied by Shlomo Argov, minister at the Israeli embassy, a persuasive diplomat and war hero.* They briefed Humphrey, and when he subsequently met Kosygin, he raised the question of Georgian immigration. Kosygin told Humphrey there would be no further problem, and indeed the gates opened for a while and Georgian Jews left Russia in large numbers following Humphrey's intercession. I learned from that first experience with the Soviets that they needed to be asked, to be prodded, to be confronted.

I knew by then that Israel needed whatever help it could get in the way of assistance from the United States. Immigrants from the Soviet Union were also necessary. Money and people were both essential. Maggie and I made our first trip to Israel in 1951. We went as the guests of a wealthy Dutch lady, Mrs. Van Leer, who was interested in adult education, of a sort, and who had recruited a friend of ours from the University of Chicago faculty to help her. Her motives were wonderful, her concept a little wild, and her style off the wall. Her intent was for Israel and Israelis to put the Jewish religious principles of morality and brotherhood and justice into daily practice. Adults as well as children were to be taught and encouraged to do that. To help, she asked my friend, Martin Diamond, a self-educated former socialist leader then teaching political science at the University of Chicago, for professional advice. He asked Maggie and me and Irving Kristol, the writer, with his wife, Gertrude Himmelfarb, a distinguished historian in her own right, to join him. One of Mrs. Van Leer's projects was to

---

* Shlomo and Chava Argov became our lasting personal friends. Shlomo became Israel's ambassador to the Netherlands at about the time that Geri Joseph, Burton's wife and my dear friend from our University of Minnesota days, was appointed by Carter as our ambassador there. I introduced them to each other in September 1980 during a visit from Madrid to The Hague. None of our spouses was present, so the three of us had dinner together at Geri's residence and then joined one another for the Kol Nidre services on Yom Kippur at the synagogue in The Hague, where we were prominently and proudly seated by the Jewish community leaders. In 1983, Shlomo was savagely shot by Palestinians in London where he was serving as ambassador and today remains gravely ill and bedridden in Jerusalem.

translate the Bible into a newspaper format, telling the stories of the Bible as though they had just happened. She thought that the ethical code and wisdom of the Bible would in that way reach and move more people.

It took only one meeting between our American group and a number of Dutch academicians she had assembled to make us realize that we could not agree on how or even whether her project should go forward. There was no second meeting. Clearly, many different kinds of people were drawn to this infant nation, enthusiasts because of its history and its nation building in the midst of hostile forces.

Israel was like a developing nation, albeit with Western traditions and values. There were food shortages, drinking water was unsafe (so we drank a tepid, bottled orange drink), and transportation was not easy. Yet there was a wonderful pioneer spirit, a sense that anything could be accomplished no matter what the odds. The story was told of a young Israeli who was asked whether he could play the piano. "I don't know," he replied, "I've never tried it." We left the country eager to be an ancillary part of its growth. That continuing association has been a special part of our lives.

Several years later, during the mid-fifties, Hubert told me he was going to meet with Golda Meir at the Wardman Park Hotel and asked me to come along. She was then foreign minister. Humphrey and Golda were a wonderful pair, filled with mutual affection, admiration, and easy camaraderie. She had grown up in Wisconsin and knew the American labor movement very well. They were like two Midwestern politicians greeting each other. Humphrey and she chattered on about people and politics in the United States.

Golda was warm and hospitable not only to Humphrey, but to me. She spoke of my help to Nechemia Levanon. She invited a first-name relationship almost immediately, although I did not find it comfortable to call her by name so soon. She involved me in the conversation and listened when I had something to say.

I arrived at the meeting concerned that the positive attitude toward Israel in the United States, though still favorable, was shifting. Our papers were filled with stories of the Arab refugee camps, with pictures of adults whose faces reflected a catatonic sort of hopelessness, of Arab children with huge dark eyes and empty stares. Churches were taking up collections for the Arab and Palestinian refugees, displaced by the 1947 war. Americans felt compassion for those who lived in the ugly conditions of the camps, where the refugees were cared for under United Nations supervision.

I suggested to Golda that she consider something similar to what had been done about American Indians here. The idea, which came to me after talks with Richard Schifter and Felix Cohen, was that all the Arabs who could demonstrate that they had owned property within the area now called Israel and who would accept the primacy of Israeli law should be compensated for their land. I thought a formula for payment could be worked out that allowed for value as of the taking or abandonment of the land plus modest interest accumulated during the years since. Disagreements about compensation would be adjudicated. The system provided compensation and permitted a government to say, "We are correcting a wrong," no matter who had perpetuated that wrong. I thought it would not only be the right thing to do, it would also elicit public support for the Israeli government. Furthermore, I believed that such a plan could be financed entirely with funds raised outside Israel.

Golda listened attentively, but indicated that she did not feel the problem was as serious as I suggested. She pointed out that the Jews had preceded the Arabs in the area and that there had never been a time in history without a Jewish presence there. It was not a simple matter of expulsion and displacement. Jews and Palestinians had come and gone for generations—indeed, for centuries. It was the Jewish national homeland created out of God's desert, not taken from Arab lands and hands.

We remained in touch over the years, even after I left the Humphrey office. When Maggie and I first took our children to Israel, Golda invited us to visit her at home. By then, she was the prime minister, but she kept her tiny house in Tel Aviv and invited the whole family to visit.

Away from her responsibilities as government leader, she was the quintessential grandmother. She hugged the children and paid attention to them and then led them off to the kitchen where she prepared hot chocolate for them and tea for Maggie and me. It was a golden afternoon I could not forget. Years later, after she left office, she asked me to represent her in the sale of her life's story for a play that unfortunately never captured the exciting qualities of the woman I knew. It survived only a short run on Broadway.

When Golda came to the United States for her first visit as prime minister, Nixon hosted a White House dinner for her; Maggie and I were invited. When Golda and I greeted each other, her eyes seemed to say, "Not bad for a girl from Milwaukee." I certainly thought it was also not bad for a boy from the Bronx. Just before she stepped down from office, we met again, and that day we talked more about Richard Nixon. In Israel, American politicians and American presidents were measured by their support of Israel. Nixon was a strong supporter and a constant friend.*

Her successor as prime minister, Yitzhak Rabin, and I had become good friends while he served as ambassador to Washington from 1968 to 1973. He arrived in Washington with a hero's aura, a victorious general in the 1967 war. It was not his military skills that attracted me. He had a keen analytical mind and is, I think, the best Israeli political analyst of Middle East problems and solutions. In addition, his insights into general East-West relations were perceptive and instructive. He also understood NATO strengths and weaknesses. In all, he had a broad view and deep understanding of world politics and dangers.

I wish he had been able to remain as prime minister of Israel for a longer period. I think he would have brought unique wisdom to the job as he became more accustomed to it. Rabin went back to Israel to be prime minister, but not before he had incurred the wrath of some Democratic Jews in the United States with his undisguised partiality toward Nixon during the 1972 presidential campaign. He felt that Nixon had been a great friend of Israel and understood the Soviet Union. That was sufficient for Rabin, even if George McGovern had not been the Democratic candidate.†

Menachem Begin was quite different from either Golda or Rabin. One cannot ignore the human dimension fully to comprehend international relations. The first time we met was soon after he had been elected, when he came here for his initial meeting with President Carter. On the eve of his return to Israel, I received a phone call from my friend and rabbi, Stanley Rabinowitz, who was then the head of the Conservative rabbinate, telling me that on the next day an official delegation of Conservative and Reform rabbis was meeting with Begin in New York to persuade him not to support the "who is a Jew" issue

---

* When Nixon's private comments about Jews became public after Watergate, I was both surprised and shocked. He was so consistently good on policy matters regarding Israel that it was hard to think of his published remarks as other than an aberration, a temporary and verbal flight of the ugly. I thought at the time that the forces of light and darkness struggled for his soul.

† After Ronald Reagan's election, Rabin was the first person to tell me that George Shultz would make a fine secretary of state as far as Israel was concerned. While I knew Shultz slightly and liked him, I was impressed with Rabin's view. He said the American Jewish community's concern about Shultz as president of the Bechtel Company, which did vast amounts of business with Arab nations, was not well founded—indeed, was clearly mistaken.

being initiated by the Orthodox rabbis. The delegation wanted me to join them. I agreed. Begin was alert with excitement as he greeted us. Then he surprised us. He informed us that Jimmy Carter was the second greatest person of the twentieth century, that only Winston Churchill ranked higher in his estimation. I had no response. The praise seemed so excessive that I listened in silent astonishment, thinking that Begin had taken himself out of Poland, but nothing had taken the Polish shtetl out of him.

I believe Begin never looked into a mirror without also seeing a small Polish-Jewish lawyer. He looked up to Carter, the American president, with awe and a sense of humility. To have been treated well, as an equal, by the American president made a great impression. Yitzhak Shamir may have some of the same quality as Begin. Reagan and Shultz understood this part of Shamir. I am not certain that the present administration does, but it will. Israel is being asked to make important decisions, ones that go to the essence of its security. Those decisions cannot be made by votes of 51 percent to 49 percent. They require consensus. Shamir and the views he represents are vital to those decisions.

Shimon Peres seems to me a competent leader, more in style like Golda Meir and Rabin, than Begin and Shamir. In the one opportunity he recently had to be prime minister during his coalition with Shamir, Peres served effectively. A brilliant political tactician, for years he suffered the cost of being considered a politician rather than a public servant. He demonstrated his qualities of political leadership as prime minister, and his popularity soared, only to drop again as he became foreign minister and then minister of the treasury in his coalition government under Shamir.

My relationship with Israeli leaders, whether in Washington or Jerusalem, has been a privileged part of my life. They are quite special people of talent and wisdom. The United States is, after all, the premier friend of Israel, without whom life there would have been more difficult, if not impossible. Their ambassadors to the United States, therefore, have been unusually gifted and well trained.

One of the most impressive of all Israeli ambassadors was Avraham Harman, who served from 1959, when Eban left, until 1968—the years when Humphrey was most prominent as a national political leader. One day in December 1961, Harman brought another Israeli, Meir Rosenne, to my office. Rosenne, a well-trained international lawyer who later became Israel's ambassador to Washington, was then based in Paris, assigned by his government to try to do something about the abysmal conditions of Soviet Jews. Stalin, his paranoia in full flower, had in late 1952 and 1953 "discovered" Jewish plots against him and had ordered that Jewish doctors and writers be executed. Stalin had then gone on to his celestial reward, but Jews in the Soviet Union continued to suffer the consequences of longstanding state-sponsored anti-Semitism.

Rosenne had come to the United States to get support from the American Jewish community for Soviet Jews. I had never been an officer or leader of the traditional American Jewish groups, but visitors from Israel were coming to me more and more frequently. Rosenne said he had found difficulty obtaining support for his project because American Jews largely took the position that Israel had a sufficient enemy in the Arab states without invoking the additional wrath of the Soviet Union. I thought Soviet Jews deserved any support we could muster and that the decision about invoking Soviet wrath was not one for me, or any other American Jew to make, but one that the Israeli government had to explore with President Kennedy.

I arranged for Harman and Rosenne to meet with Abraham Ribicoff, who was then secretary of Health, Education and Welfare; Hubert Humphrey; and Arthur Goldberg. Through them, particularly Ribicoff, an appointment with President Kennedy was arranged. Kennedy said something would be done, although he would have to overrule the entire State Department because "there are 7,000 people there who will tell me no." He thought the problem cried out for American interest and whatever American pressure could be safely applied. He arranged for Rosenne to meet with Treasury Secretary Douglas Dillon and with the State Department's Llewelyn Thompson, who had served twice as our ambassador to the Soviet Union.

Intervention worked. That marked the beginning of serious American interest in pushing for immigration rights for the Jews. Once the government was involved, it also became much easier to stir the American Jewish community to concern and support. This was a clear case in which American Jewish concern followed the government, rather than the other way around.

Rosenne had met previously with the Soviet ambassador, Anatoly Dobrynin, who claimed that Jews in Russia had long ago assimilated, and sooner or later people would get tired of raising the issue. He offered old lines: Soviet Jews are divided among themselves, some ask for immigration and some for a better Jewish life, there was no anti-Semitism in the Soviet Union. Neither Rosenne, nor Harman, nor President Kennedy bought the Soviet procrastination.

Harman and I talked frequently, and when war was imminent in 1967, he and his deputy chief of mission, Ephraim Evron, came to me with a fear that American arms and supplies that had been promised would not be sent in a timely way because of bureaucratic problems and delays in the Pentagon. Up to this time, our relationship with Israel had been a warm and supportive one, since Israel was an ally. We showered our goodwill and economic aid on the country, but we had been extremely cautious about sending military equipment.

Suddenly Israel was faced with a serious Arab military challenge led by Egypt's Nasser. We Americans realized that it was not in our own interest to permit Israel's security to be at risk. Humphrey was able to cut through layers of bureaucracy that obscured Johnson's vision of what was happening. He was able to get the quick action that was needed to enable the Israelis to win in six days. Harman, Evron, and I went to Humphrey's office immediately, Humphrey went to the president, and virtually by the end of the day, the necessary material was on its way. The Six-Day War was, for me, as for most Americans, a time of pride in Israeli accomplishment and American assistance. It is often forgotten that the distance from the Jordan River to the Mediterranean is forty miles. Before the 1967 war, Israel was only eight miles wide between Haifa and Tel Aviv, vulnerable to being chopped in half. It is hard in a country our size to comprehend what that means in terms of national security.

When Harman left his diplomatic post and became head of the Hebrew University, our friendship grew even closer, as he asked me to join the board and shortly thereafter arranged for me to become head of the American Friends of the Hebrew University. I later served on the university's board of governors at his request. The problems on campus were not so different from the problems at American campuses where I also served in a similar capacity: academic freedom, student unrest, Arab (or minority) students on campus, balancing the budget, improving or developing programmatic areas of concentration.

I joined the board of the American Friends, but before I had a chance to do much, Frank Lautenberg,* who had just been elected president of the group, called to explain that he had to withdraw from his post because compelling needs at the United Jewish Appeal required his volunteer efforts. He consulted with Harman and asked me to assume the presidency.

I began then to visit Israel more frequently—two or three times a

---

* Lautenberg was later elected to the United States Senate from New Jersey.

year—and to meet not only with the board at the Hebrew University, but with the political leadership of the nation. While I remained, in Israeli eyes, the easiest conduit to Humphrey even after I left his office, I increasingly became a counselor on my own. It was a comfortable role. I had no constituency to which to report and no power to abuse, and I never became an advocate for a group or point of view. I was an independent voice saying what I believed to be true without worrying about anything but my own judgment.

My relationship with the Israelis has always been a quiet one. I did not go to the press with stories. I did no lobbying, no organized contact work with congressional leaders. I worked in a confidential manner with every one of the ambassadors here in Washington. All of them afforded me more than thirty years of fruitful involvement with them and thus with Israel.

In 1973, Israel came close to disaster. The Israelis were uncharacteristically complacent before the Yom Kippur War, agreeing to an American request that they not engage in a preemptive strike. Israel could have suffered a catastrophic defeat, and in the first hours it seemed imminent. They asked me to help. President Nixon and Secretary of State Kissinger were committed to help Israel, but there was a critical shortage of military equipment and matériel in the U.S. arsenal. Humphrey also threw himself into the effort, using his close relationship with both Nixon and Kissinger to urge them to ship military aid to Israel from Germany and other parts of Europe even if it meant depleting U.S. resources below a previously decided-upon minimum standard. This was done. Golda was furiously active on the phones and with cables until Israel's military forces began to turn back the tide. U.S. assistance was quick, extensive, and effective.

The war took some of the edge off the Israeli reputation for invincibility. Israel was no longer seen as David in a battle with Goliath, capable of victory with a slingshot. The young nation seemed more vulnerable than ever.

The war was also instructive for me in another important way. I was struck by the intensity of rhetorical support for Israel by some members of Congress, particularly some Jewish members, who then voted against domestic defense budget items with equal intensity. They were hawks in the Middle East, doves back home, or at least an infertile hybrid. The United States had emptied part of its European arsenal to supply Israel. How could a strong supporter of Israel not appreciate that our country's military strength was vital to Israel's security if for no other reason?

It made no sense to Dick Schifter and me, so we organized the Jewish Institute for National Security Affairs (JINSA) after talking one day to Israeli General Aharon Yariv, who had just finished an arduous several days at the Pentagon, where for the first time he ran into something approaching hostility from American officers. He told us that a good bit of the anger derived from the votes of Jewish members of Congress against United States military requests. He was asked, "What are these guys thinking of when they want us to give military aid to Israel and then consistently vote against a strong America?" Our prime purpose for JINSA was to persuade Jewish members of Congress and the Jewish community to support a strong American defense.

The McGovern-led influence in the Democratic party, one that appeared to me to tend toward isolationism and pacifism, with a left tilt, had become increasingly strong during the seventies. I thought it was bad public policy for the United States, bad politics for the Democratic party, and bad for Israel. Many other Democrats agreed with me.

When Jimmy Carter was elected in 1976, Fritz Mondale was in a role much like Humphrey's during the Johnson years. Mondale was a strong supporter of Israel within the Carter administration. His task in some ways was more difficult than Humphrey's was, since Carter and others in the White House were not as consistently understanding or supportive of Israel as Johnson had been.

The historic success of Camp David, with Carter bringing Egyptian President Anwar Sadat and Begin together, was one of the president's great moments. It required avoiding endless pitfalls. While I was not directly involved, Fritz Mondale, during the talks, kept me informed to the extent he could. Israel's ambassador to the United States, Simcha Dinitz, and Meir Rosenne briefed me as well during the meetings, thinking that Mondale could help and that I could reach him. Legal questions also assumed increasing importance.

Egypt had signed treaties with other Arab nations requiring Egypt to join in war against Israel if war were to occur with one of those other countries. How could Israel be assured it was at peace with Egypt when in a moment Egypt might turn into a wartime enemy through the actions of a third party—Jordan, for example—which might declare war and insist that Egypt, with whom it might have a treaty, join in that effort? Israel felt that Egypt had to disavow its automatic involvement in such wars against Israel. That was awkward for the Egyptians, and they resisted. The State Department legal adviser said that an Israeli-Egyptian agreement would automatically eliminate Egypt's other obligations without a specific reference. President Carter was persuaded by State that to put Sadat on the spot, requiring him to repudiate treaties with other nations, was unreasonable and could harm his leadership, and even endanger his life.

Rosenne, Israel's lawyer during the talks, held stubbornly to the view that international law required the renunciation of those treaties if any agreement was to be reached at Camp David and that Israel could not live with Egypt as a friend when in a moment it might turn into a wartime enemy through the actions of a third party. Begin and Moshe Dayan, Israel's defense minister, were impressed by Rosenne's arguments but were being pressed by Carter to ignore them.

When Rosenne came to me, we agreed that he should seek an authoritative independent legal opinion from a widely respected source whose views Carter would consider, if not automatically follow. If the second opinion went against Israel's view, nothing was lost. If a legal case could be made in support of that view, then much might be gained.

I arranged for Rosenne to leave Camp David and go to New Haven to visit with Eugene Rostow, former dean of Yale Law School and a distinguished professor there, and several of his colleagues, including Miles McDougall, a world-respected international law expert. They supported the Rosenne position and rapidly wrote a memorandum explaining their reasoning.

When Rosenne got back to Camp David, memo in hand, Carter, I was told, expressed his strong irritation that Rosenne had second-guessed the State Department and used American lawyers to do so. But Carter was a meticulous man and apparently read the memo carefully. He was persuaded, and his wrath was turned on the State Department lawyer who had written the original opinion. When he did not get a satisfactory response from State, he accepted the Rosenne-Rostow opinion, and Egypt was persuaded to agree to incorporate an appropriate provision in the agreement.

This was not the first time Rosenne and I had worked together on legal questions. During an earlier negotiation with Secretary of State Kissinger, Rosenne, as Israel's lawyer, came to me with a constitutional question. Henry was referring to assurances to be made in the form of a letter from him, and another letter from the president. What assurances could Israel enjoy from such letters? How different were they from executive agreements or treaties? My partner, Richard Schifter, undertook to prepare a thorough memorandum on the question that, Rosenne later said, proved very valuable.

Rosenne and I had another opportunity to work together when I became head of the U.S. delegation to the Conference on Security and Cooperation in Europe (CSCE), meeting in Madrid in November 1980. Israel is a "nonparticipating" member of the CSCE process. In that role Israel had the right to make an opening statement when the Madrid meetings began. Meir Rosenne, who was then Israel's ambassador to France, was designated by his government to make that statement. He and I met in Madrid and discussed his desire to relate at the meeting the plight of Soviet Jews. He informed me that the Soviets had threatened to declare his appearance out of order should he do so. The reported intent to disrupt the meeting troubled me immensely, and I assured Rosenne that the United States would not tolerate such a development and that he should proceed to state what he and his government felt would be appropriate. I then made a point of informing the Spanish authorities that I would not tolerate such a disruption. Rosenne made his speech and there was no disruption.

Soon after Sadat's visit to Jerusalem in November 1977, I received a call from Ashraf Ghorbal, the Egyptian ambassador to the United States. We had met on several occasions and, despite our differences on the Middle East, became reasonably good friends, although we did not see each other often. He knew I was close to Mondale and cultivated my friendship. He asked if I would be willing to meet with Anwar Sadat when he came to Washington. This was after the euphoria of Sadat's trip to Jerusalem had worn off, leading to renewed tension, and not long before the Camp David meetings.

I told Ghorbal I would be delighted to meet with Sadat. He asked if I understood that I would be criticized by many people in the Jewish community if I did. He said he had talked to Philip Klutznick, a far more prestigious and honored member of the Jewish community in the United States than I, and that Klutznick, while agreeing to come, had warned of such criticism. I felt the invitation was an honor, and I accepted it without hesitation.

As it turned out, Klutznick and I were joined by only a couple of others when we met one afternoon at Blair House across the street from the White House. Sadat was impressive, a man of great presence and dignity. He began with an eloquent monologue describing the legacy he found in Egypt when he became its head: Soviet troops, the KGB, and a nation filled with hate for the Jews and for Israel. He spoke passionately about love.

He also spoke with strength about how he got rid of the Soviet advisers and then the Soviet troops, braving the consequences. He told us that the Yom Kippur War had restored national pride to Egypt. He paused, at that point, to tell us that Mossad, the Israeli intelligence service, had saved his life. Mossad agents had discovered a plot to assassinate Sadat and had quickly passed the details to the CIA, which had warned him, permitting him to put down the plot.

With that, he launched into a forceful and beautiful statement about the power of love. What he was trying to do, he said, was replace hate with love in the Middle East. That was no easy task. It was a moving discourse from a religious man. When he finished, there was not a sound. When he asked for questions, no one spoke.

The silence was broken when Ghorbal said, "Max, why don't you start?" I was surprised and unprepared, since I thought Klutznick, an acknowledged Jewish leader, would be called on if anyone was. But I launched on my own much briefer and less eloquent monologue. I told Sadat how impressed I was with his talk of love and that I thought the power of love in both human and political relations was undervalued and too little used.

But, I said, I was puzzled and troubled by a report from Egyptian newspapers in the *New York Times* a few days earlier that said that after Begin's visit with Sadat in Alexandria, Begin was warned by the government-controlled press that he was lucky to escape Egypt with his life. I said, "Mr. President, we all know that would not have been published without your approval and I did not see any love in the statement. I did not see any love for Mr. Begin. You can preach love here, and I believe what you say, but I don't see that you are really practicing love toward Mr. Begin."

Sadat blanched. Then he simply denied that any such story had appeared. In a moment, he regained his composure and his eloquence. He said, "The Israelis know of my love. When I rode through the streets of Jerusalem, the people of Israel knew I loved them and they loved me. I could tell it in their eyes when they held up their children."

I hesitated to challenge Sadat again. But I had decided some years earlier that I never wanted to look back after meetings of this sort with important or powerful Israelis, or Americans, or Russians, or, now, with an Egyptian president, and feel that I had failed to express thoughts important to me when I had the opportunity to do so. So I continued, "That love was real, but it is disappearing because you have essentially threatened the life of a man they elected and whom they also love. That is an act that creates hate." Then I shut up.

I sent the *New York Times* clipping to Ghorbal later in the day, and on two or three occasions after that, Ghorbal brought to my attention evidence of friendship expressed by Sadat. My next meeting with Sadat came after the Camp David agreement was signed and President Carter hosted a dinner on the White House lawn for both Begin and Sadat. That was a real love-fest.

I sat at a table with Henry Kissinger, Zbig Brzezinski; Ezer Weizmann, the Israeli war hero and general; and Lieutenant General Kamal Hassan Ali, the Egyptian minister of defense. The euphoria was universal. The normal restraint and formality of such occasions were fortunately absent. When we were all served steak, the Israelis received kosher ones, well done. Weizmann looked at the steak in front of him, cut into it with obvious concern, and mumbled with resignation, "It's kosher." He then looked up just as General Ali cut into his steak, which was rare.

Weizmann stood up and said, "On this evening of unity between Israel and Egypt, you, my dear general, must eat kosher." With that he took his steak to Ali's place and traded, carting off the rare steak for himself. At that moment, the new bonds were tested and found strong.

Well before the toasts, Ambassador Ghorbal approached, and I stood to greet him. We shook hands, and he invited me to have breakfast the next morning with Sadat at the Egyptian ambassador's residence. I accepted.

The next morning, Sadat was, indeed, filled with love and concern for Begin. He said that he was worried about Begin's health and that the United States and the Jewish community here had to take care of Begin, had to help him politically in Israel. He said that the peace process couldn't have gotten so far without Begin, whom he praised as a great man. There was no implicit reference at all to our earlier Blair House conversation. It was unnecessary.

Sadat then said the United States was making a major mistake by sending our assistant secretary of State, Harold Saunders, to Jordan to further the Camp David process. His advice was to leave King Hussein and Jordan alone. He urged that to build on Camp David we should build with Syria and its president, General Hafiz al Assad. Then Sadat said, "Assad hates me. He hates the fact that I now have my land back. He will in time agree to negotiate to get his land back. Hussein cannot and will not do anything without Assad. We must build with Assad and not irritate him by going to Jordan." I reported our conversation to the State Department and the White House.

I met Sadat only one more time. He was at Georgetown University in the office of Father Tim Healy, the university president. Sadat was there to receive an honorary degree. I was there to greet him. We embraced and spoke warmly, but only briefly. Sadat's assassination soon after set back the peace process, and it also made me mourn the loss of one of the great leaders of our century.

Sadat's on-again, off-again feelings about Begin were no more mercurial than our own relationships with Israel soon after Camp David. At one low point, Fritz Mondale decided to go to Israel in an effort to restore balance and goodwill. He was known to the Israelis as a friend and hoped he could help resolve their differences with Carter. His mission was nearly thrown off balance before he ever left home.

Fritz called me to say that he was not allowed, by U.S. policy, to go to the Old City of Jerusalem because that would offend the Arabs who disputed Israeli control of that portion of the city. The Israelis, on the other hand, would want him to visit because Jerusalem was the capital of Israel and they looked on the city as one entity. I was not that sympathetic to the U.S. position, but I understood the delicacy of going to the Old City with an official of the Israeli government. I suggested that Fritz not be escorted by the foreign minister or his surrogate, but rather by the mayor of Jerusalem, Teddy Kollek, who was elected by all the people, including those living in East Jerusalem.* The solution worked. Cy Vance approved it, Fritz enjoyed it, and no one complained about it. Human relations are an integral part of diplomacy.

In May 1989, shortly after Yitzhak Shamir had made his first visit to the United States to meet President Bush, I was invited to see him while I was in Israel. This was my first trip to Israel in two and a half years. I had then been there on a whirlwind twenty-four-hour visit after the Reykjavik summit to brief Prime Minister Yitzhak Shamir and Foreign Minister Shimon Peres. On that day, in accordance with their agreement to form a coalition government, they had switched jobs. I also met with Defense Minister Yitzhak Rabin and President Chaim Herzog. The subject was the Iceland summit from which I had just come. As we began to talk, I sensed that something was amiss. I later learned that Shamir's pride had been hurt during his visit to our country. President Bush had taken President Hosni Mubarak of Egypt to a

---

* When Golda Meir died, I was part of the official delegation sent by President Carter. The rest of the delegation included the president's mother as its head, Henry Kissinger, and Senator Abraham Ribicoff. Henry told me en route that he had never visited the Old City. I thought it was an experience well worth having and arranged for Kollek to take us on a walking tour. He introduced us to Arab leaders, stopped to chat with the Arab shopkeepers, pointed out historic sites. Though Ribicoff and I had been there before, we were all quite taken with the visit and with the respect shown Teddy by Jews and Arabs alike.

baseball game some time before the Shamir visit, but no equivalent event had been put on Shamir's schedule. Israel's advance team proposed something comparable, which was first rejected, before a routine event, clearly not similar in spirit, was agreed upon. Shamir was hurt by what he considered an affront to his dignity. Bruised feelings are sometimes a part of realpolitik.*

But for all the complications on all sides and all levels, the problems of the Middle East are sufficiently central to international stability that they must be faced. The skeptic will optimistically declare that they will undoubtedly be settled—one year after the problems of Northern Ireland are settled! The Middle East strains, however, are much more flammable. The formidable barrier to the peace process, I believe, is the refusal of the Arab states, except for Egypt, to recognize the legitimacy of Israel. Israel, with its national life at stake, cannot operate on naive trust when all the evidence clearly warns: "Be careful." Israel's insecurity today must be appreciated, and that is frequently lost in reporting and commentary on Middle East conflict, and sometimes even in national policy. The Arab nations that surround Israel have vast arsenals of missiles and chemical weapons that could kill large numbers of Israelis. No Israeli government can ignore that reality.

A double standard is at work. Israel is judged on standards that are uniquely applied to her. That may be understandable, since we demand of our friends, who share our values, far more than we do of those who have been enemies or are uneasy associates. When China kills hundreds or even thousands of its own citizens, we express disappointment, but not too harshly, and there are no UN resolutions. India killed seventy persons in the recent Kashmir riots and there were no editorials, protests, or UN resolutions. We tolerate abuses in other countries and save our outrage for Israeli actions in their efforts to hold down rioting and terrorism. American television has an insatiable appetite for confrontation between Israeli soldiers with guns and Arab children with rocks.

The Palestine Liberation Organization (PLO) turns several faces

* Sensitive egos do not reside only in Israel. Henry Kissinger, a man I admire for his many talents, once apparently wanted to discuss the Middle East with me. My secretary came in one morning and said, "I didn't know you had asked to see the secretary of State." I said, "I didn't." She said, "Well, I received a call from his office saying that in response to your request, the secretary could see you at nine A.M. tomorrow." I shrugged and said, "For some reason he wants to see me." Neither of us raised the question the next morning of how the meeting was arranged, but it was clear who had an agenda and who was running the meeting.

to the world—smiling, kindly, wronged, falsely accused; but it really offers only one to Israel: a face of hate. Its charter calls unequivocally for the devastation and destruction of Israel. There appears to be no ambiguity in what they want. The map of the Palestinian state on their letterhead is the whole state of Israel, not a part of it. To expect the Israelis to ignore the PLO's stated intent is beyond reason, and no responsible Israeli leader, of whatever persuasion, can ignore that reality.

Henry Kissinger once told the story of the biblical zoo where the lamb and the lion appear side by side. When asked how he manages that extraordinary event, the zoo keeper says, "It is simple. We keep a supply of lambs on hand."

Arab speakers frequently explain to each other that their "peace offensive" is part of their "phased plan" to achieve the destruction of Israel. Saudi Arabia's King Fahd once urged Iran to stop fighting Iraq so that the two nations could join in the fight against Israel to liberate Jerusalem. The problem is most aptly put by a commentator who said, "The Arabs have never missed a chance to lose an opportunity for peace with Israel." In the meantime, the Palestinians remain pawns and victims. When Jordan controlled the West Bank before 1976, they made no move toward a Palestine state or autonomy. Sparsely populated neighboring Arab states made no move to resettle refugees out of their miserable camps. The refugees were not wanted and are still not wanted by their fellow Arabs.

The alternative to the violence and frustration is talk and mediation. Israel should be talking to Palestinians, and that may very well mean talking to the people that the PLO wants them to talk to. That is not politically easy, but it is probably necessary. Israel must also talk to non-PLO Palestinians, and PLO violence against those Palestinians must be considered hostile acts against the peace process itself. Similarly, the United States and the observing world must appreciate that talks between Palestinian Jews in Israel and Palestinian Arabs on the West Bank must be accompanied by simultaneous talks between Israel and its Arab neighbors who now consider themselves at war with Israel.

When I became counselor of the Department of State in January 1987, my assigned horizons broadened and, on occasion, included the Middle East. The secretary and his confidential aide, Charles Hill, kept their plans and ideas close to their vests, although they also depended on Richard Murphy, the assistant secretary of State for the region. Shultz occasionally tested an idea or observation with me. We shared a commitment and deep friendship for Israel, but he was persuaded that time was not on Israel's side, given the low Jewish and high Arab birth rates. He had no illusions about the PLO, but felt restricted by a thirteen-year-old Kissinger commitment to Israel that the United States would not deal with the PLO unless it recognized Israel's right to exist, accepted UN Security Council Resolutions 242 and 338 as a basis for peace, and renounced terrorism. Shultz believed the United States should have the flexibility to talk at will with anyone if we are to play a constructive role. On the other hand, it was essential to maintain our integrity by respecting commitments made by a former secretary of State while in office.

The Swedish government began telling us in late 1988 that PLO leader Yasir Arafat was ready to satisfy American requirements after winning a power struggle within his own organization. Would we respond? That depends on what is said, Shultz answered. It was like pulling teeth. Maggie and I were vacationing in Florida. Mike Armacost, undersecretary of State, telephoned. The secretary wanted me to return. I did. We looked at Arafat's words of December 7 and 13. They were inadequate. Murphy explained that to the Swedes. Finally, the necessary words came on December 14. The combination of "I repeat for the record that we totally and absolutely renounce all forms of terrorism," plus "on the basis of United Nations Security Council Resolutions 242 and 338," plus "respect for the right to exist in peace and security for all" after referring to "the parties concerned in the Arab-Israeli conflict," made more specific to include Israel—all those did it. I urged delay in the U.S. public pronouncements so that Israeli officials and interested congressmen could be fully informed, but the president made the decision, and the White House did not want a leak.

We all knew that the 1968 PLO charter called for the complete destruction of Israel and had not been renounced. We knew Arafat had raised double-talk to an art form. Just a few weeks earlier, his deputy, Abu Iyad, had reconfirmed the PLO 1974 "phased program" strategy aimed at destroying Israel in phased stages. Skepticism was called for. After all, from Israel's point of view, if you believe the PLO is out to destroy you, you have every reason to believe they would lie to you. George Shultz, however, saw an opportunity for a break in the impasse and a break within the PLO. I agreed it was worth a shot, although I was not a bit surprised when Secretary of State Baker recently felt it necessary to call off the direct talks with the PLO. Arafat's total identification with Iraq's Saddam Hussein in the war with the United States and our coalition partners adds a major complexity to the Mideast peace process, but does not alter the need to seek stability and security in that area.

I have tried often to explain to the Israelis that American politicians who see themselves as friends of Israel come in two forms. One, represented by Truman, Humphrey, Henry Jackson, Ronald Reagan, and George Shultz have a commitment to Israel in their hearts. The other, equally friendly, find their commitment to be one of the head. The distinction was described to me by a White House friend comparing Presidents Reagan and Bush. If Israel behaves in a manner that may warrant American criticism, Reagan might be inclined to say, "There must be a reason why Israel has behaved this way. It's awful. Let's find out why they did it before we criticize." Bush, he said, is more likely to accept the report and regrettably proceed to criticize. Since I have never spoken to President Bush about Israel, I do not know if this is a fair characterization of his view, but I believe the two approaches do exist. Both approaches are likely to agree 90 percent of the time. Both groups correctly look upon themselves as friends. One Israeli who heard me give this explanation responded: "What are friends for? We don't depend on friends when we're right. It's when we're wrong that people need a friend!"*

Democracy and peace will come to the Middle East because there is no way for that region to escape for long the movement toward democracy and human dignity that is gripping all parts of the world. Change is inevitable.

The democracy movement that overwhelmed Eastern Europe so quickly will in time have its impact on Syria, Libya, Iraq, and Saudi Arabia as much as it has had its impact on Paraguay and Poland. The American people understand that Israel today is the only democracy in the region. This accounts in no small measure for the deep friendship toward Israel felt by the vast majority of our fellow citizens. This commitment, however, is under siege as Israel appears—sometimes unwittingly, sometimes regrettably contributing to that appearance— unsympathetic toward the human and political aspirations of its Palestinian Arab neighbors.

There are risks in elections just as there are risks in negotiations,

---

* Cultural differences and misunderstandings cannot be ignored in international relations. The perceptions of space are also a reality. The story is told of a Texan visiting an Israeli farm for the first time. Responding to the proud Israeli's description of his acreage in what must have seemed to the Texan as little more than an overgrown vegetable garden, the Texan said: "Let me tell you something about my farm in Texas. If I start out early in the morning in my Ford pickup truck and just travel along the four boundary lines, east to west and north to south, it would take me a full day to make the trip and it would be dark before I got back to my farmhouse." The Israeli listened sympathetically and attentively, thought a moment, and then said: "Yes, I know how it is. I had a pickup truck like that once too! It always broke down."

but there is strength and virtue in the process as well. Israel must not lose its identification with the Jewish values of universal human brotherhood, political democracy, and commitment to human dignity for all. That is not easy to do in the present geopolitical context, and it is not without risk.

It may, I hope, be easier to accomplish when the Soviet Union restores its ties with Israel. That process seems to be under way. Their respective government officials are talking to each other. There is a diplomatic presence in each country. Citizen exchanges and visits of all kinds are taking place. The Soviet Jewish immigration flow is increasing.

Israel's medical assistance to Soviet victims of the tragic Armenian earthquake of December 1988 also made a positive impression in the Soviet Union. In early 1989, Burton Joseph of Minneapolis called me to say that the Jewish Joint Distribution Committee (JDC) was having difficulty with Soviet officials about a humanitarian earthquake relief project they were prepared to begin. Could I help? I talked to Aryeh Cooperstock, JDC director, who explained that Israel's unfortunate history had made it medically well equipped and expert in burns and lost limbs. They wanted to organize an airlift of victims from Yerevan to Tel Aviv so that victims of the earthquake could receive treatment and prostheses at no cost to them. They were stymied by the lack of response from Soviet authorities. I communicated directly with Soviet ambassador to the United States, Yuri Dubinin, and also with people I knew in the Soviet Foreign Ministry. I explained the fine humanitarian record of the JDC. On May 19, a letter of Soviet approval was sent, which included the sentiment that they were "deeply touched by the overwhelming humanitarian response of the Jewish community . . . On behalf of our government and our people please extend heartfelt appreciation . . . to the government and people of Israel." Negotiations began also for the construction of a children's rehabilitation center in Armenia. The airlift began on June 27 with a direct El Al airline flight, the first time that an El Al plane had landed in the Soviet Union.

It is regrettable that the United Nations cannot play a constructive role in the resolution of Israel's problems with its neighbors. When the Soviet Union in 1975 introduced and then—with the help of the Arab and most of the third-world states in the UN—passed the "Zionism is racism" resolution, it automatically disqualified itself from the peace process in the area. Until that resolution is repealed or replaced, Israel cannot look on the UN as a qualified unbiased peacemaker.

This puts the burden on the United States. Democratic and Republican presidents have desperately tried to advance the peace process through conciliation and negotiation. This is understandable and correct, but very difficult. My own belief is that the effort requires persistence, patience, and presidential prestige. Kissinger and Carter produced direct results in the form of agreements, but it is too much to expect a president or secretary of State to lay aside other vital concerns of state to concentrate for an appreciable amount of time on the Middle East alone. It requires the full-time dedication of a senior respected and skilled negotiator who is perceived as close to the president and secretary of State. I have long felt that Henry Kissinger should have been drafted to undertake the assignment. For the United States to fulfill its leadership responsibilities conscientiously, it must raise its sights above the emotional drama that permeates the Jewish-Arab conflict and stands in the way of solution.

President Carter, after being incorrectly advised that the communities being established by Jewish settlers in the West Bank were illegal under international law, became terribly exercised over them. President Reagan corrected that error. The settlements may in the end be wise or unwise; necessary for Israel's military security or not. They may be obstacles to peace given the emotions they engender, although the Jewish settlements did not at all prove to be a serious obstacle to the successful negotiation between Israel and Egypt. But they are not illegal. To say they are is to poison the negotiating atmosphere.

The international law doctrine that governs Gaza and the West Bank is UN Security Council Resolution 242, adopted at the end of the 1967 Six-Day War, which was fomented by Egypt against Israel. That resolution was reaffirmed in UN Security Council Resolution 338, passed after the 1973 Arab attack against Israel that started the Yom Kippur War. Israeli troops moved into the areas after defeating the Jordanian attack against it, an attack that Israel and the United States urged Jordan to keep away from. The land in question was not Jordanian or Arab in any way. The last sovereignty over the area was exercised by the Ottoman Empire before World War I. It became a mandated territory under the League of Nations and its successor United Nations. While Great Britain served as trustee under the League, the land, which included the area now known as Jordan, was promised as a Jewish national homeland. After Arab protests, the British carved out the area east of the Jordan River, 80 percent of the total, and gave it to the Palestinian Arabs, calling the country Jordan. Jews considered that the remaining area, 20 percent of the total, would be part of their state.

In 1948, when the United Nations was prepared to declare and recognize a Jewish state, the Arabs refused to accept that reality and began a war against Israel, determined to destroy it, in spite of the fact that the land occupied by the Jews was further reduced in area. When a truce was declared, an armistice line was drawn that was considered a temporary border pending negotiations.

All this was understood when the UN enacted Resolutions 242 and 338 as the governing international law for the area. There was a recognition that the Israeli presence in the West Bank followed a defensive war, and there was absolutely no condemnation of that presence and no demand for withdrawal. There was an assumption that just as a permanent boundary line for Israel required negotiation following the 1949 armistice, so negotiation was still required to fix a permanent boundary after the 1967 war.

UN Resolution 242 asserted Israel's right to "live in peace within secure and recognized boundaries free from threats or acts of force" as a fundamental basis for negotiation designed to bring peace to the area. The Arabs and the Soviets attempted to include in the resolution a provision that Israel had to withdraw from "all the" territories to "secure and recognized borders" as part of the negotiation process. The words *all* and *the* were omitted. The timing and extent of any such withdrawal was to depend on the negotiation. Thus the slogan "territory for peace" is not mentioned in 242 and is not a principle or requirement of that resolution. It is an option that might or might not result from the negotiation. Israel has, of course, already withdrawn from about 90 percent of the territory when it withdrew from Sinai after successful negotiations with Egypt. Whether it withdraws from any more or all or none of the remaining area depends on further negotiations on the question and on assurances Israel does or does not receive that it can live in peace within secure and recognized boundaries free from threats of force.

We have here a complex problem surrounded by historical contradictions, legal ambiguities, and political aspirations all of which are intensified by deep emotional experiences and convictions. I suggest that the primary task for the United States is not to try to impose hasty solutions. It is rather to encourage small confidence-building steps between representatives of all the parties who are prepared to enter a relationship in which compromises are possible. Our task is to discourage violence and, indeed, to attempt to prohibit it. It is to be patient and persistent in the pursuit of that process.

The need to build confidence is clear. This should be the main thrust of a constructive American policy in the area. It is the surest way to establish a foundation for agreement. Shortcuts will not work. Indignation and anger will not succeed. Creative and imaginative leadership is what is now required on the part of our country, the strongest and most respected in the world.

The list of potentially valuable confidence-building measures is a long one. The Middle East in its entirety must be persuaded to appreciate that each of the countries and peoples in the area have a great deal to gain from economic and scientific cooperation. Disease must be conquered, food must be produced, water must be supplied and distributed, trade must be encouraged. Furthermore, we and the Soviet Union, together with the other three permanent members of the Security Council and other suppliers of arms, must cooperate by agreeing not to supply destabilizing arms and equipment to the area for at least eighteen to twenty months while we encourage an arms limitation agreement for the Middle East.

The attainment of these goals and of the fruits of modern technology requires cooperation among all who reside in the area. The task of the United States as the respected world leader and exemplar is to help establish a community of interest in the region. Within that broader context, it is time that the Arab Palestinians, who continue to face discrimination in the Arab world they inhabit, join forces with the Jewish Palestinians in a joint effort to make the entire region a land of milk and honey. No two peoples in the region are more energetic and creative.

It is not in Israel's best interest to sit back and wait. It is a mistake always to assume that time is on your side. Time is neutral and sometimes works against you. To stall for time is too often an excuse for inaction in the face of difficulty. Moshe Dayan, the legendary Israeli military and political leader, once urged that, in the absence of an opportunity for constructive dialogue between Palestinian Jews and Palestinian Arabs living on the West Bank, Israel should exercise its power and responsibility as the legal governing power by unilaterally designating as autonomous and demilitarized a specific portion of the area where the Arab populations are concentrated, since Israel's military security needs will not thereby be threatened. Israel would then withdraw its police and military from the autonomous area and say, "Govern yourselves. We are prepared to negotiate political and economic relationships with you, but only when and if you are ready." In the meantime, Israel would use its troops to protect its security interests outside that autonomous region. There would be no confrontational incidents between Israeli forces and Arab civilians in the area.

In the meantime, Jews in the United States must maintain the commitment that has kept Israel alive for more than forty years. That takes organization and political power. Power is not anathema to a democracy. Power is not evil. Power is the ability to make or influence decisions and, as an essential part of the decision-making process, is crucial, as James Madison understood in *The Federalist Papers*, to the proper functioning of a democratic society.

My own role in the American Jewish community has been a varying one. I made modest financial contributions to large numbers of American Jewish organizations and, at different times, have held office with the Anti-Defamation League, the American Jewish Committee, and the Jewish Institute for National Security Affairs. More of my time was spent working with American organizations supporting Israel's colleges and universities, particularly the American Friends of the Hebrew University of Jerusalem, where I served as both president and chairman of the board. I have avoided Jewish organizational politics in this country as well as involvement in Israel's internal political turmoils.

During this period, I developed an important relationship with the Lubavich Hasidic group. It began soon after I left the Senate, when I received a telephone call from Bernard Lander, president of Touro College. He said that he had met with my friends, Billie and Larry Tisch, who were interested in meeting the Lubavitcher Rebbe and knew that I shared the same interest. He had set up an appointment for the following Saturday evening in Brooklyn at 11:30 P.M. and invited me to join them. It was there that I met Rabbi Abraham Shemtov of Philadelphia, who impressed me by noting the names of people I knew in Philadelphia. He had done his homework. The meeting with the Rebbe, a graduate of the Sorbonne, was impressive and stimulating, although I have never particularly appreciated the Lubavitch attachment to the nineteenth-century evidenced by their traditional clothing, a sort of uniform. I also strenuously disagreed with the position they had taken in attempting to influence the Israeli government on the "Who is a Jew?" issue, which tended to make nonorthodox Jews second-class citizens. I nevertheless tried to be helpful where I could, and on issues I felt comfortable with. Our relationship continues over these years, and I cherish my friendship with Rabbi Shemtov and my respect for the Rebbe.

When I decided, before the 1988 election, that I would retire from government service as of January 20, 1989, with the change of administrations, no matter who won the election, I knew that among my private activities, I would want one active Israeli involvement. As the time approached, Mayor Teddy Kollek of Jerusalem, who had met George Schultz at a private dinner at my home, informed me that he would like to visit with the secretary of state again and then come to my nearby office for a conversation. When he did, he urged me, upon retirement, to assume the chairmanship of the Jerusalem Foundation in the United States. My enthusiasm for his work in Jerusalem was unquestioned, but I had always found fund-raising distasteful. Former chairpersons Martin Peretz, James Wolfensohn, and Martin Lipton followed through with urgings of their own: The foundation was indispensable to Jerusalem's ability to meet the needs of its citizens, Jews, Arabs, and Christians alike; the city had no tax base to speak of; there was a professional staff to raise funds.

Accepting the responsibility fortuitously exposed me to an extraordinary experience. In May 1991 I joined an impressive group of people from many different countries who met in Jerusalem to celebrate Teddy Kollek's eightieth birthday. When I arrived at the airport, I was enthusiastically greeted with the news that 14,500 Falashas, "black Jews of Ethopia," had arrived in Israel that day in a major airlift, joining 23,000 others who had migrated earlier. There was excitement in the streets as bitter partisan divisions were set aside. Israel was again fulfilling its role as a haven for persecuted Jews. The airlift had been a dramatic feat for Israel's air force following intensive negotiations, aided by President Bush, with both government and rebel leaders in Ethiopia. Israel and Israelis were aglow with excitement and pleasure.

It reminded me of an earlier visit to Jerusalem in early 1976. A French airplane, with a large number of Israeli passengers who had been kidnapped and taken by Idi Amin of Uganda, was still being held hostage. I will never forget being awakened in the early morning hours of July 4 by the telephone operator of the King David Hotel, who shouted into the telephone as she woke me, "Our boys went into Entebbe and are taking our people back home." She had awakened every single guest in the hotel with the news.

The Falashas were being temporarily housed in hotels, community centers, and wherever, so that they could be bathed, medically examined, fed, interviewed, reassured. I asked if I could personally observe and talk to some of them. It was arranged. At the entrance to the hotel I visited, there were mountains of clothing and toys brought by Israelis. We were surrounded by family reunions as those dignified, well-postured men, women, and children began their first full day as citizens of Israel. I joined in the tears and the emotion that gripped all Israelis that weekend.

My friend, Ken Adelman, columnist and former ACDA head, had

been an African expert in his younger days. In 1974 he and his wife Carol journeyed to northern Ethiopia to learn more about the Falashas, (the word for "stranger" in Amharic). He wrote that for more than 1,000 years these people believed they were the only Jews left in the world. They had never heard of Chanukah, never had a bar mitzvah, never heard of the Talmud, never seen the Star of David. They practiced a pre-Talmudic form of Judaism, including crude animal sacrifice. They observed Yom Kippur, the Sabbath, Passover.

Their own tradition, according to Adelman, told them that their ancestors fled the Holy Land with Jeremiah, who left Jerusalem after the temple was destroyed in 587 B.C. A number of Ethopian historians believe they descended from Menelik I, son of King Solomon and the queen of Sheba. Others contended that the Falashas wandered south from Egypt when Moses led the Jews eastward out of Egypt. They might well have been an indigenous people who were converted by some Jewish travelers many centuries ago. The whole story is filled with mystery and anticipation. How, indeed, is it that their dietary laws are somewhat similar to modern kosher rules?

What is not a mystery is that these people who lived in mud huts for centuries and continued some rather barbaric practices had been eager to move to Israel. The culture shock for them will be great, as they enter the mainstream of modern Jewish life and realize the ancient dream of being reunited with the Jewish people. But Israel will be the stronger and richer for it.

There is occasional reference to the Jewish lobby and Jewish power. In fact, there are several Jewish lobbies. They frequently differ among themselves and about Israel. For many years, some Jewish organizations fought not for distinctively Jewish causes, but for broad civil rights issues and causes. It was only after black leadership became radicalized and separatist, seeking disassociation from whites, that this emphasis deescalated. It is ready to be energized again.

For American Jews, however, as strong as the commitment to Israel may be, it is not our primary impetus to political involvement. It is true that Jews vote in a higher percentage, particularly in political party primaries, than other religious or ethnic groups. It is true that political leadership has a disproportionately large share of Jews compared to population. But that stems from the same source of loyalty to country that was demonstrated by those twenty-three immigrants from Brazil looking to enlist in the colonial militia in 1654. America was home and haven, and deserved full commitment and devotion.

Jewish involvement grows from the commitment of people like

my parents' generation, who saw education and social justice as part of their religious and political heritage. That's why my father helped Ed Flynn in the Bronx and received his badge. Helping make democracy work was and is a noble calling, a moral imperative of the highest order.

For my own generation, the United States has been home and democracy the nourishment that has permitted us to flower in the fullest. Our obligation is to make sure that our children can share in the glory of this society for decades ahead, and our grandchildren beyond that. It is our obligation to make certain that all the children of this land share its blessings. There is no room in our scale of values for poverty, illiteracy, bigotry, and uncared-for ill health. This is our commitment not only because we are Jews, but also because we are Americans.

12

Mr. Ambassador

When World War II ended, the Soviets quickly moved from wartime ally to postwar adversary, threatening and angry and difficult. In recent months, scholars from both the United States and the USSR have been reviewing the causes of the cold war that followed. Whether contributed to by the United States or not, certainly Stalin's personal paranoia and ambition enveloped his nation and became official policy, emphasizing Soviet expansionist views and a more pronounced police state. The Soviets made a significant investment of their resources in Eastern Europe, Africa, and Asia, as well as in Latin America.

It became clear, in that atmosphere, that a major Soviet foreign policy goal was to separate the United States from its European allies and to legitimize, in any way possible, the Soviet Union's expanded domain. In pursuit of that policy, the Soviets in 1954 proposed a European security conference. Their appeal said, in effect, "We Europeans have security problems that are unique and special to those of us who live here. Let's meet together to discuss them."

Neither we nor, more importantly, our Western European allies found the idea acceptable, since the whole fabric of European security was based on the North Atlantic Treaty Organization (NATO), which in turn was based on the active participation of the United States in the defense of Europe. Our power and concern were both vital to Europe's survival and reconstruction, and all our allies knew it. They were unwavering in their response to the Soviets—no United States, no conference.

We were not in favor of a conference at all—with or without us—if its prime, almost exclusive, concern was to confirm the new Soviet borders, which had been established by conquest, not agreement. The Soviet proposal was not picked up during the fifties and sixties. But with President Nixon's ardent pursuit of detente, it became increasingly difficult for the United States to oppose a European security conference. We muted our objections, and our allies finally agreed to consider the Russian proposal with several stipulations: that the United States and Canada be included, that conventional force levels in Europe be discussed in separate talks, and that a variety of humanitarian concerns be included in defining European security. The Soviets and their Warsaw Pact allies accepted all of that, essentially motivated by their own interest in pursuing their version of detente.

Thus, by 1973, thirty-three European nations (only Albania refused to join in), plus the United States and Canada began serious negotiations in Helsinki on an overall formula for East-West relations. The negotiations were later moved to Geneva, where agreement was reached in 1975. The rules for the conference required unanimity for any statement to be adopted. The only security issue to gain that level of support was a limited "confidence-building measures" (CBM) provision that called for twenty-one-day notice of military maneuvers to diminish the element of surprise. If the possibility of surprise attack was reduced, the chance of unnecessary and uncalled-for armed "response" would also be reduced.

The CBM agreement was a symbolic good beginning, but very limited. The agreement, at Soviet insistence, only involved the *first* seventy-five miles inside the Soviet border. The Soviets had almost endless territory beyond that where they could hide preparations and from which they could still launch a surprise attack. In effect, the mileage limitation essentially exempted the Soviets from the intended impact of the agreement.

That and other agreements were adopted as part of a package that was to be called, at the suggestion of some anonymous State Department officer, the Helsinki Final Act, although no one knew what that meant. It was not a legally binding treaty or executive agreement. It was not an act or a statute and was certainly not a final act, there being no such thing under international law, although the Congress of Vienna in 1815 ended with a "Final Act." The United States and others didn't want it elevated to the status of a treaty. It stood by itself as a unique international agreement, presumably without teeth.

Despite that, it was seen by many as a step toward a more peaceful world. The agreement was divided into three areas, called, for some reason, "baskets." The substance of Basket I came from the United Nations Charter and defined the principles of behavior between the signatories. It called for peaceful settlement of disputes, respect for territorial integrity, and nonintervention in the internal affairs of other countries.

Also in Basket I, signatories were called upon to respect human rights, including freedom of thought, conscience, religion, and belief. The West, in effect, had said that we didn't believe that a country that declares war on its own people can be trusted to maintain peace with its neighbors. Ultimately, human rights became a most vital ingredient of the continuing discussions, not just because of the United States, but through the commitment and interest of European countries that shared our values.

Basket II called for cooperation on economic, scientific, and technical questions; and Basket III talked of reducing travel restrictions, allowing family reunification, and encouraging cultural, information, and educational exchanges.

The Helsinki Final Act was important enough to have heads of state, including General Secretary Brezhnev and President Ford, sign it in 1975. It was a moving and symbolic ceremony, although many people, including me, wondered at the time if there was any substance or power behind the elegant thoughts and fine words. My doubts were serious.

When the Soviet press praised the agreement unabashedly as a significant victory, the suspicions of the "ethnics" in our country, many of whom had been driven from their native countries by Communist governments, were particularly intense, since they had heard words of emancipation for years without action to accompany them. The act, for all its fine phrases about family reunification and human rights, left them uneasy and wary since they had suffered separation, had seen their own families' rights abused and their native lands dominated by Soviet puppets, and then had endured a generation of raised expectations and failed hopes.

Some critics said the agreement was merely a Soviet ploy to legitimize the borders set in Europe after the war. That was not quite accurate. While there had never been a formal peace treaty signed, by

1975 the borders had been agreed to by the four powers.* What the Helsinki Final Act seemed to do was to protect those borders from any effort to change them by force, thus giving the Soviet position an additional bit of legitimacy. On the other hand, since only sovereign nations could sign the agreement, Helsinki also established the important fact that these were independent nations, not Soviet fiefdoms. It is interesting to note, as I write these words, that the Helsinki process now serves to reassure and provide a sense of stability to Europe in the face of concerns about the reunification of Germany on the part of its neighbors.

The irony of the agreement is that the Soviets accepted the human rights affirmations, probably never believing they could be used effectively in an attack on their totalitarian systems. As it has turned out, they could not have been more wrong.

This was a Final Act that was in its creation not final at all. Detente was considered a process, and the Final Act, as part of detente, not only implied continuing review, but called for follow-up meetings to check on compliance and examine the next steps to be taken in the process. The first follow-up meeting took place in Belgrade in 1977, and one was scheduled to begin in 1980 in Madrid. Arthur Goldberg was the U.S. representative to the Belgrade meeting.

All of that was only dimly in my mind when Fritz Mondale called on a Friday morning in December 1979 to say he wanted to see me. When I told him I would be available anytime the following week, he asked with a certain urgency in his tone if I could come over to his office that morning. I did so without asking why, since we had begun to meet from time to time and to talk about a variety of subjects after he became vice president.

I walked the mile from my office, which was then in the Watergate Building near the Kennedy Center, past the State Department, the Federal Reserve Building, the Department of Interior, and other gov-

---

* I was skeptical of Yalta in 1945 when it took place. As it turned out, it de facto resulted in tens of millions of people becoming subjugated to Soviet power. While the Yalta Agreement provided for free elections in Poland and other nations in Eastern Europe, the elections did not take place, and we accepted the consequences of Soviet force. The Soviets believed, or pretended to believe, that their control over the area was in effect legitimized by the Yalta Agreements, and by our acquiescence when elections did not occur. In Madrid, where my involvement with the Helsinki Agreement began in 1980, I used the Yalta document to keep pressure on the Soviets by accusing them of violating the agreement in not permitting elections in Eastern Europe to take place. I argued in Madrid, supported by Secretary of State Shultz's final address to the conference, that a Europe divided into East and West was contrary to Yalta and to the Helsinki Final Act.

ernment buildings to the White House, enjoying the crisp winter air, thinking not so much about Mondale's call as about how beautiful a city Washington is and how fortunate I had been in coming to it at Humphrey's invitation. Walking casually to the White House for a meeting whose subject matter I did not know, but which seemed important to the vice president, was not something I would have imagined when I first came to Washington as a student forty years before. Certainly, the thought of any significant White House role had diminished with Humphrey's defeat in 1968 and had died with him in 1978.

I was cleared at the guard station by the iron fence surrounding the White House grounds and walked to the west wing reception room, where I waited for my escort. When we settled down in the vice president's office just down the hall and around the corner from the Oval Office,* Fritz explained that every Friday morning there was a foreign policy breakfast with President Carter, attended by him, Secretary of State Cyrus Vance, National Security Adviser Zbigniew Brzezinski, and White House Chief of Staff Hamilton Jordan. Fritz, without saying who, told me that one of the participants that morning had recommended to the President that I be asked to head up the American delegation to the "Madrid meeting." He had not been the one to make the recommendation, he said, but everyone in the meeting, including the president, liked the idea.

For some moments, I didn't know precisely what meeting he was talking about. I had long before come to understand that I learned more by listening than by talking, so I simply listened as he talked on. Soon it all fell into place and I thought, "That's the meeting Arthur Goldberg ran in Belgrade," the Conference on Security and Cooperation in Europe (CSCE) under the Helsinki Final Act.

I had inadvertently been involved in Arthur's being offered that job. Late in 1977, Hubert Humphrey called me to say that he was concerned about the gyrations in our relations with Israel and the resulting friction between the two countries. He felt that President Carter needed to hear more about the history of United Nations resolutions on the Middle East, needed to understand the Israeli government and personalities better. He said that he had recommended that Carter invite Goldberg in to describe what he knew. Humphrey wanted my judgment on his suggestion, unsure whether Arthur and Carter would

---

* Vice presidents before Mondale, including Humphrey, did not have their offices so close to the president. Their offices were connected by a roadway to the White House in the Old Executive Office Building. The short physical distance made for great psychological and political separation. Proximity has its value.

get along. I thought it was precisely right, that no one knew more than Arthur about the subject, so I told Humphrey that I agreed with him. He said, "Arthur will talk a lot, but if Carter listens, he will learn a lot. Will you call Arthur and alert him?"

I did, and he was immensely pleased by Humphrey's suggestion to the president. When the president called, Arthur went in to see him, and the two of them talked about the Middle East without anyone else present. The president was obviously impressed with Arthur's detailed knowledge and asked him on the spot to become his Middle East negotiator. Arthur was delighted. He was happiest in public service, and the challenge of resolving Middle East problems was an exciting and historic prospect.

After the meeting, Vance and Brzezinski learned of the offer and apparently blew their diplomatic gaskets, fearing the appointment would conflict with their own ideas (which differed from each other) in seeking solutions. Warren Christopher, a highly efficient and broadly competent lawyer who was deputy secretary of State, came up with a logical face-saving compromise: find Goldberg a different, but equally prestigious, job. They did.

The president decided that the Helsinki review that was about to begin in Belgrade was just right. The problem was that the State Department had already selected and informed a career foreign service officer, Bud Scherer, that he would lead the delegation. His name had been sent to the Senate for confirmation. Scherer had also traveled throughout Europe, setting forth what the U.S. position would be at the follow-up meeting, based on what the State Department had decided, which placed much less emphasis on human rights than Carter apparently wanted.

The situation was chaotic. Scherer was on the verge of quitting. Finally, someone must have appealed to his professionalism and convinced him to swallow his pride and his public embarrassment, and to become Arthur's deputy. It is not the sort of thing that makes a career foreign service officer, or his colleagues, happy.

Beyond that, our allies felt confused. They wondered why Scherer had been replaced. They weren't sure what we expected from Belgrade, what our emphasis would be, how firmly we were committed to any particular process.

Arthur ultimately did not feel very much better than Scherer, believing that the State Department frequently undermined him, even though he was certain he was doing exactly what the president wanted done. In short, Belgrade certainly never jelled into a very productive meeting, although historians may well say that the shift of emphasis from detente to human rights began in Belgrade.

As Fritz talked, I remembered what skepticism the process of the Goldberg selection had raised in my mind about the Carter White House style and the depth of their interest in the Helsinki Final Act, but I verbalized none of those doubts to Fritz.

When he described the special importance the talks had for Jimmy Carter, I believed him. Clearly, human rights had become a major part of our international agenda at Carter's insistence. My reservations about taking an overseas diplomatic assignment were largely overcome by my sense that I could publicly make a difference and avoid some of the problems in Belgrade. Fritz said he and Vance knew from earlier conversations that I would not leave my law practice and felt the job would involve only several months and would not be full-time. I told him I would be interested on that basis.*

Then, with a friendly grin of the fisherman he was, knowing I was hooked, he said, "Max, there is a catch. Cy Vance has already offered the job to Bill Scranton, former Republican governor of Pennsylvania, but hasn't heard from him." It was Goldberg revisited. I asked when the offer had been made, and Fritz, this time with eyebrows raised and no grin, said, "In October, two months ago."

It was my turn to smile. I said, "Fritz, I did not have the job when I came over this morning, and I don't have it now. If Scranton says yes, I would be delighted to step aside as though nothing had ever been offered. If he says no, I would be pleased to do it." Fritz thanked me for my understanding and asked me not to talk about the job with anyone. That was easy to do since I expected nothing to come of our morning's visit. I walked back to my law practice.

I told only Maggie and never spoke about the job to anyone else until March when Fritz called with the information that Scranton had been in that morning to tell the president he would take the chairmanship. Although I had by then concluded, with the passage of time and the absence of a call, that Scranton had probably accepted the assignment, I was relieved to hear it from Fritz. It seemed that a job I hadn't

* While Mondale and Vance obviously supported my appointment, I believe it was proposed by Zbig Brzezinski. We had been friends for some time, occasionally had lunch just to talk, and held similar views of the Soviets. Some of my friends were suspicious of Zbig, assuming a Polish Catholic who was on occasion critical of Israel was anti-Semitic. I once introduced Zbig at a Hebrew University dinner and told the audience that before World War II his father had been an official in Danzig who had saved the lives of large numbers of Jews, at great personal risk. I had learned that from sources in Israel, not from Zbig himself. Zbig shared his father's views and his father's courage. Anti-Semitism was a bad rap and its own form of stereotyping and prejudice.

sought was now gone. Before I could respond, Fritz quickly added that the president would now like me to become co-chairman with Scranton. I assured him that the gesture, if it was that, was not necessary. But he said it was not a gesture, but a sincere desire on their part that I do it. My immediate, but unspoken, assumption was that, with elections imminent, bipartisan leadership of the delegation had become more politically appropriate. I said okay, asking innocently whether Scranton knew he was to have a co-chairman.

More Goldberg. Scranton didn't know anything about it, but I was assured that Cy Vance would be calling him if I accepted. Fritz asked me to call Vance, confirm my willingness to serve, and chat with him. I arranged to see Vance. He and I and his counselor and chief aide, Matt Nimitz, talked about the meetings and the co-chairmanship. I foresaw no problems with the arrangement and looked forward to participating.

Cy said he was certain there would be no objection from Scranton and that the assignment should take us no more than three to five months. That seemed perfect to me, and Vance subsequently called Scranton to confirm our arrangement.

When Scranton and I finally got together, he was gracious and friendly, a gentleman about the arrangement. From the start, we worked well together. Our first task was to find a chief deputy. That brought us up against our first problem and our first negotiation.

In 1976, Congress had created the Commission on Security and Cooperation in Europe, consisting of six representatives, six senators, and executive branch representatives from the Departments of State, Defense, and Commerce. It was to be an oversight committee. The idea for the commission had come from Republican Congresswoman Millicent Fenwick of New Jersey and Democratic Congressman Dante Fascell of Florida.

These two were an odd couple in more than their political affiliations. Mrs. Fenwick was an aristocratic lady, properly schooled in surroundings of affluence, an Eastern liberal Republican at home in the salons and summer spas of the upper class.*

Dante, the child of Italian immigrants, had been in Congress since 1954, a party loyalist too rarely given credit for his talents and knowl-

---

* She has been parodied in the comic strip "Doonesbury," but not as she was in real life. When I first met her and we talked of the meeting in Madrid, it was apparent her knowledge of human rights problems was clear and deep, her commitment to deal with those problems sincere and thoughtful. I liked her and we became very good friends, sharing ideas on human rights and other issues as well. I later learned that when Reagan won the election in November 1980, she led a bipartisan group of members of Congress who wrote asking him to keep me in Madrid.

edge of the world. He was not as polished as Millicent, but he had an intense, good-humored charm, and he knew government extraordinarily well. We had been friends for years, since he had early become an enthusiastic Humphrey supporter.

What they had in common was a combination of feistiness and independence. Together with a number of their House colleagues, they shared a deep commitment to human rights and, it appeared, a deeper suspicion and mistrust of the administration's philosophy and style of government. Even without Kissinger there as secretary of State, they believed that the State Department itself was so traditional and cautious that no waters would be churned, no challenges to other countries made in the clear cause of human rights. Striped pants and human rights fights did not, in their view, go together.*

Kissinger's emphasis on realpolitik led many House members to believe he would sell out human rights considerations if he saw them as adversely affecting American security interests, as he defined those interests. Henry apparently viewed the idea of the commission as a constitutional abomination and reportedly wanted President Ford to veto the law creating it. Ford's connections in the House were still close, and he decided not to offend his old friends but to live with the commission, averting what he saw as an unnecessary confrontation.

The staff director of the commission was the son of my friend Bob Oliver, a highly effective labor lobbyist from Texas. I had recommended Spencer Oliver to Fascell at Bob's request and was pleased when Dante chose him. Spencer was young, competent, ambitious, and a serious human rights advocate. He had gathered a dedicated, hard-working staff around him that reflected his own strong commitment.

I had been told by one of the commission members that Spencer had wanted Dante Fascell to be the chairman of the delegation to Madrid, knowing that Dante could not be in Madrid for more than a few days at a time and that Spencer, de facto, would become the head of the delegation.

When I met with Dante alone, I told him that I knew of his rumored interest in the chairmanship, although I couldn't figure out

---

* The belief that the State Department is populated with the privileged and elite whose lightly held convictions are derived from ideas taught in private schools, not values learned by personal experience and real life, persists. There is certainly some of that, but it is clearly exaggerated. I found in most of the foreign service officers I met a deep, visceral commitment to human rights, just as honorably motivated as that of the rest of us. Indeed, I was and am continually impressed with the competence and dedication I find among the professionals. Our country can be proud of them.

why he would want the post in addition to his other duties. He said that he really didn't care about it and we agreed that, since the president had gone in a different direction, the question was behind us.

I praised his commission staff, indicating that we would certainly work closely with them. He recommended Spencer for our top deputy. It was a bad idea on several counts. I explained to Dante my view that Spencer was too aggressively anti–State Department, and that we needed an experienced diplomatic hand with good relations at State at our sides since neither Scranton nor I could be effective without ardent and active State Department cooperation. We agreed to make Spencer one of two deputies.

We were fortunate to enlist as our chief deputy Warren Zimmermann, an experienced foreign service officer who had served in Moscow, spoke Russian, and was then the political officer in Paris. He had the maturity, the language skills, and the diplomatic experience that was essential to us.*

I also suggested to Fascell that he and Senator Bob Dole, as chairman and co-chairman of the commission, also ought to be vice chairmen of our delegation and attend the sessions whenever they could. I wanted their input and their experience. But I felt that I could not permit any other members of Congress who might show up in Madrid to make speeches at our sessions. I thought that could become confusing to friends and opponents alike and destroy any hope we had of being taken seriously by other delegations. Fascell agreed. Fortunately, a number of members did show up, and all accepted our understanding.

Everything seemed in order, until on a Friday night soon after, Scranton called me at home to say he had informed the president that morning that he was resigning as chairman for health reasons.† I urged him to stay on the job, assuring him that if illness kept him away some, I would be there in his stead. He responded by saying that he had anticipated my response and to avoid any reconsideration, he had gone

---

* Some years later when the next Final Act review was to take place in Vienna, the State Department asked me for suggestions for someone to head our delegation. They wanted someone like me from the public, but I could not think of anyone who would be better than Warren. The department, in light of Bud Scherer's earlier problems in Belgrade, hesitated on the grounds that it was not appropriate for a career foreign service officer to hold that job, since it was associated with a great deal of public sensitivity. They felt that his career could be derailed, but they ultimately appointed him. He did superbly and went on to become ambassador to Yugoslavia.

† I did not ask him for specifics and he did not offer them. I was aware, however, that he had an inner-ear problem that made him dizzy from time to time and observed the discomfort it caused him on a number of occasions when we were together.

to see the president first, and the matter was now settled. There was nothing to do but say I was sorry.

During the next few days, I heard from Mondale, Vance, Jordan, and Brzezinski, each one saying he wanted me to be the sole chairman. By then, I was no longer indifferent to the job. I was confident we could become a "bully pulpit" for freedom and democracy. I was both intellectually and emotionally committed to the project and was prepared to go it alone as chairman.

I started to plan two journeys of explanation and exploration. I wanted to meet with appropriate officials in every one of our allies' countries to avoid the misunderstandings of Belgrade and to gather the strength of unity. I also wanted to meet with the leaders of religious and human rights groups within the United States. I needed to learn from them what their concerns were and what they wanted us to accomplish. They needed to hear from me what I thought we should be trying to do and that we were quite close to one another in our goals.

My political instincts told me that the Madrid meetings needed a constituency to support our efforts. All of these groups had ardent participants and a long history of contacts with the media and on the Hill. If they disapproved of what we did, they would be an obstacle difficult to overcome, but if they understood what the delegation was after and accepted what we accomplished, they could be indispensable supporters and advocates.

Then there was another call from Mondale, this time to say that the president had decided to appoint former Attorney General Griffin Bell, Carter's good friend who had resigned from the cabinet in July 1979, as co-chairman with me. It was on-again off-again—first Scranton, then Scranton and me, then me, now Bell and me.

Bell seemed pretty good company to me, having been both a federal judge and attorney general of the United States. I thought that he added luster to our mission and that I was made stronger by the association. I once again accepted the situation, with only a little shrug of wonderment at how we got to where we were.

Presidential appointments are a little like sausage making. The end product looks pretty good, but you don't want to know in detail what goes into making them. The Carter administration seemed to me at the moment to have been somewhat more awkward in that process than other administrations, but not by very much. In the most organized of administrations, personal and political considerations inevitably change with the moment and affect the ultimate choices.

I subsequently was told that in this case, Mrs. Bell had earlier been furious with President Carter when the White House announced the judge's voluntary resignation at about the same time as Carter sent two of his other cabinet secretaries unceremoniously packing. Carter had spent a long weekend at Camp David visiting with various "leaders" about conditions in the United States and particularly about energy problems. He came down off the Catoctin Mountain with a strange speech that seemed to blame our problems on a national "malaise," and fired Secretary of the Treasury Mike Blumenthal and Secretary of Health, Education, and Welfare Joe Califano. It was not a fine hour in either personal or national political terms. He gained nothing politically, seemed to blame everyone but himself, and almost lost a friend.

In an effort to show that Griffin Bell was still in favor, and to assuage Mrs. Bell's lingering anger, Carter apparently looked around for a job that was available and that would fit the judge's commitments and obligations to his law practice. The Madrid assignment, with its ambassadorial rank to boot, seemed to meet both requirements, and Carter offered it to him.

When I called to congratulate Bell the day after I talked to Mondale, he asked, "What is this all about? I got a call from Jimmy, but he didn't explain anything. Why do I want to do this?" I explained to him why he should want it, but he remained unconvinced, neither rejecting nor agreeing to participate. He clearly was not looking for a job. When I asked to meet with him, he began to talk of trials and travels that would prevent our meeting in Washington, so I said, "Judge, why don't I come to Atlanta? Will you be there tomorrow?" When he said yes, I simply asked if he had time to see me. The next morning I flew to Atlanta.

I did not know Bell personally. We had been introduced at some Washington event once or twice, but that was about it. Bell conveys both the drawling Southern gentleman judge and the good old boy of the country roads, an interesting combination of smooth and rough that sometimes disguised his superior intelligence, fine instincts, and exceptional talents.

What is most distinctive and almost immediately obvious is his directness and his refreshing candor. They were there in good supply when I sat down in his office. He explained that he had been in the shower when the president phoned about Madrid. His wife had called him to the phone, where he stood wet and impatient while the president told him about the appointment and not much more.

Bell asked again as he had the previous day, "Why do I want to do this?" He explained that he was tremendously busy, had court commitments, and couldn't figure out what he could contribute that was so special, or, more importantly, what could be accomplished in Madrid.

I was able to convince him during the several hours we were

together in his office and over lunch that President Carter's commitment to advancing human rights around the world might be seen by historians as the most lasting mark of his administration and that Bell's closeness to the president would indicate to everyone Carter's seriousness in a way that my appointment might not. We talked more about what was at stake, and he agreed that he would accept the appointment and do what he could.

There was one remaining problem that inadvertently surfaced. During the course of our conversation, I referred to a Senate confirmation process for our ambassadorial appointments. His face became grim as he firmly declared that he would not take the job if it required a Senate confirmation hearing. Memories of the embarrassment caused him and his wife in 1977 when the Senate held up his appointment as attorney general because of clubs to which he belonged came to mind. There was no mistaking his determination not to risk a repetition of that experience. I would have welcomed a Senate confirmation of my ambassadorial rank, but it would have been inappropriate for only one of us to go through the process. I therefore hastened to assure him that I would return to Washington and persuade the State Department that both of us would be content with ambassadorial designations by the president without Senate confirmation, a process permitted by law for short-term appointments.

When I told him the preparatory session to establish the rules of procedure would begin in September, he said it was impossible for him to be there. I responded, "Okay, don't be there for the preparatory session. It's all about the rules and guidelines, and I can handle it alone." I told him that the substantive meeting started in November, that I hoped he would join me for the opening sessions, but that I would be there when he couldn't. That made sense to him, and we agreed that I would keep him informed of what I was doing, and he would join me in Madrid in November.

I also explained to him what I had in mind visiting European capitals and American cities. I said we needed to build unity, as best we could, from the beginning of the meetings. That could happen only if our allies saw us as having a considered, consistent, and sensible plan. More importantly, they had to feel that they had been consulted and taken seriously.

Back home, it was not so different. People who cared about the Helsinki Final Act wanted to know what we expected to accomplish and how we were going about reaching our goals. The groups existed in large part because they did not feel comfortable with any administration whose promises were made, but not, in their eyes, kept. I wasn't seeking unity so much as simply understanding. Out of that I hoped we could find broad-based support.

Bell saw the value of those trips, so I continued what I had begun, traveling to Europe with Warren Zimmermann and occasionally with Roger Harrison,* another able foreign service officer working with us but based in Washington. During our trips within the United States, we were also accompanied by two or three members of the commission staff. Our diplomatic group—citizen-led with State Department support and congressional involvement—communicated a sense of coherence in American policy that had been difficult to achieve in Belgrade.

That was central to my strategy. At the core of our message was a demonstration that we took the Helsinki Final Act seriously by insisting on compliance with its provisions. Our agenda for the meeting would have to provide the time for review of implementation. We needed evidence to build the case of Soviet noncompliance. But to do that successfully required that we avoid division and strains of misunderstanding among the West as happened in Belgrade.

On the central issue of human rights, my view was that we had to specify the names in Madrid, talking of specific people jailed or otherwise abused by Soviet and other Eastern European authorities. Suffering is not faceless or impersonal. Families kept apart were flesh and blood cruelly separated by artificial boundaries and capricious political restrictions.

I believed that proper dramatization of the human rights problem in the Soviet Union had been deficient in Belgrade, since we were the only country to name names and had stopped at six. We had to go from statistics to people, and beyond the most illustrious and well known of them to lesser known people and causes as well. I did not view general talk of human rights as adequate. Our allies had to understand our objectives and not be taken by surprise. It was not an easy idea to sell. It was a more aggressive tactic than most diplomats were accustomed to pursue.

When I first met with Foreign Minister Hans Dietrich Genscher in West Germany, he persuasively pointed out to me that more than 50,000 Germans had been repatriated in 1979 without any public clamor, leading him reasonably to conclude that for his government, quiet negotiations were most effective. The issue, he said, was not principle or morality; it was how best to save human lives. I pointed out that an equal number of Jews had been permitted to emigrate that same year only after protests and a great deal of notice had been given

---

* Roger Harrison, as I write this chapter, is U.S. ambassador to Jordan.

to their plight. I also pointed out that neither group had been faring well in 1980. Our talk was healthy and his comments were reasonable. I therefore decided to assure him and his associates that we did not wish to do anything in Madrid to diminish the number of emigres by even one person and that I certainly did not want the Federal Republic of Germany (FRG) to do so if it meant one more German was kept in the Soviet Union. If silence was effective for them, they should remain silent and pursue our common goals the way it worked for them. Yet I told the minister that we intended to pursue our tactic aggressively, because we believed it would work for us, unless and until it was shown to be harmful to the people we wanted to help.

I then urged him to think of our joint effort toward freedom as a symphony orchestra in which there were different sounds. Some musicians played the trumpets and the tympan, others the harp and violins. Some played *sotto voce,* some *forte.* Even a single instrument, like the piano, was played loudly sometimes and softly others. Whatever instrument they or others chose, our purpose was to maintain harmony and create beautiful human rights music together. Genscher accepted the analogy, repeating it later, although some at first seemed to think I ought to play the trumpet solo.

During July and August, I visited about a dozen American cities—including Chicago, Philadelphia, Seattle, New York, and Detroit—to talk to ethnic, religious, and human rights groups. The groups were not necessarily close to one another, but they shared at least some common interests although they arrived at their focus from very different points of concern.

The Captive Nations groups—a descriptive term more in vogue in earlier decades, but still applicable—each cared about a single country or ethnic group. They were seen by some as conservatives, right-wing zealots, even anti-Semitic. Some of their members may have been all three, but not those I met. They were an argumentative agglomeration, often suspicious of one another, even questioning whether certain groups belonged among them. I had long thought they deserved to be heard and encouraged to seek their goals of emancipation for their native countries.* With the help of the commission staff and Spencer

---

* Captive Nation declarations were passed unanimously by the Congress year after year. Some people thought these were empty gestures, but others of us thought it was important to keep peoples' spirits up and hope alive both here and in the various countries in Europe. Humphrey agreed with that view and had worked with the ethnic organizations over the years when many Democrats preferred to keep their distance. It was good politics in some ways, but it was really not more than an extension of his nights as mayor in the East Hennepin Cafe.

Oliver, who knew the leaders well, I met with Ukrainians, Lithuanians, Latvians, Estonians, Romanians, Poles, Hungarians, and Czechs, overcoming their initial suspicions when I sensed any and making them allies in our efforts. What impressed me was how many of them were young and American-born. They were coming together with one another and with the more traditional human rights groups.

The human rights groups—led by Helsinki Watch, a citizens' group chaired by Robert Bernstein, a New York publishing executive whom I respect—were somewhat easier to approach since they tended to be less suspicious of Carter's commitment to the human rights battle. They came to the question without the same personal involvement as the ethnics, but with a deep moral and ideological base. Some had wanted their own candidate selected for Madrid and were a little resentful that Carter had not accepted their recommendation of Orville Schell, Sr., a distinguished New York lawyer.*

As much as I thought of myself as a human rights supporter, the professionals did not identify me as a champion or advocate. That label, in their eyes, applied to people who shared their passion and their singular focus. I had not been an active participant in any of their groups, and that was a basic measure, an ideological litmus test. One of them, Ed Kline, whom I did not know personally but knew was close to Andrei Sakharov, seemed particularly upset at my appointment. He apparently persuaded a friend who was an editorial writer for the *Wall Street Journal* to criticize my appointment, as did Vladimir Bukovsky, a deserved hero of the Soviet dissident movement who knew me not at all. For the most part, I was a stranger to them. They had been the foot soldiers, and I was their general brought in from outside their ranks. I had to overcome their reservations as much as I did those of the nationality groups. Bernstein, Schell, and Jeri Laber of Helsinki Watch helped me.

I tried to supply both hope and focus to people who had carried on a lonely, almost hopeless, fight for years without giving in to despair. I invited some of them to come to Madrid as public observers, knowing they would go back home with a better understanding of what we were doing.

Beyond that, I liked a great many of the leaders and respected their passion. I remember coming away from a meeting in Chicago, where I had met a nun, Sister Ann Gillen, believing that we could accomplish great things with people like her behind us. Sister Ann was a person on a mission. Human rights, and particularly the cause of

---

* I invited Mr. Schell to be a public member of our delegation and to join us whenever he could arrange it. He did, and his presence was always helpful.

Soviet Jewry, was her passion. Religious persecution was to her the devil's work and needed to be eradicated as thoroughly and as quickly as possible. She was saintly in her devotion to making the lives of others full and free, and was tough in a gentle way. I thought that the answer to the ancient question of how many divisions the pope had was irrelevant as long as one of them was led by Ann.

By the autumn, Judge Bell and I had became increasingly comfortable with each other. I had accomplished what I wanted to do in my trips to the Continent and across our own country. I was ready for my part-time, three-month assignment.

As it turned out, that job turned into a three-year stint, under two presidents and four secretaries of State. It was challenging, educational, exciting, and, I think, valuable in affirming Western values, in teaching about those values, and in holding their banner high for those in Europe who aspired to attain them in their own countries.

All my preparations and plans were consistent with my democratic political convictions, my anti-Soviet views, and my commitment to a strong national defense for the United States. My own views were open and clear. After the McGovern nomination in 1972 in Miami, I joined in the establishment of the Coalition for a Democratic Majority (CDM), aimed at returning the Democratic party to its traditional anti-totalitarianism, with a strong emphasis on defense. Woodrow Wilson, Franklin Roosevelt, Harry Truman, John Kennedy, and Lyndon Johnson represented that tradition. An examination of public opinion survey data showed that most Democratic party voters remained loyal to that tradition and were uncomfortable with the left trend that reared its head in 1968 and asserted itself decisively in 1972. George McGovern's candidacy for the presidency in 1972 left me reluctantly lukewarm, mostly because I felt his program for reducing our military spending, coupled with what I perceived to be a third-world foreign policy that ignored the totalitarian nature of the Soviet Union, was dangerous. I was less concerned about Carter's position in 1976 because he had been a naval officer and had supported Henry Jackson in 1972. His foreign policy statements and positions, however, disturbed me during his first two years in office. But the Soviet invasion of Afghanistan seemed to set him on course, and I had an opportunity to confirm this personally at a meeting with him in early 1980.

Lane Kirkland, the eloquent, impressive leader of the AFL-CIO, encouraged the formation of CDM and identified himself with it. Many elected public officials did the same. Dick Schifter and the columnist Ben Wattenberg assumed leadership roles, as did Jeane Kirkpatrick, then a political science professor at Georgetown University beginning to earn a national reputation through her writing. Hubert Humphrey and Scoop Jackson became honorary chairpersons.

Yale Law School Professor Gene Rostow and I also began to talk about the need to develop a prestigious nonpartisan foreign policy group aimed at developing support for a stronger national defense and a more sensitive awareness of growing Soviet military strength. Gene had also been talking with Paul Nitze, the immensely respected banker turned public servant; Henry Fowler, former secretary of the Treasury; James Schlesinger, former secretary of Defense; and others with the same goal. After much discussion and correspondence and many telephone calls, an organization meeting was held at the Metropolitan Club in Washington on March 12, 1976, chaired by Rostow. It included, in person or by personal commitment, in addition to those mentioned above, Sol Chaiken of the AFL-CIO, David Packard, Admiral Elmo Zumwalt, Ronald Reagan, Richard Allen, Charles Burton Marshall, George Shultz, Charles Tyroler II, former Secretary of State Dean Rusk, Professor Richard Pipes, Charles Walker, Herbert Stein, and scores of other prominent scholars and people of public affairs. Tyroler was the consensus choice to assume the day-to-day operations of the committee. I became its general counsel and a member of the executive committee. Between that date and November 11, 1976, when the creation of the organization was publicly announced at a press conference, we met ten more times, hammering out word by word a manifesto, "Common Sense and the Common Danger," which effectively set forth the objectives of the group.

Our purpose was to persuade the country that international stability and peace with freedom required a strong America, one that could and would deter Soviet adventurism and aggression. We thought of ourselves as an emergency committee that might last for a year or two. We withheld the announcement of our organization until after the 1976 election because we did not want to be involved in partisan politics. We were Democrats and Republicans, labor and management, liberals and conservatives. We decided to accept no funds from corporations engaged in defense work. Our expenses and overhead, under Tyroler's careful guidance, were always minimal. The only members we had were members of our board of directors and we initially limited that number to 100, although we were forced to raise it to 150. We did not look upon ourselves as a lobbying group and did not testify before Congress except on rare occasions by direct invitation.

We called ourselves the Committee on the Present Danger (CPD).

The studies we undertook and released analyzed America's military strengths and weaknesses as well as those of the Soviet Union. The studies were extremely well received here and abroad and led to wide respect for CPD in the press and government circles. I know of no private public affairs organization that has had a greater influence in such a short period of time on U.S. foreign and defense policy issues.

13

Jaw to Jaw with the Soviets

By the time the Madrid meetings began in September 1980, even the optimists knew there was no semblance of detente. The Soviet invasion of Afghanistan had turned Carter icy cold toward the Soviet Union. U.S. relations with the USSR were at a standstill. The Soviets continued their human rights abuses at home, disrupting the lives and livelihoods not only of dissidents, those seeking to emigrate, and members of various religious and nationality groups, but also the population as a whole. Helsinki monitors, the men and women who were urging their own country to abide by the standards set down in Helsinki in 1975, were being particularly singled out and punished.*

Few thought much good could come from our Madrid meetings. Why talk of human rights, critics asked, while those rights were so sadistically being abused throughout the Soviet bloc? It was a reasonable question. For all that, I arrived in Madrid in early September 1980

---

* During the Madrid meetings, the Soviets imprisoned more than 500 people who were working for Helsinki-related goals. These monitors, protected in theory by the Final Act, showed great courage in standing up for human rights, knowing the possible consequences. In March 1982, about halfway through our meeting, fifty-two members of the Helsinki Watch were in prison or in internal exile. Fifteen had been in jail since the meeting began. We and our allies kept careful tabs on these developments and expressed our outrage both in Madrid and outside the meetings.

with some hope that a firm and united Western negotiating posture could alter Soviet behavior. The West, furthermore, most particularly the NATO states, seemed ready to agree that Europe should be made fully aware of the Soviet Union's reprehensible behavior. I felt that to the extent that European public opinion was reminded of the true nature of the Soviet system, the more likely Soviet political influence would be damaged.

I had never negotiated on this diplomatic level before, but I felt I knew the Soviets well, and I was a good negotiator. I was inspired by the challenge, by being an ambassador appointed by the president of the United States, by heading one of thirty-five delegations dealing with serious questions affecting the lives of millions of people. I was determined to behave with dignity, consistency, and equanimity, but that did not, in my mind, preclude aggressively pushing for our goals and demonstrating that Soviet violations of the Helsinki standards were threatening the peace and stability of Europe.

My hope had a solid foundation. Unlike Belgrade, where no unity ever evolved, a relatively united Western group of nations, speaking in many languages but finally in one voice, was prepared to join us as we documented the Soviet record of slave labor camps; psychiatric hospitals used for political punishment; government-sponsored anti-Semitism; armed aggression in Afghanistan; religious persecution of evangelical Christians, Baptists, Seventh-Day Adventists, Pentecostals, and Catholics; strangulation of scientific freedom; destruction of cultural and national heritages; and defiance of agreements against the use of chemical and biological weapons.

Our uniform message was that the Soviet Union had to comply with the agreement it made in 1975 if it wished to be accepted as a responsible member of the international community. To lead that charge without letting the negotiations fall apart was not easy. I began with certain preconceptions about negotiations, and I believe those principles made me a tougher adversary than many, on both sides of the debate, liked.

Negotiation without confrontation, where the objective facts require blunt talk, is not a serious negotiation at all; it is a charade, good for college evenings, but inexcusable where lives and liberty are at stake. Charades have no place in serious international conferences.

One purpose of negotiation obviously is to reach agreement. Where difficult issues are involved, however, that agreement may not be possible in the short run. Therefore, it is equally important to use the negotiating process to communicate existing concerns and firm goals, so as to increase the likelihood of agreement in the future. Absent firmness, there is no reason for the other side to take seriously the message that is being conveyed. I was determined to be firm, to confront where it was necessary, to conciliate where it was possible.

Another principle became apparent in negotiating with the Soviets. Repetition is crucial. If an issue that is important to us has been raised a dozen times, but has received neither response nor rejection, unless it is raised yet another time, the Soviets will believe we no longer consider it important. Understanding that, if an issue is vital we must continue to raise it—patiently, persistently, consistently, even to the point at which we bore ourselves.

Our negotiations in Madrid were not impeded by a permanent CSCE secretariat, and I took further hope from that. Although the Soviets originally proposed that a continuing staff be hired, the decision was made in 1975 not to have one. We opposed the idea for several reasons: it was certain to be infiltrated by KGB operatives; beyond that, experience suggested that staffs of international organizations begin to establish their own policy and goals. Too quickly, the participating governments become captives of their own creation. Furthermore, states then begin to claim jobs for their nationals. The numbers get out of hand. Some dimension of intellectual corruption begins. Keeping the process loose made it stronger. Instead of a permanent bureaucracy, the host government for each review supplied the secretariat, including selections from other nationals with experience, and that meant no one was manipulating the process or anticipating the outcome.*

Just before I was to leave Washington for Madrid, the Romanian ambassador to the talks, Ian Datcu, had come to the United States on an official visit. Our meeting seemed to establish a friendly bond. When I reached Madrid, I decided I needed some contact with the Warsaw bloc countries and invited Datcu to lunch with me and Warren Zimmermann. He came with several of his deputies. After lunch, he said, almost apologetically and apparently expecting rejection, that he had informed the Soviet ambassador that he was having lunch with me. I said that was fine and that I had told our allies I was having lunch with

---

* As I write this chapter, the United States has abandoned this position and approve the idea of a "small" CSCE permanent staff. I believe this is an error and will create later problems for us. My present view is that we should first decide what additional functions we wish CSCE to assume—environmental monitoring, terrorism investigation, conciliation of nationality disputes. Once deciding on the function, we should next address how best to carry it out. My guess is that we would find less onerous options than a permanent staff.

him. He then asked if I would consider having lunch with the Soviet ambassador, who had asked him to make the inquiry. I said I would be pleased to do so.

Datcu said, "You know that the United States has not been talking to the Soviets." I said I knew that. I also explained that I did not intend to function as the head of the American delegation at a conference of thirty-five nations and not talk to each participating country, particularly our counterpart on the Communist side, when the Helsinki Final Act required unanimous understandings.

I had made that decision with the approval of the State Department and the White House. I decided I was in a unique position to begin a dialogue with the Soviets and that I could not succeed in my mission without doing so. Datcu barely contained his excitement and asked when I might be available. I said, "I am free tomorrow." He was gone only a short time when he called back saying that Ambassador Yuri Dubinin, the head of the Soviet delegation who later became ambassador to the United States, would be pleased to join me for lunch and asked where. Innocently, I said that I did not know Madrid or its restaurants, that Dubinin also served as ambassador to Spain and thus knew Madrid. "Let him choose the place," I said. That apparently seemed reasonable to Datcu. It didn't to Dubinin. When Datcu called back a short time later, he sounded chastened and said I would have to choose the place.

I pointed out to Datcu that Dubinin probably felt if he chose the place, it would seem that he had invited me. If I chose it, he was being invited. I had no interest, I said, in this diplomatic waltzing. I told Datcu that we would simply have lunch in my apartment at the Hotel Castellana.*

Lunch went on late into the afternoon, slowed by the need for translation. Dubinin brought with him their number two man, Sergei Kondrashev,† who spoke fluent English and ran their delegation. I had

---

* The Hotel Castellana had once been a preeminent hotel in Madrid, but was now off its prime. It was like an old aristocrat fallen on hard days; the elegance was tarnished, but the good name remained. My suite had been refurbished but it was not quite what I wanted. A number of delegations stayed in apartments, including members of our own staff, in the building where we had our offices, and since that building was closer to our meeting place, I ultimately moved there.

† Kondrashev, a large man about six feet tall with a ready, engaging smile, was, according to our reports, a KGB general, and I believed that to be true. One book on the KGB named him its disinformation chief, but I never found that he told me anything untrue. I grew to like him. At one time during the meeting, he came to me quite agitated about an article critical of him in the *New York Times*. When I read the

Warren Zimmermann, who spoke fluent Russian, at my side. I told Dubinin and Kondrashev what they already knew: I had a long career of anti-Soviet activities. I talked about Afghanistan and our feelings about their invasion. I talked about human rights violations. I named names. Dubinin responded just as firmly, but it was an intense, not angry, confrontation and broke the ice in important ways.

Since we were on the eve of the preparatory meeting to set an agenda, I said, "We will have much to argue about in the main meeting, so let us both accept the procedural rules and the agenda of Belgrade which neither of us found fully satisfactory, and thus save a lot of time." They rejected that suggestion. It was a long afternoon, but a useful one. It was the first of more than 400 hours I spent in private talks with Soviet representatives during the Madrid meetings, outside the formal sessions.

That night Kondrashev telephoned Warren, asking if we could continue the conversation the next night at their place. After a moment's thought, I decided to take the opportunity to emphasize that I was Jewish, which I was certain they already knew. I told Warren to tell them that I could not meet because I would be at the synagogue the following evening attending Jewish New Year services. I said I would be available the following evening after sundown.

That dinner was interesting for the insight it provided into how Soviet negotiators deal with their American counterparts. Dubinin—a cultivated man who spoke good Spanish and later learned English when he became ambassador to Washington—was often unable to resist the temptation to take advantage. That evening, after caviar and beautifully broiled fish with a delicate white sauce, he offered me a chocolate out of a red box with a large picture of the Soviet Olympic mascot, Misha the bear. The United States had just boycotted the Moscow Olympics, but he unnecessarily explained to me just who Misha was. Not wanting to offend, but compelled to make a point, I reminded him (in some detail) of the reason that my country had not taken part in the Olympics, after which I felt free to take a chocolate, and did so.

There was one continuing source of friction with the Soviets during the preparatory meeting. We in the West wanted the agenda for the

---

piece, the only criticism I could recognize was the KGB reference. I urged him not to be so sensitive and reminded him of some rather insulting and inaccurate articles about me that appeared in *Pravda* and *Izvestia*, including a story that I had received training leading animals to follow direction during my early years as president of the Friends of the National Zoo. He insisted he had played no role in their publication.

main meeting to afford the opportunity to undertake a detailed review of how the Helsinki Act was being implemented. The Belgrade rules allowed that, although with some ambiguity as to the duration of such a review. What the Soviets wanted was simply to talk about the future. It was a classic case of propaganda versus reality. They would be on the carpet if we reviewed implementation; they would be in the clouds if we fashioned beautiful words about the future. To discuss the Helsinki Final Act without evaluating its implementation would be fatuous. Since all decisions in Madrid required unanimity, we sat and kept at it until the Soviets were ready to consent to review as part of the main meeting agenda. Instead of ending the preparatory meeting in days, it went on for many weeks, with tempers frequently becoming raw.

Soviet intransigence helped force NATO unity and provided me opportunities to prepare for the main event scheduled to begin on November 11. There were moments of interest and challenge and amusement.

I recalled, from my briefings, that Janos Petran, the Hungarian representative in Madrid and a frequent fiery spokesman for the Soviet bloc, was among many Soviet and Warsaw Pact leaders who had, after Belgrade, praised the Belgrade meeting. Spencer Oliver assembled those earlier statements and editorials for me. At an appropriate point in the Madrid preparatory meeting debate, after listening again to Soviet arguments about how bad Belgrade and its rules had been, I asked for the floor and began reading the earlier Soviet bloc testimonials. The silence and embarrassment were conspicuous. Petran, sitting across from me, fidgeted. He knew what was coming. On the spur of the moment, I decided not to read or refer to his earlier statement. I had made my point, and it was effective. He was surprised when I sat down and looked at me meaningfully and, I thought, appreciatively.

That night, when I reached my hotel room, I found a case of Hungarian wine and no note. The next morning, in an effort to acknowledge the gift, and without telling him that I had distributed a bottle of the wine to each member of my staff, I came to him with a sober look and said he had caused me a long and difficult night since we had a rule against accepting gifts that could not be eaten or drunk within a twenty-four-hour period. We both laughed. While I could not expect Petran to become an ally, the experience led to many good and useful conversations between us. In any event, this was one of the several gestures I made to distinguish between the Soviet Union and its satellites and to let the latter know I had done so.

The argument over rules went on not just for the three weeks we had anticipated would be the maximum length of the preparatory meeting, but for an additional and unexpected eight weeks, leading up to November 11, when the general meeting was to begin. Our allies remained firm as the NATO caucus met frequently. I used those weeks to get to know my colleagues. I wanted a sense of their individual interests, problems, foibles. I spent a lot of time with the other thirty-four delegations, politicking, listening, and encouraging large countries and small ones to understand our views and aspirations for the meetings. We were in an extended political convention, and I lined up support as I could and learned more about both our allies and our opponents.

International multilateral negotiations require as much concern for the feelings and ideas of one's allies as of one's adversaries. That effort had broken down in Belgrade for a variety of reasons, and as a result, I made a special effort to be in touch with all our allies. I worked, for example, to involve the Canadians, who are too often treated casually by the United States. Their ambassador, Louis Rogers, was a man beset with personal problems that made him appear sour. But at his curmudgeonly worst, he was a most capable diplomat, with a fine intellect, good insights, and a lot of experience. When I discovered he had a large conference room in his quarters—indeed, the only one among us—I proposed that when the main meeting began, we hold all our NATO meetings in his office. That pleased him and met our needs. It gave him points back home and us a more central and comfortable meeting place in Madrid.*

Our NATO group usually met three or four times a week and sometimes three and four times a day when necessary. The meetings usually lasted about half an hour, but they might go an hour or two when there were serious questions before us. The Canadians would always provide the coffee. When our rotation system brought the United States to the NATO chair, I, as host, supplied American doughnuts for morning meetings and small Baby Ruth or O. Henry bars from the U.S. Embassy commissary for afternoon meetings. They laughed at my American chauvinism, but our allies consumed the doughnuts and candy with alacrity.

We consulted on all aspects of the general meeting and kept one another fully informed of strategy, intentions, and concerns. We also

* Rogers often said that the United States frequently ignored Canada, resulting in a substantial amount of resentment. I visited Canada on several occasions to make sure they felt involved. Indeed, I also did a great deal of traveling throughout Europe; keeping in contact with the capitals of our allies and the neutral governments.

worked closely with our neutral friends who shared our values, since the West is stronger in dealing with the Soviet Union when it speaks with one voice and repeats a consistent message.

NATO, as an alliance of sovereign states, is not free of sensitivities. The potential for hurt feelings, particularly with the French, hovers like storm clouds. When free and sovereign states with differing histories and cultural backgrounds attempt to formulate common policy, there will be differences. Our task was to raise the vision of the West above the minutiae of our relations, important as they might appear to be at any moment, to the realization that our common values were at issue.

When I talked to the head of the British delegation on the eve of the preparatory meeting about gathering the fifteen NATO countries, he said the French wouldn't come if I called the meeting. The French commitment to NATO was real, but since de Gaulle, they had preferred to communicate independence and aloofness. That had been my concern. The British delegate suggested that he host the first meeting, feeling the French would come to that. He also warned that French attendance at the first meeting didn't guarantee they would come to the next one if I called it.

At the first NATO caucus, I reported on my lunch with Datcu that day, leading to my plan to meet with the Soviets for lunch the next day, but I emphasized that I was prepared to cancel the meeting if our NATO colleagues thought I should. I said, "I don't want anyone among us to feel that the United States is into a side bilateral negotiation with the Soviets." They unanimously urged me to proceed with my luncheon, as I had suspected they would. I proposed that I report to a NATO caucus at the end of my meeting with the Soviets. Since we rotated the hosting duties alphabetically, the United States would follow the United Kingdom and host the next caucus. I therefore proposed that we meet at our embassy, during which I would make a full report on my meeting with the Soviets. In fact, I continued the practice of informing our allies about my meetings with the Soviets throughout the entire Madrid meeting. Our allies pursued the same practice. The French did show up. With the precedent of these two meetings, the question of French involvement in our caucus never came up again, and they participated constructively whenever and wherever we met. Indeed, as a courtesy to me and without a fuss, the very able French ambassador, Jacques Martin, began speaking English rather than French at our NATO meetings.

I had come to Madrid with an additional U.S. goal of expediting

Spain's entry into NATO. It was not part of my official duties, but a parallel objective given to me by the State Department to work on. I thought a good first step would be to caucus with our NATO group, but Spain couldn't be invited into a NATO caucus, so I suggested that we call our group a Western caucus and avoid diplomatic niceties. Javier Ruperez, the Spanish CSCE ambassador and a canny political observer, was a strong champion of NATO within Spain and ably used his role as host to become an integral part of our caucus.

My hope was to invite the Irish to join our caucus as well. They were proud of their neutrality and their membership in the European Community and anxious in Dublin to keep themselves free of NATO and the United States. Ann Anderson, the Irish representative, was a young professional diplomat and the most eloquent speaker at the conference. I asked her to join our Western group. She said she would have to check with her government, but doubted that it would be approved. It wasn't. The only time I was able to get the Irish to join us was when some official visitors came to report on an important meeting of ministers. I called the meeting at dinnertime. I told the Irish that the event was social, although we both knew it might also turn into a working and planning dinner. While never a member of the caucus, Ireland was always an ally and Ann Anderson a stalwart whose down-to-earth clarity of speech and intelligence effectively strengthened us on human rights matters.

At the end of the eleven weeks, with still no agreement on the agenda and with the main meeting about to begin, the Spanish foreign minister sent me a message that the Soviets had replaced Yuri Dubinin with Leonid Ilichev, a seventy-five-year-old deputy foreign minister, who had come to find a way to end the impasse. He did so by accepting a mediating proposal by the neutral countries, Sweden, Switzerland, Finland, and Austria, which actually gave us more implementation review time than we had expected or requested and more than I had proposed to Dubinin eleven weeks earlier.

The Soviet objective at the preparatory meeting was to save themselves from human rights criticism by minimizing the time to be allocated at the meeting for a review of implementation. Their objective at the main meeting was a decision for CSCE to hold a disarmament conference, in large part, I suspected, so that they could oppose our deployment of Pershing and cruise missiles in Europe. They could then say to the publics of Europe, "Look, we are interested in disarmament, while the United States is pushing ahead on nuclear arms for Europe." It made sense from their point of view. Clearly, some citizens and leaders in Europe would have found the Soviet argument compatible with their own anti-deployment views.

The French, partly in anticipation of this Soviet position, also urged NATO to support a Conference on Disarmament in Europe (CDE), but one emphasizing confidence-building measures (CBM), the precedent for which was established by the 1975 agreement. The United States seemed to be the only holdout, skeptical of any "disarmament" meeting while Soviet troops were still in Afghanistan. When I went home on a quick review trip in October, the issue came up at a White House meeting of the National Security Council to which I was invited. The preparatory meeting was still on, but we knew the main meeting would begin in November and we would have to face the issue.

The NSC meeting was held in the White House situation room. It was my first time at such a meeting, and I must admit to a sense of involvement in policymaking that I had never felt before. The mystique of power is great, and I sensed then how intoxicating it can be on a daily basis. There is something seductive about the tight security and the secrecy. It is difficult to avoid a sense of self-importance.

Brzezinski was opposed to the French proposal; Cy Vance was in favor of it; and Carter had decided to put off the issue when the Soviets invaded Afghanistan. There had been a ministerial meeting of NATO the previous December, just before the invasion, where Vance had voiced his support of the French proposal. Brzezinski felt that Vance had exceeded his authority. It seemed to me from what I learned that the president had actually given Vance the authority to do so. Brzezinski, immediately upon the invasion, persuaded the president to set the Vance decision aside. That was the context of our meeting, and the question to be decided was what the United States would do about the French proposal.

As I listened to the detailed and intense discussion, someone—either Warren Christopher, deputy secretary of State, who was in the chair in Cy Vance's absence, or Zbig—said, "Let's hear what Max has to say now that he has heard the discussion." I responded that we probably could make some desirable changes in the French proposal along the lines of what I had heard if we used the leverage we now had. I liked the French desire to correct a weakness in the 1975 agreement that virtually exempted the Soviet Union from responsibility under the military confidence provisions of the agreement. The French did this by redefining Europe to cover the total area from the Atlantic to the Urals. I then said that as a negotiator I'd like bargaining leverage so that, at the appropriate time, our support for the CDE would be contingent on our getting the changes we wanted in the French proposal and full support from our allies on our human rights concerns.

Brzezinski unexpectedly said, "I am prepared to let Max be given the authority to make the decision and to decide when as a negotiator he wants to make that decision." Christopher said, "I agree." The issue was resolved. When we left the meeting, Roz Ridgway, then the counselor of the State Department, with more than two decades of experience in the department, said, "Max, do you have any idea what has just happened? I have never seen any negotiator given this kind of latitude before."*

On November 4, 1980, with the preparatory meeting still dragging on, Reagan defeated Carter. I had, during the previous weekend, returned to Washington to vote and for consultations. When I arrived in Madrid the next morning, Warren Zimmermann was at the airport to meet me. There was great uncertainty among our allies, he said, with no sense of where our country would go under Reagan. I was driven directly to our conference center, where I decided to take the floor and provide assurances that American policy with respect to Europe ,and CSCE would remain constant. I did so on the basis of my own strong instincts. Since the assumption of my colleagues was that I spoke under instruction and with knowledge—although I made no such claims—my assurances worked. They also proved to be correct.

I did not tell anyone that I had the authority to make the decision on the French proposal, but talked to our allies about the issue, using the possibility of support for the disarmament conference to get solid support for our human rights positions. After Carter lost the election, the State Department put great pressure on me to announce our support for the French proposal, fearing that Reagan, once president, having been a critic of the CSCE process, would also oppose the French proposal. I didn't think that made good political sense. I sent a cable to President Carter explaining my position. I said that I had been given

---

* Several months later, following Ronald Reagan's defeat of Jimmy Carter, Bud McFarlane, whom I didn't know, succeeded Roz, and was astounded, I learned, at my freedom. Bud also complained to others that I didn't clear speeches, although I did send daily cables to the department. Just before my first formal session with Al Haig, the new secretary of State, in February 1981, I called Bud's office from Madrid for an appointment. When we met, I did not acknowledge that I knew of his concern, but simply described how I operated. When it was time for my appointment down the hall, he came along at Haig's invitation. When Al gave me a welcoming embrace and spoke cheerfully about what I was doing, Bud watched, understood, and never pulled the reins any tighter. We became good friends.

the authority to support the French disarmament conference if I thought it wise, but I thought doing so at such a late date might sour the idea for the incoming administration. Certainly, they could reverse me and him, thus putting our country in an unfavorable position. Carter put national interest above his own personal interest and agreed. I looked forward to finishing my obligation in Madrid, expecting it would soon end.

14

Serving Two Presidents in Madrid

The main meeting began on November 11, 1980. Griffin Bell gave the opening U.S. statement. I delivered mine a few days later. We were off to the races.

Spanish working and eating traditions defined our days. Our morning meetings broke for lunch at one P.M. We returned at four and continued until six or seven o'clock, or later if necessary.*

Daily plenary sessions lasted several hours, with the chairman rotating according to the alphabet. Delegates would ask to speak ahead of time or simply raise a hand during the course of the plenary. Later, plenaries met just when there was a need, sometimes only two or three times a week, while working groups concentrated on specific issues.

While I was back home just before the main meeting began, Senator Pat Moynihan of New York asked me to come to his office to meet Raoul Wallenberg's half sister and half brother. Wallenberg, a

---

* Early during my Madrid stay, I was invited to dinner by a member of the Spanish delegation. I was the first to arrive at the designated hour, ten P.M. When dinner was still not served at midnight, even though the conversation was engaging, I apologetically explained to our hostess that I had to leave because of an early morning meeting. Thereafter, my staff made arrangements with a few restaurants that when I hosted a dinner, they would agree to serve us at eight-thirty or nine P.M.

Swedish diplomat who had saved thousands of Jews from death before he was arrested by Soviet troops during World War II and never heard from again, had just been made an honorary American citizen by Congress. It was an interesting meeting, which included Pat's wife, Liz, and reaffirmed my conviction that Wallenberg deserved a spotlight at the Madrid meetings.

When I returned to Madrid, I visited the Swedish representative to explain that I was going to mention Wallenberg's name, but I thought it was appropriate that the Swedes do so first. I knew that they had been opposed to mentioning names in Belgrade and probably still were, but I told him that I did not want to upstage them, and the opportunity was there to mention this heroic Swede first if they wished to take it.

During the first week of the main session, when the foreign ministers were there for opening statements, the Swedish delegate approached me and said, "You will be pleased when you hear my foreign minister." The foreign minister did indeed highlight Wallenberg when he spoke. This had quite an impact on the other Western countries. The delegates knew of Sweden's prior unwillingness to name names. It made it easier for other countries later to join in.

When Griffin Bell delivered the U.S. opening speech, a carefully prepared statement, in his deep Southern drawl, our English-speaking colleagues, including the British representative, very quickly switched to the French or Spanish translation channel so that they could understand what was being said. The joke traveled the corridors that we needed another translator—one who knew both English and the language Judge Bell spoke. He was as amused as the rest of us by the reference.

The plenaries were, after the first week, closed sessions. Whenever I spoke formally at a plenary I distributed my text, when there was one, to the press. I also met with the press whenever they wished. One day, early on, Ilichev, the new Soviet head of delegation, asked for the floor and complained that I was violating the CSCE rule on closed meetings. I answered that a closed meeting did not mean I could not talk to the press about what we believed and what we said. I explained that our democratic ways called for me to tell the American people what I was saying and doing in their behalf, but that I did not disclose what other delegations were saying at the closed meetings. This ended the exchange. After a few days, I noticed Ilichev talking to the press as well.

I had begun to think about my own opening speech some weeks earlier. One evening in Brussels, after hearing my ideas, Roger Harrison, a senior foreign service officer assigned to European affairs, eagerly volunteered to do a first draft. I unhesitatingly agreed. There is a saying in Washington that career advancement means moving from speeches you write for others to speeches that others write for you. Roger knew what I wanted. I was not interested in insulting the Soviets, or engaging in polemics, but in accuracy and candor. I wanted, I told him, to call a spade a spade. I wanted facts and evidence from which I could draw specific conclusions. By the end of the talk, I wanted all who heard to know that the United States was committed to peace with liberty, and to know why the Soviet system was a menace to that peace.

Shortly before I was to deliver the speech, I learned from Roger that his other duties had left him no time to prepare a draft for me. Since I knew of the pressure on him and how capable he was, I could not complain. The following day, a Sunday, I asked my secretary to my hotel and dictated the speech for delivery the next day. It was a good speech, tough and effective. Indeed, a month later at a Christmas reception sponsored by the Finnish delegation, the head of a Warsaw Pact country delegation took me aside to say that my talk on November 17 had made a profound impression on him. "I'm taking it home for my seventeen-year-old son to read," he said.

The essence of the talk was not only a criticism of Marxist-Leninism and an analysis of why we considered Soviet behavior since the end of the war to be contrary to the norms of responsible international behavior, it was also designed to make this criticism on the political rather than the cultural or national level. I was aware of the pride that Russians had in their nation and history. I therefore emphasized that the United States and Russia had much in common. The values that so many describe as Western have been strengthened and reflected by Russian thinkers throughout history. Our two countries, I pointed out, are both continental, sprawling across a vast land mass. We are both traditionally explorers, settlers, cossacks and cowboys of many nationalities and ethnic backgrounds. Millions of Americans come from Russian stock. We never fought a war with each other and were allies in the largest foreign war in which either of us had ever been engaged. There was, therefore, nothing inevitable about conflict between us. It was the totalitarian injection of Marxist-Leninism that undermined both of our values, I concluded.

I released the speech to the press; the Reuters man in Madrid thought it was the toughest speech on the Soviets he had heard from an official voice. One of my staff members proudly told him I had written the speech myself. The reporter reached his counterpart in Washington and asked him to find out at the morning State Department briefing whether I had cleared the speech before delivering it. The spokesman at State responded without hesitation that of course it had been cleared. The Reuters man said he had reason to believe that was not true and asked to see Roz Ridgway, who, since the reporting cable had not yet arrived in Washington, called me so that she could talk knowledgeably to the journalist. I explained that I hadn't cleared the speech, that it had never occurred to me to clear it, and that nobody had ever said that I should. I assured her that it was perfectly consistent with President Carter's policy on human rights and told her, in essence, what I had said. We had no disagreement or difficulty.* The issue of clearing speeches was never again raised.

A Reuters dispatch did go out, however, saying my tough speech had not been cleared with Washington. Griffin Bell was furious. He thought someone at State had leaked the story to undercut me and that I was being criticized. He liked the speech and announced to me that he was going to protest. "I'll tell Jimmy." A few days later, I heard from the president with praise for the speech, words obviously inspired by Griffin's friendship and support.

Very early in the meeting, the Soviets and their allies insisted that we were violating the Helsinki Final Act by interfering in their internal affairs when we criticized them for their human rights behavior. They claimed that the Helsinki Final Act clearly made such "interference" unacceptable. I was eager to speak to this issue because their argument had appeal to some of the delegates.

My response was that nothing concerns the issue of internal affairs or sovereignty more profoundly than one's military establishment and the defense of country. In effect, I explained to the Soviets: "You want arms talks and disarmament. Suppose we agree. Then you do not go forward with agreed-upon reductions and we raise the issue of your noncompliance. Will you say that we're interfering in your internal affairs? If that's the case, a disarmament negotiation becomes a farce. The same concern applies here. You willingly signed the Helsinki Final Act in 1975. We didn't force you to sign. You willingly assumed certain obligations. To the extent that you assumed these obligations, haven't you agreed we could inquire about your compliance? That inquiry is not an improper interference in your internal affairs." The argument was clearly effective with the delegates who heard it.

* Several years later when Roz was named assistant secretary of State for European affairs, her appointment ran into trouble on Capitol Hill. The State Department told me that one of the criticisms of her was that she was critical of my Madrid speech of November 17, 1980. I assured them that was not true, and did what I could to put the rumor to rest.

The Soviets then made a tactical move that I welcomed. They and their friends began to criticize the human rights record of the United States on blacks, Indians, and women. I welcomed the criticism, declaring that it legitimized the review at the meetings of a state's compliance with the human rights obligations of the Helsinki Final Act. We proceeded to present our case in response. The implementation review we sought was at hand with mutual agreement. It was a breakthrough. Furthermore, we had about twenty public members on our delegation during those early weeks, and they included blacks, Indians, many women, and other minority representatives.

We had decided to raise the issue of the Soviet Union's antireligious policies against its own citizens. Griffin Bell, who increasingly liked his participation in Madrid, suggested that he, as an active Baptist, make the speech on anti-Semitism and that I make the one on anti-Christian activities. I had received a draft of a speech on Soviet anti-Semitism from a friend who was a fine scholar in the field, but it did not particularly suit my style. I shared it with the judge, nonetheless, and he thought he could work with it. The night before he was to deliver the speech, he called to say he was urgently needed in Atlanta, was leaving in the morning, and could not give the speech. He urged me to do so.

I felt that I could not deliver a speech, especially on anti-Semitism, with which I was not fully comfortable. I arranged to see Sergei Kondrashev that morning and told him that I had a speech to deliver that day on anti-Semitism. His face fell, but before he could speak, I said, "You have told me that we attack too much. So I'll tell you what I am going to do. Instead of delivering this speech on the floor, I will deliver it to you. Here it is. You act on it as you can and I will then judge whether quiet diplomacy works."

He brightened up, saying, "Moscow will appreciate this gesture, Max." That was the last I heard on the matter. More than a year later, after writing the speech I wanted, I decided that sufficient time had passed without a positive response from Moscow, and I therefore went forcefully after the Soviets on anti-Semitism. The attack, filled with facts, was devastating. When Kondrashev that day complained to Spencer Oliver, Spencer reminded him of our exchange a year earlier. The talk was reprinted in booklet form by interested organizations and widely distributed. Dealing with the Russians, not with our allies or our own government, was the ultimate challenge. I found Ilichev, his successor Anatoli Kovalev, Dubinin, and Kondrashev all interesting and very capable men. I particularly enjoyed Kondrashev because of his impressive skill as director of the Soviet working team, no doubt abetted by his knowledge of English.

I learned a great deal about Soviet thinking from him and shared it with Washington. He had an awareness of what the West was all about. At one point, he said to me, "You do not understand, but you should understand that you and your government have many friends in my country and among my associates."

Ilichev was quite different. He was from the old school, but even he was willing to listen. He sometimes had a bullying manner; he also loved to hear himself talk. During one lunch, he treated us to a one-hour monologue on the negotiations he had conducted over many years with the Chinese. This included a section on Chinese cooking. Dubinin, who was also in attendance, fell asleep about halfway through it. I found myself hoping that Ilichev would not notice, but he did and berated Dubinin for not listening. One day, well into the second year of our talks, Ilichev said he had been reviewing the negotiations and felt that the Soviets had made essentially all the concessions and we very few. That, he said, did not seem fair to him. I replied, "You have indeed been doing a great deal more moving than we. You are correct, but I want to explain why this is so."

I put a pen on the table and said, "Let's assume that this is where you are willing to end up." Then I put a second pen down not too far away and suggested we assume this was where we wished to end up. "But, where do we each start from? You set up a beginning position at an extreme end, way off the table. Nobody is there to stop you. We can't do that. We cannot begin with an extreme position. We have to convince our Congress, including our political opposition, that we are reasonable. We have to answer the questions and criticism of the press. Then we have to go to our allies in Europe—not client states, but independent nations with different traditions, aspirations, and problems. They want to have input. They want their views taken seriously. We move some more. Each move brings our starting position closer to our end position, while you're off the table. You then suggest we meet each other halfway. That cannot work!" Ilichev made no gesture, spoke no words. But I think he understood the truth of what I said.

When we broke just before Christmas 1980 with the election of a new president, Griffin Bell and I both submitted our resignations to the State Department. Our NATO allies, figuring they had seen the last of me, asked if they could have a goodbye party, and I agreed. It was a warm and grand event for me, and we all assumed it was the end of my career as ambassador.

I returned from Madrid in December, believing that we had done a good job in setting the tone for the meeting and that I was finished with my assignment. I arranged to meet with Richard Allen, who was to become Reagan's national security assistant. I needed to tell him what we had done and to offer my assistance in briefing my successor whenever that person was selected. To my surprise, Allen said he expected President Reagan to ask me to stay on.

Allen and I had been among the co-founders, along with Reagan, of the Committee on the Present Danger, and were friends, if not particularly close. My only close contact with Reagan had come just about a year earlier in 1979 when Allen had called to ask if I could arrange for Reagan to speak before an important Jewish audience.

I was then president of the American Friends of the Hebrew University, so I arranged for Reagan to speak in Palm Beach before major Jewish philanthropists, most of whom were, or had been, successful businessmen. This helped produce a crowd for the university and a good audience for Reagan. Allen hoped I would sit next to Reagan and introduce him. Reagan gave a strongly pro-Israel speech, as Allen had said he would. I found Reagan knowledgeable about the Middle East and more than charming. He was certainly not the fool or ogre some of my friends described. Now he was about to be president, with Dick Allen his assistant on national security matters.

After visiting with Dick Allen, I also telephoned Alexander Haig, who had been announced as the new secretary of State. I thought it important to brief him on what we had done and to offer my help to my successor. I went to both because I assumed this administration would not be different from earlier ones, where some tension and even some lack of clear communication between the NSC and the State Department was usual.

During the campaign, at a meeting I was able to attend of the Committee on the Present Danger, Allen asked me if I had any ideas for secretary of State. I suggested Scoop Jackson, the senator from Washington—a Democrat. I said that the country needed healing, and a bipartisan foreign policy would provide the consensus necessary for a healthy foreign policy. Allen was enthusiastic and later came back to ask me if Jackson would accept. I talked to Scoop, who said he would accept, but only after the election was over so that it would not influence the election. He was also convinced he would never be offered the post. Allen then told me that Reagan was attracted to the idea but his campaign advisers were not.

On the morning of January 19, 1981, a day before the inauguration, Al Haig called to say officially that Reagan wanted me to continue as his ambassador at Madrid. A week or two earlier, our close friend Jeane Kirkpatrick, who was deeply involved in the transition, told me there was some talk of having former Senator Jacob Javits replace

Griffin Bell to serve as co-chairman with me. I explained that I would remain as sole head of the delegation or not at all. I had control of the delegation and saw no reason to introduce a new figure who might complicate the negotiations and my life.

I was aware when Reagan reappointed me that there were friends and Democrats, particularly in Washington, who would disapprove of my decision to accept. I had learned from Humphrey's example, however, that we had only one president at a time, and Reagan was my president. Furthermore, I concluded that Reagan was a serious and sincere man who was not devious. Whether he was an intellectual and learned was irrelevant. Not many political leaders are, and not all the critics are, either.

As no time in the eight years that followed did I feel uncomfortable as a part of the Reagan administration. I was never asked to become a Republican or to modify my personal views. Indeed, I found myself, at the very beginning of our relationship, quoted in the press as differing from the president's decisions on two separate occasions. The *Washington Star*, in an article in April 1991, referred to the fact that I opposed lifting he grain embargo against the USSR which had been imposed following the Afghanistan invasion, and I asserted my dissatisfaction with the decision to provide AWACS to Saudi Arabia. In the main, however, I strongly supported the Reagan foreign policy or I would not have remained with him.

Al Haig brought Lawrence Eagleburger back to Washington with him to serve as assistant secretary of State for European affairs. Larry, one of the most able professionals in our government, took over the responsibility for CSCE matters. I told Larry that from the beginning of the Madrid meeting, I had paid special attention to Spain, meeting with their government officials as frequently as I could. U.S. interests included easing the way for Spain to become a member of NATO and also arranging for diplomatic relations between Spain and Israel. Larry asked me to do what I could to expedite movement in both areas. I told him that Spain was already an integrated part of our Madrid NATO caucus. I welcomed the opportunity to broaden my political horizons beyond CSCE.

King Juan Carlos of Spain will most certainly be recognized as a bright light in Spanish history. He was trained by Franco as a youngster, but his supervised education ironically seemed to be steeped in democratic ways. When Juan Carlos succeeded to the throne, the message to the country was that Spain's future would be that of a parliamentary constitutional democracy.

One evening, during the first few months of our Madrid sessions, I was preparing to leave my hotel for the apartment of Mauricio Hachuel Toledano, a leader of the Jewish community, who was hosting a dinner for a visiting Israeli delegation, when U.S. security people in our embassy called to say that a military coup was under way against the democratic Spanish government. I was advised to remain in my hotel.* By morning, the king had faced down the coup leaders and coalesced support for the elected government. The Spanish government asked for a one-minute period of silence throughout the country promptly at noon the following day. It worked, as people throughout the country stopped what they were doing, indoors and out, and stood still for a moment to express their determination to save their democracy.

A few weeks later, I received a telephone call from the palace, inviting me to come by for a private visit. I did not know what the subject matter would be, but I assumed the king was interested in being brought up to date on the CSCE meetings. Our ambassador to Madrid, Terence Todman, was a very capable diplomat born in the Virgin Islands; he and I had been on a committee creating the College of the Virgin Islands. I asked Larry Eagleburger for advice. Should I suggest to Terry that he join me, or should I take literally the invitation's directive that the talk be private? We agreed that I would inform our ambassador, who graciously suggested that since he had other opportunities to meet with the king, we should now take advantage of the special invitation and limit it to my presence alone. It was a good meeting. Our agenda covered democracy and foreign policy; his own role as a constitutional monarch without actual power but with a strong symbolic presence and evident democratic leanings; and the Middle East.

The king spoke candidly about his close relationship with King Hussein of Jordan and his affection and admiration for Israel. Spain wanted to play a significant role in bringing about peace in the Middle

---

* The issue of my personal security kept coming up during my three years in Madrid. Our U.S. security reports were continually reassuring even though the Madrid airport was "open" and terrorists could freely come and go. The Spanish police would sometimes ignore me, which I would take as a good sign. On other occasions, my car would be surrounded by police vehicles, and an armed guard would be placed in my car with me. The big concern was whether I was a PLO target. At one point, the police rented an apartment immediately next to mine, which was occupied twenty-four hours a day. Since I love to walk, this was restrictive, but I learned the importance of unpredictability in scheduling. On most weekends, when I was alone, I would sneak out of the hotel and walk in the beautiful parks and streets of Madrid for hours.

East. I urged that the best way to begin assuming such a role was for Spain to recognize Israel and exchange ambassadors. Our government wanted Spain to recognize Israel diplomatically, and I considered this objective relevant to my portfolio as well. He made it clear to me that this decision was beyond his power and responsibility. Of course, I knew that; I also knew he had influence beyond the formalities of his office. Toward the end of our talk, he mentioned that the president of Israel, Itzhak Navon, who had Spanish ancestry, would be popular if he decided to visit Spain. I passed that on to Israel via Larry Eagleburger.

The king and I had one other meeting during the course of the Madrid sessions and another during a trip I made on February 20, 1987, to brief the Spanish prime minister, Felipe Gonzalez, on our Geneva negotiations. These meetings were extremely interesting and worthwhile, and I found him to be very bright, alert and informed. At one point as we concluded our meeting, he asked me to pass on a joke to the president, whose appreciation of humor was well known to those who visited him. I did so, although I must confess that I was not particularly taken with the humor. The president, however, when I next saw him, thought better of the joke than I had.*

Spain's relationship to its Jewish population and to Israel was and remains complex. Franco treated the Jewish community by and large with respect. Maggie and I were impressed with the number of Spaniards we met, particularly among the "old" families, who believed they had some Jewish ancestry. One political leader, out of this conviction, was tutoring his children in Jewish culture and Israeli history, even as they all remained practicing Catholics. For years, Spain held out the prospect of Israel's diplomatic recognition, but Arab cultural influence, oil, and economic interests slowed the process.

Israel, under the Helsinki Final Act, was a "non-participating Mediterranean state,"† with no voting rights but with the opportunity

---

* I will leave it to the reader to judge. It seems, went the yarn, that a parachutist jumped from a plane, tried the ripcord, and found it would not work. He tried again as he was hurtling toward the ground, and the parachute once more did not open. At that moment, he noticed a man shooting straight up toward the skies with his hands and body tightly wound around a large container. As they were passing each other, the parachutist yelled: "Hey, do you know anything about parachutes?" The other fellow yelled back: "No, but do you know anything about butane gas?"

† The countries falling within this category are Algeria, Egypt, Israel, Morocco, Syria, Tunisia, Lebanon, and Libya. These states can make formal statements at the opening of follow-up meetings, can participate in working groups dealing with Mediterranean issues, but cannot vote by either joining in or denying consensus for decision making.

to attend and speak at a designated few of the formal sessions. Meir Rosenne, Israel's ambassador in Paris, was assigned by his government to attend Madrid's opening sessions as their official representative, but the government also designated Spanish-speaking Samuel Hadas to be a continuing presence. With the help of Javier Ruperez and at my urging, the Spanish government permitted Hadas a de facto presence in Spain under the CSCE umbrella. He worked quietly and effectively with all the major political parties and leadership, and diplomatic recognition slowly worked its way. When I could be helpful to him, I made myself available and, in the meantime, I kept our embassy and Washington informed of my activities. The first major agreement between Spain and Israel provided for direct air transportation between the two countries. This then led to full diplomatic exchange in January 1986.

Our first year was an intensive one filled with tension. A charming and welcome break came late in 1980. As Thanksgiving approached, it was clear that our delegation and staff would not get home for the holiday. Maggie and I decided to arrange a traditional dinner for the entire U.S. delegation. I turned to an American, Robert Pecka, who owned a superb small Spanish restaurant we enjoyed, La Mesa Redondo. I asked Bob if we could reserve it for a Thanksgiving dinner with all the trimmings. He agreed enthusiastically and did a great job of preparing the food, from turkey to sweet potatoes to pumpkin pie.

It would have been a warm get-together in any case, but it received an unexpected boost when I learned that Joan Baez was coming to Madrid as part of her human rights concerns. I suggested to Warren Zimmermann that she be invited to join us. She not only came, but sang for us in her clear and beautiful voice, making it a memorable dinner and an incredible morale booster for staff far from home.*

One evening in early February 1981, the Norwegian ambassador, Leif Mevik, a close associate, hosted a dinner for a number of us, including the French, German, British, and Soviet representatives. The guest of honor was the Norwegian deputy foreign minister, who spoke, I believed, in a theoretical and somewhat obsequious way that I felt might leave the Soviets with an impression of division on our

---

* Joan Baez, whose soft, lovely voice seemed to reflect the pure spirit of traditional Quaker pacifism that moved her, impressed me immensely as a person of principle. I had read that her opposition to our military involvement in Vietnam was matched by her unsuccessful efforts to persuade her fellow protesters publicly to repudiate North Vietnam's brutality against the Vietnam refugees and boat people. She said: "People disappear and never return. People are. . . . fed a starvation diet of stale rice, forced to squat bound wrist to ankle. . . . People are used as human mine detectors. . . . For many, life is hell and death is prayed for . . ."

side. I thought it necessary to challenge some of the minister's views, while maintaining diplomatic niceties, although I could not refrain from raising questions about Soviet human rights violations and Soviet aggression in Afghanistan.

Ilichev was surprisingly candid and much less ideological that night, far beyond anything I could have expected. He said on a number of occasions during dinner that it was essential for the United States and the Soviets to assume the primary responsibility to face each other seriously and privately in dialogue and negotiations. I had made the point that national self-interest was a priority in all international negotiations. Beyond that, we also had to understand that there was a fundamental difference in values and approach between the West and the Soviets. The big question was whether we could interrelate within agreed-upon rules. Ilichev said that he agreed with me on both issues.

What was additionally fascinating to me was that Ilichev approached me after dinner to say he understood my purpose in intervening and my candor through the evening. He emphasized the need for the United States and the Soviet Union to meet privately either in Washington, Moscow, or somewhere else to resolve the present overall impasse that existed between our two countries.

Ilichev reminded me that an important goal for the Soviets in Madrid was to schedule a disarmament conference. I was already aware that this was essential for them. He made it explicit. A conference made tactical and propaganda sense for them. I believed that the Soviets would use the fact of such an impending conference as a way to discourage our deployment of Pershing and cruise missiles in Europe. They would say to the citizens of Western Europe: "Why are we spending money, increasing nuclear dangers, encouraging anger and confrontation when we're about to start serious disarmament negotiations?" Knowing this, I felt we had leverage.

This was one reason that, as a practical matter, the Soviets worked so surprisingly hard to try to keep the discussions alive in Madrid, a compelling reason for them not to walk out as they sometimes threatened. They took the heat on human rights as a price they were willing to pay. Because I had sensed that all along, I wanted a significant price for that post-Madrid disarmament meeting and was certain we could get it. In the meantime, I carefully and persistently noted at our meetings that Madrid itself was not a disarmament conference, and we should not mislead the people in the West into believing that it was or could become one.

Ilichev responded to my position by saying that without such a conference, he didn't see much useful purpose for the Madrid meeting. As it turned out, of course, by the time we finished the Madrid meeting in 1983, the issue of deployment of Pershing and cruise missiles was already moot, since they were being deployed. An agreement in 1981 would have been helpful to them; an agreement in 1983 was not a bit helpful.

At about this time and, I believe, as part of the same effort, Kondrashev took me aside on January 29, 1981, at the apartment of the Finnish ambassador, Richard Mueller, and his wife, Leni, to say that he and I had to have a private talk. We had to find a way to overcome existing combative rhetoric in Washington and Moscow and restore direct diplomatic discourse between our two countries. This was vital, he said, for our children and grandchildren.

We met privately on February 10. Saying he was speaking for Moscow, Kondrashev initially complained about Reagan's "insulting" language and Secretary of State Al Haig's "erroneous and damaging" allegation tying the USSR to international terrorism. Moscow's chief concern, however, was whether and when the United States would be ready to negotiate normally about our broad bilateral and international concerns. I reminded him that as long as Soviet troops remained in Afghanistan, I believed a "normal" relationship was not possible. He asked me to inform Washington of Moscow's inquiry and desire.

He then moved to the immediate Madrid concerns and emphasized Moscow's requirement for a decision out of Madrid to establish a European disarmament conference. Otherwise, Moscow would lose interest in the Helsinki process. The USSR, I responded, had a far greater need for the CSCE than the United States, but if the process should end, we would, of course, place blame squarely on Soviet shoulders. He then complained that the Madrid meeting had turned into "a total Western show." I agreed and suggested that Soviet violations of their international responsibilities were the reason for that development. The future, I said, depended on them and their behavior. He said he would forward my views to Moscow.

During the spring, Ilichev and I found ourselves embroiled in a bitter and sharp debate, the most intensive of our experience together. Because Maggie's arrival in Madrid had been delayed by her father's terminal illness in Milwaukee, it was just a few weeks earlier that I had introduced her to Ilichev at the magnificent home of the duke of Alba, where we had been invited to view his impressive art collection. While I was viewing the collection, I heard Ilichev's loud voice and looked up to see him dragging Maggie toward me, saying "See, she too agrees with me that you're a terribly stubborn man!"

Soon thereafter, his tone lost all traces of such playfulness. For reasons unclear to me, Ilichev decided to attack the United States fiercely at one of our morning plenaries. My custom was to respond immediately to criticisms, particularly those with a political orientation. I did so now. Under our usual practice at these meetings, my right of reply would have ended the exchange, and the formal meeting would go on. Ilichev, however, insisted on continuing the attack in a manner I considered irresponsible. It irritated me.

My pattern was to carry in my briefcase stacks of documentation about Soviet abuses. By the end of the Madrid meeting, I was determined to have all the evidence move from my files to the record of the proceedings for my colleagues to know about and for history to record. There were limits, however, to what the meeting could absorb at any one time. I also did not want to appear fanatic or obsessive. I therefore looked for occasions, or excuses, to move appropriate data from my briefcase to my tongue. Here I was being provoked, so out came my briefcase.

My retort to Ilichev was now a fully documented countercharge. He and I went at it for about two or three more rounds. The meeting became quite tense and silent. When we both sat down, nobody else asked for the floor, and the formal session ended. There was a pall. Out of the corner of my eye, I could see some of my colleagues approaching me. They were worried. There was the perennial concern: "Would the Soviets walk out and destroy Helsinki?" My response was that I did not know but would soon find out, since I was due for lunch with Ilichev at Dubinin's residence in an hour. If the door was locked, I'd know they were angry. I met this head-on, because I was convinced there was far too much concern in the West about Soviet sensitivities, coupled with a pre-accommodation to anticipated reactions.

Ilichev was a smiling, gracious host upon my arrival. I did not refer to our debate, since I had had the last word and I was a guest. Ilichev, Dubinin, and Kondrashev did not refer to it either. Our conversation was interesting and lively. It was also somewhat productive. As I rose to leave, Ilichev, a smaller man than I, put his arm around me, called over his interpreter, and said something similar to: "What I like about our relationship is that we can exchange [the word was finally translated as "pleasantries"] in the morning and do serious business in the after-noon!"

In December 1981, our meetings were complicated by the decla-ration of martial law in Poland. My closing talk of the round on De-cember 18 warned of the seriousness of that declaration, the Soviet pressure that provoked it, and its effect on our meeting. The Polish ambassador took me aside to say that his government was reacting to Soviet pressure only temporarily and intended to withdraw martial law.* When we resumed our meetings the following February, the situation had deteriorated, casting gloom over both East and West.

NATO, at our urging, had decided during the recess to use the Madrid meeting as a loud, effective and unified voice of Western protest against the declaration of martial law in Poland and to warn about the threat of Soviet military aggression there. All the NATO foreign ministers agreed to attend the opening day of the renewed round on February 9, 1982. Al Haig spoke for the United States and laid a good foundation for us. We had all decided that this would be a special session at which we would not do business as usual. This meant that we would not continue working on the draft concluding document submitted to us some weeks earlier by the neutral and nonaligned nations. Instead, we agreed that we would address ourselves directly to the repression taking place in Poland and continue with specific documentation of other Soviet excesses in defiance of the Helsinki accords. Our resolve was fully respected by the neutrals, each of whom saw Polish martial law and Soviet pressure on Poland as an indirect threat to its own security. This resolve was intensified when the Soviets persuaded the head of the Polish delegation, whose turn it was to serve as chairman, to ignore the rules of procedure. For six hours, he refused to recognize any Western speaker, all of whom were foreign

---

* Professor M. Dobrizelski was the first head of the Polish delegation to Madrid. Aiding him were two former students of his, Jerzy Novak, a career foreign service officer who served as his deputy, and Adam Rotfeld, a CSCE university expert. Since they were thoughtful people, I managed to spend some time with each of them. Rotfeld's father had been the mayor of their small village just before the war. Knowing he was Jewish, the nuns of a nearby convent, on the eve of the Nazi invasion, offered to hide the Rotfeld baby boy. It wasn't until after the war that young Rotfeld learned his true name and that he was Jewish. The nuns gave him the option of going to Israel at their expense to live or being educated at their expense in Poland. He chose the latter, but he found that anti-Semitism in Poland had damaged his career and travel opportunities. He was first in his class in the foreign service exams, but was advised that his religion would keep him from a career position.

Novak found himself in personal difficulty during Madrid with the growth of Solidarity and the imposition of martial law. He was personally sympathetic toward Solidarity. His wife had volunteered for public relations work in behalf of the union; and his seventeen-year-old son was a Solidarity youth leader. When he felt free to talk about his worries, I tried to be helpful. He was fortunately able to arrange an assignment to the United Nations in New York so he could take his family out of harm's way.

When I reached Copenhagen in June 1990 to head the U.S. delegation at the CSCE meeting, I found Novak there as head of the Polish delegation. When we greeted each other, he said he would never forget our talk in Madrid on December 6, 1980, a date fresh in his mind, when I offered my help to him.

ministers. The indignation was overwhelming, and the Pole retreated in embarrassment. During this period, *Newsweek* quoted me as saying to the Polish chairman: "You are behaving as if martial law has been imposed on the Madrid meeting."

I looked for and found an opportunity to speak about Bronislaw Geremek, who had served as a fellow at the Woodrow Wilson International Center for Scholars and was recognized as an outstanding historian. I pointed out that his "great scholarship" was accompanied by a free mind and a free soul, as with many scholars. In 1968, he had turned in his Communist party membership card to protest the Soviet invasion of Czechoslovakia. In 1980, he had joined Solidarity. With the declaration of martial law, he was jailed. The Soviet press, as part of a virulent attack on his reputation, assailed his remarkable scholarly work on the role of the gypsies in late medieval culture as "writing about degenerates," which I characterized as "another blatant example of the racism" that governed the Soviet Union. A Jew, he was also attacked in the Soviet press as a Zionist. *Pravda*, on March 21, 1982, wrote that Geremek "underwent training in anti-communist centers, including a Zionist Masonic lodge in Paris," which I ridiculed at our meeting.

I pointed out that at the time I was speaking, I was also serving as chairman of the Woodrow Wilson International Center for Scholars in Washington, D.C., and that I joined all the past presidents and the current president of the American Historical Association in expressing our concern about Geremek. I stated that we would judge the Polish government's good intentions by the fate of Geremek. "We say to our friend Bronislaw Geremek, a historian, that the teachings of history demonstrate that at no period can we say 'it is over.' The Polish people have seen this inhumanity before in their lifetime. Today is not the last day. It is just today. And there will be tomorrow."*

Tempers flared as a united West pummeled the Soviet Union and the military government of Poland for their violations of the Helsinki agreements. The Soviets would frequently respond in anger. At one point, Ilichev stood up and declared that he noticed tension in my voice, which meant, as far as he was concerned, that I was straining the truth. I responded that it was not tension that he heard, but rather

---

* I later met Dr. Geremek's wife, who visited my office, but I had not as yet met him. In May 1990, as I was chairing a conference on the CSCE at the Woodrow Wilson Center, Dr. Geremek, who had just arrived in Washington, came into the meeting room, strode to the dais, embraced me, and thanked me for what I had done in Madrid. He is now a major figure in the Polish parliament. It was a thrill for me to see his photograph on the first page of the *New York Times* alongside Lech Walesa soon after Solidarity took control of the Polish government following free elections.

"anger at the system of repression" that his society represents. When the Soviets urged that we go back to "constructive work here," I called their statements "sheer hypocrisy." The "only work I know they are doing on the Act is flagrantly to undermine it."

The forum also gave me an opportunity to talk about the Soviet Union's illegal annexation of the Baltic states after the Molotov-Ribbentrop Pact, stating that the United States does not recognize the forcible incorporation of the Baltic states into the Soviet Union. I pointed out that those nations of the world that, in the course of their own histories, had experimented with imperialism, learned that there are decided limits to imperial attainments. Those countries that have abandoned the imperial mode, I suggested, have found relief from the burdens and do not regret the loss.

Finally, on March 12, the neutrals obtained the consent of the Soviets to end this particular round without doing any further business. This was what we wanted. The neutrals suggested that we return in November in the hope that the situation might have improved by then. We agreed.

I prepared my closing speech of the round with great care. I felt that the Soviets in Moscow would study it carefully. I therefore reaffirmed our desire for peace, which I emphasized required compliance with the provisions of the Helsinki Final Act. To illustrate the strength of our system, I said, "We need no walls, no rigid bureaucratic regulations, no threats of punishment to keep our people from leaving our shores. Millions come to us to become American citizens. I suspect that those who build walls of brick and paper know full well that a large number of their citizens would choose our way of life, the way of democracy and liberty, were they given the chance." I asserted that "rulers who fear the people they govern end up fearing one another, fearing their nightmares, fearing the unknown, fearing the future, fearing for themselves and their states. They then try to instill fear in others. But fear does not produce loyalty." Pride in a country, I pointed out, must be earned by respect and not by fear.

A few weeks before the round ended, I attended an important conference in Munich sponsored by a foundation in the Federal Republic of Germany known as Wehrkunde. It is an annual gathering of arms control and foreign policy experts, government and private, from within the NATO states. The U.S. Senate Armed Services Committee serves as the co-sponsor. Judge William P. Clark, the new national security assistant to President Reagan, was the star U.S. attraction.

During the course of the Wehrkunde Conference, which I found very instructive, the FRG chairman, noticing me listening attentively toward the rear of a filled meeting room, unexpectedly asked me to come forward and brief the meeting on developments in Madrid. I did so, attempting to relate our experiences to what I had been hearing from the experts during the course of the day. I returned to my seat and noticed Judge Clark, whom I had never met, coming to greet me. We talked, and he asked me if I had ever had the opportunity to provide a similar briefing to the president. I told him I had not. He said he would arrange such a meeting.

Several weeks later, I found myself in the oval office briefing President Reagan; Vice President Bush; Judge Clark; his deputy, Bud McFarlane; the chief of staff, James Baker; and counselor Ed Meese. During the thirty- to forty-minute session, most everybody, particularly the president, asked direct and penetrating questions after I made my presentation. It was clear to me that little was known of the Helsinki Final Act, other than a negative impression of its origin, and little really known of what we were doing in Madrid to strengthen Western resolve and undermine Soviet political strength in Europe.

As I walked out of what I considered a successful briefing, the vice president took my arm, thanked me, and asked if I could spare additional time with him. We then went to his office, where we spent an additional forty-five minutes talking about the Soviet Union, how it is to negotiate with them, and how Europe looked to me. I had known George Bush, but not too well. I was impressed.

The break in the talks resulting from the declaration of martial law in Poland lasted for eight months. During the summer, we began to hear rumblings from our allies that even though the objective facts in Poland had not changed, it was necessary to deal with a final document upon our return to the Madrid table in November. In Washington, however, we saw no justification for returning to "business as usual."

In the interim, I traveled to Europe on three separate occasions to meet with the NATO caucus in Norway, Portugal, and Belgium. Our differences were sharp and clear, but I felt that our relationship was a constructive one. Our allies came to understand that our view was firmly held and began to think about how to accommodate us. At the Norway meeting, we started in the morning by having each delegation express its views. The United States seemed to stand alone. The British ambassador, Sir Anthony Williams, a very capable and experienced diplomat, joined the others in pointing out to me that we could not risk undermining the Helsinki process because it was still a vehicle that could produce results for us. As the afternoon session began, he was called to the telephone. He returned, took me aside, and said that Margaret Thatcher, the British prime minister, had read an item in the *International Herald Tribune* referring to our differences and had instructed her foreign minister to have their ambassador side with me. He very candidly explained his shift of position to our colleagues.

The European Community (The Ten) had been quite active in Madrid alongside our NATO caucus. Nine of them were also a part of NATO (Ireland was not). During the second half of 1982, the Danes were in the presidency of the European Community. They made a special effort to meet U.S. concerns, and during the Portugal meeting, their ambassador asked me to consider how we could overcome the impasse between us. After all, he pointed out, we had all agreed to return in November, so that was no longer an open question. It was unproductive and perhaps pregnant with misunderstanding, he acknowledged, for us to return after the recess in the same mold we had left. He agreed we could not do business as usual. What developed during the conversation was that we would add a series of new requirements for concluding the Madrid meeting, ones associated with the Polish problem, such as provisions for free trade unionism. This appealed to me, and I suggested that he and his colleagues might try to come up with a program. In a few weeks, he sent along a good text of additional requirements. By the time the NATO group met in Belgium, we had an agreed-upon program that we were all ready to support when the Madrid meeting reconvened in November.

The round that began on November 16, 1982, lasted until mid-December. During that time, we pressed the importance of the new amendments that had been proposed by the West. The neutral authors of the draft concluding document had no problems with most of our amendments. The Soviets, obviously, wanted none of our changes.

Just then, Leonid Ilichev was called back to Moscow to work on new Soviet discussions with the Chinese. He had spent many years in China negotiating with them and was an expert on Sino-Soviet relations. In some ways, I felt that he was the most racially biased person I had ever met, in spite of his smiling exterior. He warned me frequently about the "yellow peril," saying that the Chinese were untrustworthy and that the United States would soon learn that lesson.

Ilichev was replaced by another deputy foreign minister, Anatoli Kovalev, younger but more senior than he, a very somber, serious man with a long, earnest face that seemed to be weighed down by the burdens of his office. His wife once told Maggie that he was a poet and a songwriter. This interested me very much, so I asked to see some of his poetry, which I then had translated. I was disappointed to discover that the poems were in the old Stalinist mode, extolling the Soviet lifestyle, with little warmth or humanity in them. I might have felt differently about them were I able to understand Russian, but I doubt it. They heightened the contrast with Ilichev, who frequently did not wish to be serious in our conversations. Kovalev always was.

Yuri Andropov was, by now, the Soviet leader in Moscow, and Kovalev brought Andropov's son, Igor, to Madrid, in an effort to give him stature. Conversations with the young man soon led to a general feeling that he was not a heavyweight in spite of the protection afforded him by the rest of the delegation. He was pleasant, with an attractive wife, but he appeared uncomfortable with himself. Many rumors surrounded him, including some about his drinking, but I was unable ever to verify any of them.

When we returned to Madrid in early 1983, it was increasingly clear to all of us that we were not far from an agreement. The Soviets now indicated their general support of the neutral document, which overwhelmingly reflected democratic human values. We might once have been prepared to accept it, but we now had our new amendments stemming out of Polish martial law. They were prerequisites for an agreement. The time was approaching as we reached the finish line for Spain to play its card as host in support of the NATO amendments.

The elections in Spain had brought to office Felipe Gonzalez, the dynamic young socialist leader who had expressed public skepticism about Spain's membership in NATO. His foreign minister showed signs of impatience in his desire to produce a final CSCE document. Such a result would make his government look good. We had to make certain that this eagerness did not lead the Spanish to give up certain goals that were attainable and important to us.

Ambassador Javier Ruperez left government service with the election of the socialists in Spain. He was replaced by Ambassador Pan de Soraluce, an experienced Spanish diplomat from an aristocratic background who was a good friend of the United States. Indeed, soon after the Spanish socialists came to power, he told me he was worried about his new foreign minister's impatience for an agreement. Would I talk to him? I did, and at that meeting I acknowledged our awareness of how important it was to Spain for the meeting to end successfully. I promised we would help Spain receive appropriate credit for that result. I persuaded him of our seriousness in requiring a document better than the one then being floated by the neutrals. I promised to work with him, but he had to be guided by our combined NATO sense of timing. He agreed.

The FRG ambassador to our meetings, Jorge Kastl, has become a close working partner of mine. He and his wife, Eva, were senior diplomats and had been kind to Maggie and me. We also developed a very close political relationship that led Kastl, on a few occasions, to arrange for private meetings between me and the FRG foreign minister, Hans Dietrich Genscher. Kastl and I looked on the Soviet Union in the same way and with the same political goals in mind. He proposed a weekend meeting with our Spanish colleague, who invited us to spend a Sunday at his country home outside Madrid.

The visit was relaxing and convivial. The country house was not far from Madrid, among pastures and fields ready to turn green with spring. We talked about the current state of play, and I listed our concerns. Referring to my promise to his foreign minister, I also said I thought the host government was in a unique position soon to be the resolver of differences, thus getting credit and prestige for breaking the stalemate. I was convinced that agreement could be reached and that the Soviets were more flexible than they seemed, and I conveyed that belief as strongly as I could. We agreed on a plan that would culminate in the Spanish prime minister arranging a reception at which he, as host, would present a formula to resolve all the issues that remained open.

My conviction that the Soviets wanted to end the Madrid meeting with a concluding document and that they would be prepared ultimately to give us what we wanted to obtain that document had come to me more than a year earlier, following my conversations with Ilichev. They very much wanted to stop the U.S. deployment of Pershing and cruise missiles and expected that the agreement in Madrid would give them the ammunition to do so. I had mentioned this to Al Haig when he was secretary of State and told him I felt we should add to our demands a very private item to be discussed only with the Soviets: the release of a significant number of imprisoned political and religious activists from the Soviet Union. Haig told me he was sympathetic to that objective and, after he talked to President Reagan about it, informed me that I was authorized to try to achieve that goal.

I began the process with Kondrashev, who listened attentively but did not respond affirmatively. Now that I was seeing other concrete signs of the Soviet eagerness to end the meeting, I used the occasion of my return home for a break between rounds to brief newly selected Secretary of State George Shultz, who had replaced Al Haig, about the details and complexities of the Madrid meetings. Since I felt our requirements would be met by the Soviets, my primary question was whether President Reagan wanted an agreement with the Soviets. This was a fundamental threshold question, and his immediate response was, "Why don't you ask him? I'll arrange for you to meet with him." We did meet, and the president's response was unequivocally affirmative, assuming that we could come up with the proper agreement. I then said to the president that I needed more than an agreement if I was to satisfy my own conscience. I needed people to be released. I had to set that forth to the Soviets as a condition for a final agreement. The president gave me that authority. Shultz was very pleased with this new development.

There comes a time when negotiations must die or reach a conclusion. Energy and patience run out. More talk means increased aggravation. We had certainly reached that condition by the spring of 1983. What had been intended to be a meeting of no more than several months had gone on now for almost three years. We were also by now fairly certain we had won Europe's big political battle and that our allies would deploy the Pershing and cruise missiles in spite of the massive Soviet effort to force a reversal of that NATO decision.

The meeting that had opened under the shadow of the Soviet invasion had continued with the armed occupation of Afghanistan and martial law in Poland. Soviet repression of human rights had increased. Emigration from the Soviet Union—and thus family reunification—had declined drastically from the highs of a decade before. In defiance of prior Helsinki agreement, the Soviets jammed radio broadcasts. They talked reasonably but behaved abominably. Yet we kept working, session following session. We worked in spite of the frustrations, the disappointments, the arguments, even the occasional personal calumnies that occurred.

Western European countries considered the Helsinki meetings important for their future and feared that a repeat of Belgrade at Madrid would significantly diminish the stature and viability of the CSCE process. The Soviets wanted some form of a disarmament conference, and the West wanted gains in human rights and family reunification, among other things. The question remained after months of meetings and volumes of talk whether we could finally agree on a document that, at least in words, improved upon the original 1975 agreement.

In May 1983, the neutrals came up with a new proposal that embraced nearly all our requirements. Indeed, it was good enough for us to declare victory if we were inclined to do so. Our original humanitarian goals were in the main included, as were the additional provisions agreed upon by NATO after Polish martial law was declared; and the military section met the requirements of our Joint Chiefs of Staff. NATO considered this development a triumph.

The neutral proposal was a major step forward, but we had already told the Soviets we wanted more. Soviet President Andropov sent a letter to the thirty-four other heads of state, saying we ought now to proceed with the neutral paper without any further amendments. The Soviets expected this to carry the day. The United States refused to agree. The Soviets were angered by my recalcitrance, saying that Andropov had put his reputation on the line with his letter, and their hands were tied. They could accept no other changes. This was a rather persuasive argument with some of the neutral countries, who also didn't want further amendments to their handiwork. I pointed out to the Soviets that the decision for Andropov to sign such a letter was obviously based on a recommendation from the Madrid negotiating team and was simply a mistake in judgment on their part. We could not be bound by their error. Slowly but surely, with NATO unity behind us, the neutrals came up with a new paper supporting more of our requests.

The private agenda item that had absorbed my attention for most of the thirty-three months I had been in Madrid was slowing taking its course. I wanted the Soviets to do something concrete to demonstrate their verbal commitment to human rights and family reunification. The standards of the Helsinki Final Act are based on the principle that the human being is the center of our quest for peace. I wanted a Soviet act to recognize that basis.

While I did not believe or pretend that our U.S. society was perfect, I also knew that six decades after the Soviet revolution, the span of my life, Soviet citizens enjoyed neither bread nor freedom, the promise that came from Bolshevik bloodshed. The search for a more abundant life for the many in the Soviet Union had yielded to the accumulation of military, political, and police power in the hands of a few.

Sergei Kondrashev became the key player for the Soviets. He warned me on a number of occasions to keep our talks private even in Washington and to talk to nobody else in his delegation about our discussions, including the head of their delegation. The message was clear. The KGB was in charge and was the direct channel to Andropov.

Kondrashev had already demonstrated a willingness to take on individual human rights cases. We had been trying to get Natan Sharansky released. Kondrashev reminded me that he had followed up on our conversations, and that Sharansky's mother, Ida Milgrom, had been called in by the KGB, treated courteously in February and March 1983, and had received letters from her son in February, March, and April. Mrs. Milgrom was also now permitted to visit her son. The Soviets, I was told, were prepared to release Sharansky himself if he would simply write a letter that the Soviets had told us would be necessary to initiate the process of release. Kondrashev accepted my draft of the letter, which omitted words such as "pardon," that might imply guilt. Instead, in effect, it said, "I request my immediate release from prison on the grounds of poor health." Sharansky's mother carried the plan and the draft letter to her son (since he might not believe someone else), but he refused to write the letter. He heroically would not place himself as a supplicant before the Soviet state.* Kondrashev reminded me that all of that had been done at my request in behalf of the president.

Kondrashev also helped with the release of a group of people of special interest to the president. A small number of Pentecostal Christians, nine members of the Vashchenko and Chmykhalov families, had found safe haven in the American embassy in Moscow. The president told me he had talked to Dobrynin in March 1983, indicating that he would look upon the release of the Pentecostals as an important signal that serious dialogue and improved relations were possible. It had irritated the president that he received no response at all, not from Dobrynin or anyone else.

The president had asked me to make certain that Kondrashev

---

* Sharansky's report of this event is found in his book, *Fear No Evil* (New York: Random House, 1988), in which he describes a visit to him in jail on July 5, 1983, by his mother and brother (p. 357):

> Lenya [Sharansky's brother] continued: "The Helsinki Review Conference is now drawing to a close in Madrid, and the Americans made it clear that they won't sign the final document without a resolution of your problem. The head of the Soviet delegation has informed Max Kampelman, the head of the American delegation, and Kampelman told Avital [Mrs. Sharansky], that if you sign a statement requesting a release for reasons of health, the request will be granted. In Moscow, the KGB told us the same thing. Kampelman thinks the Soviets are serious, and that this is a major concession. They aren't asking you to admit guilt, or to recant, or to condemn anyone else. Elena Georgievna [Bonner], in the name of herself and her husband [Andrei Sakharov], asked me to tell you that in their opinion it's possible to accept this proposal."
>
> I interrupted Lenya: "And what about Natasha? Did Natasha ask me to do it?"
>
> "No, she asked nothing," he said. I sighed with relief, for otherwise it would be the first time I had to disagree with Avital since my arrest, which would have been a terrible blow to our spiritual unity.
>
> "Mama and I won't advise you what to do," said Lenya, "but I must convey your answer to the American embassy in Moscow. They're waiting for it. So think about it and let us know by the end of the meeting."
>
> "I can tell you now," I replied. "I committed no crimes. The crimes were committed by the people who arrested me and are keeping me in prison. Therefore the only appeal I can address to the Presidium is a demand for my immediate release and the punishment of those who are truly guilty. Asking the authorities to show humanity means acknowledging that they represent a legitimate force that administers justice."

knew of his interest and his previous request. I decided that I would not limit myself to the few people who were at the embassy. I learned from Warren Zimmermann, who was now in Moscow as our deputy chief of mission, that by counting members of their extended families not in the U.S. embassy, the number of Pentecostals whose release we requested amounted to about sixty people. I gave all the names to Kondrashev in April. He came back and said that they would be released if they went to Israel. That seemed odd, but if we did it his way, he explained, the decisions could be made in certain quarters in Moscow rather than in other less favorable ones. On April 12, the Pentecostals left our embassy for Siberia. On June 26, all the members of the two families were given permission to leave Siberia for Israel. They did so by July 18, 1983.

In that connection, an exchange with Kondrashev illustrated for me the extent to which irrationality was frequently a factor in complicating negotiations with the Soviets. Florida Congressman Dante Fascell, chairman of the CSCE Commission, had urged me to try to persuade the Soviets to release a Soviet lady named Kaplan who had relatives living in his state. I made the case to Sergei, pointing out that Fascell would likely soon be chairman of the House of Representatives Committee on Foreign Affairs, one of the most important posts in the American government. He agreed to pass the request on to Moscow. A few weeks later, he firmly told me Moscow had said no. There was no chance she would be released. I repeated my arguments and pointed out that Moscow was being foolish. In agitated fashion, he broke in to say: "Max, you don't understand. Kaplan tried to kill Lenin!"—referring to a 1922 shooting attempt by a lady with the same name.

During this period, I received an urgent message from Warren Zimmermann. His wife, Teeny, a vivacious woman of strong convictions, had gone to the Moscow apartment of Ina and Naum Meiman, her dear friends. Ina was teaching Russian to Teeny and other Americans. Naum, a world-renowned mathematician and dissident whose desire to emigrate to Israel had been refused, was an active champion of human rights. While Teeny was visiting Ina, the KGB police entered the apartment and took many of Naum's papers, despite Ina and Teeny's protests. The police threatened Teeny as they left. Warren was concerned that the Soviets might distort the event into a cause célèbre.

I made arrangements to see Kondrashev. He seemed to be familiar with the incident that had just taken place. I said that if the KGB was going to make trouble for the Zimmermanns, I would bring the whole story to the attention of the Madrid meeting. A few days later, he told me that the incident was now ancient history and was best forgotten. I decided to adopt the Meimans and their cause, using as many occasions as seemed appropriate to push for their release from the Soviet Union.

Maggie and I later visited the Meimans in Moscow and became good friends. Ina, tragically, developed a relatively rare form of cancer. The Soviets delayed so long in giving her permission to leave for treatment in the United States that, when it came, it was too late. Teeny arranged for treatment at Georgetown University, where Ina died. Maggie and I were in Geneva at the time, but our daughter Julia was able to visit Ina at the hospital in behalf of our family. Soviet authorities refused to give Naum permission to attend her funeral.

Naum is now in Israel at the Weizmann Institute. In 1989 he made his first visit to the United States, and Maggie and I were pleased to host a dinner at our home in his honor.

Our list with Kondrashev was not by any means a large one, but it was meant to be representative. We also kept pressing very hard for significant increases in the number of Soviet Jews who could leave their country. In that context, a harassed Kondrashev asked to have a cup of coffee with me one morning. "I thought we were going to keep our talks secret," he said. "You've now spoiled it. I cannot do any more." I did not know what he was talking about and reminded him of my recount of some weeks earlier that Ambassador Dubinin had asked me to lunch when I was last in Washington and began pumping me about Madrid, obviously suspecting he was being kept in the dark. Kondrashev had at that time laughed, said he knew of the lunch, and then went on to say that his ambassador always liked to stick his nose into matters not of his concern.

In any event, through Kondrashev's concern and disappointment, I learned that Dubinin had continued to pry. Only George Shultz and two or three of his top aides with whom he consulted knew of my talks with Kondrashev. One of them, thoughtlessly assuming that Dubinin was aware of the talks, responded to the wily ambassador's probing and confirmed his suspicions. Dubinin complained to Andrey Gromyko, the Soviet foreign minister at the time, who may well have also been unaware. Now that the Soviet Foreign Ministry knew what was going on, Kovalev had that morning received instructions to read a message to me verbatim. Kondrashev said the message had been worked on carefully in Moscow, and there was one "ray of hope" in it. I told Kondrashev to set up the meeting with Kovalev.

In a few moments, we met. Kovalev, serious and unsmiling, began to read. In effect, the United States was being criticized for interfering in Soviet internal affairs; the Soviets would not change their policies or practices just to please us, or to end the Madrid CSCE meeting; we should disabuse ourselves of any illusions that the Soviets had promised or would promise us anything about their behavior; if, in pursuit of their national best interests, they do adopt a policy that pleases us, it is purely coincidental and nothing more. I accepted the Soviet document, said I would study it and forward it to Washington, and decided I would say nothing more.* My conversations with Kondrashev continued.

On a Saturday morning, I received a phone call from Kovalev apologizing for the late invitation but asking me to join him for dinner that evening. I accepted and asked the interpreter if there was a special reason for the invitation. Kovalev responded in Russian that his wife had just decided to return to Moscow since our meeting was coming to an end and did not wish to leave without saying goodbye to me. I looked forward to a significant conversation.

This was the first time I had been in Kovalev's apartment, since we usually met, when the Soviets were hosts, at their elegant embassy. His apartment was small, informal, and comfortable. We were in shirtsleeves and sat on the balcony. This was a relaxed and smiling Kovalev. The conversation was wide ranging, but a bit difficult for me to follow, given his tendency to speak in allegories, suggesting hidden and cosmic messages. What did come across was a message that they hoped a Madrid agreement could lead to improvements elsewhere in our relations. From this evening's conversation, I came away convinced that the Soviets would be willing to abandon Central and South America. The United States had been concerned for some time about a growing supply of armaments being sent from Moscow to Cuba, El Salvador, Nicaragua, Venezuela, and other countries in Latin America. We looked on this as disruptive and destabilizing. His message, it seemed to me, was that the Soviets would walk away from our part of

---

* The internal Soviet bureaucratic overtones of this incident became increasingly evident when I learned a few weeks later that Alexander Bessmertnykh, until quite recently the Soviet Union's minister of foreign affairs, but then one of Foreign Minister Gromyko's aides, had told one of our embassy officials in Moscow that "Max talked to the wrong person," implying that I should have dealt with the foreign minister rather than the KGB. I was certain this was wrong. I had probed with Ilichev, Kovalev, and Dubinin, all of whom had sternly rejected my overtures. Both Al Haig and George Shultz found Gromyko totally cold on human rights issues. Gromyko was far less flexible than Andropov, who had indeed permitted Kondrashev to deal with me and had, at least minimally, delivered.

the world if we walked away from Afghanistan. I reported the conversation to Washington, and not until I went to Geneva in 1985 did I have another opportunity to speak to a Soviet official about Afghanistan and a broad United States–USSR agreement.

The neutral proposal, known as RM39, called for a human rights experts' meeting, but did not provide for such a meeting on human contacts and family reunification. This was the single remaining substantive issue for the United States. The Soviets adamantly refused to support such a meeting. I explained to friends and foes alike that the idea for an experts' meeting on family reunification originated in Congress, and I could not ignore the wishes of the Congress. It was time to put into play our suggestion in the Spanish countryside.

On June 17, at a cocktail reception, Felipe Gonzalez, the Spanish prime minister, offered what he called a final compromise that met the key U.S. demand for an experts' meeting on human contacts. Kovalev was visibly angry as I came to him at the end of the reception to say we both had a great deal of thinking to do overnight. He understood what had happened, and the following day Moscow accepted the Spanish solution. We did, too.

All the countries except Malta soon agreed to the draft. Since the rules required unanimity, Malta was in a position to block the conclusion of the meeting, holding us hostage to its private agenda, which was to heighten its Mediterranean leadership role. It was a ludicrous moment. I told the Maltese foreign minister, Alex Trigona, who felt free to talk to me openly because we were both friends of Victor Reuther, the labor leader, that I was going home, leaving a junior officer to protect our interests, and would not return until Malta was ready to agree. I left the next day. They finally concurred, after a petulant and undignified performance that lasted several weeks. I returned with George Shultz for the concluding proceedings on September 7, 1983.

George Shultz sent a memorandum to the president, calling the agreement "a good one from our point of view." He noted that the agreement was based on a Spanish initiative and that "it provides the balanced result which we have long sought—significant improvement on the humanitarian provisions of the Helsinki Final Act and provision for human rights and human contacts experts' meetings, as well as agreement to hold the first stage of the European Security Conference dealing with surprise military attack."

The secretary then discussed with the president the "performance" issue that I had been emphasizing. He indicated specific steps that had been taken by the Soviets and referred to assurances to me about the release of a number of specifically named Soviet citizens who were in prison for their activity on behalf of the Helsinki Final Act.

The Madrid concluding document was accepted by the thirty-five countries during three days of meetings on September 7, 8, and 9, 1983, where many of the foreign ministers who had been there when the meeting began in 1980 spoke again. The tone of that meeting was set by the shooting down on August 30 of a Korean civilian airliner by the Soviets. It dramatically illustrated the point that despite an agreement on paper, the nature of the Soviet Union had not changed, and its system remained a threat to Helsinki values.

I left Madrid believing that history would proclaim the Helsinki Final Act of 1975 as a "moral tuning fork" and one of the most important milestones on the path to peace. It proved to be significantly more. Its distinction is that it established a set of Western values agreed to by thirty-five sovereign nations as standards by which to judge responsible international behavior. When those standards are met and their promise fulfilled, we will truly have achieved the positive peace that is more than the absence of war.*

In reviewing Madrid, I should expand on my relationship with former Justice Arthur J. Goldberg. When it became known that I would participate as our country's representative to the Madrid CSCE meetings, he urged me not to accept that assignment and to join him in urging the United States not to attend the meetings in the light of the Soviet invasion of Afghanistan and continued blatant human rights

---

* The satisfactions from Madrid continue. In July 1990, I received an autographed book from Dr. Alexander Lerner, a distinguished scientist with whom I had talked by telephone from Madrid while he was cruelly being denied an exit visa to Israel by a stubborn Soviet bureaucracy. The inscription reads: "Everybody in the Refusnik community understands and recognizes your noble efforts on our behalf. You played an important role formulating and executing the policy of the United States government in this battlefield. Thank you very much for all you have done." It was postmarked from Israel, where he is now at the Weizmann Institute.

On March 6, 1991, I received the following message from a United Nations Association officer: "Forgive my intruding on your time with this, but a Polish member in a group USIA brought to us yesterday—a Wiaderna Kolodziejcza, foreign editor of *Rzeczpospolita* magazine—*insisted*, simply *insisted* that I had to promise to report to you her words:

> Please tell Mr. Kampelman that for all of us who were in prison [during martial law], to say the name "Kampelman" was like mentioning God. "Kampelman, Kampelman"—it meant there was hope for us, it meant that there were people outside who were remembering us, it meant that there really was an "international law." You can't imagine how important Max Kampelman was for all of us at that time. He gave us hope. You must tell Mr. Kampelman that."

violations. Henry Kissinger was the only other person who suggested that I not accept the assignment, using the same appealing reasons. I disagreed.

When Arthur, after testifying, could not persuade the congressmen on the CSCE Commission, he ceased his efforts. Furthermore, his wife, Dorothy, had decided to write a book on the CSCE process following their experience with the 1977 predecessor Belgrade meeting. I proposed to Dorothy, for whom Maggie and I had deep affection, that she visit Madrid as often as she could and participate as a public member. She frequently joined us. I came to see that she felt it was correct for us to be in Madrid doing what we were doing.

Not only the presence of Dorothy, however, brought Arthur occasionally to my mind. The more successful we were perceived as being, either in holding the Soviet feet to the fire, or in strengthening Western unity and cohesiveness, or in producing results that improved upon the original 1975 agreement, the more some people would unfavorably compare Arthur's Belgrade performance with mine in Madrid. This must have hurt Arthur, who resisted criticizing me or what I was doing in Madrid because of our friendship. I attempted to meet this potential source of tension between us by publicly and privately asserting that I was building on what Arthur had initiated in Belgrade when he highlighted our human rights concerns.

The Goldbergs had, in effect, sponsored us when we came to Washington in 1949 by introducing us to their friends, many of whom were "important." Maggie and I had met them at the University of Wisconsin's School for Workers in the summer of 1948. We were frequent visitors to their home. He and I strongly disagreed politically following his deep attraction to the Kennedys in the late 1950s, but we kept our friendship going. We occasionally took long walks together on a Sunday, talking public affairs. He shared his personal concerns with me regarding his role at the time of the AFL-CIO merger. He had been the major harmonizing force in bringing those two major labor organizations together. Yet he was not certain he would any longer enjoy a special place of leadership in the merged federation.

I knew of Arthur's early difficulty in adjusting to the pace and restriction of Supreme Court life. He missed being at the center of high-level political decision making. When President Johnson and he talked of his replacing Adlai Stevenson as our ambassador to the UN, he came to our home to escape the incoming phone calls, and we spent hours walking and discussing his decision. (I had no doubt after listening to him that he welcomed the challenge and would leave the

Court.) Following his appointment to the United Nations, he asked me to serve as a senior adviser to the U.S. delegation, which occasionally brought me to New York. When he felt it was time to leave the UN and he came to understand that Johnson would not reappoint him to the Court, we discussed his joining our law firm. I never understood why he decided to go to the firm he chose, which proved to be a mistake, instead of our firm; and, particularly, why I had to learn about his decision in the newspapers, rather than directly.

One day, Arthur called me from his New York law office. He wanted to meet, and we agreed to have breakfast together in his apartment at the Hotel Pierre. The Democrats wanted him to run for governor of New York. He told the press that he had talked to no New York politicians and wanted to maintain that posture. Would I talk to Stanley Steingut, the powerful Brooklyn leader and legislator, whom I knew? I agreed, but to say what? I felt Arthur should not run for governor against Rockefeller, but should run for the Senate, where his extensive and intensive life's experiences would be employed. He and Dorothy fully agreed. I explained all this to Steingut, who logically reasoned that a governor was more important to a political party than a senator—and the polls showed Goldberg ahead of Rockefeller. But it would be the Senate, Steingut continued, if that's what Arthur wanted. The Goldbergs were pleased when I reported to them. A few days later, I read in the papers that Arthur had decided to run for governor. His defeat, accompanied by his loss of the Jewish vote, made him bitter. He soon left New York and rejoined us in Washington. Life was never again as pleasant and exciting for him as it had been. Maggie and I visited them on occasion during Dorothy's bout with cancer. After Arthur died, on January 18, 1990, I was honored to be a speaker at a memorial service for him at the Department of Labor. I could never think of Madrid without thinking of Arthur Goldberg.

I have some very strong additional recollections about Madrid. There comes to mind the day I delivered a statement documenting the terrible growth of offensive Soviet military power. At the conclusion of our session that afternoon, a Warsaw Pact delegation head came to me in the corridor and said: "I did not know any of that." He believed me. The statement had its impact.

I will also long remember a brief coffee session I arranged for a visiting congressional group with the head of the Soviet delegation. The meeting continued for two and a half hours. Its theme was set by one member of Congress, a Catholic priest, wearing his collar, talking with vehemence, conviction, and eloquence about Sharansky and Soviet Jews. Father Robert Drinan of Massachusetts made a profound impact that day.

I remember an intense conversation with a determined and relentless Avital Sharansky in our delegate's lounge where others could see her, urging that it was not in our interest to sign a Madrid concluding document. And I remember a few days later a tearful exchange on the phone with the sister of Ida Nudel, a woman whose constant efforts to leave the Soviet Union for Israel were continually rebuffed, leading to her exile to a labor camp. It did not take any effort to persuade me to mention Ida's name at our meeting.

There is the exchange with an Eastern European ambassador, during which I turned over the names of 1,200 families seeking to leave his country for ours, whose applications had not been acted upon. I urged him to communicate with his government, saying that it made no sense for me to be taking this issue up at our meeting or for the issue to be an irritant between our two countries. A week or ten days later, he came to me with about 600 names, saying their visas had been issued and the remaining families on the list would be acted upon within a matter of weeks. They were.

I still possess and cherish a letter to me written in minuscule handwriting on what appeared to be thin toilet tissue. It came from Balys Gajauskas, a Lithuanian political prisoner in a special regime camp in Kuchino, Perm Oblast, USSR, in 1982. It urges me to continue the struggle for "basic human rights." Gajauskas pleads the case for Lithuania's freedom, the right of workers to organize trade unions, and the abolition of religious discrimination in the Soviet Union. The letter, framed, hangs on my wall as a constant reminder of the strength of the human spirit. Gajauskas was not released from jail until 1988. In 1989, he was able to visit the United States, where he was warmly received. He now lives in Lithuania.

Madrid also gave me a special insight into the vulnerability of totalitarianism in the face of the modern communication revolution. During the early days of our meeting, the Soviets released from jail a Jewish dissident, Josef Mendelevich, after more than ten years' imprisonment. The press reported that he had gone to Israel.

The next weekend, I was back in the United States to speak at a luncheon in New York sponsored by one of the groups organized to defend Soviet Jews. I arrived at the banquet hall early and went up to the dais, where I located my assigned seat and looked at the nameplates to learn the identity of my neighbors. I noticed the name of Mendelevich next to me and assumed that it could not be the recently released man but was perhaps a relative. A few moments later, a young man came by and seated himself alongside the Mendelevich nameplate. When he saw my name, he stood up and kissed me. He began to talk about the Madrid meeting. It was the same Josef Mendelevich. In surprise, I asked how he knew so much about the Madrid meeting, having been in jail for such a long period and only released within the past few days. He responded: "We in the jails—we know!" The lesson was clear. No society could any longer have a monopoly of information.

Finally, I remember a Chanukah in Madrid. It was the second night of this Jewish holiday celebrating ancient heroes. A number of women from the United States, the United Kingdom, and elsewhere, active with Soviet Jewry concerns, had arranged a reception at a local hotel. As I rose to light the candles, the phone rang. It was Moscow. Arrangements had been made unknown to me to gather a number of Jewish refuseniks in the apartment of Abe Stolar. I was brought to the phone. Other delegates from Western states followed me. We told Dr. Lerner, Mr. Stolar, and their friends gathered around the phone that evening, that they had friends. They were not alone. They were not forgotten. There was hardly a dry eye in that room. The candles were in our room, but the flame of hope burned where they gathered in Moscow.

Looking back at Madrid, I believe that this meeting—held during a period when relations between the United States and the Soviet Union were at an all-time low—was a major stage-setter for the East-West progress that followed. When we first convened at Madrid, human rights as a major Western policy objective was still a new concept. When Arthur Goldberg insisted—rightly—on the primacy of human rights at the Belgrade meeting in 1977, the NATO allies were hesitant, and this difference in Western approaches caused considerable tensions within the alliance. At Madrid, I was convinced that human rights had to be a part of a combined and coordinated Western policy, and by the end of the meeting, it was. From Madrid onward, the Soviet Union could entertain no further hope of splitting the West over human rights. I take satisfaction that the United States led the way in this effort, but it would not have been possible without the splendid efforts of European colleagues in the negotiating arena and back home in foreign ministries.

Madrid, I believe, also helped to create a more realistic perception of the Soviet Union in Western Europe. The pussyfooting diplomatic circumlocutions that marked previous CSCE meetings gave way at Madrid to a hard-nosed cataloguing of specific human rights abuses.

Facts were laid bare, names named, crimes cited. While the U.S. public and press were barely aware of what was going on at Madrid, this was not the case in Western Europe, where the negotiation was followed carefully. The Soviets, of course, condemned themselves by their own actions against Afghanistan and their own citizens, but for nearly three years Madrid was a permanent mechanism for keeping the truth before the eyes of Europe's people. I have no doubt that this contributed to the extraordinary Western solidarity with which we confronted the Soviet Union during the Reagan years. This solidarity includes the remarkable (some thought impossible) decision by our European allies to deploy intermediate-range nuclear missiles in spite of an intense continent-wide campaign by the Soviets and peace activists who joined them. Once it was clear that NATO was going to deploy those missiles, the Soviets agreed to a negotiation that led to the elimination of this entire class of nuclear weaponry, ours as well as the Soviets'. Without Madrid, I do not think European publics would have been ready to support such a momentous decision.

More recently, a newspaper reported that Secretary of State James A. Baker III said CSCE was "the conscience of Europe."* West German Foreign Minister Hans Dietrich Genscher wants it to serve as "a framework of stability for the dynamic, dramatic and sometimes revolutionary developments in Eastern Europe and the Soviet Union." Soviet President Mikhail Gorbachev calls it the right address for his "common European home."

It is hard to disagree with any of them.

---

* On September 19, 1989, Secretary of State James Baker wrote to me: "I was delighted to hear . . . that you have agreed to lead our delegation to the Copenhagen and Moscow Human Rights Conferences. You are 'Mr. CSCE,' and we will rely on you greatly." I spent the month of June in Copenhagen. There were no conflicts between the United States and the Soviet Union. We and our allies pressed for an understanding that the human dimension of the Helsinki Final Act requires a commitment by all thirty-five states to the principles of the rule of law, political pluralism, and free elections. Those principles were accepted in Copenhagen by consensus. I believe historians will say that this document equals in importance the Helsinki Final Act of 1975.

The Moscow CSCE meetings on the Human Dimension will bring Maggie and me to Moscow for the whole month of September 1991.

It had been my intent that these two meetings serve as my last assignment. In early May, however, I received a message from Secretary Baker asking me to head the U.S. delegation to a CSCE meeting in Geneva during July 1991, dealing with the vexing and potentially dynamite issue of ethnic and other minorities. I agreed. Once again, we arrived at a unanimous declaration, expanding the Copenhagen agreement and providing the basis for CSCE's constructive involvement in resolving the serious ethnic problems that once again plague Europe.

15

A New Challenge: Reducing Nuclear Arms

I came home from Madrid content. My children were grown and pursuing their own lives; I was in my early sixties and healthy, with no real financial worries and no need to return to the practice of law under the pressure of the old high-intensity daily bustle. Maggie and I could enjoy ourselves even as I practiced without pressure. I could pursue my interest in public affairs as a private citizen, without stress. And I had met a fine king in Juan Carlos.

In an age in which monarchies are decreasing in numbers and importance, I nevertheless confess to a feeling of some excitement when I think of the "kings and queens in my life." In addition to Juan Carlos, with whom I spent the most time on two occasions and whose intelligence and grasp of public issues impressed me, I recall a majestic evening with King Hassan II of Morocco in one of his grandiose fairytale palaces.

It was, I believe, in 1984 when one of my clients, a Saudi businessman close to the Saudi royal family, asked me to meet him in Morocco. When our business was done, he suggested I join him for a meeting with the king so that I might share with him my observations about Israel, the PLO, and Middle East peace. When I arrived at the palace, I was overwhelmed by the surroundings as well as the conversation. With time, we moved away from discussing international politics to the king's interest in the United States. He told me of property he had purchased in our country. This led to a discussion of American politics.

When I rose to leave at the end of our talk, the king asked me if I knew Vice President George Bush and his wife Barbara, both of whom he obviously knew and liked. I said I did. After a moment's hesitation he responded that on more than one occasion he had been tempted to kidnap Barbara and bring her to Morocco with him. I was never certain that he did not mean it! In any event, when I returned to Washington, I sent a note to the vice president passing on the king's greetings and final comments.

I don't count King Hussein I of Jordan in my inventory of acquaintances because our meeting and conversation was a brief one. It was at a White House state dinner in June 1980, to which Maggie and I had been invited. As I went through the reception line, President Carter, in introducing me, graciously noted that I had been helpful in the Camp David process and could be again. The king politely suggested that I visit him when I was next in the area. Regrettably, I have yet to make my first visit to Jordan.

In late 1989 I was invited to lecture at the Peace Palace in The Hague before a prestigious audience of Dutch officials, including the foreign minister. Among the sponsors were the Roosevelt Study Center and the Joseph Foundation, organized by Burton Joseph, my longtime Minneapolis friend, in honor of his wife Geri, who had been our highly regarded ambassador to the Netherlands. When I reached Holland and was given my schedule by our embassy staff I was told that I had an audience with Queen Beatrix. I assumed our ambassador had arranged the session and that the Josephs, who knew the queen well, would be at the meeting, as well as the ambassador, who explained, however, that the palace had suggested the audience and that neither he nor the others would be present.

I arrived at the palace in the early evening of November 19 and was greeted by the queen's military aide, who explained, in response to my question, that the session was likely to last about fifteen minutes and that the Queen would make it very clear to me when it was time for me to leave. He was obviously impressed by her majesty. So was I. Our conversation lasted for close to an hour as she powerfully and decisively ignored the signals from her aide who opened and closed the door on two occasions without entering the room.

It is, I am told, not proper to discuss or report on a conversation with the queen. Mindful of this, I will continue to keep to that propriety and only relate the broad concerns of our discussion. The queen had apparently been invited to attend my lecture, but she was unable to do so. We could now make up for that lost time. Our conversation was about world affairs, events in the Soviet Union, the roles of our respective countries, and her own perception of her responsibilities to her country. As I finally left her presence, it was with the thought, "Believe me, this is a strong, well read, and very intelligent lady."

In contrast, I did not even scratch the surface in two brief encounters with Queen Margrethe II of Denmark. At the beginning of the Copenhagen CSCE Conference on the Human Dimension which I attended as head of the U.S. delegation in June 1990, the queen hosted a reception at her Palace for all the delegates. Danish Foreign Minister Uffe Jensen-Ellemann introduced me to the queen. The occasion did not permit more than brief small talk, and it was my impression she was bored and somewhat frustrated at not being able to pursue a continuous intelligent conversation with anybody. Shortly thereafter, Mr. Jensen-Ellemann introduced me to the queen's son, whispering that the queen had suggested it.

The following year, in February 1991, Maggie and I were invited to a White House state dinner for the queen, who was visiting the United States. We were on a brief vacation in Florida that week and, rather than return with me, Maggie suggested I invite our daughter-in-law, Nina Bang-Jensen, whose father had been a distinguished and famous Danish diplomat before his death, to join me for the evening. As we went through the receiving line, Nina spoke some Danish to the queen and her husband, Prince Hendrik, while I whispered to the president and then to Mrs. Bush Nina's Danish connection. The president quickly briefed the queen, who seemed, it appeared to me, to recognize the Bang-Jensen name, but neither she nor her husband permitted themselves to open up.

My most unexpected contact with royalty came with a phone call to my secretary in April that the king and queen of Romania were in Washington and wanted to come by for a visit. A few days later, former King Michael and Queen Anne, sprightly but with dignity, stepped into my office. I was jacketless and in shirtsleeves, which they insisted I not improve upon. They asked me whether it was true that my parents had been born in Romania, and we proceeded from there to a very pleasant and informative discussion. To my statement that ours was an age of declining royalty, the king pointed to the success of Juan Carlos of Spain and said that he too would bring democracy and free enterprise to Romania under a constitutional monarchy. I liked them both. They had a seriousness and determination I had not expected to find. In this changing world, who knows? Prophecy is certainly not one of my strengths.

A few weeks later, Queen Elizabeth II of England and her husband, Prince Philip, came to Washington. I had not expected to meet or see her and made no effort to do so. Our friend Dr. James Billington, the librarian of Congress, had other ideas. He telephoned and invited us to lunch with the queen and the prince at the library. Maggie had no interest in canceling her plans in order to attend the lunch and suggested that this time I invite our daughter Julia to accompany me. Julia, who loves England and works as a paper conservator at the Folger Shakespeare Library in Washington, was delighted to accept. We were very pleased to be in the company of a decidedly gracious couple.

I cannot leave this discussion of royalty without noting the Dalai Lama, whom Tibetans look on as an integral part of the Kingdom of God. Freedom House, the bipartisan national organization, which I serve as chairman, took a keen interest in the Dalai Lama and Tibet immediately after the Chinese invasion of that small country in 1951. The cruelty visited upon these people by the Chinese communist rulers included desecration of their Buddhist monasteries, forcible removal of tens of thousands of Tibetan children to the mainland of China to lose their cultural and religious identities, the uprooting of millions of Chinese from the mainland into Tibet, where they would dilute Tibetan culture and traditions, and the expulsion of the Dalai Lama, the spiritual leader of Tibet. While much of the world accepted the realpolitik of Chinese control, Freedom House identified itself with the aspirations of the Dalai Lama and the people of Tibet.

In 1989 the Dalai Lama won the Nobel Peace Prize, which served dramatically to highlight the issue in a manner not experienced previously. We decided to host a luncheon for the Dalai Lama at the Capitol in Washington in April 1991. We urged the Congress to participate in our luncheon and to sponsor an official function of its own. We similarly were immensely pleased when President Bush agreed to visit with the Dalai Lama.

Our luncheon was a great success with approximately 500 people attending or attempting to gain entrance into our meeting room in order to hear the Dalai Lama and express their support for him. I had the privilege of sitting next to him for a part of the lunch and of introducing him to the many members of Congress and journalists who were present. He was a splendid conversationalist with a ready smile and a light touch. He knew a great deal about the members of Congress he met. The atmosphere he exuded was one of nonviolence and human warmth. That was also the essence of his message. It was a privilege to be with him.

During the lunch, chicken was being served to the guests. I noticed that the Dalai Lama was eating the vegetables and not the chicken. I suggested that I could arrange for the chicken to be replaced with fish or a vegetable plate. He looked at me with a smile and said that he was not a vegetarian; that he had been a vegetarian for a few years in his younger days, but was no longer a vegetarian. He explained that he ate chicken. He then looked at the plate and quietly said: "But this chicken looks too much like a chicken!" He won me over.

Madrid had been special. I had taken on a short-term, almost pro forma, job for President Carter and turned it into a useful and successful human rights effort. When my work concluded under President Reagan, I had received good international press and favorable diplomatic recognition. Through their moving letters asking for help or merely telling me of their conditions, I had become "friends" with large numbers of dissidents I had never met. I cherished those friendships. No one had expected much when we began, but, over three years, with persistence, cooperation from our allies, and the desire or need of the Soviets to reach agreement, we had done exceedingly well in placing human rights firmly on the world agenda as it had not been for decades or perhaps ever.

Beyond the substance, I was pleased with how effectively we had organized our forces and accomplished what we did. I felt we had exacted as much as we could from the Soviet bloc, and had exposed both their leaders and many of their people to Western values. We had provided great psychological sustenance and at least minuscule political clout to the longtime human rights activists and movements in the Communist world. Oppression, exile, abuse, and imprisonment were still widespread, but the concentrated attention we created helped lift some of the misery.

I had applied my negotiating skills and had demonstrated my patience and perseverance in an international forum; and these had worked to strengthen our national interests and the cause of human rights. Through it all, I had learned a great deal, too, from working with and against the Soviets, and with our allies.

Back home again, I settled into my law practice, although the firm no longer depended on me as it once had. The management duties of hiring and firing had long been in the hands of others. Even though I had been for years the lead man (or rainmaker, in lawyerly slang) in attracting clients, others had now developed their own strengths. Our reputation for solid work was substantial and sufficient to bring in a steady stream of clients.

While I had remained a partner in the firm during the Madrid meetings, choosing not to receive a government salary, my attention had been almost totally on the negotiations and hardly at all on our law business. Once back, I started working again for clients, but government opportunities continued to divert me.

In the fall of 1983, President Reagan asked me to carry a personal letter from him to the heads of government of our European allies to assure them and their foreign ministers that our interest in human rights had not ended with Madrid, but would be an aggressively continuing one. His emphasis was on Soviet Jews. The president wanted our allies to know that he was not satisfied to rest with what had been accomplished. He was already looking ahead to future Helsinki Final Act meetings and to continued pressure in between meetings. He wanted them to look ahead with us. The opportunity to meet and discuss these issues with the heads of free Europe was a special one.

In early May 1984, I went to El Salvador as co-chairman of a presidential delegation to witness and monitor the first free elections for president. Despite physical threats from the leftist guerrillas, the citizens lined up at the polls, some of them having traveled for hours to stand in line for additional hours, all of them determined to seize the democratic opportunity afforded them. Our helicopter would drop into some remote rural village, a symbol of American power and interference for those who didn't like us, but a greater symbol of American concern and Salvadoran hope to those who did. Because we might appear at any time, our presence helped keep the balloting honest. My flight, as a matter of fact, was not without adventure. At one point, our ambassador to El Salvador, Tom Pickering, who now serves as our ambassador to the United Nations, and I were on the same helicopter when the pilot suddenly swerved, climbed, dropped, and moved away. We were being shot at by the guerrillas. When we landed shortly thereafter in a rural area, the pilot showed us the artillery nicks on the plane. It was a close call.

On this trip, incidentally, I first learned of the heavy Palestine Liberation Organization (PLO) involvement with the rebels. Jose Napoleon Duarte, a Christian Democrat who won that election, was with us on the eve of the balloting and spoke about the PLO and Soviet activity in support of the rebels.

At the end of the month, I returned to El Salvador as part of the official party led by Secretary of State George Shultz, to attend the inauguration of Duarte. En route on an air force jet, Shultz invited me forward to his cabin to talk with him. During the course of our conversation, he told me that our intelligence agencies had learned of a possible assassination attempt planned during our visit and aimed either at him or at the new president. The attack purportedly would come from the right wing and was intended specifically to generate social chaos.

I suggested he confide in Senator Jesse Helms, who was with us on the plane as part of the delegation, since Helms was close to D'Aubisson, the right-wing presidential candidate. Shultz did. I did not sit in on their discussion, but a subdued, stern-faced Helms came back to his seat next to mine, obviously troubled. When we landed, he left us and apparently went directly to perform his duty. The rumor may have been false, or the Helms visit may have had the effect we hoped for. In any case, there was no assassination attempt, although a good deal of tension remained throughout the visit.

En route, Shultz also told me that he had suggested to the president that a meeting between Shultz and Daniel Ortega in Nicaragua might be useful, but the trip hadn't been cleared before we left. Word finally came from the president that a meeting had been set up, and two days later, after the inaugural ceremonies, I was on my way to Nicaragua with Shultz simply to keep him company on the plane and to discuss Central America.

Shultz and Ortega met at the Managua airport, and I spent my time visiting with other Nicaraguans while Shultz and Ortega talked. It was an unproductive and disappointing meeting for Shultz, although it did lead to a temporary resumption of diplomatic talks. We then flew back to El Salvador to pick up the rest of our delegation and the press, and then proceeded on to Andrews Air Force Base outside Washington. By the time we arrived, around midnight, I was exhausted and eager to get home. Shultz waved a cheerful goodbye to us and bounded across the tarmac to another plane that carried him for another six hours to a meeting with Reagan in Dublin the next morning.

I had other occasional State Department meetings with Shultz, Eagleburger, and others as I settled back into private life, intending to combine it with a continuing commitment to work on foreign affairs matters and yet to avoid long and arduous travel—leaving that to those who shared Shultz's level of stamina. Several months later, Lynn Hansen, who had worked for me on military matters in Madrid, called to ask if I would like to attend the University of Edinburgh Conversations on Arms Control.

Maggie had never been to Edinburgh, and I thought she would enjoy the visit, so we agreed to go. The "conversations" also fell between a meeting on religious freedom in Rome sponsored by the Seventh-Day Adventists, to which I had been invited to speak, and a meeting in London where I would talk about the problems of Soviet Jewry. It seemed an interesting package tour. I, of course, assumed the meeting was in Scotland, since it was under the direction of the University of Edinburgh's John Ericson, but when it came time to go, I discovered that the meeting was not in Scotland but in the Soviet Union.

Maggie and I had made our first trip to the Soviet Union almost fifteen years earlier. That visit had taken us to Moscow, Leningrad, and Kiev. Each day had been more depressing than the previous one, the rigidity of the society was oppressive, and the atmosphere of the police state was almost unbearable. We had brought Jewish prayer books and calendars with us to distribute at synagogues we intended to visit in each city. Had the Soviet customs officials looked into our luggage on arrival, they probably would have confiscated the religious contraband and conceivably declared us unacceptable, but they did not inspect our baggage. We knew the Soviets would frown on the distribution of religious material, but it seemed right to us, and we did it.

At the synagogue in Moscow, while Maggie sat upstairs in the orthodox tradition, I sat among the men on the first floor. When my distribution of the calendars and prayer books to the appreciative elders caught the attention of the "leaders" of the synagogue, they invited me up front from my rear seat, ostensibly as "an honored guest," but in fact to keep me from mingling. Even within the synagogue, there were Jews who played the government's game.*

In Kiev, that became explicit. Maggie and I had arrived at the synagogue before the services were to begin, and I chatted in broken Yiddish with a handful of the older Jews. I gave them some of my religious items, and they seemed excited by them and by our presence. Suddenly, they grew silent and left me, hurriedly taking their seats. The sexton, obviously a feared man, had come in and was surveying the scene. When he approached, we exchanged greetings, and I of-

* For years, the United States had a political officer from the embassy stand outside the synagogue to observe and talk to those who wished to talk. It was a demonstration of our concern and witness, immensely heartening to the Jewish community.

fered him a calendar. He rejected it coldly, saying, "The state provides us with what we need."

When the services were over, we headed for a bus stop, wishing the congregants a *Gut Shabos* as though we were in the Bronx. Their response, with the sexton still near by, was restrained, but when we got to the bus stop, we found that one of the congregation had taken a shortcut and was obviously eager to talk out of sight of the synagogue. Since Maggie did not understand Yiddish, she took out a pad of paper and a pen, and turned her attention to writing down her thoughts about the morning. The man blanched and seemed ready to flee. He thought she was taking notes of our conversation and that he was trapped. I assured him that was not the case, but it was not easy to calm him down.

We were struck by the age of the Jews in the synagogues. They were generally elderly, survivors of the angry anti-Semitism of the Stalin years, and the persistent, if less virulent, form that followed. They were old enough to remember firing squads and the decimation of their numbers. Yet they were determined to assert their Jewishness at whatever cost. The younger ones did not seem to enter the synagogue at all, satisfied on Friday nights and Saturday mornings to congregate outside, talking among themselves and in particular to visitors. They ignored the obvious KGB notetakers standing among them.

A few younger people in the vicinity of the Moscow synagogue could speak English. They surrounded us, and several asked to meet us away from the synagogue despite the danger to them. Their spirit and daring were heartening. Our visits with them were rare bright spots in the darkness of the Soviet system.

In Kiev, we had wanted to visit Babi Yar, where thousands of Jews were murdered by the Nazis during World War II and buried in huge trenches they had been forced to dig before being shot. The Soviets, who for years had denied or distorted the facts of the slaughter to minimize the victimization of Jews, discouraged visits to that grave of horrors. Our Soviet guide always found a reason that we couldn't go. First she told us it was too far away, then that our schedule was too crowded to fit it in.

Finally, we asked the desk clerk in the hotel to tell us how to reach Babi Yar. He was as uncooperative as the guide, offering a similar set of reasons. We considered giving up, but our irritation at their complicity with the old lies led us to make one more try. We stepped into a cab outside the hotel and simply said, "Babi Yar," fully expecting another rejection. The cabdriver turned with a big smile and said,

"Bist Yiddish?" When we said we were, using German and Yiddish to converse, he said he was, too. He had been born in Kiev and had lived his entire life there. He took us on an animated trip to the nearby site, happy to meet Jews from America; happier still, it seemed, to flaunt the wishes of the government. He waited solemnly as we looked across the vast area that covered the Jewish remains, quite possibly including his own relatives, and then brought us back, talking seriously about what it was like to be a Jew in the Soviet Union.

When Maggie and I arrived in Moscow in 1984, we remembered that earlier trip and its Big Brother quality. The first night we were in Moscow, a reception had been arranged for everyone attending the conference. As Maggie and I talked with new friends and had a drink, Sergei Kondrashev, my Madrid counterpart and friend, suddenly appeared. We greeted each other warmly, and I asked, "Sergei, what are you doing here?" He said with a straight face, "Max, you know I am interested in arms control."

We both knew it was only vaguely true. He asked if we might get together to talk, and we arranged to meet the next day at the Soviet Foreign Ministry. That night after the reception, Maggie and I asked our guide, "Why was Sergei Kondrashev at the reception?" He shook his head and said, "I don't know. He called up and said he wanted to be there. We were surprised."

In his office the next day, Kondrashev had two colleagues with him and no discernible agenda. I had hardly settled in my chair when he said, "I see you attacked us in Rome." He was right. I had gone after the Soviets quite strenuously for their abuses of their own citizens' religious rights, recalling in my mind the meetings Maggie and I had at the synagogues on our earlier trip, and what I had learned about the Pentecostals and others during the Madrid meetings.

I told him that the Rome speech was nothing compared to the one I was scheduled to give in London on the treatment of Jews in the Soviet Union. I said I was puzzled why the Soviets kept providing me with ammunition. He raised his eyebrows and made some reference that the Reverend Billy Graham did not agree with me.* I asked if he would like a copy of my advance text, which I had prepared before we

---

* During the latter days of the Madrid meeting, Billy Graham had gone to the Soviet Union on an evangelical mission. I was told that a serious effort was made in Washington to discourage the trip, or, at a minimum, to brief him on the facts of religious oppression in the thought that he could assist its victims. The effort failed. Soviet dissidents reported back that they could not talk to the minister during his visit. He drew large crowds, with USSR official assistance, and chose not to offend his hosts. To the press, who noted his omission of any support for the victims of religious discrimination or persecution, he said he was "understanding of Soviet problems."

left home. He said he certainly would and remarked to his colleagues something like: "He fights us, but you can do business with him." I took that as a compliment. I sent him a copy of the speech after I returned to the hotel.*

Of course, 1984 was a presidential election year, with my friend, former Vice President Walter Mondale, challenging Ronald Reagan's bid for a second term. During that summer, following the Democratic convention that nominated him for president, Mondale telephoned me to say that I would receive a call from Bud McFarlane at the White House. Bud had called Mondale to set up the accustomed national security briefing that all recent incumbent presidents have made available to official candidates running to succeed them. This was good practice, healthy for our democracy and for reducing partisan excesses in foreign policy.

Mondale accepted the offer and was apparently told that he could select three additional people to receive the briefing, ostensibly people he would depend on in some fashion should he be elected. Mondale had provided McFarlane with the names of David Aaron, who had been his staff aide and the deputy national security adviser under the Carter-Mondale administration; Dr. James Schlesinger, former CIA head, secretary of defense, and secretary of energy; and me. I was, of course, surprised and pleased to be included, particularly since I had deliberately excluded myself from the political campaign in light of my Madrid service under both Carter and Reagan and the fact that I was still performing occasional chores for the president and George Shultz.

Later in the day, McFarlane telephoned me. He said that the president was very pleased that Mondale had included me, and they both hoped I would agree to attend the briefing. My selection demonstrated Mondale's desire for continuity, which they appreciated.

McFarlane, Schlesinger, and I flew to Minnesota to meet with Mondale at his home in suburban Minneapolis, and Schlesinger, Aaron, and I had dinner with the vice president that evening in preparation for the briefing. I was again impressed with how much Mondale had grown and developed as vice president. He was obviously sophisticated and experienced, knew a great many details, and had a broad vision of America's responsibility in the world, which I welcomed.

---

* Several times in subsequent years, Kondrashev and I met and talked. The State Department encouraged me to visit CSCE meetings, and Kondrashev would often be there. He was a master of the subject matter. We would talk for a while about whatever was current in United States–Soviet relations, we would part cheerfully, and he would disappear from my life again. I don't know that I ever told him anything new, but I certainly tried to help him understand what we meant and what we sought in a developing relationship.

The briefing, which lasted practically all day, provided an excellent summary of all parts of the world and all areas of existing and potential international tension. On our return to Washington, McFarlane, too, expressed both increased respect for Mondale's grasp of the issues and satisfaction with his obvious competence.

When the Edinburgh Conversations ended, I believed I had seen the last of the Soviets in any official capacity. But back home in Washington, on January 9, 1985, at five A.M., I received a wake-up call I had not anticipated. The New York bureau of CBS News was on the phone. An apologetic woman said she was sorry to call so early, but they had just received a cable from Dan Rather, who was in Geneva with George Shultz. Rather's scoop was that I had been selected to head the upcoming arms negotiations with the Soviets. It was a scoop for Rather and CBS. It was a surprise for me.

I told CBS I had no comment. Not only had I not been asked to take the assignment, I had never had any discussions with anyone about it. Before that call, I had never even heard a rumor of my involvement. I said they were misinformed, and ended the conversation with the suggestion that they not air a totally erroneous rumor. The reporter seemed to believe me, but she suggested I should turn off my phone if I didn't want to receive more calls, since they were going to run with the story at six A.M. in any case. As I talked to CBS, I recalled silently that I had lunch with George Shultz not a month before, and he had said nothing of the talks. Certainly, he would have done so if there was any substance to what I was now hearing.

My skepticism also came from two prior experiences during the year. Some months earlier, the *New York Times* had reported that I was slated to succeed Jeane Kirkpatrick as UN ambassador. From time to time, Jeane had indicated an intention to resign. While they were not idle threats, they did not come to pass. No one ever talked to me about replacing her, and when she continued in her post, it was all moot anyway.

On another occasion, Joe Kraft, an esteemed newspaper columnist and a friend, phoned to ask ingenuously, "When are you going to the Middle East?" It seemed an odd question, but I said I had no plans to go there, because I was tired of travel. He said he knew the president was going to name me his special negotiator for the Middle East, so I needn't be coy or secretive about the appointment. He explained that he had just come back from Saudi Arabia, and a high-ranking member of the royal family had told him how pleased they were about my forthcoming appointment. Joe said that since his return he had checked with friends at the State Department, who had confirmed the rumor. I told Joe I hated to disappoint a friend *and* a prince *and* his anonymous source, but it was all news to me.

That rumor died like its earlier companion, but the arms negotiator story did not. TV cameras were in front of my home as I left for the office and cameras were in my office when I arrived. More reporters called. My answer to them was the same as it had been at five A.M.: no offer; therefore, no comment.

Neither Maggie nor I wanted an overseas assignment. With continued press reports of my appointment, Maggie urged me to call Shultz and tell him that I did not want the job, but I felt I just couldn't do that. To turn down a job that hadn't been offered seemed odd and presumptuous. If the rumors were inaccurate or if I had been considered and rejected, I would look like a fool and would have put a friend in an awkward position.

I did what I thought was the next best thing. I called Larry Eagleburger, who had just left the State Department as undersecretary to work with Henry Kissinger's private consulting firm. I asked him to call Shultz to tell him I didn't want the assignment. I didn't have to convince Larry that I shouldn't take the assignment. He felt it would not be in my interest to undertake what would likely be a fruitless effort.

When he paused for breath, I assured him that I had not been offered the job or accepted it. I told him I was not looking for another government post and that I did not want to live in Europe again.* I also noted that I was not an arms expert. Larry seemed relieved and said he would follow up, but asked if I would take the job as United Nations ambassador if Shultz asked. He reported that Shultz had, in fact, sent my name to Reagan as a replacement for Jeane Kirkpatrick when they thought she was leaving and that the president had approved. I asked him why someone hadn't told me, and he expressed surprise that he himself had not. I told him that the UN job was intriguing and that my Madrid experience might be useful there, although Jeane seemed quite settled for the moment.

The next day, Larry called with the message: "Mission accomplished." I could relax. Soon after, Maggie and I went to Aspen,

---

* I gave that same reason when, in 1984, Helene Van Damm, working as head of the White House personnel office, said the president wanted to appoint me to an ambassadorship. I turned her down without even asking which country. I later learned it was Poland, where my contacts with Solidarity would have made the post interesting, but still unattractive to Maggie and me.

Colorado, where I had been invited to speak to a group of young business leaders headed by Gary Rappaport, the successor to his father, Max, at my old client, NAPCO.

While we were in Aspen, a call came from the White House in its distinctive fashion: an operator's voice saying, "This is the White House. Is this Ambassador Kampelman?" I said yes and she asked me to hold for a moment. Both George Shultz and Secretary of Defense Cap Weinberger came on the line. They said that the president wanted me to head the arms negotiations in Geneva and he was going to call me in ten minutes. It was a call I had hoped to avoid because I knew I could not turn down the president.*

After I listened to Shultz and Weinberger, I told them I did not want the assignment and thought that message had been conveyed to them. They said they were aware of my reluctance, but I could not say no to the president. I knew that, which was precisely why I didn't want to receive the offer. I also said that I did not know enough about the subject matter and, further, I was about to have cataract surgery. For all of that, both secretaries urged me to accept the job, not only offering their encouragement, but assuring me of personal and agency support.

The arms talks were to begin on March 12, 1985, fifteen months after the previous set of talks had been broken off by the Soviets. The talks were the successor negotiations to those started in the early 1980s after Reagan became president. All the talks shared a common concern: fear of nuclear destruction. Hawks and doves both acknowledged the existence of incredible destructive power in the world's nuclear arsenal. We lived with a real threat to civilization. Some scientists thought the danger of annihilation was exaggerated, but other scientists and segments of the general public were sufficiently fearful to cry out, "Let's do something." However, it was also generally appreciated, particularly by political leaders, that the existence of nuclear weapons probably provided the deterrent to both conventional and nuclear war, thus making their use less likely.

The traditional position taken by those who could make a difference was to talk about limiting numbers and the further development of those weapons, not reductions. The emphasis was on keeping down increases in the numbers of offensive nuclear weapons. Then, in 1983,

---

* George Shultz never directly referred to Larry Eagleburger's call. About a year later when we were just chatting about a variety of issues, he noted in an aside that he thought the Geneva role I was playing was of greater national importance than being the U.S. ambassador to the United Nations would have been, because it would have more lasting results.

President Reagan injected another ingredient. Reagan's presidential insight, garnered from scientists he spoke with, was that if missiles fly in space, the way to defend against them is to put something in space to stop them. He said, in effect, "Let's explore whether a defense is possible. We know the Soviets are looking at the defense question, maybe we should too." He had, in fact, been persuaded by some scientists that a virtual shield might in time be put in space to protect against nuclear annihilation.

Reagan understood that it would require enormous amounts of money, but his view was that we should spend whatever was necessary if it might result in a world safe from nuclear destruction. While the idea got mixed reviews at home, the Soviets came to Reagan toward the end of 1984 and proposed discussions about Reagan's Strategic Defense Initiative (SDI).

His response was somewhat unexpected. He agreed to talk, but said that talking about defense alone was inadequate. We ought to talk about reducing offensive weapons as well; then he pointed out that the Soviets, not us, had walked out of the talks in 1983.

In Geneva in January 1985, Secretary Shultz and Foreign Minister Gromyko agreed to begin talks covering three disarmament subjects. One set of talks, dealing with intermediate-range nuclear force (INF) missiles, would pick up basically at the point reached when the Soviets walked out in 1983. These missiles had a travel range roughly from 300 to 3,300 miles. These, of course, were barely relevant to American soil, except possibly for Alaska.

The second set of talks was aimed at those so-called strategic missiles that could threaten the United States by crossing the ocean in minutes, traveling more than 3,300 miles to their targets. Here, too, the earlier Strategic Arms Reduction Talks (START) from which the Soviets walked out in 1983 would be resumed. The third area they agreed to discuss was space and defense questions, focusing largely on SDI.

Maggie and I had hardly had time to discuss the situation when the president called. I had barely put my thoughts in order, but it didn't make much difference. The president told me that he wanted my help, that by taking the job I might contribute mightily to a nuclear-free world and advance the search for peace. I simply said, "Of course, Mr. President, I would be honored to head the negotiations."

Meanwhile, word of the White House call had traveled from the switchboard at Aspen to my meeting, where I was scheduled momentarily to speak. By the time I reached the dais, there was excitement in the room. Since I had not been asked to keep the content of the call a secret, I told Gary about it when he asked. When the audience was informed, there were emotional cheers, led by Gary and Susan Rappaport, who could not hold back their tears. It was the first clear indication to me that my assignment carried with it heavy emotional baggage. It also made me acknowledge my own excitement, albeit with some ambiguity, about the opportunity.

Maggie and I packed our bags and headed home that afternoon, less rested and a good deal more troubled by the turn of events. It reminded us of an old Abraham Lincoln story of the man who had been tarred and feathered and was being carried out of town on a rail. When asked how he liked the experience, he said, "Except for the honor . . ."

When I had talked to Shultz and Weinberger, I learned that former Senator John Tower and an experienced foreign service diplomat, Maynard "Mike" Glitman, would handle the START and INF assignments, respectively. I would be the overall head of the delegation and would handle the third area of defense and space. That brought with it a potential for problems.

The three of us were equal in the sense that we each had an area of responsibility, but since I was specifically designated as the head, I was more equal than the others. Yet they both had substantial careers much more related to the substance of the negotiations than I. There was bound to be some tension between us, and we had no past associations on which to build.

I had never spent much time talking to Tower face to face, although I had recently been asked by a mutual friend to help Tower find a professional home in Washington after he left the Senate. By then, he had been in the Senate for twenty-four years and had become a power, particularly through the chairmanship of the Senate Armed Services Committee.

Glitman was a younger diplomat who had been our deputy chief of mission at NATO, where I had worked with him, if only casually, when I had visited there during the Madrid meetings. He had been chief deputy to Paul Nitze when Paul was negotiating INF, and Paul thought highly of him, which made me favorably disposed toward him.

From the beginning, I took my role as head of the negotiations seriously, particularly as it became clear to me that the president, the secretary of State, and the congressional leadership were looking to me as the one with prime responsibility. My determination to be in charge made Tower and Glitman understandably nervous, even though I had no intention of interfering with how they pursued their own substantive areas of responsibility.

My relations with John Tower were made more difficult than they needed to be because of tensions emanating from his staff. Once we were in Geneva, I decided to talk to him about our relationship, which showed signs of becoming adversarial. I said, "John, neither you nor I made this decision and I know it is not easy for you, but if we both work at it, it will work." Through my actions, I assured him and Glitman that I did not want to run their negotiations. What I did want was to make sure we were coordinated. We met together almost every day and reported to one another to maintain consistency in the three groups. If either of them remained seriously distressed, I was not aware of it.

From the president's telephone call to the first meeting with the Soviets was only a matter of weeks. Since I was not an arms expert, leading the negotiations meant absorbing a lot of information quickly. As an executive committee member of the Committee on the Present Danger, I had learned a great deal in general about arms questions, but I had always assumed the technological details were for the experts, not for me. I had dreaded the tediousness of mastering the complexity of weapons. That could no longer be the case in the negotiations ahead. I didn't need to know everything, but I did need to know a good deal more than I already did.

My predecessors, Paul Nitze and Ed Rowny, had been technically highly qualified, with extensive experience in arms control matters. Nitze particularly was the guru of arms control in Washington, having spent virtually his entire adult life thinking, writing, and speaking about it. He had an extraordinary mind, backed by a deep institutional history of our negotiations with the Soviets. Paul might have been expected to do the job I was being asked to do, but his wife had become seriously ill. Rowny, a retired general, was blunt, direct, and highly regarded, and he held his opinions strongly. For whatever reasons, Washington had decided to go with a clean slate. Instead of being sent to Geneva, both men were designated as special advisers to the president and the secretary of State on arms control, and were extraordinarily helpful to me. Paul and I had worked closely with the Committee on the Present Danger. Ed and I had met when he was a scholar at the Woodrow Wilson Center and I was its chairman. We were not particularly close, but I certainly thought of them as friends.

I was concerned about my staff. I had learned in Madrid that complicated issues required strong staff support, people who were smart—which was not so difficult to come by—and could work together with political sensitivity. I had watched too many staffs in Washington compete among themselves to the detriment of their shared goals. When turf battles did not aggravate me, they bored me. Tripartite negotiations held infinite opportunity for unnecessary competition, misunderstandings, and jockeying for position.

I needed an overall deputy in my role as delegation head to avoid all that, and I turned once again to Warren Zimmermann. He had left Madrid to serve as our deputy chief of mission in Moscow, and with that tour of duty over, he was now returning to Washington. His value would be not only that he spoke Russian fluently, although that was, of course, terribly important, but that he knew my methods for pursuing a negotiation and was comfortable with my habits and instincts. He also knew the State Department even better than he had when we first met and was quite familiar with arms control questions.

I asked Shultz and Weinberger about a deputy for me in the defense and space areas for which I had special responsibility, and they both recommended Dr. Henry Cooper, an assistant director of the Arms Control and Disarmament Agency (ACDA). Cooper was an engineer with extensive military and scientific experience and a hardliner, which seemed a good combination to me, but I had to assure myself that he understood that being a hard-liner did not mean he was in principle hostile to an agreement. When we met in my law office for the first time, I was impressed that he was serious and an expert of obvious competence. I explained that the president wanted an agreement if it was in our interest. I told him that I was a negotiator, and if I were given the task of negotiating something, I took it seriously and did not try to find reasons not to succeed. He assured me that he understood.

Hank was invaluable from the start, although he operated only in high gear. When he was briefing me before the meetings began, he was soon over my head and unrelenting. I tried to keep up, but just couldn't. Finally, in desperation, I said, "Whoa! Stop! I am not training for a hundred-yard dash. I'm training for a marathon. Take it easy." He slowed down some, but I thought to myself, "If he's that tough on an ally, what will he do to the Soviets?"

Hank is a big man with a lot of nervous energy, always drumming his fingers or his feet, moving around when he could, never sitting still. He is also impatient with fools, which is not the best stance for a negotiator, and he is more than a little stubborn when arguing for his own views, which isn't bad if it is not excessive.

Hank never stopped working. He had no inclination or talent for small talk. He didn't seem to have a lower gear, but he tried to adjust down, although not always successfully. I liked the fact that he was a religious man with a deep sense of morality. We made a very good team, I thought, because he taught me a lot about the substance, and I taught him a lot about international relations, about politics, and about dealing with the Soviets.

I depended on him to find the staff we needed for our defense and space group from State, the Arms Control and Disarmament Agency, the Joint Chiefs of Staff, the Office of the Secretary of Defense (OSD), and the intelligence agencies. While those agencies would make their own recommendations, Hank knew the strengths and weaknesses of the people and could help influence the decisions. Furthermore, I had veto power over their selection. They were my technical support.

Having agreed to the job, I reviewed my strengths and weaknesses. While I was by no means an expert on arms control matters, I had learned as a lawyer how to cram, becoming a mini-expert who knew what he knew and what he didn't. I also felt I knew the current Soviets about as well as anybody as a result of my college studies, my teaching, and hundreds of hours of meetings with them in Madrid, both in groups and one-on-one. I had a sense of how they negotiated, what restrictions were imposed on them, how to divine what they really thought behind the bombast of their rhetoric.

Finally, Madrid had confirmed my opinion that I was a good negotiator. I had spent a long time, really all my life, thinking in terms of negotiation and conciliation rather than confrontation. My enthusiasm for the job increased, and I found myself eager to begin. I was prepared for a long haul, having learned in Madrid that serious negotiations take time.

In late February, the Senate Foreign Relations Committee held confirmation hearings at which Paul Nitze, Tower, Glitman, and I all appeared. Nitze summed up our feelings, "It is important that we keep our expectations in check and that we prepare ourselves and the public for a long process." Each of us also supported the administration's view that the MX missile and the SDI research and development program should be funded.

I talked of "mutual assured security" to replace "mutual assured destruction" as my goal in the negotiations, which I called "the most important assignment in my life." I was determined that if the Soviets turned out to be bona fide negotiators, I would try to find a way to reduce the number of nuclear arms in the world and diminish the threat of nuclear disaster.

The chairman of the committee, Senator Claiborne Pell of Rhode

Island, a highly sensitive public servant who correctly looked upon himself as a good personal friend of mine, asked a most perceptive question about my qualifications. He listed the names of the Soviet negotiators and the impressive number of years each had spent in negotiating arms control. Would I not be at a decided disadvantage, he asked, given my lack of arms control expertise? After a moment's pause, I acknowledged the legitimacy of his concern but pointed out that with all the experience and expertise on both sides, we had still been unable to reduce nuclear arms. Perhaps, I suggested, my own talents might make a difference.*

We were unanimously confirmed.†

When the president invited the congressional bipartisan leadership in for breakfast on the eve of our departure for Geneva, I sensed a strong surge of personal support combined with a sense of realism about the difficulties ahead. I assured them that I would not produce an agreement just for the empty satisfaction of saying we had one. I told them they would not be asked to support anything that did not serve U.S. interests. But I insisted that I would explore all avenues that might open up. They appeared to like what they heard. I felt I was departing for Geneva with their good wishes, and that was encouraging.

Democratic suspicions about Reagan's intellect and commitment to arms control remained strong, and I knew there were some questions about my continued willingness to serve him, but my Madrid experience had convinced me that he was a serious man and by no means

---

* Another friend, Senator William Proxmire of Wisconsin, a maverick who prided himself on his independence and integrity, wrote me on September 8, 1987: "Although I did say a critical word about your qualifications when you were appointed, there is no question that your fundamental and extraordinary intelligence has overcome any lack of experience you had and you have done a bang-up job." A few months later, on November 20, he repeated his compliment in a statement to the Senate, referring to "an excellent blend of toughness, substance, and willingness to bargain in good faith." He concluded: "I give Mr. Kampelman high marks . . . I believe he has done as professional a job as any other person that could have been named."

† With the U.S. Senate making my ambassadorial rank official, I daydreamed a scene of my coming home and informing my deceased Aunt Rose that I had been appointed an ambassador of the United States. There was a moment of incredulous disbelief. When the seriousness of my message sank in, Rose composed herself and quietly said: "Good, Max, good." Then, came: "Good. By me, you are an ambassador. By you, you are an ambassador. By Momma, you're an ambassador. But, tell me Maxie, by an ambassador are you an ambassador?" Rose would always have a way of coming to the essence of the matter. I never forgot this story or the need to prove myself to the professional foreign service officers. As time went on, it was clear to me that I had.

irresponsible. Furthermore, I agreed more with Reagan than with the new mainstream of the Democratic party about the need for a strong defense in light of the aggressive totalitarian nature of the Soviet Union.

I flew into Geneva for the March 12 meeting to learn that the Soviet leader, Chernenko, had just died. I immediately telephoned my Soviet counterpart, Victor Karpov, whom I had never met, to suggest that if he needed to return to Moscow or wanted a day or two of mourning, we would be pleased to accommodate him. He thanked me, but said we should start as planned, exhibiting a "show must go on" attitude. He also noted that the Politburo meeting that had given him the instructions for negotiating had been chaired by Chernenko's successor, Mikhail Gorbachev.*

Clearly, the Soviets wanted no delay and, indeed, apparently wanted to communicate a sense of continuity as power was transferred in Moscow. Since the first meeting was to be held at the Soviet mission, I indicated that we would like to begin by signing their book of condolences. The next morning while we were doing that, Karpov took advantage of the delayed arrival resulting from our gesture by having a mini-press conference. It was not of major importance, but irritating. I expressed my displeasure to Karpov and proposed a "confidentiality agreement." It was the U.S. view, I suggested, that we should be talking to each other and not to the public, that we should not be scoring points outside but pursuing serious negotiations inside. We both agreed to refrain from public comments on the contents of the talks.

The purpose of the confidentiality agreement was to allow both sides, in their efforts to make progress, to speak openly and to try out alternative solutions without fear that everything they said would appear the next day in the press. Our American objective, of course, was to persuade the Soviet Union that we were serious about the negotiations and to prevent grandstanding and reckless playing to public opinion. It was important for me to make this proposal because in Madrid I had met with the press daily and had publicly criticized the Soviets

---

* George Shultz and George Bush attended Chernenko's funeral and met Gorbachev for the first time. At their second meeting not long thereafter, Shultz was astounded at the intensity of Gorbachev's anti–United States bias, fueled by misconceptions. Gorbachev said, in effect, "I *know* your people sleep on the streets because I have seen it on your television. You have millions of homeless." He apparently referred to the incident of the serial killing of black children in Atlanta as evidence of our racism. Anatoly Dobrynin, who should have known better, was present and reportedly encouraged Gorbachev's misperceptions.

relentlessly. That would not work here, and I wanted the Soviets to understand that I had the distinction between the two meetings clearly in mind.

The Soviet delegation had, like ours, a three-man leadership team. Karpov was the head of their delegation and would handle the strategic arms talks with John Tower; Alexei Obukhov would negotiate the INF with Mike Glitman; and Yuli Kvitsinskiy, who had negotiated the earlier INF talks with Paul Nitze, would be my counterpart in the defense and space talks.*

Karpov's maiden plenary speech was filled with old-style bombast, posturing, and anti-American slogans. I was outraged and responded immediately, attacking the speech as a terrible way to begin a serious negotiation.

Karpov listened stolidly, waiting for me to finish. At the end of the meeting, he said, in essence, "Don't confuse the messenger with the message." I took heart from that in the hope that he might be a more reasonable man than his words had indicated. Karpov also suggested that diplomatic protocol would have called for me to listen, wait, and come back with a defense later. I said I didn't need time or protocol to define how I would react to excessive rhetoric attacking my country.

I also sensed from our exchange that the Soviet negotiators were on a short tether. They moved their lips in Geneva, but the words were written in Moscow and were intended for a Soviet audience as well as for me and my colleagues. I obviously had a freedom that Victor and his colleagues did not have. Until that changed to some extent, I understood that there would be a long time of shadowboxing like prizefighters in the early rounds, taking each other's measure.

The formal negotiating process consisted of two ingredients. The most formal and most important was the plenary session. Each side would sit around a long rectangular table on which would be placed

---

* It was Kvitsinskiy with whom Paul had taken the "walk in the woods" in 1982, seeking agreement outside the traditional negotiating room. Their efforts were later chronicled in a play by that name. Kvitsinskiy, according to Paul, prided himself on being part of an intellectual Polish family that had been sent to Siberia by Stalin and "rehabilitated" during World War II. Kvitsinskiy spoke German before he learned Russian, was a physicist, a lawyer, and an outstanding musician who studied the cello for five years. Paul later wrote that Yuli carried the party line in formal meetings, running on illogically, but Paul said, "In private discussion, away from the ears of his associates, and presumably of the KGB as well, he was generally quite a different man. He could be charming, a good conversationalist, interested in an amazing array of subjects. He appeared to be surprisingly frank in his discussion of Moscow politics, of the character and ability of his superiors, and of speculative possibilities." I found him to be incisive and pleasant, very shrewd.

pads, pencils, bottles of water, glasses, fruit juice, nuts, and candies. Sessions alternated between the United States and USSR missions. The host state would call on the visitor to speak. The head of the delegation would read in his native language a formal paper, which would be translated every few sentences by an interpreter from the delegation that had the floor. The host state would repeat the process. An exchange sometimes, but not always, followed. It might be an expression of disappointment, or a question, or a reassertion of position, or a rebuttal. The formal plenary would then end and was usually followed by the delegates breaking up into smaller groups, previously arranged within each delegation. This would usually be our military with their military, our CIA with their KGB, and so forth. Variations might take place if specific subject matters crossed those delineations. Informal discussions without prepared statements would here take place. With time, there were fewer plenaries and more informal sessions. All of this interchange was occasionally supplemented by private dinners, receptions, lunches between delegation members on both sides. At all times, the facts and essence of these exchanges were requested to be reported to me and cabled to Washington.

The opening of negotiations also brought visitors from Washington. The Senate had created a bipartisan arms control observer group of ten members plus the majority and minority leaders.* The House appointed a similar group, but the senators, because of their treaty responsibilities, were more conscientious as a group. Executive branch people often fear that legislative presence means interference, but I was delighted. I needed their support. The Senate observer group said in one of their reports, "The Group is not a Committee of the Senate, and has no legislative or formal oversight function," but they would have significant influence in interpreting the agreement to their constituents and, of course, ultimate power in approving it.

I first heard of the move to create Senate and House observer groups at a White House meeting shortly after I was appointed. It was raised by Richard Perle, assistant secretary of Defense, who understandably characterized it as interference by the Congress in the presi-

---

* Senators Robert Byrd of West Virginia and Robert Dole of Kansas, the majority and minority leaders, were ex-officio members. The rest of the original members were Claiborne Pell of Rhode Island, Ted Stevens of Alaska, Sam Nunn of Georgia, Richard Lugar of Indiana, Pat Moynihan of New York, Ted Kennedy of Massachusetts, Al Gore of Tennessee, Don Nickles of Oklahoma, Malcolm Wallop of Wyoming, and John Warner of Virginia. Other senators and congressmen showed up from time to time, and I tried to make sure they were treated well, briefed thoroughly, and, when appropriate, given the opportunity to talk informally with the Soviets.

dent's prerogative to manage foreign policy. He had been informed that the congressmen intended to be integral parts of the negotiating process. Richard's recommendation was that the president call in the leadership and kill the idea. My own view was that I had gained in Madrid from the active interest of those congressmen who were part of the commission. The president authorized me to explore a solution. While talking to the Senate majority leader, Robert Byrd of West Virginia, I learned that he and the president had already agreed on the desirability of the idea. It was not difficult to work out the details. The Senators were to be observers and not negotiators. They would not be included in the sessions when they were in Geneva, but we would provide them with full briefings on a continual basis.

A visit by the congressional leaders and the observer groups on opening day proved immensely helpful. They met our Soviet colleagues and impressed upon them that our negotiators had their complete bipartisan support. They read Karpov's unhelpful opening comments and my rejoinder. We briefed them on our objectives and approach. They then held a joint press conference in which they voiced their strong support for us and our position.

I was pleased to note in the senators' public statement the following:

> In fulfillment of our constitutional responsibility in providing advice and consent in the making of treaties, we believe it is necessary to become completely conversant concerning the particular issues under negotiation. . . . We believe the Senate will be in a far better position to evaluate any agreement which may be reached and that such agreement might benefit from the reactions of the Senate as it is being formulated. . . . In the event that the negotiations fail, the Senate will be in a better position to understand and to make comprehensible to the American people just why that failure occurred. This is particularly important in light of the staggering complexity of the issues . . .

The senators took their roles seriously and were continually briefed in Washington through meetings with various people of differing points of view. They studied, they considered, they did not interfere. It was an example of the Senate at its best. I knew some of the senators reasonably well, others almost not at all, but those days in Geneva cemented a relationship that would prove valuable in a variety of ways as our negotiations proceeded. Led by Senators Ted Stevens of

Alaska and Claiborne Pell of Rhode Island, they visited Geneva frequently and were of immense assistance to our negotiating efforts.

Our delegation was provided space in an office building known as the Botanic Building in Geneva. It had housed earlier arms talks, but none of the earlier talks had had three separate negotiations taking place simultaneously. We hardly had room to turn around. More important, it soon became obvious that we were vulnerable to terrorist attack and Soviet technical espionage. The senators, led by Stevens and Nunn, noted this and entered statements into the *Congressional Record* urging a supplemental appropriation for a new building to be constructed on the grounds of the U.S. mission. This was approved by the Congress. In the meantime, however, I began to negotiate to obtain underused space in the existing U.S. mission building. Ambassador Gerald Carmen at the mission was both cooperative and understandably reluctant. We ended up with three floors there—most of the building. It seemed to work for all of us, so I later arranged to meet the budget crunch by postponing and probably thereby killing the new building project.

One Friday soon after we began, I received a call from Ken Dam, deputy secretary of State. He said there was talk of asking me to return to Washington to lobby in the House for an appropriation for twenty-six MX missiles that had been authorized, but not funded, the previous year. I told him how totally inadvisable I thought that was. I did not want to jeopardize the strong bipartisan consensus behind our negotiations, even though I supported the MX appropriation. In addition, I had serious doubts whether I would even be effective at lobbying, and suggested that John Tower might be a better lobbyist considering his long congressional service. Ken said George Shultz had also expressed reservations, but the decision would obviously be up to the president. Neither Shultz nor I carried the day. That night Ken called again to say the president wanted me to return to Washington immediately. I flew to London the next morning in time to get on the Concorde for a speedy trip home.

On Monday morning, I checked in early at the White House to get my marching orders. I was told that we were twenty-five to thirty votes shy and given a list of people to visit on the Hill. I noticed that Speaker Tip O'Neill of Massachusetts was not among them. I informed my schedulers that I would not set foot on the Hill without first calling on Tip, as a proper courtesy if nothing else. They responded by saying that he was the opposition, but gave in to my request and arranged for me to start with the Speaker.

Tip and I were not close friends, but we shared an affection for

Hubert Humphrey and the social programs of a generation of Democratic leadership. I explained my mission: to garner as many votes as I could for funding the MX. I also said that it did not help the Democratic party or the Democrats in Congress to be seen as anti-defense. I thought we gained nothing as a party by destroying a weapons system like the MX. He did not argue the point, but said that members were free to vote their own conscience. I told him that was not the general perception, that most observers viewed the contest as purely Tip O'Neill versus Ronald Reagan.

Tip then took from his desk a list of members, looked it over, and said I needed about forty more votes and would probably not get them. I urged him to help produce them. We soon moved away from the matter at hand as he lamented the state of Congress. He said, "You know, Max, it is different from when you were up here. The institutional loyalty, the memory isn't there. The sense of history isn't there, too many personal ambitions, too much irresponsibility." Then he said sadly, "The role of leadership is not as strong as it once was, and you need that."

I went from meeting to meeting all day, some one-on-one, some with small groups. I met with members from both parties, and I returned to the White House with sufficient assurances to tell the president we would get the votes we needed if he made a few phone calls.* He immediately picked up the phone and made the calls.

While we chatted, someone said, "We have our meeting now, Mr. President." He popped out of his chair, said, "Let's go," and I settled into step beside him. I simply followed him, not knowing where precisely we were headed, and as we walked, we talked about Geneva and Hollywood and our mutual experiences with American Communists. I saw we were approaching the east room, where Lincoln met Grant, which was now used for large meetings or functions. The president, while walking, turned to me and said, "Max, all I'm going to do is stand up and introduce you. Then you take it from there." I thought, "What the hell is this?" No one had said a word to me about speaking at a meeting. By then we were in the doorway, and the television lights made it difficult to see what was inside. I blinked and then focused on a platform where Vice President George Bush, George Shultz, Cap Weinberger, and Bud McFarlane were waiting for us. In front of them

---

* I remember, in 1981, making a courtesy call one evening on Senator Orrin Hatch of Utah. It was about eight P.M., and the senator had left the floor to meet me in his office. During our talk, the phone rang. It was newly elected President Reagan, squeezing Hatch very hard to get a vote on extending the debt limit. This surprised me, since the press had portrayed Reagan as a nine-to-five president.

was a roomful of congressmen and the press. This was to be a major performance by an unrehearsed understudy before a powerful audience while Ronald Reagan, the real star, wished to step aside and be the supporting actor.

The president said, "I don't have to introduce you to our good friend who agreed to come back here from Geneva . . . Let me turn you over to Max Kampelman." I didn't have time to be speechless. I looked out at the audience, my eyes focused on Senator Howard Metzenbaum of Ohio and Congressman Steve Solarz of New York, two friends and liberal Democrats on the other side of the MX issue, who were often critical of Reagan.

I responded to the president's introduction by saying that I did, indeed, have old friends in front of me, and they were all patriotic Americans. I purposely said this because one of the themes I picked up during the day was that people inclined to vote against the MX did not like having their patriotism questioned as some MX supporters were implying. I continued, "They are patriotic, but in this case they are wrong, Mr. President." Instinctively, I tried to build a nonconfrontational platform from which I might persuade. I spoke of the importance of the MX missiles to our negotiations. I urged bipartisan support.

The cameras were grinding away, the reporters were scribbling, the congressmen were applauding, Reagan and Shultz were obviously pleased, and I headed for Andrews Air Base where an air force plane stood by to fly me back to Geneva. When the vote was taken, I was back at my post, and we had won. I could never prove it, but I felt that I could discern the hand of Tip O'Neill in that final count. After that, I focused entirely on what we were doing in Geneva, resolving never again to lobby on issues not directly a part of our negotiations.

I learned or confirmed several items of importance during the first round of our meetings. For example, although the plenary sessions were formal and repetitious, they served a useful purpose. They probably did not persuade either side to change its views, but I was speaking to Moscow with these formal statements as much as to the negotiator in my presence. Everything written would be sent to Moscow precisely as delivered. The plenaries permit you to make a case and lay out a position; in something as complex as nuclear arms and disarmament, that takes time.

I came to the meetings knowing that a serious negotiator needs to accomplish two objectives. First, a negotiator must understand the other side, where they are going, how far they are ready to go, and what they are after. Second, a negotiator must persuade the other side that his proposals are reasonable and not hostile to their purposes, nor contrary to their interests. If a negotiator cannot do this the other side certainly will not accept what is offered, and no agreement short of capitulation will be possible.

I also knew that I did not like to bluff and, therefore, was not good at it. I preferred to be straight and honest as the only way to avoid contradicting myself. To remember old lies, distortions, and deceptions would strain my memory and my intellect. If you don't bluff, it is much easier to be consistent, and consistency is vital in negotiations with the Soviets. A lack of consistency leads to confusion and miscalculation; it is self-defeating. I never called a position unacceptable if there was a chance I might later accept it. If I ultimately accepted something I had called unacceptable, then the Soviets would have every right to believe I would accept other items I call unacceptable.

I also found that informal sessions were immensely important in finding new directions for the negotiations. A lunch away from the meetings or a ten-minute coffee break after a two-hour negotiating session was often more valuable than the tailored speeches, but even those periods had their own protocol.

I urged my staff to leave meaningless debating points and cosmically macho demonstrations to others. A serious negotiation was not a time to outsmart or outmuscle your opponents, but to listen. We tried to listen to everyone who seemed to have something to say. A related lesson, inscribed on a sweatshirt given to me as a birthday gift by my staff, was "We don't fail until we stop trying."

We learned early that the Soviet KGB and military people felt freer to speak informally and informatively than those in the Soviet foreign service. They may have felt more secure. Much later in the negotiations, one of our State Department negotiators in the START talks developed a friendly relationship with a Soviet START negotiator whom I had not thought of as a key player, but whom I later decided was probably KGB. He obviously wanted to explore ideas directly with me and found a way to do so through his new friend in State.

He provided very useful information. He was not being disloyal to his country. On the contrary, he knew precisely what he was doing and where his information would go. Occasionally, he would explicitly say, "Give me a reaction." A great deal of successful negotiating depends on the comfort level people have with each other.

Karpov and I developed the pattern of holding press conferences at the beginning and end of each round of talks. The Soviet approach was their traditional one of bewailing a lack of progress. Their reasoning was simple. I always felt that if there was a Soviet primer on "How to Negotiate with the Americans," the first lesson would be to wait until the forces of the democratic process produce U.S. concessions without the need for the USSR to pay a price for those concessions. They believed the old adage that "the apples will fall without the need to shake the tree." If there is a negotiating blockage, the U.S. tendency is both to look for a solution and to blame ourselves for the impasse. I saw that early on with some members of Congress who should have known better accepting the Soviet assertion of an impasse and immediately publicly calling on the United States to make concessions by changing its position.

My own public position during the opening rounds of our talks was to assert that the initial talks had increased our understanding of each other's position, an indispensable ingredient for any later agreement. I also explained the Soviet effort was to panic us into making concessions that the Soviets would not have to pay for, and I said that would not happen in Geneva. Finally, I pointed out that we needed to give the Soviets time to clarify their own position in the light of Chernenko's death and Eduard Shevardnadze's becoming the new Soviet foreign minister in place of Gromyko. I found the press ready to accept these realities and to treat the negotiations in that light.

At the end and beginning of each round of talks, Tower, Glitman, and I also briefed the North Atlantic Council in Brussels. We needed the support and understanding of our allies, and there was no better way to earn it than by a full discussion of our problems and our accomplishments. The NATO meetings were very important. Our allies, whose lives and land were obviously involved directly in any decisions made at Geneva, needed to be informed to prevent fears of a sellout. I felt this obligation keenly.

Even though I saw the president before and after each round, I did not believe that I had to see him frequently or even regularly. It is currency in Washington to be able to say, "I said to the president yesterday . . ." If everyone who says that did, in fact, meet with the president, his schedule would be an impossible one. Once I told Bud McFarlane, who succeeded Judge Clark as national security adviser to the president, that it was not always necessary for me to see the president. Bud replied, "Well, you may not think so, but the president does." These sessions were usually liberally photographed, and I did sense their utility in persuading both United States and world public opinion that the president wanted to reduce nuclear weapons.

McFarlane (or occasionally John Poindexter, his deputy, in his behalf) would call me at least once a week to obtain a report for the president. McFarlane and the president met at nine-thirty A.M., which was three-thirty P.M. in Geneva, so I would get a call in midafternoon from Bud. He would try to get a feel for what had happened during the week, which might not have come across in the cables. At the beginning, he would invariably say, "The president is going to ask me whether you have any new insights as to their seriousness."

I liked and respected McFarlane. I still do. He is serious, careful, and direct, and he was always trying to find a consensus to present to the president on any particular issue. When interagency meetings became hot and contentious, he remained a calm and soothing influence. Although exceptionally firm in his convictions, he was always willing to listen to new ideas and to consider new directions. He worked constantly as best I could tell, ignoring weekends and holidays. He was immensely loyal to the president. At the end of his time at the NSC, he had reached the ragged edge, nervous and exhausted, carrying the burdens of the NSC, the country, and the world on his shoulders.

Vice President Bush came to Geneva during the second round of our talks and met with the Soviet negotiators to indicate President Reagan's seriousness of purpose. He impressed me immensely, just as he had during my Madrid days when we discussed the Soviet Union. He also impressed the Soviets.

At the end of the round, Karpov said to the press that he was "unsatisfied" because there had been no "progress," but I believed the atmosphere had in fact improved. I said, "We do note a greater emphasis on dialogue and a lesser emphasis on polemics." I was also not discouraged by the slow pace.

Part of my confidence grew out of discussions with Yuli Kvitsinskiy. In the summer of 1985, we had lunch shortly after the Union of Concerned Scientists had written to Gorbachev and his response was reported in the *International Herald Tribune*. Gorbachev had just begun his anti-SDI offensive. I told Yuli that I didn't understand Gorbachev's response. He said, "It is very simple . . . what didn't you understand?"

I said, "Gorbachev wants us to reaffirm the Anti-Ballistic Missile (ABM) Treaty. I don't know about Soviet laws, but we don't reaffirm treaties. A treaty is a treaty. In your country, would a treaty that is reaffirmed be stronger than one that has just been affirmed once? Is a treaty that is reaffirmed twice better than one only reaffirmed once?" Kvitsinskiy, who knew English well, said, "Stop pulling my leg. You know what we want."

I said, "I do not know what you want." He responded, "We want to make sure you don't withdraw from the ABM Treaty while we are reducing our offensive arms." I said, "The ABM Treaty is a permanent treaty. We must have a vital reason and then give you six months' notice to withdraw." He replied, "That's not enough. We want to make certain you will stay with the treaty for at least ten years." The ABM Treaty, which was ratified by the United States and the Soviet Union in 1972, was premised on the assumption that peace could best be assured if we both agreed not to deploy defenses against ballistic missiles. This would deter an attack, in that an attacker would be defenseless against retaliation. SDI and a space defense would undermine that premise.

That was the first time the Soviets departed from their slogans and propagandizing about abolishing "space strike arms." I had frequently told Yuli that I could not negotiate political slogans, which was all I heard from them for most of the first year. Now I knew they would go beyond slogans at some point. I sent a cable to Washington immediately, repeating Kvitsinskiy's comments, discounting the ten years to seven or eight, and concluding that we would know they were serious when they put this on the table. I urged Washington to start immediately to define our own position so we would be able to react when it was desirable to do so. I was now certain the time would come, and it did, in fact, one year later.*

Kvitsinskiy continued to be an interesting mirror on Moscow's thinking, reflecting their direction when it was clear, and occasionally and inadvertently their confusion when it was not. On one occasion in early 1986, I was scheduled to visit FRG Foreign Minister Hans Dietrich Genscher in Bonn. A few days before my departure, Yuli said he would be gone from Geneva for a few days and would not be attending our plenaries. He didn't say where he was going, and I instinctively asked, "Going to Bonn?" He smiled and nodded. He wanted to get his points across to the Germans before I did.

A vital procedural issue that preceded our Geneva negotiations and remained with us for nearly two years was the Soviet desire to place pressure on us to drop or seriously curtail our SDI program by holding hostage the INF and START treaties. At the January 1985 Shultz-

---

* By then, Kvitsinskiy had left to become the Soviet ambassador to West Germany, and Karpov and I were having lunch when he said, "Max, I am putting in a new proposal tomorrow." I said I appreciated the alert and asked what it was going to be. Victor said, "We want both of us to agree not to withdraw from the ABM Treaty for a period of time, twenty years." Remembering my lunch with Kvitsinskiy, I just nodded. By the time Gorbachev and Reagan met at Reykjavik, the Soviets were at ten years and the United States at about seven years.

Gromyko meeting in Geneva, which reopened the arms reductions talks, the Soviets unsuccessfully tried to formalize this linkage. They kept trying when our formal talks began in March. We successfully resisted, arguing that we should complete and put in effect any steps of significance that could be finished without waiting for a total package in all three areas. It took a while before the Soviets finally accepted our approach, and then they did so with obvious reluctance.

In Geneva, it became increasingly clear to us that the INF talks were understandably proceeding more expeditiously than those in START or defense and space. The subject matter was more compact and manageable. The linkage issue, however, kept reappearing as a puzzling irritant. On January 15, 1986, Gorbachev, in announcing some sweeping arms reduction initiatives, had renewed the idea of linkage. A few weeks later, using the media-worthy visit of Ted Kennedy to Moscow, he reversed himself and announced that a separate INF treaty was indeed possible. In November, after the frustrations at Reykjavik, Moscow began to relink the treaties. Indeed, Karpov, thinking that the issues had been delinked, told the British and French that the no linkage position was still in effect. When he got back to Moscow, he was apparently chastised for saying so.

During this back-and-forth period, Kvitsinskiy went to Bonn. In Geneva, he was stating that the Soviets demanded linkage between INF and SDI. There could be no INF treaty, he stated, without an SDI agreement. Neither Mike Glitman nor I believed Kvitsinskiy to be correct. Mike's counterpart at the time in the INF negotiations was Ambassador Lem A. Masterkov, a relatively young Soviet arms control expert, who was cautiously avoiding the subject. This led Mike and me to believe that the whole question was under review and that the Soviets in Geneva did not quite know where Moscow was heading. Mike, therefore, proceeded on the assumption that there would be no linkage.

Kvitsinskiy, however, went to Bonn publicly and privately insisting that linkage was Soviet policy. When I visited Genscher the day after Kvitsinskiy's visit, Genscher was once again concerned about Kvitsinskiy's statement reaffirming linkage. Moscow took time getting its act together.* Finally, on February 28, 1987, Gorbachev definitively delinked INF and SDI and START, and we proceeded toward a sep-

---

* During one informal lunch with Kvitsinskiy, I mentioned that I thought it was in his personal interest to avoid being personally pigeonholed into arms control work alone. I knew he was fluent in the German language, culture, and politics and suggested he try to become his country's ambassador to Bonn. Some months later, in March 1986, I received a note from him saying he took my advice. Within a few days, the announcement of his appointment to Bonn was made.

arate INF treaty. Not until 1990 did Gorbachev finally agree to delink START from SDI and defense and space.

Visiting European capitals and making speeches was a part of my agenda.* SDI had become increasingly controversial, and, I thought, increasingly misunderstood. I found it useful in talking about SDI to quote a 1964 speech by Soviet Major General Nikolai Talenskiy, a member of the Soviet Senior Staff, who had written, "When the security of a state is based only on mutual deterrence with the aid of powerful nuclear missiles, it is directly dependent on the goodwill and designs of the other side, which is a highly subjective and indefinite factor. . . . The creation of an effective anti-missile system enables the state to make its defenses dependent chiefly on its own possibilities and not only on mutual deterrence." I used Talenskiy to make a point that prevention was far better than retaliation. It was one thing to be so heavily armed that any first strike would bring a devastating response. It was yet another to be able to prevent destruction in the first place.

On two occasions, I was asked to extend my trips beyond Europe. In the spring of 1986, Indian Prime Minister Rajiv Gandhi visited Washington. During his meeting with President Reagan, the issue of our Geneva arms talks came up. The Indians had for too long been critics of the United States and shown a decided tilt toward the Soviet Union. Gandhi was demonstrating some signs of shifting sentiment, with the result that the president apparently offered him an opportunity to learn firsthand what was happening in Geneva and what we in the United States were striving to achieve. I received a cable urging that I find the time to travel to Delhi to meet with the prime minister. In view of the fact that our negotiations were increasing in intensity, I felt I had to capsule the trip into a weekend.

On Thursday, June 12, I left Geneva and arrived in India the next morning, where I was met by our ambassador, John Gunther Dean, who had set up appointments for me to meet the prime minister and the minister of defense. It had been at least twenty years since I had

---

* On one occasion, I was invited by Italian Foreign Minister Giulio Andreotti, now prime minister, to speak at a special meeting of his party's parliamentary body in Florence. A day before I was to leave, I received a cable from the U.S. embassy in Rome, informing me that they had learned of a plot to assassinate me in Florence and suggested I cancel. I thought about it and decided to proceed with my plans since I could make an equally available target in Geneva. A few hours later, my secretary saw the cable, and before I knew it, our embassy's security chief was in my office for a serious talk. We agreed on my wearing a bulletproof vest as I got off the plane in Florence and throughout my brief visit to Italy. Since I flew on an air force plane, the pilot reminded me to put it on. There was no incident in Florence, although the police were everywhere. My son Jeff joined me there. It was the only time I wore such a vest.

been in India, and I was impressed with the obvious changes for the good that I could see, driving from the airport to the ambassador's residence. Ambassador Dean also told me that the "brain drain" that attracted bright young Indian scholars and engineers out of their country toward more lucrative opportunities elsewhere had virtually stopped. The Indian economy was increasingly using that talent.

My first visit was with the minister of defense, a bright young man whose probing questions were impressive. On the spur of the moment, I decided to go into some detail on the SDI question, pointing out that India was concerned about potential nuclear threats from China and Pakistan. I suggested that they were ill-advised to depend on Soviet propaganda to the effect that SDI could not work. The Soviets themselves were spending large sums on their own SDI program. If our approach could not work, why were they concerned? India, I pointed out, now had its own young and imaginative scientists. Why not have them talk to both American and Soviet scientists and decide for themselves whether an SDI program could be helpful to the Indian defense forces? I could see that my argument did not fall on deaf ears, although I had no further indications from anybody that the minister had indeed pursued the exploration.

When I later that day met with Prime Minister Gandhi, I found a more reserved, cautious, and wary response. His quiet smile was appealing and his face seemed soulful as well as pretty. It was disappointing, however, quickly to learn that he had at least a residue of his mother's bias against the United States. He raised with me all the criticisms of the American approach that he had heard from the Soviets and other critics. I believe I responded to them effectively, but he gave me no indication that he would consider my responses. I told him of my discussion with the minister of defense on SDI, and I had the impression that this approach was indeed falling on deaf ears. He was pleasant, and our conversation was interesting. He obviously was hearing from me an American commitment to arms reduction that was running contrary to his own tendencies and what he had been told.

My day in Delhi was an active one and included a rather lengthy and detailed press conference as well as meetings with top government and community leaders who were interested in foreign policy. I left early the next morning, exhausted but satisfied that I had done as much as I could. When I returned to the Geneva negotiation table on Monday, I found the Soviets were aware of my trip to Delhi and my meetings there.

Earlier in 1986, the prime minister of Australia, Bob Hawke, had visited Washington and told the president that he wanted to come to Geneva to talk about the arms negotiations. Reagan encouraged him to talk to me. When Hawke found that he could not come to Europe, Reagan assured him that I would be pleased to visit him in Australia. Maggie and I and our daughter Sarah, therefore, planned a journey to Australia and New Zealand during the August break. The trip had been set up by the State Department, but when George Shultz saw the itinerary, he urged me to cancel the New Zealand portion of the trip to reflect our continuing dissatisfaction with New Zealand's policy about our naval presence in its ports. I did as he asked.

The purpose of my visit was to persuade the Australians that we were serious about arms reductions and that our efforts at negotiations were genuine. My travels within the country were extensive. My interviews were many. I left Australia convinced that both United States and Australian interests had been well served.

Just as I wanted my message heard in Moscow, I also hoped it would have some effect back home. Democratic debate frequently tends to exaggerate and dramatize issues, sometimes beyond recognition. The SDI debate had taken on that distorted character. During the seventies, the Soviets had launched the largest military buildup in history with deployment of three new types of intercontinental ballistic missiles (ICBMs), eight improved versions, five new and five improved types of nuclear ballistic missiles, and a new intercontinental bomber. By contrast, we had deployed no new types of ICBMs, one new type of submarine-launched ballistic missile, and no new types of heavy bombers. The Soviets, furthermore, seemed to be preparing a nation-wide defense against ballistic missiles. They were proceeding with an intensified program of research on their own SDI.

Our research on strategic defenses had also been well under way when Ronald Reagan took office; he simply intensified that work. It was prudent to do so in light of the Soviet buildup, but it also provided a new target for critics. Somehow the argument back home ignored the fact that what we pursuing was research, which might or might not lead to the production of strategic defenses. SDI was not an attack on deterrence, as I saw it, but a way to make deterrence work better in light of modern technology.*

The desire to end or learn more about our Strategic Defense

* Long before there was any thought or talk of my being the arms control negotiator, at a long and useful lunch with Zbigniew Brzezinski, we found ourselves in agreement in support of SDI. We thought it would be unfortunate if the issue turned into a partisan one. We decided, therefore, to do a joint article for the *New York Times Magazine* on the assumption that a piece by a senior aide to Jimmy Carter and a close associate of Hubert Humphrey might contribute to a broad consensus. We were joined by Dr. Robert Jastrow, a leading scientist in the field. The article appeared on the Sunday after the announcement of my appointment.

Initiative seemed to be a major reason contributing to the Soviet decision to return to the Geneva negotiating table in March 1985. That was clear during the opening months of the talks.

I supported our SDI program before I had any idea that I might become a government negotiator. We were defenseless as a nation against nuclear missiles crossing the ocean, and it seemed to me irresponsible for us not to see whether science could develop an adequate and cost-effective defense, particularly since we had overwhelming evidence that the Soviets, traditionally defense oriented, were well on their way with their own program.

Opponents of SDI attached the misleading but effective label of "Star Wars" to the program, declaring simultaneously that it was threatening to the Soviets and scientifically impossible. Scientists from many disciplines, in fact, seemed to be in the lead against SDI. I was not a bit persuaded and felt most Americans would agree with me that we would all be better off if we could defend ourselves effectively, albeit not perfectly, against a nuclear attack. This was certainly preferable to depending only on revenge after the attack by retaliating with a nuclear strike of our own.

As for the "experts" who said the task was impossible, I was not impressed. It was not too difficult to find evidence of expert fallibility:

- Thomas Edison once wrote: "Fooling around with alternating current, as we know it, is just a waste of time, no body will use it . . . It's too dangerous. Direct current is better."
- Simon Newcomb, the astronomer, wrote in 1903: "Aerial flight is one of that class of problems with which man will never be able to cope."
- Rear Admiral Clark Woodward said in 1939, two years before Pearl Harbor: "As far as sinking a ship with a bomb is concerned, it just can't be done!"
- Admiral William Leahy, President Truman's chief of staff and a munitions expert, wrote to the president shortly before the Manhattan Project demonstrated its success: "The atomic bomb will never go off, and I speak as an expert in explosives."
- Dr. Ernest Rutherford, Nobel Prize winner in physics for his work on the atom, said as late as 1930: "The energy produced by the breaking down of the atom is a very poor kind of thing. Anyone who expects a source of power from the transformation of these atoms is talking moonshine."

• And Albert Einstein in 1932 wrote: "There is not the slightest indication that nuclear energy will be obtainable. It would mean that the atom would have to be shattered at will."*

None of these examples is intended to denigrate the expert, but to illustrate why policymakers do not have an easy time of it when they evaluate the expert advice they receive. They must ultimately rely on their own judgment, instincts, and experience. The prudent policymaker will remember that when Napoleon met Robert Fulton around 1800, he reportedly exclaimed: "What, sir? Would you make a ship sail against the wind and currents by lighting a bonfire under her deck? I pray you, excuse me. I have no time to listen to such nonsense." Hubert Humphrey handled the dilemma by his belief that "experts should be on tap, but not on top."

* I am indebted to Kenneth Adelman, a scholar, journalist, and former director of the Arms Control and Disarmament Agency, for assembling these expert illustrations.

16

We Are on Our Way

We went back to Geneva in mid-September of 1985 determined to push the intensity of negotiations up a notch. My instincts told me we could obtain the INF and START reductions we sought without having to give up our SDI program or the testing we would have to perform to judge its effectiveness. I increasingly came to believe that this was so for several reasons.

The reduction of offensive nuclear weapons was important to the Soviets as well as to us. Furthermore, I believed the Soviets were beginning to appreciate the complexity associated with addressing new technologies. I had been hammering away at the futility of their emphasis on SDI and had urged that we face the more crucial and significant task of how to achieve stability in the face of any and all of the new technologies that would emerge. In addition, they had an SDI program of their own. We knew that, and they knew we knew it. And my luncheon conversation with Yuli Kvitsinskiy early that summer was a clear signal that we could arrive at an SDI agreement on the basis of deployment rather than testing.

In addition, I began to receive other Soviet signals to that effect—

or at least I thought I did. These were finally confirmed to my satisfaction on February 28, 1987, a Saturday on which a senatorial delegation visited. I will report on this development now, even though it is out of chronological order.

Early in the day, the Soviets had called my aide to say that the deputy foreign minister, Yuli Vorontsov, recently appointed head of their delegation, wanted to call on me at five P.M. that afternoon. After I greeted him in my office, he said he had been instructed to give me an advance copy of a statement Gorbachev was to issue that evening. I began to read it and noticed that General Secretary Gorbachev was identified rather as chairman of the Soviet Defense Council, a rarely publicized equivalent to our National Security Council, which presumably had the dominant influence on defense matters along with the Politburo itself. I told Vorontsov that I did not recall any other Soviet declaration with that designation for Gorbachev, although I had assumed he was the chairman. Yuli confirmed it was rare and emphasized the importance of the message. I asked him whether he had reason to believe that the Politburo held its regular Thursday meeting that week. He said it had. He also seemed to agree with my assertion that the policy in the statement had been developed by Gorbachev and the powerful Soviet Defense Council, and then ratified by the Politburo, making it a very important policy statement to be taken seriously. Vorontsov asked me to emphasize to Washington that it was indeed an important statement.

One sentence struck me as vital: "The conclusion of a START agreement, as has been repeatedly emphasized, should be conditioned by a decision on the prevention of deployment of weapons in outer space." There was no reference to testing, no conditions designed to limit it. They were concerned about deployment and we could all agree that deployment was prohibited by the 1972 ABM Treaty. This is what I had been emphasizing to all who would listen, and it was at the root of my negotiating approach. Did a Soviet typist or translator inadvertently leave out the word "testing"? Not at all likely, but I had the Russian text carefully examined. The message was clear. This was the Soviet bottom line, whatever else might be said about testing at the Geneva negotiating table or public forums. The Politburo and the Soviet Defense Council had spoken. This, to the best of my knowledge, was the authoritative statement on the subject from Moscow, although practically all of my Washington colleagues, including people I respected highly, did not accept my conclusions because they were not "logical" or consistent with their view of Soviet self-interest. Since

when is politics—and international relations is a political process—
logical and rational?*

The president in the meantime continued to say that SDI was not
and would not become a bargaining chip in the negotiations. Critics at
home and abroad continued to seize upon such occasions as indications
of recalcitrance and rigidity. Reagan would then be painted as a pred-
atory hawk and an obstacle to any agreement when he was, I was
certain, on the right track. SDI had helped bring the Soviets to the
table, and I was convinced by my experience in Geneva that we could

---

* Hank Cooper, my deputy, fully shared this conclusion and arranged for a
further search of the record a few months later. This is what he found and passed on
to me (emphasis added).

November 28, 1986—Soviet Field Marshal Sergei Akhromeyev, interview with *Stern* (not
published in Soviet press): "If there is no agreement *to ban deployment of a nationwide
ABM system*, there will be no START agreement."

February 28, 1987—Gorbachev statement: "The conclusion of a START agreement, as has
been repeatedly emphasized, should be conditioned by *a decision on the prevention of
deployment of weapons in outer space*."

March 30, 1987—TASS on Gorbachev talks with British Prime Minister Thatcher: START
agreement linked to 'non-placement of weapons in outer space.'

April 15, 1987—*Pravda* reporting on Secretary of State Shultz's visit: "If the U.S. begins *to
deploy ABM systems in space* there will be no agreement of any kind on strategic
offensive arms."

April 28, 1987—Soviet negotiator Alexei Obukhov, press conference: "And should the U.S.
proceed *to the deployment of space ABMs*, there will be no agreement on strategic
offensive arms."

May 7, 1987—Soviet Deputy Foreign Minister Vorontsov, meeting with me: "If either side
deployed, reductions would go out the window."

May 12, 1987—British Labor Party leader Dennis Healey, at Moscow press conference,
citing the Soviet arms control director, Victor Karpov: "The USSR could negotiate 50
percent reductions with the provision that if the U.S. broke the ABM Treaty or
deployed SDI, the terms of the agreement would no longer apply."

May 13, 1987—Memorandum of conversation summary by U.S. negotiator citing Soviet
negotiator Masterkov: "A strategic reductions agreement would become invalid immediately upon *deployment of strategic defenses*. Therefore, the START treaty must
contain some language to this effect."

May 18, 1987—U.S. negotiator referring to Soviet negotiator luncheon conversation: "On
Soviet linkage between termination of a START agreement and SDI *'deployment,'*
Rosylakov affirmed this linkage and said that if the USSR had reduced its offensive
forces by 50 percent and then *'the U.S. deployed SDI,'* the USSR would then have to
build back up again."

May 19, 1987—Vorontsov interviewed in Bulgarian press: "The Soviet proposals concerning
preserving the regime of the ABM Treaty provide for agreement to be reached on a
list of installations that will be *permitted or forbidden to be deployed in outer space* in the
course of scientific research activities in the field of the space ABM system."

June 16, 1987—Soviet ministry of foreign affairs arms control and disarmament directorate
counselor to U.S. embassy official in Moscow: "Loukiantsev said that there had to be
agreement on *no deployment of ABM systems in space*. Such *deployments* 'would make
strategic offensive arms reductions impossible' and 'if either side violated the ABM
Treaty, e.g., *by deploying space-based ABM systems*, the other could withdraw from
START reductions.' "

obtain INF and START treaties without abandoning our SDI research program.

Partisan critics of the president began to believe they could play for advantage. When my friend, the very able Congressman Steve Solarz of New York, made a speech asserting we could not get an INF or START treaty without giving up SDI, I knew he was wrong. When he then blamed what he perceived as the negotiating stalemate on us, I saw red. I may have overreacted. Even though we knew each other well, he had not alerted me to his intentions, as he might have. He was inadvertently playing right into Soviet hands. I was sorely disappointed in him. Inevitably, the Soviets used the story to their advantage, pointing out to me in Geneva that even our congressmen agreed with them and not with us. That and similar statements and speeches by others were a burden we could have done without.

The Soviets did not know how to read events in a democratic context. For all their sophistication, they were victims of a *Pravda* complex, believing that if something important appeared in the paper, someone in power had approved its appearance. They were inveterate analyzers of cosmic tea leaves and chicken entrails, rather than objective observers. Moscow read the American press diligently, particularly on military matters, and fed their negotiators a constant stream of questions and interpretations. Frequently, in both formal and informal sessions, I would be asked the "meaning" of a press item. Often there would be no "meaning" beyond the facts. When I said so, they were suspicious, and a few, I suppose, just thought I lied.

Fortunately, my credibility with most of the Soviets had become sufficiently high to overcome some of these obstacles. As the negotiations proceeded, I said with intensity that "we both have more nuclear weapons than we should have, more than we need, more than the safety of the world requires. We should be reducing these offensive nuclear weapons." I knew that I reflected accurately what the president felt, and I spent part of virtually every meeting with the Soviets trying to convince them that was so. I wanted them to understand that we were committed to substantial reductions in offensive nuclear missiles, no matter what some partisans had to say. In communicating this message, I was helped when members of both parties in Congress who visited Geneva worked hard at understanding the negotiations and expressed support for our efforts.

To return to chronology, what really drove the pace of both sides was a planned meeting between Reagan and Gorbachev in November 1985. Summits create their own kind of pressure. Heads of state look for something momentous to declare, sign, or initiate. It is a moment of high drama that, if at all possible, must play well back home for both leaders. Preparatory staff meetings were often the crucible where differences were ground away and agreement made possible.

Both countries were well served in this regard by their foreign policy ministers, George Shultz and Eduard Shevardnadze, and their ability to get along with each other. When they met for the first time in Helsinki at the beginning of August 1985, as part of the tenth anniversary celebration of the Helsinki Final Act, Shultz chose to meet Shevardnadze without staff present in their initial session. As is clear from the interpreter's report, Shultz looked to a warmer, better relationship with Shevardnadze than had been possible with his predecessor, Gromyko, and said directly that they had a special opportunity to accomplish great things.

The other Soviets were obviously nervous when the two foreign ministers were absent from our meeting place. When the two returned, I was surprised at the patronizing attitude shown toward Shevardnadze by others in his delegation and particularly by former Ambassador Dobrynin, who repeatedly interrupted Shevardnadze in a manner that some of us thought rude. The new foreign minister had risen to power too quickly for them, and the old hands seemed intent on making certain he made no errors and kept his inexperience hidden.

Theirs was a losing effort. Both Shultz and Shevardnadze had a healthy inclination for bypassing bureaucratic obstacles and were extraordinarily good at resolving differences. With time and increased self-assurance, they broadened their agenda to include even the technicalities of arms control. In a real sense, the time came when our negotiations in Geneva essentially refined the options and polished the conclusions that, in turn, prepared both sides, under the leadership of the two ministers, for reconciliation of differences. I encouraged this development even though it met with resistance from some of my fellow negotiators and from representatives of the Defense Department.

The one time during our negotiations when I was seriously at cross purposes with the White House did not involve our negotiations at all and had no lasting impact, but demonstrated how easy it is for bad decisions to be made in complex relationships. The annual meeting of the Socialist International, an organization in which many of the governments of Europe participate, was approaching. It is a high-powered and important group of considerable influence. Soon after our negotiations began, the president of Finland asked both Vice President Bush and Secretary of State Shultz to encourage me to attend and speak about our negotiations. They did, and I accepted.

Out of the blue, I received a cable from Admiral John Poindexter, deputy national security adviser at the White House, that said my speaking there would be inappropriate. He clearly did not know two things: the importance of the Socialist International and that both Bush and Shultz had urged me to be present. I guessed at the time that one of his minions in public affairs who was without good sense had not known the invitation's background, didn't like being a fringe player, and recommended that I not go. It was a case of ignorance compounded by bureaucratic insecurity.

With my labor background, which the leaders of the Socialist International knew about, I was the ideal spokesman to make the case for the United States. I couldn't believe that Poindexter would intrude, and certainly not in the direct, unambiguous way he did. His action aggravated me, but I just didn't have the time to hassle with him and the National Security Council. I fired off a sharply critical cable to Poindexter and found an excuse not to go. Our friends in the Socialist International were offended. Later conversations with Poindexter made clear to me that he recognized that he had made a mistake, which, though not serious and permanent, was needlessly irritating in our relations with Finland and other countries. We also missed a good opportunity to make our case. Poindexter later called the matter "a classic case of lack of internal communications."

When the round ended early in November 1985, I thought there were some seeds of agreement to nurture, but we had not moved forward nearly as much as I had hoped we would. The negotiations continued to be a dance: two steps forward, one step back, and a pause. The most important step forward had come near the end of the round on November 1, when the United States placed a comprehensive set of proposals on the START table that called for reducing ballistic missile warheads and air-launched cruise missiles. Our proposal gave them something to think about as the Gorbachev-Reagan meeting approached.

Back in Washington, the pre-summit days took on a special urgency for creating an agenda, preparing the president, and making certain that our Geneva point of view was heard and understood. I had no problem having our views heard because George Shultz was so much on top of what we were doing. From my own visits with the president, I was comfortable and confident that we were in step with what he wanted as well.

The president's scheduled speech to the United Nations General Assembly was looked upon as a preliminary step to the summit. When asked for my ideas about what he ought to say, I joined those who urged that our emphasis be on the invasion of Afghanistan and human rights, since these were among the causes of the tensions that lead nations to take up arms.

While my responsibility was now arms control, I was pleased that the president agreed that our agenda should give priority to regional problems, such as Afghanistan and Central America, in addition to human rights, prior to dealing with our arms negotiations. For me, Geneva followed Madrid; it did not supersede it. That not only made me feel good about our work on human rights, but gave me further reason to believe that Reagan and Shultz would stand staunchly behind what we had set out to do in Geneva. They had long-range mentalities, and I liked that.

The Geneva summit was, of course, vital in defining the direction for our negotiations. I did not attend the Geneva summit, even though George Shultz, in response to my inquiry, said I would be welcome. I sensed that he felt the presence of the negotiators at this first summit would be premature and extraneous. Since I have always avoided the role of "camp follower," I readily took the hint and passed the word on to Glitman, who lived in Geneva and would be in the area if needed, and to Tower, who clearly wanted to be on the scene and decided to go. Tower later complained to me that he had been humiliated at not being permitted to be even in the vicinity of the talks. George Shultz saw to it that I was informed by phone of developments. We knew that little of substance would be agreed upon, but sensitive wording was checked with me, particularly with respect to Gorbachev and Reagan calling for a 50 percent reduction in the nuclear arms of the United States and the Soviet Union, "as well as the idea of an interim INF agreement." The media focus on the statement gave us the impetus I thought was needed to lift the negotiations to a higher plateau.

What turned out to be even more crucial was Reagan's personal reaction to Gorbachev. They spent several hours alone with interpreters as well as more time together in larger group sessions. Like Shultz and Shevardnadze, they were immediately comfortable with each other. Reagan liked Gorbachev, and he told people that he did. It is virtually impossible to trust someone you dislike; obviously Reagan was later willing to work with Gorbachev in ways he would not have been before Geneva. Without that kind of personal good feeling, our negotiations would have been much more difficult. Inevitably, Reagan's attitude trickled down and affected our negotiating environment.

When we returned to Geneva for the fourth round on January 16, 1986, both Victor Karpov and I expressed a desire to speed things up in keeping with the spirit of the summit. Karpov clearly began the round in a proper frame of mind. He privately told me that Gorbachev liked Reagan and believed in his sincerity. Moscow, he said, had instructed Karpov to treat our president with respect. I thought that was encouraging news and a shift away from Soviet posturing and idle attacks.

Both sides offered new proposals, particularly in the intermediate range (INF). It seemed to us that the Soviets were more prepared to move in this area than in START, and that was fine with us. Gorbachev's proposal came in mid-January, and ours soon after. Together the proposals called for the total elimination by the end of the decade of U.S. Pershing II and ground-launched cruise missiles and Soviet SS-20 missiles. Those statements of goals were exciting. It was now time for serious technical study of both proposals, which required patience and diligence. The process was slow.

By now, we had spent nearly a year together, getting to know one another, taking measure of one another, team testing team, traversing old dry ground endlessly, occasionally discovering little oases of agreement.

I had assumed, from the beginning, that there would not be much movement during the first year, but I had used that time to educate the Soviets about our position. I spent a lot of time talking about national interest. They would be foolish to expect us—just as we'd be foolish to expect them—to do anything contrary to our perceived national interest.

International negotiating is an interesting discipline—putting yourself in someone else's shoes, defining how they see the world, and then stepping back, arguing for your goal within that context. You have to explain and understand how national interest is involved before you can discern a way of narrowing the points of difference. Agreement comes when both national interests appear to be served, or at least not harmed.

John Tower and Mike Glitman did the same thing as well, explaining, explaining, explaining so that every doubt about where we really stood or what we meant was dealt with and resolved. Tower, probably because of his training in the Senate, did this particularly well. He worked very hard with Karpov, patiently spending hours with him.* The process was doubly important because everything we said was cabled back to Moscow, and we wanted the Kremlin to know why we took the positions we did.

That first year had been an educational one for us all, not just for the Soviets. In a three-pronged negotiation, with often differing views coming from State and Defense and a variety of positions on the Hill to consider, a great deal of adjustment was necessary. Our negotiating group in Geneva and our advisers in Washington had to learn to cooperate and, for the most part, to trust one another. John Tower's prestige as a former senator served us well, as did my obvious good relationships with the secretary of State and the Congress.

A negotiation of any kind is a delicate and usually subtle process. My Madrid experience had somewhat spoiled me, in that Washington rarely interfered and I was able to develop a staff whose primary loyalty was to me—they would follow my lead, criticize when appropriate, and not undermine my approach. This was partly because Washington paid scant attention to our negotiations in Madrid, expecting little, if anything, to materialize. Although a similar skepticism existed about our Geneva talks, particularly in the Office of the Secretary of Defense (OSD), there was no similar inattention.

At some point during our second year, it appeared as if an INF agreement might develop. This, it seemed to me, caused disquiet in OSD, and concern that they might be under pressure to concede something in SDI as we moved toward that agreement, and possibly a concession in START as well. I could feel the freeze not only from the OSD people working with us in Washington, but also from those on our Geneva negotiating team. The conventional wisdom that "the military" resist arms reduction agreement is simply wrong. Some do; some

---

* After George Bush was elected president in 1989, he announced the appointment of John Tower as his secretary of Defense. This brought a number of phone calls from journalists and others including Senators Sam Nunn and Carl Levin, both members of the Senate Armed Services Committee. They referred to rumors about John's behavior and drinking habits and inquired about my experiences with John. I told all who called that I had no knowledge of what was in his FBI files, but that, based on my experience with him in Geneva, were I a member of the Senate, I would vote to support the president's nomination. He was fully qualified and experienced. He had been a serious and highly competent negotiator. I said I had never seen Tower drunk and, indeed, recalled that he would frequently ask for soda water when offered an alcoholic drink. I also knew of no unusual, aberrational, or questionable conduct relating to women. The senators and I were aware of serious problems in Geneva between John and his wife, which led to a bitter divorce. In looking back at this period, I believe that John Tower's problems with the Senate were compounded by what many considered a feeling of contempt on his part toward them, a feeling that he did not hide.

don't. In this case, a distinction must be made between those civilian and military people who represented the secretary of Defense and the military people assigned to our delegation from the Joint Chiefs of Staff, the formal military establishment. The former seemed to be supervised by those who probably opposed any agreement with the Soviets; the latter clearly worked under instructions to help me find an agreement, if we could, in our national interest.

The first sign of difficulty was unexpected and came from a very capable air force colonel assigned to me by OSD. Early in the talks, and soon after U.S. Army Major Arthur Nicholson was killed by the Soviets in East Germany, he came to me to say he could not in good conscience accept a Soviet invitation for a reception at the Soviet mission, even though the event was a cover for informal negotiations. I respected his position and told him to follow his own judgment. His zeal, however, propelled him further. He started to be indiscreetly critical of John Tower, falsely accusing him of excessively wining and dining the Soviets. The comments came close to questioning Tower's patriotism. That was not only unsettling to the atmosphere I had tried to encourage but aggravating to Tower and to his staff. It was also nasty and mean-spirited. When I heard of the attacks, I was outraged. I immediately sought out Tower to discuss the sniping. He said he didn't take it at all seriously, although I knew he did, and he did not accept my offer to fire the man and send him home. I warned the colonel that any further evidence of his immature behavior would lead to his dismissal, in spite of my high regard for his talents. Later, he also got crosswise with Hank Cooper, at which point I decided to have him removed. Only a plea from Richard Perle, the assistant secretary of Defense, that I give him another chance prevented that from happening.

Some expected that I would have a problem with Cap Weinberger, and ultimately they were right, but that wasn't the case at the outset. Cap and George Shultz had both called to urge me to accept the job, and I considered Cap a friend. I made a point of seeing him whenever I came home. He can be most charming. Our visits were more than a courtesy—they were necessary for mutual understanding, valuable to me, and always pleasant. Cap and I shared a strongly skeptical view of the Soviet Union and watched their actions with suspicion.

During the first year, nothing much happened substantively that could divide us or create tension between Cap and me. The Soviets were not moving in our direction, and I was as yet uncertain as to their seriousness. Indeed, during the first year, I was closer to Cap's view than to that of the State Department, which wanted us to move in ways they mistakenly felt would encourage agreement. I did not wish to make any concessions that early in the negotiations. Paul Nitze, to whom I looked for counsel as the wisest and most experienced veteran, did not seem to share my view, however. I thought State's suggestions were tactically wrong. A premature move would have left the Soviets wondering where else we might move, and what else we might give up. I had no problem with repackaging our position and had ideas how best to do that, but I was opposed to changing our position. Some might have considered that stonewalling; I thought it was consistency. I held my ground with Cap's silent approval.

As the negotiations began to pick up steam, it became apparent to me that Cap was unhappy about my efforts and did what he could to thwart an agreement from evolving. This led me to depend more on Ken Adelman, the very capable director of ACDA,* and his professional staff than on the OSD for technical information and advice.

Soon after the fifth round began in the spring of 1986, Karpov asked me to meet a small group of Soviet visitors: a member of the Central Committee, a prominent television commentator, and the head of a prestigious Moscow research organization. It was the first time that any of us could remember such a request and was probably an early sign of *glasnost*. I immediately agreed to see them. I had frequently invited the Soviets to visit with groups of Americans, particularly legislators who came to Geneva.† That was helpful to both sides, and I hoped my visit with the Soviets would be useful to them as well as to me in the same way.

Unfortunately, Karpov was called to Moscow just as we were to meet, so his deputy, INF negotiator Alexei Obukhov, who had studied international relations under Hans Morgenthau at the University of Chicago, was host. Obukhov could be stiff and obdurate one day, then

---

* The Arms Control and Disarmament Agency was the product of Hubert Humphrey. The logic for its creation was that no agency within the government had disarmament as its prime responsibility. ACDA would, as an independent office. I thought it was wrong when it was created, and my experience since confirms that feeling. There are voices for and against disarmament elsewhere, and they are heard. ACDA is frequently a bureaucratic hindrance to policymaking. It should be an integral part of the State Department headed by an undersecretary.

† Two congressmen, Norman Dicks of Washington and James Moody of Wisconsin, showed the most interest in our work among House members. They visited Geneva more frequently than others and kept abreast of our negotiations. Since the House, unlike the Senate, has no treaty approval responsibility, it was understandable that House members would have other priorities, but these two were extraordinarily informed and helpful.

filled with humor and sensitivity the next. I usually tried to be as informal as possible within the constraints of diplomacy and language barriers, but the Soviets were always more controlled, sitting straight in their chairs, facing us across the table like arm wrestlers about to compete. That was the scene and atmosphere of the meeting to which we were invited at the Soviet mission.

Obukhov began with a long opening statement, and I could see the looks of distress and discomfort among his three guests. They had come to talk and to learn and were being subjected, as we were, to meaningless doctrinal nonsense, the death rattle of an ailing regime. When Obukhov finally finished, I essentially ignored his speech and spoke to the trio as though nothing had preceded my greeting. I said that I was pleased to meet them and that I thought this was an auspicious moment in United States–Soviet relations. Noting that Andrei Sakharov had just been released from Gorky, I said, "I want to commend you and your government on what you have done. I think that it is an important step toward bringing understanding between us." I went on to a fairly specific, but brief, discussion of the issues in the negotiations and indicated that I would be glad to answer any questions.

Before they could respond, Obukhov launched into an attack on my comments about Sakharov and my "interference" in Soviet internal affairs. It was a sad performance by an intelligent man eager to please the visitors from home, but one who totally misread them and their attitudes. When he finished his criticism, we simply talked around him. John Tower and Mike Glitman concisely set forth the U.S. position. We responded to questions about SDI, we expressed the hope that our countries could create a safer and more secure world and said that we were eager to find common areas where neither side's national interest was threatened. They were the most open government Soviets I had met, less doctrinaire than most, and demonstrated real intellectual interest in the subjects at hand.

Other Soviet visitors came from time to time. I met for two hours one afternoon with Georgi Kornienko, who had been deputy foreign minister, but who now worked as deputy to Dobrynin in the international department of the Communist party Central Committee. He was a mild, grandfatherly type who smiled a lot, but he had a reputation of being anti-American. He brought me personal greetings from Ilichev and Kovalev, Soviets I'd worked with in Madrid. We talked a bit about the Helsinki Final Act, and then he asked to be brought up to date on the negotiations as I saw them.

He was one of a number of pulse takers who came in to gauge the seriousness of our negotiations. Obviously Gorbachev, like Reagan, regularly asked his people whether we were serious. It was important to convince the visitors of our determination since, we feared, the Soviets in residence might not reflect our views accurately. Karpov and his associates had to worry about their careers and their future in a society that provided them with no safeguards. It was only natural for Karpov to cover his vulnerability, and that meant he might be putting an undeserved onus on us for lack of movement. It also occurred to me that he thought the visitors could carry back views about what we said that might help him as a negotiator.

Slowly, in mid-1986, the atmosphere began to change. With the preliminary process behind us, serious negotiating began. Proposals were refined and discussed. A few areas of agreement were established, and points of disagreement identified for solution. Movement was not overwhelming, but it was there. At about this time, in early spring, SDI was unlinked from INF. It seemed to us that the Soviet negotiators were waiting for new proposals from Moscow, which were not forthcoming.

In midsummer, the Soviets proposed that a smaller group of experts meet in Moscow in an attempt to push things along. We accepted, but the White House refused to impose adequate discipline. With every U.S. agency and office that had any interest in the negotiations seeking to be included, our team was unfortunately too large for the informality that was needed. The group met first in Moscow and then in Washington. This represented a subtle shift in emphasis away from Geneva toward the two capitals, but very little of substance came out of the process. It seemed to me as if the United States, with its large numbers, was demonstrating an inability to cope with its bureaucratic anarchy. What was, of course, behind all this was a concern that some movement might be imminent, and no agency wanted to be left out of the process. We all agreed that Paul Nitze would chair the Moscow and Washington "working groups," but the meetings remained overpopulated and unfocused.

My attention shifted a bit as well. Before we went to Australia in 1986, Shultz, who was vacationing at his home in Palo Alto, suggested that Maggie and I stop by on our way back to Washington to have dinner with him and his wife, Obie. However, Maggie and our daughter Sarah, as tourists, decided to go on to New Zealand. I stopped in Palo Alto to visit George Shultz. It made sense to break the long trip and give George and me a chance to talk about many subjects. We spent the afternoon alongside his pool and then had dinner. The secretary had seen the complimentary cables from Australia. We talked more about my visit to Australia, about what we might expect in the arms negotiations, and about his plans to reorganize the department, particularly the Seventh Floor—the traditional understated identification of where he and his top aides had their offices.

He told me that he was going to shift Ed Derwinski, a former Illinois Congressman who was then counselor, to undersecretary of State for security assistance, to make continued use of his contacts on the Hill. He wanted someone he could trust to replaced as counselor, someone he felt close to in terms of policy and who knew the substantive aspects of foreign policy. He wanted someone who could work with Congress, help build a stronger foreign policy constituency, and relieve him of some of the burdensome travel and speeches around the country necessary to this effort. Did I have any suggestions?

I made some suggestions about people we both knew. He took careful notes, but as our conversation continued, I sensed that he was indirectly asking me to consider the job. I decided to ask if that was what he had in mind, and he said that, in fact, he wanted me or a clone.

I suggested a few names, and he raised the names of several others. We then talked about the consequences of my leaving Geneva in the hands of someone else, both of us believing that the negotiations were bound to shift to some degree from Geneva to Moscow and Washington. We did not reach any conclusions, and he asked me not to discuss the question with anyone other than Paul Nitze, since he first wanted to talk to the president about various options.

Shultz soon reported back that he and the president thought my leaving the Geneva post would be a mistake. They felt that I had gained public credibility on the issue and bipartisan support on the Hill. My departure might be misunderstood or misinterpreted, and they did not want to take a chance on losing those strengths. Did it make sense for me to have both jobs?

I focused entirely on the negotiations, and, slowly, during the second half of the year, the Soviets began to be more forthcoming. In INF, it became evident that they would drop their demand that British and French weapons of a similar range be part of the negotiations. We said that we were not authorized to negotiate on behalf of the British and French, and that the Soviets should deal directly with those countries involved. (Gorbachev had raised the issue in Paris with French President François Mitterand and had already been thoroughly rebuffed.)

In October, the issue of my appointment as counselor of the Department of State came up again. Shultz and I agreed that negotiations in Geneva were moving along well, and indeed would increasingly shift in emphasis to Moscow and Washington as we anticipated, and that I could handle both jobs. In a sense, the negotiations had broken the sound barrier and now it was a matter of flying straight and keeping the plane under control. An INF treaty was in sight, although complicated details had yet to be worked out. Negotiations were likely now to be resolved at the ministerial level, between Shultz and Shevardnadze, and it might even serve our interests better for me to be principally in Washington.

The counselor's job, although it is the second oldest in the State Department, has no fixed statutory responsibilities. Shultz said he would have Derwinski take to his new position most of his current assignments and that we would redefine the counselor's job to fit Shultz's new needs and my strengths. I found the new job an exciting prospect, but once again was asked not to say anything about it while various other arrangements were made.

Our assumption in 1986 was that Gorbachev would be visiting Reagan in Washington during the year. We and our Soviet colleagues in Geneva acted under that assumption. At the Geneva summit the previous November, Reagan had invited Gorbachev to visit the United States in 1986 and he accepted. No conditions were expressed in that acceptance. There had been a few exchanges of letters between the two, but the relationship had turned formal again and rather cold. Shultz and Shevardnadze had expected to meet in Washington early in the year, but we could obtain no date from Moscow. We assumed that Gorbachev was facing domestic challenges but could not be certain of their nature. I had noticed an item in the European press that when Gorbachev landed in Moscow after the summit, he was met at the airport by most of the Politburo, and all had gone directly to a meeting room at the airport. There were reports that some in Moscow felt Reagan had done better than Gorbachev at the summit. All sorts of rumors abounded, but nothing definitive, other than that the Soviets seemed reluctant about a 1986 summit in Washington. Finally, a date was set for a Washington visit by Shevardnadze, but the Soviets used our April 1986 aerial attack on Libya, in response to terrorist acts, as an excuse for canceling. The Chernobyl tragedy occurred later that month. Then, in mid-September, Gorbachev proposed that he meet with President Reagan in London or Reykjavik the following month to advance arms control and prepare for the promised summit. Iceland was selected.

I looked forward to Reykjavik for answers to the puzzling Soviet behavior. Shortly after the meeting was agreed to, I had separate lunches with Fred Ikle, the undersecretary of Defense, and Richard Perle to learn of the Defense Department's current views. Ikle suggested going to zero on all ballistic missiles. It superficially appealed to me, and I felt it would put us in a favorable light. I had picked up a term of the diplomatic trade and urged Fred to "staff it through." I did not think acting on my political instinct (or his) was sufficient on a matter of this importance. Someone had to measure its military implications, its political implications in terms of our allies, and its effect on the negotiations. I talked to George Shultz about Ikle's idea and urged Paul Nitze to discuss it with Ikle, knowing that he would ask the proper questions, fruitfully challenge the assumptions, and anticipate the consequences.

The staffing process apparently showed that it was in our interest to pursue the approach. Shultz, an old marine, was concerned about the effects on our navy, but when Cap Weinberger brought it up at the White House, Shultz went along with it. In July 1986 Reagan proposed the idea in a letter* to Gorbachev before Reykjavik, and we all prepared for the trip.

* A number of letters were exchanged between Reagan and Gorbachev. The process was initiated by Reagan, whose early letters were personally handwritten. They then became mechanically typed products produced by the interagency process and lost some of their effectiveness.

17

Reykjavik and Beyond: The Counselor

I had been to Iceland only once before, immediately after Madrid to thank the Iceland government for its cooperation. I liked the country and the people immensely. It had some characteristics like Minnesota. But a meeting of major powers so far off the beaten track had a certain surrealistic quality to it. The physical arrangements added to that feeling.

The meetings in Reykjavik were held in an old two-story building, Hofdi House, which is neither elegant nor ancient. It is big by Icelandic standards, but quite unpretentious and a little cramped for heads of state and their entourages. The main floor has a reception area that served as a living room, with additional quarters to its right and left where Reagan and Gorbachev and Shultz and Shevardnadze met.

A curved wooded staircase leads to an area in which most of us loitered or more often met for hours on end throughout the day and night. The Soviets had several small rooms to the right, and we had several to the left. When we met together we used the open area in the middle, or if the two delegations or members wanted to chat, we mingled there. We were like two large families in a bed-and-breakfast inn trying to stay out of each other's way, but wanting and needing to socialize some and learn a bit more about one another.

The Soviet group included Marshal Sergei Akhromeyev, their army chief of staff; Dobrynin; Alexandr Yakovlev, their former ambassador to Canada, who was obviously close to Gorbachev; and several information and propaganda people. Our group included Don Regan, Paul Nitze, Ed Rowny, John Poindexter, his able aide Robert Linhard, Admiral John Howe, Richard Perle, and Ken Adelman. The chemistry on that second floor of Hofdi House was fascinating to watch. Without plan or purpose, we each soon found someone to talk to. My conversation was mostly with Yakovlev, a relative unknown to us but believed to be excessively anti-American. When I learned he had studied at Columbia, we talked about New York and the university, and I searched unsuccessfully for clues to what might have made him so hostile to the United States. He and his colleagues were not interested in personal history, but in "selling" Gorbachev to us as a domestic innovator genuinely interested in improving relations with the United States.

Reagan and Gorbachev, accompanied by Shultz and Shevardnadze and two notetakers and two interpreters, began talking on Saturday morning, October 11, and continued through the day. At no point did anybody else from their delegations join them. The rest of us were on the second floor of Hofdi House talking to one another or reading.

During a lunch break, we returned to our respective embassies. Our U.S. group crammed into a small secure room, known as "the bubble," to receive a report from Shultz. The report was encouraging, the opening talks had been totally private between Reagan and Gorbachev, and he and Shevardnadze did not join them until later in the morning. The spirit was good; Gorbachev seemed anxious to proceed constructively without polemics, but he had come with a position paper, even though the Soviets had originally told us the meeting would not be substantive.* It was beginning to look more like a summit than a meeting to prepare for a summit. In the midst of the briefing, Reagan walked into the overcrowded bubble. He wanted to give us his perceptions, which seemed encouraging as well. Shultz proposed that Reagan explore whether a "working group" might meet that evening to go into detail on how to narrow the arms control gap, since the

---

* We had received reports in Washington of Dobrynin bragging that Gorbachev would surprise us with new proposals designed to trap us and make us appear unresponsive. Actually, the Gorbachev paper presented to Reagan repeated the 50 percent reduction in strategic offensive missiles that we had been working on, the zero INF missiles for Europe proposal which brought them closer to our position, and a limit on SDI research to the laboratory, coupled with an agreement not to withdraw from the ABM Treaty for ten to fifteen years.

Soviets obviously had the appropriate people present, that is, the down-to-earth and powerful Akhromeyev.

The working groups met at eight that night. We broke about two o'clock in the morning to report on an impasse to Shultz and Shevardnadze and reconvened an hour later. Paul Nitze and I returned to the hotel, where we woke Shultz and brought him up to date. At times we verged on dramatic breakthroughs; at other times we appeared to be miles apart. What did impress most of us was Akhromeyev's serious and no-nonsense approach to our meeting. He tolerated no polemics or speeches from his side.

Our meeting, which began at eight o'clock Saturday evening and ended at six-thirty Sunday morning, lasted too long, even with two recesses, and took place during the wrong part of the day. I have always despised, mistrusted, and avoided all-night meetings, with their tension, exhaustion, and potential for unclear thinking.

Gorbachev and Reagan met at ten o'clock Sunday morning. The summit was scheduled to end at noon. Twelve noon came and went. Reagan, Gorbachev, Shultz, and Shevardnadze were still talking. Upstairs, we thought it was a good sign; particularly after, at one point, Shultz came out briefly to say that it looked as if we were close to an INF agreement, with a maximum of one hundred warheads for each side in Europe and another one hundred in Asia, although Gorbachev wanted zero in Europe and one hundred in Asia. We were prepared to accept most any number in Europe as long as it was an equal number for each of us. We also wanted equality in Asia; we could not favor Europe over Asia by going down to zero in Europe alone. Shultz also reported that there had been "fireworks" between Reagan and Gorbachev on SDI, and they were going back to talk about it some more. The meeting finally broke up at one-thirty that afternoon. As most everyone rushed to their automobiles, we were told that another meeting was scheduled at three. Shultz signaled to some of us to remain behind, as the rest left for the embassy.

The morning meeting had faltered over differences on SDI. The Soviets threatened that all the agreements on INF and START were contingent on an SDI agreement on Gorbachev's terms. Shultz asked what we thought we could do. Shevardnadze would soon join us to see how to salvage the summit. When he did, he was obviously distressed. We reviewed the situation, and Shevardnadze said that it would be tragic to have all the work accomplished in Reykjavik go down the drain. Shevardnadze turned to me and said that since I had the reputation of being a creative negotiator and mediator, why did I not come

idea on Sunday morning when it was proposed. The president had been adamant: no extension. His instinct was that another meeting would not have brought agreement. He may have been right. He was also quite irritated at Gorbachev's behavior.

My own view was that things were moving too fast in Reykjavik. I had no problem with the inability to come to an agreement. I felt that the progress we had made on INF and START issues would remain on the table in Geneva and that there was no need for us to rush into something for which we were not adequately prepared.

I also felt the Soviets had deceived us. Gorbachev's letter to Reagan recommending a meeting in Iceland did not call it a summit, but suggested that the meeting would be useful as preparation for a summit. He had given no indication that we would take up serious matters in a true summit fashion. I kept thinking of the Moscow press reports after the Geneva summit, criticizing Gorbachev for having been bested by Reagan. Was this a Soviet effort to even the score?

Many people were critical of what went on in Reykjavik, feeling we had been ill prepared to deal with Gorbachev and his proposals. But I saw movement and sensed the chance for fruitful follow-up discussion. There is no doubt that the Reykjavik talks on SDI, START, and INF laid the groundwork for the INF Treaty and for the basic agreements in the START draft treaty. For all the argument, I thought it had been an important conference, and that's what I told the press.*

Ronald Reagan was disappointed and angered by the failure to arrive at an agreement in Iceland, even though he had not come expecting one. He understood that, as president of the United States, he had the opportunity to help the world in its search for peace. His international vision had as its centerpiece a world without nuclear weapons. I had been in meetings where his staff tried to talk him out of that position. I do not know of a single adviser to the president who agreed with him that a nuclear-free world was a real or proximate possibility. Reagan had his private dream, however, and he pursued it in his own fashion.

Since nuclear weapons had unquestionably been a deterrent to war, our allies and many in the Congress were terribly concerned about

---

* The reporting on the Reykjavik summit illustrates the difficulty and limitations faced by historians as they try to recapture events. I watched a well-done BBC show on Reykjavik and have now read two published reports written by participants. The tendency to emphasize one's own role is too overwhelming to overcome. I could sometimes barely recognize events in which I had participated; and, in some cases, I obviously did not participate as far as the author was concerned, even though I could have sworn I was there!

any kind of move that would remove that nuclear restraint. Our allies feared Reagan's impulse to go down to zero, feeling that as the danger of nuclear war decreased, the danger of conventional war rose, and they knew a conventional war would be fought on their territory at the expense of their people and their countries.

For all the differences and confusion, there was movement in Geneva. A month after Reykjavik, just before Christmas 1986, the sixth round ended. It had been the most productive round, and important areas of agreement had emerged during those two months. We had agreed on an approximate 50 percent reduction schedule in intercontinental-range missiles and bombers, leaving each side with a maximum of 6,000 warheads and 1,600 delivery vehicles. In INF, we agreed on the elimination of intermediate-range missiles in Europe and a global equality level of 100 warheads for each side. This, in effect, was a reduction of 100 percent of the Soviet SS-20 missiles that threatened every European city, and a reduction of 80 percent of the Soviet SS-20s in Asia.

I went home for consultation, but was back in Geneva at the beginning of December for four days of special talks designed to summarize where we stood. This had not been requested after previous rounds, but since we were moving faster, both Karpov and I thought it would be useful to take inventory. I surmised the Soviets might be ready to make some further concessions, but these were not forthcoming.

With this movement, there was increased anxiety in Washington from the Office of the Secretary of Defense. It appeared to me they would be prepared to accept an INF agreement, particularly if we did not move rapidly, but they were greatly troubled by the prospects of a START agreement. Their concern was that as we moved closer to START, pressures would mount that we sacrifice SDI for such an agreement. I felt we could resist those pressures. OSD differed. From the Joint Chiefs of Staff, furthermore, we were hearing that a START treaty was very much in our interest because of our vulnerability to the Soviet SS-18 weapons that could cross the ocean in minutes.

All "instructions" to me—essentially the official position of the government—were largely influenced by me and my staff, and, in some cases, even drafted by us. But they were discussed in Washington, cleared by the interagency process there, and approved by the National Security Council and the president. I was part of the process that helped define and refine our national interests, but I never presumed to make policy decisions. Nobody had elected me or appointed me to establish policy for the United States. All I wanted as a negotiator was significant participation in the decision-making process and the right to probe for openings after those instructions were decided on by the president.

My freedom to probe apparently worried some Defense Department people, the secretary of Defense among them. With growing concerns about the movement toward agreement in Geneva, I learned objections were being raised to my being "instructed" to probe the issues we were negotiating with the Soviets. The right to probe meant, to me, the right to discuss and explore, without binding our country.

Without that right, I did not feel I could fulfill my responsibilities as negotiator. Weinberger, in his book about his experiences as secretary of Defense,* asserts that the president decided that our delegation should not offer "any" space control proposals and that my discussion with the Soviets of "outer space arms control," including a possible ban on anti-satellite weapons, undercut the president's decision. I am surprised about how far he apparently distanced himself from negotiating details, since the president did forward specific proposals for us to offer the Soviets, and we did. Those were the only proposals we made on the subject in Geneva. I recall one such instruction dealing with open laboratories, which arrived without an explanation. When I cabled for guidance, the response I received was "wing it," which Cooper and I did successfully.

Furthermore, the agreement between the United States and the

---

* The book contains an inaccurate reference to me. He identifies me with a position taken by Paul Nitze in 1986 that we should negotiate an agreement with the Soviets defining what would be permitted or prohibited in space research under the ABM Treaty. He gives his source for that information as Colonel Dan Gallington, his representative at the Geneva talks. He was misinformed.

I openly disagreed with Paul Nitze and with the State Department recommendation that the United States propose a "permitted-prohibited" agreement. Hank Cooper and I felt that would be entering a swamp, and there would be no constructive way to get out of it. At one point, I received a telephone call in Geneva from either Poindexter or McFarlane or Linhard at the White House saying that Nitze and the State Department had made such a recommendation and they did not find my name associated with it. What was my view? I explained that I thought it would be bad for our negotiating objective for us to make that proposal; there was no way I could see the United States at this point agreeing internally on a position; the likelihood of an agreement with the Soviets on the questions was remote if not nonexistent; and finally it was unnecessary for us to go through the anguishing and unproductive process at this time, since I was convinced we could obtain an INF and START treaty without dealing with SDI. I consistently maintained that position.

Immediately after I brought this inaccuracy to Weinberger's attention, he said it would be corrected in the next printing of his book.

USSR in January 1985 that led to the Geneva talks specifically included space as a subject matter for negotiation. It is elemental that the word "discuss" is not a synonym for "agree." Regrettably, some people at OSD never seemed to comprehend the subtle but important difference between being an earnest and honest negotiator and still holding firm to positions of vital national importance.

One day, I received a phone call from then Air Force Colonel Robert Linhard at the NSC, informing me that Frank Gaffney, a Defense Department official who worked for Richard Perle, had strongly objected to my instructions. Could I resolve the problem? I said I would talk to Perle, which I did, and the objection disappeared. I had always found Richard supportive of my personal efforts, but I was aware that this problem was institutional, and Richard was capable of working through others. Gaffney was perfect for that role. I was convinced that Gaffney was in principle opposed to any agreement with the Soviets, so when developments began to look as if they were moving in Geneva, he would send word to his people to slow things down. Frank was technically able, charming when appropriate, unyielding, irritating, frequently confrontational, and a most competent and intelligent adversary.

Both Weinberger and Gaffney seemed concerned that my probing would open up some new line of discussion they had not anticipated. I, of course, felt that finding new possibilities was one reason to probe, and was the purpose of my endless meetings with the Soviets. I also knew that Hank Cooper* and I would not "sell out" SDI.

I continued to work closely with friends at Defense. Fred Ikle had been an acquaintance from the time when he was the director of the Arms Control and Disarmament Agency. We got to know each other better when we were both involved with the Committee on the Present Danger. He is Swiss by birth and accent, but an American citizen who is scholarly, imaginative, and creative in foreign affairs and military affairs. His willingness to soar where others walked put some people off.

Fortunately, my friendships with Ikle and Richard Perle were strong enough to overcome the Gaffney impediment. They knew I was not naive, nor would I sell out our interests to the Soviets simply to get an agreement. Richard Perle was one of the most brilliant people in our government, suspicious of many, but masterful in carrying out his responsibilities.

Perle had an undeserved reputation, which he personally enjoyed,

* As a matter of fact, Hank is now director of the Strategic Defense Initiative Organization at the Pentagon.

for closing the door to agreement with the Soviets. It was my impression, after working with him closely for four years, that this was unjustified. He could be a heckler and an irritant from the sidelines; he had done that often enough to have attracted more enemies than he needed. He did mistrust the State Department and felt that their emphasis was more on obtaining the fact of an agreement and much less on the substance of the agreement. He therefore looked on himself as the protector of the national interest from State's detente tendency. I was convinced, however, that if he were given the responsibility of negotiating an agreement, he would creatively arrive at one rather than destroy its prospects.*

Cap did not want SDI negotiated. I felt that he carried it to extremes. In 1986, after listening to Yuli Kvitsinskiy make some inaccurate comments about our SDI program, I told him I would be pleased to arrange a briefing by General James Abrahamson, who was in charge of our SDI program. Yuli was noncommittal, which did not surprise me. Such a meeting would require approval from Moscow, and he needed time to check. I had made the offer without conferring with anyone, so while I was in Washington, I asked Abrahamson if he would like to come to Geneva for that purpose. He indicated that he would be pleased to do so; I then mentioned it to the NSC staff and to the secretary of State, all of whom thought it was a good idea.

I had not had a chance to raise the question again with Kvitsinskiy when I heard that Abrahamson was going to be in Bonn. I cabled the general and suggested he come to Geneva after Bonn. I told Yuli what I had done, and he responded in formal diplomatic talk, "If the American delegation invites the Soviet delegation for lunch, we will, of course, accept." I explained that I was being specific about it because I did not want to embarrass him in any way and did not want him to be surprised by General Abrahamson's presence. He repeated his formal response, and I interpreted it as an acceptance.

* For example, Perle, along with Linhard, was given the responsibility for negotiating an agreement with the Soviets on a plan presented by Senators Nunn and Warner for a nuclear risk reduction center. When the senators heard that he had the responsibility, they both talked to me about their disappointment and anger, assuming that Perle would kill the prospects for an agreement. I assured them that the reverse was probably true, and indeed Perle expeditiously negotiated the treaty and made a very favorable impression on the Soviets, who also had looked upon him as a bête noire.

Roz Ridgway, now president of the Atlantic Council, once told me that when she was assistant secretary of State for European affairs and she and Perle were assigned to work with the Soviets on a concluding statement at the 1985 Geneva summit, Perle was much more conciliatory than she was.

Then I began to hear static from Washington. The general, I was told, was finding it difficult to schedule Geneva. I called him and sensed why that was so. Secretary Weinberger was opposed to his visit. I knew Abrahamson wanted to come, and in conversations with the White House I prevailed.

The lunch took place. The American delegation invited; the Soviet delegation accepted. Abrahamson's briefing was superb. He is thin, attractive, with a ready smile. His warmth and friendliness and competence were all evident. He started by referring to some important research work in the SDI field undertaken by Soviet scientists, mentioning their names and where they had done their research. The Soviets recognized the names and places, but seemed to know essentially nothing about their own program. I could see their eyes register surprise and their curiosity surge. Their notebooks came out, and their pens began to work actively. They were eager to hear more. Abrahamson told them what he could. I am convinced that his appearance helped us immensely in educating the Soviets not only about our plans, but about their own activity. After this highly successful briefing, Hank Cooper and I decided to prepare as complete a U.S. plenary statement as appropriate about the Soviet SDI program.

The reluctance of either Weinberger or his staff to permit General Abrahamson to join me in Geneva was only one occasion when Defense was wrongheaded. Because I was the chief negotiator on defense and space issues dealing with SDI, the Department of Defense's searchlight was on my statements. I certainly felt the responsibility to vent my ideas and intentions with my delegation, but I obviously could not always follow the lead or automatically accept the wishes of those who represented the secretary of Defense alone. The responsibility was mine. It was not like the first year when we agreed so thoroughly. One weekend in early February 1987, before I was to deliver a plenary statement on SDI, I went to a conference near Oxford, England. Dan Gallington, the secretary's representative in my defense and space group, reached me with the message that he had to see me when I returned on Sunday evening. "Cap is very unhappy about your proposed statement," he explained. I looked again at what I had dictated and said I would stand by it. I explained that I spoke when I thought I should, covering what I thought was appropriate, and left it at that.

The next morning, just as I was heading for my meeting with the Soviets, I received a cable from Cap ending with "warm regards," urging me not to give my intended talk, saying that I was going beyond my instructions. I was never certain if it was Cap on his own or if his name was used by Frank Gaffney. There were not many statements more likely to annoy me. I cabled back, saying in effect that I appreciated his views and respected them, but I was not going beyond my instructions. I explained my position and said that by the time he received my cable, I would have delivered the statement. I sent copies to Frank Carlucci, then national security adviser to the president, at the White House and to George Shultz, who responded with: "you have my gratitude and support . . . Thanks for your help in working out this position."*

The purpose of SDI was to stop destruction, to stop the threat of nuclear war. That was what the defense and space negotiations were all about. They were not a charade or a mock negotiation as far as I was concerned. I was in favor of research and development to see whether such defenses were feasible and practical. It would be years, I had reason to believe, before the issue of deployment need be decided. I wanted the Soviets to know that the United States was ready to begin talking about how we might jointly manage the transition, should the research be successful, from a force structure that is overwhelmingly offensive and destructive in nature to one that had a mix of offense and defense and perhaps, in time, would become defense dominant. I wanted them to know that President Reagan felt we were well within the obligations agreed to in the 1972 ABM Treaty in continuing our research. I also felt there was a strong consensus of Democrats and Republicans in the Congress supporting SDI research and saw no reason to undermine that consensus by unnecessarily threatening to violate the ABM Treaty and prepare for deployment before we were ready.

For reasons still not clear to me because they were counterproductive to support for SDI, the secretary of Defense and his associates decided to press the president toward breaking away from the ABM Treaty, with the assertion that new SDI technological developments

---

* One of the consequences of the Iran-Contra controversy during this period was John Poindexter's replacement by Frank Carlucci as national security adviser to the president. A career foreign service officer with great success as ambassador in helping Portugal become a democracy, Frank served as number two at the CIA and the Department of Defense, where he served with distinction. He was an ideal choice for the president. We had met when he was in private life. I trusted him. At one point, after I heard some static from Defense about a minor issue involving an interview in *Die Welt*, I cabled him suggesting he might wish to disown me if it was in his interest. He responded: "No Problem . . . Your comment is first rate. You have my admiration for all you are doing."

now required steps beyond the restraints earlier imposed by the president on the program. This, I was convinced, would break apart the broad coalition in support of SDI. Furthermore, I was told by people working in the program that the drive for change was motivated by "politics" rather than technology.

This problem first hit me on January 23, 1987, in a speech to the Royal United Services Institute for Defense Studies in London. A questioner informed me that the wire services were carrying a story that Caspar Weinberger had just announced "dramatic results" in SDI experiments that had created deployment opportunities earlier than previously thought possible. I quickly responded to my critical audience that SDI was an exploratory program, a decision on deployment was still years ahead, a decision to deploy was not foreordained, and the president's pledge not to make a decision prior to consultation with our allies remained operative.

My comments were carried by the press. Our embassy officers seemed pleased. At least one senior British official expressed relief. But, I was told, the response did not sit well in OSD. I was, however, saying nothing more than the president had been saying.

In this atmosphere and with movement toward INF and START treaties evident in Geneva, a bitter and unnecessary controversy erupted in the United States that did serious damage to our SDI research program. The United States had persuaded the Soviet Union in 1972 to join us in the ABM Treaty, under which neither of us would try to defend ourselves against nuclear ballistic missiles, the theory being that if we were both defenseless against each other's weapons, the deterrence would assure us peace. Greater safety, it was said, lies in greater danger.

During the ABM Treaty negotiations, the United States urged a total ban on all defense-oriented anti-ballistic missiles. When our executive branch explained the treaty to the Senate as part of the ratification process, we asserted that we had achieved what we sought. That interpretation became known as the "narrow" one. The Soviets opposed a total ban and insisted on exceptions for new technologies; when they explained the treaty to the Supreme Soviet, their Marshal Andrey Grechko asserted the treaty met their objectives, an interpretation known as the "broad" one.

Each country went forward with its own view of what the treaty meant. Over the years, we claimed the Soviets clearly violated the ABM Treaty while we abided by the narrow interpretation. In authorizing the SDI program, President Reagan limited the research program to that permitted by the restricted narrow definition of the ABM Treaty.*

Richard Perle, looking ahead to how the SDI research would evolve, concluded that necessary testing would not be consistent with the narrow interpretation, but would be consistent with the broad. That was the crux of a controversy that evolved in the United States, lingered, intensified, and adversely affected the SDI program. There was indeed strong reason to believe that both the United States and the USSR had their own differing interpretation of what was agreed in 1972. There was no meeting of the minds. Furthermore, a good case could be made that the Soviets were correct in 1972 in arguing that the text reflected their broad interpretation. The Defense Department attorneys came to that conclusion, as did Judge Abraham Sofaer, the brilliant State Department legal adviser. Yet, as Judge Sofaer pointed out to the president, the Senate, in ratifying the treaty, relied on what the executive branch had reported: that the ABM Treaty was to be narrowly interpreted.

At a Friday meeting at the White House, Paul Nitze, who had been one of the chief U.S. negotiators in 1972, said that after reviewing the record, he agreed with the conclusion that the broad interpretation was correct, thereby reversing his former position. Much to our surprise, Bud McFarlane announced on a talk show the following Sunday that the president accepted the broad interpretation as the legally correct one, but would, nevertheless, until further notice, keep SDI research confined to the narrow interpretation. There had been no consultation with the Senate on the president's decision to reverse what had been the U.S. interpretation since 1972. Senators on both sides of SDI, therefore, united in opposition on constitutional grounds. Opponents of SDI also suspected that the president intended to withdraw from the ABM Treaty, thereby complicating our arms talks in Geneva. My own view was that the move by the White House was unnecessary at the time. There was a great deal of research yet to be done under the narrow definition. Why be divisive prematurely when it might never be necessary? Why be confrontational before the SDI research program is better established and accepted?

The question of what the ABM Treaty meant, how it was to be interpreted, became an acrimonious part of my life. In our negotiations in Geneva, we were taking the position held by the Soviets in 1972 and they were taking the position held by us in 1972. Back home, consen-

---

* As I write, the Soviets are dismantling their giant radar at Krasnoyarsk, which we have said for the better part of a decade violated the ABM Treaty.

sus behind the SDI program began to disintegrate, and relations between the Hill and the executive branch became strained.

On the last day of February 1987, members of the Senate observer group were in Geneva, as were Richard Perle and Paul Nitze, who were on their way to Brussels. During that Saturday morning gathering, Senator Ted Stevens, who had impressed me from the beginning as a highly effective de facto leader of the Senate observer group, said that intense controversy was building on SDI appropriations and he did not know where it would end, although he believed it would inevitably result in reduced SDI appropriations. In any case, he felt certain the controversy could not make my life as negotiator any easier. I agreed with him that reduced SDI appropriations would adversely affect the negotiations.

After a long discussion, I suggested that we try to help resolve the question since all the various points of view were reflected within the Senate observer group and among us at our meeting. I proposed that the SDI appropriation continue with an agreed-upon modest increase for a year and a half, without a legislative fight. In return, the president would give assurances that we would not go beyond the narrow interpretation for that period of time. That seemed a reasonable position for the administration to take since we were not then beyond the narrow interpretation and had no immediate plans or need to exceed those limits. The congressional critics would receive, in fact, what they wanted on the interpretation question, would avoid a public wrangle with a popular president, and would put the administration on notice about future funding. I thought everyone could win.

Senator Claiborne Pell thought the formula acceptable, but said that he could not commit any other Democratic senators, and would want to consult with Alan Cranston. Senator Gore reported that Senator Nunn, the most influential senator on these matters, was about to make a series of three speeches critical of the administration's ABM position, which would, of course, be confrontational rather than conciliatory. Gore volunteered to call Nunn to see if he would hold off, and quickly reported that Nunn was prepared to delay his speeches for a couple of weeks if that were necessary and if a compromise was really the goal of the White House. Ted Stevens liked the approach, as did Paul Nitze. Perle also liked it and made a few suggestions for improvement. He then said that he would push it when he returned to Washington.

That day was also former Senator Howard Baker's first day as chief of staff at the White House. At Ted Stevens's suggestion, he and I went back to my office to call Baker and to seek his advice. We explained what was involved, and he thought our posture, as we explained it, was an intelligent compromise that he could support. We expected him to talk to Nunn. In the meantime, I cabled the details of our proposed understanding to George Shultz and to the national security adviser, Frank Carlucci.

When I returned to Washington the following week, there was a message for me from Al Gore saying the agreement was coming undone since neither he nor Sam Nunn had heard from the White House. Gore and I had breakfast the next morning at his father's apartment. He had stuck his neck out not only with Nunn, but also on the House side, where many of his former colleagues accused him of selling out to Reagan. He was embarrassed politically and personally and concerned that the White House was leaving him exposed by withdrawing from the deal he thought was in the making. I could not understand what had happened.

I requested a meeting with the president to try to reactivate the plan. Shultz asked me to carry the ball, as I had hoped he would. The president seemed to be unequivocally in favor of our compromise after I explained it. SDI would not be jeopardized. The negotiations would not be harmed. There would be no fight with Congress. Reagan would look good. I further suggested to the president that I thought we ought to have a single administration voice, and that it ought to be Howard Baker's. He agreed. Baker agreed.

Cap Weinberger took a contrary view. He said he thought it was imperative that we embrace the broad interpretation immediately and that we were going to get the money we needed in any case. I thought that his argument was faulty, based on a gross misreading of Congress and the nation, and that he gave the president inaccurate information on SDI's readiness for the broad interpretation. I knew he was inaccurate, as did others in the room, although I could not judge whether Cap knew that what he was saying was not so. I thought as he spoke that it was a crime for any of us who advises a president knowingly to mislead him or provide him with inaccurate information. Once again, I felt the secretary was badly served by his staff.

Yet the president, for all Cap had to say, seemed to accept my views. I went away pleased and expecting Howard Baker to put the pieces together. But, again, nothing happened. Weinberger, after our meeting, had persuaded the president that our compromise would do serious damage to the SDI program and convinced him to call off the Baker negotiation. It was a mistake. Gore was ill used and justifiably angry. Nunn felt deceived and gave his intended speeches, which cut the legs off a great deal of SDI support in the Senate. Beyond that, Nunn's mistrust lasted through the end of the Reagan administration. We ended up with far less money for SDI than we would have under my formula. And we are, as of this writing, more than three years later, still operating SDI under the narrow interpretation.

The Soviets, of course, looked with interest on the Washington break within the ranks of SDI supporters. Quite possibly, they interpreted Washington's internal controversy on the question as a reason for them to be less concerned about SDI and how soon it would be deployed. In any case, by late 1986, the Soviets were communicating to us in Geneva a desire to step things up. At about this time, too, we received informal suggestions in Washington that it might be time for the two capitals to develop a private back channel for conducting informal probings about how to expedite the arms talks as well as other outstanding issues between our two countries. This would be outside the normal diplomatic channels. The value of a back channel is that fewer people are involved, information can be better kept to those who really have a need to know, and exchanges can be informal. The Soviets suggested having someone come to Moscow who could perform that function.

George Shultz talked to me about the idea, and we agreed it could be a useful method of exchange. He decided that Paul Nitze might be the person for it, but we both understood that it would be hard to sell Paul to the Defense Department. I suggested we might be able to overcome Defense fears by adding Richard Perle, thus giving the back channel double status. I knew that Richard was a responsible negotiator despite the hostile press label as the "Prince of Darkness."

Neither suggestion worked. Defense would not accept Nitze alone, and the Soviets would not accept Perle in any fashion. What later evolved after the Soviets introduced a new leader for the Geneva talks was that I took on a modified back-channel role from Geneva, working with my new Soviet colleague.*

The Soviet interest in back-channel communication was not a surprise. Ambassador Dobrynin and Senator Ted Kennedy had devel-

---

* Every American negotiator knows how Henry Kissinger and Andrei Gromyko settled issues between themselves while negotiators were struggling for compromise, unaware that they were wasting their time. John Tower worried about that each time Shultz met with Shevardnadze. I, as a matter of fact, had urged Shultz to get involved. He said, "John will not like that." I said I knew that, but as head of the delegation, I was sure it was essential.

oped a special relationship that had matured over time. The Soviets were as fascinated by the Kennedy family as any American aficionado. The Soviets saw them as more powerful than they probably were, but the Kennedys were millionaires, presidents and senators, glamorous celebrities of legend. The Soviets, as a result, had wanted to work with Kennedy as a back-door conduit of information during earlier arms negotiations and on other occasions as well. This relationship had permitted the senator to get a number of people out of the Soviet Union when efforts by others had not been successful. Furthermore, I learned that the senator never acted or received information without informing the appropriate United States agency or official.

Some in the White House tried to discourage or end any intermediary role for Senator Kennedy. They suspected a self-aggrandizing effort. Their distrust of him clouded their judgment. I disagreed and spoke to George Shultz about it. I noted that the Soviets like to work through back channels, that it did not have to affect our negotiations except as a positive means of learning what the Soviets wanted and emphasizing our requirements. We could use the senator's good standing, I suggested, to our advantage.

Shultz talked to the president, who thought working with Kennedy informally was a good idea. I found the arrangement useful. Kennedy always let me know when he received a message from Dobrynin, and I, in turn, would brief Ted and suggest what would be helpful to pass on to Dobrynin. Messages passed back and forth, and I believe the negotiations were helped. The senator's personal friend and former aide, Dr. Lawrence Horowitz, served as an important conduit in developing the relationship. He frequently traveled to Moscow at either Kennedy's or Dobrynin's suggestion and met with me before and after each trip. On every occasion, I learned some useful information. I kept George Shultz informed of every contact.

I disagreed with many of the senator's foreign policy positions, but I had met Ted through Senator Henry Jackson, who liked and trusted him. Scoop at one time asked me to participate in a private seminar with Ted on the Soviet Union, which is when I first talked seriously to him. Scoop, a hard-liner on the Soviet Union, told me at the time that Ted was much more knowledgeable and sophisticated about the Soviet Union than he sometimes conveyed publicly, and I realized that in those first meetings.*

* Our friendship grew during the negotiations. He was a member of the Senate observer group. We spoke regularly, and I made a point of keeping him informed. When I returned to my law firm, he and Ted Stevens had a bipartisan senatorial dinner

In January 1987, after the Reykjavik meeting, Gorbachev sent a letter to Reagan saying that he was replacing Victor Karpov with a more senior official, Yuli Vorontsov, a first deputy foreign minister. Karpov was asked to put his arms control knowledge and experience to work in their foreign ministry, creating an office to deal with disarmament. Arms control issues had always been a part of their defense ministry, most recently under the direction of Colonel General Nikolai Chervov, a leading Soviet bureaucrat who had headed the arms control group within the defense ministry for many years. Shevardnadze, I assumed, may have come to understand and appreciate countervailing U.S. disarmament structure, with both civilian and military opinions measured and considered.

Vorontsov, now the Soviet ambassador to the United Nations, is a distinguished diplomat who knows the United States and the West well, having served in both Washington and New York. He had limited experience in arms control, but obviously was a Kremlin heavyweight. That could only mean they were more serious than ever about reaching agreement.

Shultz was traveling overseas, and the White House press office, apparently in an effort to match the Soviet news, announced that I was to be appointed counselor of the Department of State, even as I continued to head the arms control negotiations. The press, having been informed that the counselor position was at the rank of undersecretary of State, concluded that I was being promoted so that I would match Vorontsov's rank.

In fact, the counselor position is a lower rank than the executive level I held as ambassador and head of the U.S. delegation, and this is reflected in a lower pay grade. When Vorontsov and I met for the first time, he apologized for his responsibility for what he believed was a cut in my pay. It was the first demonstration of his light touch, but it also showed how familiar the Soviets were with our structure.

We talked by phone as soon as I arrived in Geneva, and he invited me to the Soviet mission for lunch. Because he is fluent in English, there was no need for an interpreter. He is a charming, pleasant, direct person. After his joke about my salary, he got right to the point. He said, "Gorbachev thinks the negotiations are going too slowly. You and I must get things moving."

I told him that his negotiators, as a practical matter, were not of a

---

in my honor at his home, with Vice President Dan Quayle and Secretary of State James Baker present.

high enough level to make any significant decisions. They were capable, but we no longer expected them to move outside the beaten path. He said he knew that, and we would have to take matters into our own hands.

He then said that he wanted me to know about his other jobs. He explained that he was still first deputy foreign minister, and his primary duties included dealing with both Iran and Iraq as well as Afghanistan, highly sensitive areas for us. When Shevardnadze was out of town, he sat in his chair. He, therefore, could not spend a lot of time in Geneva, but he would spend whatever time I thought was necessary.

Then he asked how much time I would spend in Geneva. I said I, too, would not be there full-time because my counselor's position involved other duties as well. I proposed that we both try to coordinate our schedules so that we were in Geneva at the same time. I thought our presence was required in Geneva every four or five weeks. He agreed.*

Vorontsov said he had some suggestions for improving the negotiations. He proposed fewer formal meetings. He said we really didn't need to make speeches and that it was time to just talk to each other. None of these suggestions was surprising, since they were the very suggestions I had made to Karpov in 1986, and which, I assume, he cabled home. We were already on a first-name basis, so I said, "Look, Yuli, with all your suggestions, I agree. I don't care who gets credit for them." With a twinkle in his eye, he said, "Moscow gets credit." I responded, "Okay, Moscow gets credit, but we both know who deserves credit."

We relaxed then and talked about many areas of United States–Soviet interest. We had both been informed that our agenda was broader than arms control and that we would be conduits for a privacy channel. Afghanistan and Central America were part of that agenda. At one point, he said, "You're being misinformed if you think the Afghans you are supporting are going to move in and take over if we move out. That is not what is going to happen. They are going to kill each other. There is going to be a bloodbath." I was not inclined to believe him at the time. That was the first of a number of discussions on Afghanistan and I always passed on his views to Mike Armacost, our undersecretary

---

* We were probably in Geneva together about half a dozen times in 1987, but more time wasn't necessary. It was invaluable time together. When we were there, we spent concentrated periods outside of formal, time-consuming meetings. We would take stock, figure out how to get where we wanted to be, and then go back to our respective capitals to work on details with others.

for political affairs, who had a continuing responsibility in that area. Mike had no turf-protection instinct and on several occasions invited me to his meetings with Vorontsov.

Our private arrangement received the name Project Five in Washington. During these early days of the relationship, Frank Carlucci cabled me that Soviet Ambassador Dubinin in Washington was not aware of the project. On the other hand, our Ambassador Arthur Hartman in Moscow was informed. Arthur was asked by Carlucci to inform Gorbachev via Anatoly Dobrynin, who was now an aide to Gorbachev, that I had two responsibilities paralleling Vorontsov's. In addition to heading the U.S. delegation, I represented and served as the president's personal emissary in a confidential dialogue. Vorontsov informed me that he had received word from Moscow of that communication. It strengthened my status.

At some point during this seventh round, General Chervov arrived in Geneva and asked for a meeting with me. Our first meeting about a year earlier had been a disaster. I felt then that Chervov's every word was hostile and unrelated to what we might have discussed. If I spoke in a friendly fashion, he responded harshly. When I spoke up, it got worse. At one point I said, "It seems very clear to me that your hostility is so deep that even when I pay you a compliment, you interpret it as a hostile charge. I can understand why we have never been able to come to terms with you and your people over the years."

We never had another angry meeting. We developed a good and warm relationship. It is as though he had gotten the venom out of his system, taken my measure, and was prepared to entertain rational discussion and negotiation. Chervov and I met with Mike Glitman and Ron Lehman, who had been John Tower's deputy and now replaced him after John resigned to return to private life. Later, Chervov met with each of them separately. He stayed nearly a week, and we made significant movement toward understanding. It was an additional sign of the Soviet intent to reach agreement.

Vorontsov had been in Moscow while Chervov was in Geneva. They met at the airport in Geneva on a Saturday as he arrived and Chervov left. At dinner that evening, Vorontsov abruptly informed me that any understandings we had with Chervov were misunderstandings. Clearly, something I did not understand had set off a reaction at the foreign ministry and Vorontsov was directed to undo what Chervov and we had begun.

I met with Glitman and Lehman the next morning, briefed them about my dinner conversation, but added: "We now know what the bottom line is. It is what Chervov told us. We may get things better than Chervov offered, but the Soviets will at least get to the Chervov point because Chervov would not have said what he did unless he had authority to do so." All three of us proceeded from that assumption.

When the seventh round ended early in March 1987, I was certain of our INF success, or as certain as one can be. I publicly noted our satisfaction that the Soviets had abandoned their insistence that agreement on INF reductions had to be linked to agreement in the two other areas of the Geneva talks—START, and defense and space.

Two weeks later, back in Washington, on March 19, I came down off that high with a crash. I had a serious heart attack. My father's death at an early age made me aware always of my own mortality. Ever since the starvation days in Minnesota, I have taken vitamins and educated myself on nutritional and health matters. While I had never become seriously overweight, I had also been to a Pritikin diet center, and that had made me even more aware of my physical condition and nutritional requirements.

Life in Geneva made my health routines more difficult. I had a treadmill at home in Washington that I used daily as I watched the morning news. I bought one in Geneva, but it turned out to be inadequate. So I tried to walk outdoors as much as possible. I'd walk to work or to lunch, and take longer strolls on the weekends, but to walk meant avoiding my car with its bulletproof protection and cheating on my security people by slipping out. That was restraining.

It was nearly impossible to find a bad restaurant in Geneva, and that meant wonderful French cooking, heavy on cream sauces, red meats, and fat. I cannot deny possessing a sweet tooth. This is known by my friends and enemies alike. I have never been able to turn down a piece of chocolate, and the Soviets made certain there were chocolates at hand when I met at their mission. Beyond that, my days were long and stressful. I arrived by nine o'clock each morning and frequently ended up without dinner still at the office at a late hour. At ten P.M., it is just four P.M. in Washington. Cables and phone calls would often flow back and forth all day and all evening. The pressure was unrelenting.*

The attack itself was preceded by warning signs that I was unable, or unwilling, to piece together into an accurate reflection of my condition. One morning back in Washington, I got on my treadmill for my

---

* My skimpy diary, recounting the days' substantive events, often reflected an aside that I was tired. Looking back, it is clear that fatigue was chronic, the result certainly of the most aggravating and stressful job I ever had in my life.

regular workout and felt a little weak. I spent no more than a minute
on it instead of my normal twenty minutes. I sat down but felt no pain
except for a little heartburn and thought I had indigestion. I went to
work. I asked for some Alka-Seltzer and settled for Tums, which someone in the office had. I worked that morning with a little discomfort and
then proceeded to lunch with Meir Rosenne, who was then the Israeli
ambassador. When downtown traffic turned to gridlock a block from
the International Club where we were to meet, I told my driver to let
me off. When I got to the club lobby, I was dizzy and sat down until
it passed. I walked up a flight of stairs, had lunch, and then went out
to rent a white tie for the White House correspondents' dinner, which
was coming up that weekend.

I felt dizzy again but got measured anyway, waited for my car, and
went back to the office. That night, Maggie and I were invited to
dinner at the Charles Corddrys' home and we went, since Corddry, a
Baltimore Sun reporter and a member of my "Washington Week in
Review" panel, was a good friend.

When we got home, Maggie, seeing I was not well, insisted I call
my doctor. I described my symptoms and my day's activities, and he
said, "It doesn't sound like a heart attack." Since my annual physical
was scheduled for the next day, we agreed that I would wait to see him
then.

When I got into his office, he took an EKG and said, "You had a
heart attack yesterday." In a matter of minutes, I was in an ambulance
and headed for the hospital. The damage, which might have been
tempered by drugs if we had caught the attack quickly, was serious.

I was scheduled to go to Moscow with Shultz about three weeks
later. Since I was not able to go, Shultz visited me at home after my
discharge from the hospital and before he left, telling me what he
intended to do and say. A few weeks earlier, seeing that our visit to
Moscow was scheduled to overlap the Jewish Passover holidays, Dick
Schifter and I recommended to the secretary that he arrange his schedule to attend the annual Passover seder services held in the apartment
of one of our U.S. foreign service officers, to which many of Moscow's
Jewish refuseniks were invited. He readily agreed. Shultz, as he was
leaving Washington, wanted me to know that he was looking forward
to the seder. I later learned that it was a moving experience for everyone involved and an outstanding success. In the hour he was with me,
I grew tired, but I was exhilarated at the same time. The following
week, when the Moscow meeting ended, Paul Nitze, Roz Ridgway,
and Hank Cooper came to my home to brief me on developments.

I am convinced that the concern Shultz and others showed in keeping me informed and involved helped me to think about the future and not about my condition, which, in turn, helped me heal. The secretary's visit was a great morale booster. I was ready to return to Geneva for the next round, which began on May 8. Maggie was afraid that I was moving too soon, but my doctors indicated I had recovered sufficiently to go if I did not overwork, and I felt strong. My son Jeff went along to look after me should that be necessary and to enforce moderation.

I slowly worked myself back to a full schedule as counselor of the department, with its responsibilities, and as head of the Geneva negotiating team. It turned out that for the remainder of 1987, I spent about 20 percent of my time in Geneva, meeting with Vorontsov or arranging to be there when the Senate observer group was planning a visit. The Vorontsov sessions were crucial to an agreement; the Senate to its ratification.

I also liked to be on hand to encourage informal conversation between the Soviets and the senators. They both learned a great deal when they got together, although there was also room for good fellowship. On one occasion, the senators hosted a dinner at a restaurant Ted Stevens recommended on the outskirts of Geneva. Vorontsov had made quite an impression on them, since he was so debonair and charming, the antithesis of the stereotypical Marxist of the Eastern bloc.

I arranged for him to sit with the senators and their spouses and sat myself at the far end of the table. I paid scant attention to what was going on until I heard raised voices and highly animated conversation. Civility and normal tones returned quickly, and I relaxed. I later discovered that Vorontsov had engaged the senators in a discussion of President Kennedy's assassination, proclaiming that he and particularly his wife were well versed on the matter. They had been in the United States during the assassination and had apparently read all they could on it afterward. They seemed to be convinced that the Warren Commission was a cover-up. One of the senators, Arlen Specter of Pennsylvania, had been an attorney on the commission and had been deeply involved in studying the evidence. Vorontsov was reportedly unwilling to accept any of Arlen's arguments or facts. When they explained the argument to me later, one senator shook his head and said to me, "Do you have to go through that all the time?"

On one occasion, during the summer of 1987, George Shultz called me to say that Shevardnadze had sent word that he was going to be in Geneva for a UN meeting on August 7 and wondered if I was going to be there, too. That seemed a command performance, and I made plans to go to Geneva. Vorontsov remained in Moscow.

Shevardnadze and I were to meet at nine A.M., and I was told by one of my press people that he had a scheduled ten A.M. press conference. It was an extraordinary meeting for me. None of the Soviet negotiators was present. We first went through the details of the negotiation. I explained carefully why we held certain positions and what our goals were. He set forth his views, his problems, and his goals. It was neither negotiation nor argument. It was an exchange of information that transcended normal diplomatic parrying. With respect to SDI and defense and space, I suggested it was useless to argue about what the parties intended in 1972. We should arrive at what today is in our respective interests and proclaim that to be the 1972 intention. I was impressed with how well Shevardnadze had mastered the subject matter.

Despite his press conference, Shevardnadze seemed in no hurry to leave. He wondered aloud why the negotiations went so slowly when our goals were clear and amenable to agreement. I explained what he knew: that even if you know your destination in negotiations, you must choose the route carefully, avoiding potholes and pitfalls. You travel by tortoise and not by hare when the nitty-gritty must be worked out. We continued to talk about United States–Soviet relations in general and about the state of the world. It was twelve-fifteen in the afternoon when we finished one of the most intriguing days in my negotiating career. He then went to his press conference. That morning persuaded me further that the process would be laborious, but that both sides wanted an INF agreement and would in time arrive at one. The deal, however, would have to be made at the ministerial level and not at the Geneva table.

There were other interesting days during that year. By the summer, I was back at my desk after the heart attack and in high gear, fulfilling my role as counselor of the department of State. It proved to be a highly gratifying conclusion to my decade of public service with the State Department that began with President Carter and would, I assumed, end with President Reagan. I was proud to serve as counselor, working with a man I considered one of the most able secretaries of State in our history. To work with George Shultz was a splendid experience. His intellect, openness, fairness, public spiritedness, energy, purpose, and friendship were inspiring. He was the finest of public servants, the most decent of men.

When he first talked to me about the counselor position the previous August at his home in Palo Alto, he mentioned it was the second-oldest position in the State Department. As a matter of history, the title first appeared in 1909 and then disappeared from 1919 to 1937 after the Congress replaced the title with that of undersecretary of State. When I assumed office, a sheet of paper given to me quoting regulations, defined the position as assisting the secretary "in the handling of special, unusually complex, international negotiations and consultations requiring the highest degree of experience and skill"; serving as a senior adviser and consultant to the secretary on diplomatic and foreign affairs problems; and performing "special assignments as directed by the Secretary."

As a matter of practice, I learned that counselors had varied historic roles: second in command within the department; head of policy planning; representative on the National Security Council; adviser on Soviet affairs; in charge of congressional relations; coordinator for international conferences and visits; overseer of speechwriting for the secretary. As George Shultz's counselor, I performed at one time or another a great many of these duties.

Being counselor to George Shultz meant carrying only one burden I didn't like: getting up early in the morning. When Frank Carlucci replaced Cap Weinberger at Defense, he and Shultz began a regular seven A.M. meeting with Colin Powell, then national security adviser to the president, at the White House. By seven-thirty, Shultz would be ready for a breakfast meeting to which I was invited. The cast of characters changed each day: the joint chiefs, Jim Baker from Treasury, a congressional group, Bill Webster from CIA. They were important educational meetings for Shultz and played a vital policy coordinating role for the administration. They were also of immense value to me.

At eight-thirty, for about fifteen minutes, Shultz would meet each day with a different assistant secretary and follow that with a half-hour meeting with the undersecretaries; the executive secretary of the department; the legal adviser, Abe Sofaer; his press spokesman, ACDA Director Ken Adelman; USIA Director Charlie Wick; Paul Nitze; Ed Rowny. The press spokesman would review the important news events of the morning and people would suggest responses for the press. Wick would report on the important stories in the foreign press. We'd go around the table for reports and observations. At nine-fifteen, there would be a brief meeting with someone within the State Department bureaucracy—a report on the physical plant, or security, or the budget, for example.

Frequently, Shultz would invite me to join him at a lunch or a meeting, and, indeed, I was free to check his schedule and attend anything that interested me. He encouraged collegiality and open doors so that John Whitehead, the deputy secretary of State,* Mike Armacost, the undersecretary of State for political affairs, and I shared our schedules with each other as well as with Shultz. We also coordinated our travel schedules so that at least one of us was always in the department.

The rest of my day would then include attention to the continuing arms negotiations, reviewing incoming cables from around the world, talking to the experts and assistant secretaries from the various bureaus, meeting people who could not fit into the secretary's schedule. I kept my eye on the Congress, where we would need support and approval when we were ready, and I made myself available to the press whenever there were inquiries.

I became a kind of "utility infielder" at State so that people could bring problems or visitors to me when Shultz, Whitehead, and Armacost were busy or away. I became one of the contacts with the business community whenever there were mutual concerns involving our department, and I kept up my contacts with the human rights organizations still interested in the Helsinki Final Act. In that connection, my correspondence with refuseniks and dissidents and their families continued. It was a source of satisfaction to know that the human rights effort was in the highly competent hands of my close friend and former law partner, Richard Schifter, our assistant secretary of State. I knew he was on top of all the pending cases, that they were being handled with compassion and dispatch.

Dick Schifter and George Shultz were effectively freeing Soviet Jews from the Soviet Union and breaking the back of repression against dissidents and refuseniks. It was a logical and beautiful continuation,

---

* John Whitehead came to the department of State from a lifetime of investment banking at Goldman, Sachs. He demonstrated the ability to transfer his talents and proved to be of immense assistance to George Shultz as deputy secretary of State. We worked closely together, and when we both left government service on January 20, 1989, he became chairman of the United Nations Association and shortly thereafter invited me to be chairman of the board of governors of the UNA, where we continue to work closely together.

When Jim Baker resigned as secretary of the Treasury to serve as George Bush's campaign manager in early 1988, Shultz told me that John Whitehead was being considered as secretary of the Treasury to replace Baker for the duration of the Reagan presidency. He wanted me to know that should this transpire, he intended to appoint me deputy secretary of State to replace Whitehead. John, with obvious pleasure, passed the same information to me.

on a higher dimension, of what I had energetically pursued in Madrid a few years earlier. The personal joy and gratification it brought me cannot be adequately described. At every visit to Moscow accompanying the secretary of State, Dick Schifter arranged a reception for refuseniks at one of the apartments within our embassy compound. With time, fewer attended as the numbers emigrating increased, and we would exchange news about those who had left. My participation in this process was now minor, but it was vicarious, and I felt I had helped begin a successful process.*

Public diplomacy was also one of my responsibilities. I had been active and successful with the press in Madrid and Geneva. This led the United States Information Agency and its director, Charles Z. Wick, to call on me frequently for press conferences and overseas television appearances. Wick, a very energetic and wise public relations expert, would conscientiously send me a written report of embassy and foreign press reactions following each appearance. On December 22, 1987, for example, he sent me a copy of a letter he had sent to the president following the first television press conference with the People's Republic of China, in which he referred to "Max Kampelman's incisive exchange with journalists in Beijing."

While my trips to Geneva were now fewer and briefer, there were special assignments, including time in Central America talking to the leaders of Costa Rica, Honduras, and El Salvador. Panama and Noriega were also on the agenda. I was brought in to smooth over problems the department had with members of Congress on the Haitian revolution. I remember well a long meeting in Greece with Prime Minister Andreas Papandreou, an old and not always friendly acquaintance from my Minnesota days.

In June 1988, before deciding whether to make one final effort at coordinating the Central American democracies in a joint campaign to rid Nicaragua of its Sandinista dictatorship, George Shultz asked me to go down there to speak with each of the presidents. I did so and came away persuaded that the key figure was the sad, Hamlet-like, indecisive Oscar Arias of Costa Rica, who persuaded me to encourage Shultz to fly to the region. Shultz did so, only to find when he reached

---

* There is in my hands now a letter from Israel typical of scores I have received in recent years. It is from a lady whose name never reached the newspapers: "My son and I just received the good news that my refusenik husband . . . has been given permission to leave the Soviet Union. Thank you for helping make it possible for my family to be together again. May God bless and watch over you and your dear ones always." The letter is certainly blessing enough.

Costa Rica that Arias was again in a depressed, uncooperative frame of mind.

Elliot Abrams, our assistant secretary of State for Latin American affairs, asked me to help him in his efforts to persuade the head of the military junta ruling Chile, General Augusto Pinochet, to give way to a democratic regime. At different times, he brought to my office three members of the military junta running the country. I believe our efforts helped.

I kept abreast of Middle East problems, offering my advice where that was appropriate, but taking great care not to intervene where others had responsibility. On one occasion, George Shultz expressed his concern about the safety of our people in the embassy in Tel Aviv. Our embassy is in a public building not far from the sea, vulnerable to terrorist attacks, and Shultz asked me to find a solution. I did, overcoming problems that derived from the old argument about recognizing Jerusalem as the capital. The solution was to put up a new secure embassy structure in Tel Aviv and a much-needed new consulate building in Jerusalem that could serve as a formal embassy should political developments lead the president to have our embassy in Israel's capital. With Senator Jesse Helms's help, the Congress unanimously supported the solution, but I regret that the Israeli government has still unwisely not followed through on its end of the move. It rejected all sites for the Tel Aviv embassy proposed by the United States, while the sites it suggested were clearly unfit for Israel's best friend in the world. It was one of the incomplete tasks of my time in government, and both George Shultz and I were disappointed at Israel's shortsightedness.

The many varied and challenging responsibilities I assumed as counselor were highly satisfying, but it was evident to me and understood by all that I could not take my eyes off the talks continuing in Geneva. My work with Vorontsov when we would meet in Geneva was very important, but the prime attention clearly shifted to Washington and Moscow as 1987 matured. Shultz and Shevardnadze began to meet more frequently, and the Reagan-Gorbachev summits became a pattern. The Geneva negotiators increased the tempo of their work and, even though the most troublesome of the remaining issues were for the ministerial meetings to decide, the issues for Geneva were increasing in complexity and required meticulous attention and difficult bargaining. Last-minute snags inevitably developed. As major issues fell into place, issues that had earlier been considered minor became major. At one point in early summer 1987, Shultz and Shevardnadze decided to meet in Geneva to see if they could push the negotiations along and over the last hurdles. The secretary asked me to assert myself in his behalf and be creative. Karpov and I virtually took over the deal making and believed we had settled the remaining issues. We informed our principals. I took a rare sleeping pill and went to bed at about midnight, exhausted, while the working group was to put pencil to paper and record the agreements made. At about three A.M., I was awakened by a phone call. The working group was in sharp internal disagreement. A troubled Shevardnadze had called Shultz. Shultz asked me to return. I showered, and in a daze worked with Karpov. We put it together and obtained final agreement just as we were about to leave for the airport and the flight home. INF was in place and ready for signature when Gorbachev came to Washington on December 8, 1987.

The Gorbachev visit was exciting. My own role in it was satisfying and eventful. During the day, the ceremony at which the INF Treaty was signed by Reagan and Gorbachev was impressive and symbolic of what we hoped would be a new era of good feeling. On the last evening of the visit, the president and Mrs. Reagan hosted a grand dinner for the Gorbachevs to which Maggie and I were invited. Maggie, recovering from back surgery, relinquished her place to our youngest daughter, Sarah, who joined me as my date.

In the morning of the next day, during the last hours of the visit, we had problems over the wording of the final communique. We found it necessary to telephone Shultz, Carlucci, and Shevardnadze, who were having lunch with the president and Gorbachev at the residence quarters of the White House. We asked them to join us in the cabinet room. We were running into Soviet intransigence from its military with respect to the wording of the communique on the space negotiations. Shevardnadze quickly withdrew the Soviet objections, since our proposed wording was practically verbatim from a statement made by Gorbachev.

It rained during the closing afternoon ceremony, which took place on the White House lawn. I left the cabinet room to observe that ceremony and was drenched, in spite of an umbrella loaned to me by a Secret Service agent. A couple of days later, I received a handwritten card from Vice President Bush, which read: "Last Thursday in the rain, I looked up and saw you standing off on the side. I said to myself, something is out of whack here. There is the man who did as much as anyone, standing there without proper recognition or credit. You did a superb job, and I just wanted you to know how grateful I am to you for giving peace a chance."

It was a most satisfying end to a long process.

The next task was to persuade two-thirds of the Senate to support the INF Treaty during the ratification process.* Shultz sent a memorandum to all the appropriate offices in the building, putting me in charge of the ratification process for the Department of State. Since I saw no movement in the White House and was aware that our work product would receive careful scrutiny in the Senate, I assembled a group within State to meet regularly, daily when necessary, to prepare for the long detailed hearings we anticipated.

I was convinced we had the votes, but one could never be certain. We knew that Senator Helms headed a small group who would not trust the Soviets to comply with any treaty. Senator Malcolm Wallop of Wyoming, a Rhodes scholar and a conservative critic, would scrupulously examine every minute detail of the treaty. Most troublesome, there were deep scars flowing from the controversy on the meaning of the ABM Treaty, exacerbated by the inept way the White House treated the February 28 effort temporarily to rescue the SDI issue. Democrats like Sam Nunn of Georgia and Albert Gore of Tennessee were angry with the administration and would demand their pound of flesh.

Our job was cut out for us. Senator Alan Cranston, the Democratic whip, was very helpful in lining up Democratic senators and in keeping us informed of trouble spots as they arose. Senator Richard Lugar of Indiana was also extremely helpful with the moderate Republicans and with valuable information as to where we should concentrate our efforts.

George Shultz asked Paul Nitze and me to deal with a growing problem among the Democrats stimulated by Senator Nunn's understandable irritations. He took the position that since the president was establishing his right to interpret the ABM Treaty in a manner contra-

---

* During an appearance before the Committee on Foreign Affairs of the House of Representatives, I was asked whether the administration had given any thought to having the results of our arms reduction negotiations with the Soviets take the form of executive agreements requiring a majority approval of both houses of Congress rather than a two-thirds vote of the Senate. This was an expression of a House desire to play an increasing role in foreign policy, but it also had a pragmatic cast to it in that it might be easier to receive congressional approval for an executive agreement than for a treaty. I dodged the question, passed it on to the legal adviser at State, whose response, implying that a permanent rather than an interim agreement required a treaty, I forwarded to the committee. We all understood, however, that the Senate would institutionally insist on a treaty and would not act on an alternative. The House committee, however, to keep its oar in the process, did ask probing questions about the treaty, to which we always courteously responded.

dictory to an interpretation provided the Senate in 1972 by Richard Nixon, and, furthermore, that the change was announced without consulting the Senate, a serious constitutional issue was being raised that required clarification if the integrity of the Senate was to be maintained. What assurance would the Senate have, he asked, that some future president might not reinterpret the INF Treaty that was now before them for ratification? This position was receiving growing support in the Senate, particularly with the powerful Democratic leader, Senator Robert Byrd of West Virginia. Paul and I met with Nunn, Gore, and Byrd in an effort to deal with the problem. They understood that there was no way President Reagan could bind future presidents. We came up with a formula that we took back to George Shultz, who liked it.

In the meantime, the White House set up a clearing committee on ratification, which I was asked to join. I informed the committee of what Paul and I were undertaking. The next step was a breakfast meeting in Senator Byrd's office between Shultz and the leader plus the three chairmen of the committees with ratification responsibility: Nunn, chairman of the Senate Armed Services Committee; Dave Boren, chairman of the Senate Intelligence Committee; and Claiborne Pell, chairman of the Senate Foreign Relations Committee. Paul and I laid out our understanding of the agreement, and Shultz undertook to write a clarifying letter to the Senate setting forth our willingness to open up our records on the negotiations so that the Senate would have access to the history of the negotiations in the event interpretation problems arose. Everybody agreed.

Shultz left Byrd's office and walked immediately to the Senate Republican leader's office, where he brought Senator Robert Dole of Kansas up to date. We thought we had the problem licked until I heard from the White House that a number of Republicans, led by Senators Malcolm Wallop of Wyoming, Don Nichols of Oklahoma, Dan Quayle of Indiana, and Pete Wilson of California complained that we were working with the Democrats and not the Republicans in obtaining ratification. There may have been some feeling on the part of the White House that, since I was a Democrat, I could not be adequately sensitive to their problem. In any event, this caused some further strain and delays until it was resolved in accordance with our earlier agreement.

The questioning by the Senate was careful and intense. Moscow cooperated. At one point, I called in Soviet Ambassador Dubinin and handed him nine technical questions raised by the Senate to make

certain that the Soviets agreed with our interpretation of those technicalities, many of which dealt with on-site inspection. Shultz raised a
question with Shevardnadze about future technologies, and a day later
Dubinin came to me with a response: "I would like to confirm to you
once again that the Soviet side's understanding of this question is the
same as that of the U.S. side."

We received at the State Department about 1,500 questions from
senators. I insisted we respond to all of them as quickly as we could.
Many required clearance with the Defense Department and the White
House. Since the answers committed the president, there could be no
mistakes. But it all came together. The Senate vote for ratification was
overwhelming, with only five recorded opponents.

Prior to the Senate action, however, another problem arose. One
of our accomplishments in the INF Treaty was to authorize intrusive
verification procedures to make certain that our zero-zero agreement
would be complied with and that there would be no further production
or testing of nuclear missiles with a range of between 500 and 5,500
kilometers.

In late April, just as the treaty was to be presented to the Senate,
I was informed by the U.S. technical team, which had begun discussions with its Soviet counterpart on how to begin implementing the
treaty once it was operative, that serious differences had arisen about
the treaty's inspection provisions. The talks were secret, but there was
no way or desire to withhold the news from the Senate. Senators Robert Byrd and Robert Dole, the Democratic and Republican leaders,
jointly announced that the ratification debate would be postponed until
May 11 in order to help us resolve the inspection issues. I immediately
asked Soviet Ambassador Dubinin to meet with me and gave him a list
of issues that required a change of Soviet position, four of which we
considered urgent. The response was inadequate, and the solution to
the problems required a Shultz-Shevardnadze meeting in Geneva,
where Karpov and I were asked to step in. The Soviet negotiators
relented, with Shevardnadze accepting Karpov's position and overrul-
ing the Soviet military. Colin Powell, the national security adviser, and
I flew back to Washington on May 13 with satisfactory results and the
Senate proceeded with its deliberations on ratification.

Inspection, of course, not only permitted us to have observers in
the Soviet Union, but also permitted the Soviet Union to have observers in the United States. The chosen production facility agreed upon
by both countries was a Hercules plant in Magna, Utah. We had met
with the Utah senators, Orrin Hatch and Jake Garn, who agreed to

cooperate with us fully. Both then telephoned me to say that the Hercules Company, which wanted to cooperate, did not know how to begin. I met with the company officials in Senator Hatch's office so that they could have some feeling of having talked to a responsible official, but as a matter of fact, our government was still in the process of setting up the verification office within the Department of Defense. We were breaking new ground. The unknowns and questions were many. The company and the community did not know what was expected of them. I recommended that the Department of Defense undertake an immediate visit to the community, meet with the city officials and newspaper editors, as well as with community leaders to explain the desirability of the proper hospitality merged with proper security concerns. This was done, and a proper mechanism was established quietly and without further difficulty.*

There was optimism that the next treaty, START, designed to reduce strategic nuclear weapons by approximately 50 percent, would rapidly fall into place. That proved to be an impossible goal. We learned a great deal from our INF negotiations, particularly with respect to verification, but it is a great deal easier to verify an agreement that provides a zero result rather than one that would permit 6,000 warheads to remain after the agreement. If you have zero agreement and see one missile, you know there is a violation. If you permit 6,000 and see 500, the task remains of determining whether the 500 is part of the 6,000 or above that number. The verification task is formidable, particularly when we have never done it before.

It became clear to me that a START agreement in our interest was probably inevitable, given the rapidly developing political changes in the Soviet Union, but I also now saw that it would take time. The Senate understood the issue's complexity and would be suspicious of speedy movement. Our Defense Department also had a great deal to absorb and learn about how to preserve our national security in light of those contemplated reductions. On the other hand, too much of a delay would risk having an agreement in our interest derailed should there be further less favorable internal Soviet changes.

* Brigadier General Roland Lajoie, director of the On-Site Inspection Agency, after visiting Utah, responded to my concerns on July 5, 1988: "Just as you had suggested earlier this visit was beneficial in informing and reassuring the local residents . . . some people are delighted at the warming of U.S. and Soviet relations and the presence of Soviet inspectors in their midst; others expect the Soviet presence will bring economic benefit to the area; and of course there are others who feel threatened and concerned about a possible negative economic effect on the sensitive industries in the area and the presence of 'Soviet spies' in their midst . . ."

When I left government service on January 20, 1989, I expected a START agreement by the end of that year or shortly thereafter. It was then anticipated that the agreement would be signed by Presidents Bush and Gorbachev in February 1991, at a Moscow summit, but that was postponed. It is now a reality facing probable Senate approval. The position that I developed shortly after our negotiations began, that a START agreement would be achieved without an agreement on SDI, was confirmed. The agreements provided by START are important to us, but we should go farther.

We should also continue our negotiations on defense and space, but I believe that they should be expanded beyond SDI to examine how best to maintain stability in the world in the light of new and evolving technologies. In the meantime, it is important that the United States and the Soviet Union begin working on confidence building measures between us, such as annual exchanges of relevant data, meetings of experts, frequent briefings, notification of test satellites, mutual visits to laboratories, and opportunities for observing the work in which both countries are engaged in the field of strategic ballistic missile defense. We will all be helped if we can reduce the risk of technological surprise. I am convinced that a safer world is possible through defense, coupled with a reduction in weapons. The way to get there is through a negotiated cooperative transition with the Soviet Union. Instead of continuing to argue about how to interpret the ABM Treaty by referring to what we each think was the intent of those who drafted the agreement in 1972, we should assert what is in both of our interests today and decide that to be what was intended in 1972. This is really what we have been doing with our Constitution, and it has worked for us.

To have overseen our successful arms negotiations and to have established the groundwork for future arms agreements is gloriously satisfying. To receive recognition for it is especially satisfying. Reviewing the Geneva negotiating results on top of the successful CSCE Madrid talks with its resultant concluding document, the *Times* of London editorialized: "The achievement is very much Kampelman's own. In many ways, he has been the perfect negotiator—patient, cunning and unfailingly courteous." I don't know what I could have done at this time of my life that would have been more useful, or could have better employed my talents to serve my personal and lifelong hopes or our national interests. I look back knowing I did my best, having followed my heart and my conscience, in pursuit of worthy goals. With satisfaction, I think especially of the

than seventy-five years, an increase greater than has occurred in
revious ten thousand years of human history. Advanced comput-
ew materials, new biotechnological processes are rapidly altering
 phase of our lives, deaths, even reproduction. Looking ahead,
imensions of the changes to come during the lifetime of today's
gsters are probably beyond calculation or imagination. I read only
 weeks ago that a single computer chip just developed can hold
 than 64 million bytes of information.

These developments are stretching our minds and our grasp of
y to the outermost dimensions of our capacity to understand them.
we have had only the minutest glimpse of what our universe really
ur ignorance remains a sea. Our scientific knowledge is indeed a

We are brought up to believe that necessity is the mother of
tion. I suggest the corollary is also true: invention is the mother
cessity. The awesome technological and communication changes
ve have observed during our lifetime have made the world much
er. More than $1 trillion a day is instantaneously exchanged in
 twenty-four-hour period between one part of the world and the
—a sum nearly as large as the total annual budget of the United
s. There is no escaping the fact that the sound of a whisper or a
per in one part of the world can immediately be heard in all parts
 world. Canada cannot constructively deal with its acid rain prob-
without assistance from the United States. More than eighteen
ries pollute the Mediterranean. A drop in the Tokyo stock ex-
e has immediate repercussions in London and New York.

Wherever I go to speak, people who are aware of my negotiating
iences with the Soviet Union ask whether I ever predicted the
 changes we are now experiencing. I readily admit that prophecy
 one of my gifts. I agree with the alleged Chinese proverb that
iction is difficult, especially with respect to the future," and I
always rejected the advice that if you can't predict accurately,
t often. On the other hand, there is an explanation.

Technology and science and communication have all experienced
nse revolutions that have propelled humanity forward into "the
new world" of tomorrow. But there was no similar forward move-
in the world of politics and social organization. Indeed, when we
ler that men and women are still killing each other in wars and are
stilled with hate, our politics remain in many ways back in the
Ages. What we have been seeing in the last four or five years, it
 to me, is the world of politics catching up with the world of
e and technology.

day when a memo was distributed in the State Department announcing that I would be acting secretary of State that day while George
Shultz was away and that all outgoing cables to the world would go
out over my signature. It was only a symbol, but it measured a milepost on a long journey.

18

Beyond Pacifism to Peace: A Memorandum

To: The Reader

From: Max M. Kampelman

Re: The Coda Chapter

I sit down to write this concluding chapter a few hours after receiving a phone call from Simon Michael Bessie, my editor, publisher, and friend. He and I will meet in a few days to review his editorial comments and suggestions. In the meantime, he proposed that I prepare a short summary concluding chapter, putting it all together for myself and the reader—a coda. It's a good idea. Let me get started.

The call came on the eve of my seventieth birthday. Maggie and the children arranged to celebrate it at a Sunday daytime party in our home in Washington, attended by our personal and political friends and neighbors. Reunions are a luxury of longevity, a celebration by-product of surviving another year or another decade. I remember lying in my hospital bed in March 1987, wondering whether I would make it to my seventieth birthday. Mortality intrudes itself after a serious heart attack, never far from one's thoughts. To paraphrase Samuel Johnson,

it concentrates the mind wonderfully. Mine has
fulfilling life that has taken me places and allowe
never could have imagined in my wildest dreams

A friend recently talked to me about Henry S
three presidents—Taft, Hoover, and Franklin Ro
retary of State and twice secretary of War. Towar
he was deeply concerned with arms control. Mr. S
man who tries to work for the good, believing in
while he may suffer setback and even disaster, wil
The only deadly sin I know is cynicism." It is
avoid.

It is also appropriate that I quote here an u
hammmad Ali is reported to have said: "The man
at fifty the same as he did at twenty has wasted th
That remark has great truth and relevance for me
tieth year.

All human beings since the beginning of tim
been actors in a history, living it, but not necessa
Those of us living today have been fortunate in
have seen history change before our eyes ever
Every morning's newspaper is a dramatic page in
period since the beginning of human life, proba
riod in which fire was discovered, has experience
the period in which we live.

In my early years, there were no vitamin tal
no transcontinental telephones, no plastics, no
pantyhose, no fluorescent lights, no airlines, i
copies, no fax machines, no contact lenses, nc
antibiotics, no frozen foods, no television, no
chips, no computers. These developments and c
commonplace and have deeply altered our lives

During my lifetime, medical knowledge a
has reportedly increased more than tenfold, an
understatement. More than 80 percent of all sci
are probably alive today. Gene splicing has re
than 100,000 scientific journals annually publ
knowledge that pours out of the world's labo
lifespan is now nearly twice as great as it was v
were born. Indeed, in 1888, the year my mother
ancy at birth in the United States was about forty
below the current levels in India. Today, the life

When I retired from government service to rejoin my law firm on January 20, 1989, I agreed to serve as chairman of Freedom House, an organization founded by Eleanor Roosevelt and Wendell Willkie, designed to champion a bipartisan and nonpartisan approach to the advancement of freedom in our country and all over the world. One of our tasks is to issue an annual survey grading every country in the world, using well-established criteria for freedom. Our latest survey shows that there are more countries and people today who are "free" than there are those governed by societies that are "not free." This is the best human rights report card that the world has ever received. Liberal democracies, even in a fragile or embryonic form, far outnumber any other political system. We are seeing dramatic changes taking place or evolving in Chile and China, Poland and Paraguay, the Soviet Union and the Union of South Africa—different cultures and different parts of the earth. Not all people striving for human dignity have attained it, but the goal is universal because it is an integral part of the human character.

We are, furthermore, moved by the growing realization that democracy seems to work best. Governments and societies everywhere are discovering that keeping up with changes requires openness to new information, new ideas; it requires freedom that enables ingenuity to germinate and flourish. A closed, tightly controlled society cannot compete in a world experiencing an information explosion of technology and science that knows no national boundaries. During the period I was growing up, when one thought of Latin America, one thought of macho military dictators. Today Latin American governments are, in the main, democratic. In the Middle East, although Israel remains for the moment the only democracy in the region, the picture is changing, as elections and competing political parties intrude in Algeria, Tunisia, Egypt, and Jordan. Even in remote Africa, we note recognition of a "hurricane of change [toward democracy] which is now irreversible."*

Nations of the world are becoming inexorably interdependent. We are clearly in a time when no society can isolate itself or its people from new ideas and information any more than one can escape the winds whose currents affect us all. National boundaries can keep out vaccines, but those boundaries cannot keep out germs or ideas or broadcasts.

Until quite recently, the label "Made in the United States" or "Made in Japan" meant something. Today, the global economy evolving from the new world of science and technology means that items of vital importance and high value can be produced essentially in many

* Statement by the executive director of the sixteen-member Economic Community of West African States. *New York Times*, April 14, 1991.

different locations, serving peoples and industries efficiently in all corners of our world. Dr. Robert Reich of Harvard University recently illustrated the change, referring to precision ice hockey equipment. He pointed out they were designed in Sweden, financed in Canada, assembled in Cleveland and in Denmark, for distribution in North America and Europe, respectively, out of alloys whose molecular structure was researched and patented in Delaware and fabricated in Japan.

He continued that when an American buys a Pontiac automobile, which he believes to be American, he automatically engages, knowingly or not, in an extensive international transaction. Of the $10,000 he probably paid his General Motors dealer, about $3,000 goes to South Korea for routine labor and assembly operations; $1,850 to Japan for advanced components, engines, transaxles, and electronics; $700 to Germany for styling and design engineering; $400 to Taiwan, Singapore, and Japan for small components, $250 to Britain for advertising; and about $50 to Ireland and Barbados for data processing. This leaves less than $4,000, which goes to strategists, lawyers, bankers, insurance brokers, healthcare workers, and General Motors shareholders in many countries all over the world.

In response to these realities, nations are by agreement, knowingly or not, curtailing their sovereign powers over many of their own domestic and security affairs. Under the Universal Declaration of Human Rights and the Helsinki Final Act, nations undertake to behave humanely toward their own citizens and to recognize the right of other states to evaluate that internal behavior.

When I began negotiating with the Soviet Union in Madrid, the Soviets protested my intense criticism of their human rights record, saying that the United States was improperly interfering in their internal affairs. Three years later, by the end of 1985, the Soviets were accepting the discussion of human rights as part of the agenda of meetings between President Reagan and President Gorbachev and between George Shultz and Eduard Shevardnadze.* That pattern continues

---

* The dramatic change became vivid for me during one of the early meetings between Shultz and Shevardnadze in Washington. The secretary of State, consistent with his continuing effort to develop a good personal relationship with his counterpart, suggested an informal chat over coffee in his private office before the nine A.M. opening of the formal talks. Our two delegations were mingling and waiting in the beautifully spacious and historic eighth-floor reception rooms. Finally, as host, Shultz said to the Soviet foreign minister: "Well, it's time to get started. They're waiting for us. Now, let's see. What's the first item on our agenda?" Without a moment's hesitation, Shevardnadze responded: "We have an agenda. We always start with human rights!" The significance of the moment was overwhelming as the secretary, Roz Ridgway, and I looked at one another and smiled.

today with George Bush and James Baker in their dealings with the Soviets.

Nothing is more sacred to the more traditional concept of sovereignty than control over one's military forces. Yet today, as a result of the INF Treaty that we negotiated in Geneva, observers and on-site inspectors are given the right to inspect military facilities and maneuvers within each other's boundaries. We are accepting "interference" and "infringement" with vital ingredients of traditional sovereignty. The Soviets are now struggling and anguishing over how to further adjust the doctrine of "sovereignty" to the demands of the Baltic republics and other national groups demanding and receiving independent recognition.

It took a failed coup, but the current Soviet leadership fully appreciates the urgent need for drastic internal changes if the Soviet Union is to be a significant part of the twenty-first century. The Soviet economy is working poorly. Massive military power has provided the Soviets with a presence that has reached all parts of the world, but this military superpower cannot hide the fact that its economic and social weaknesses are deep. The Soviet Union's awesome internal police force provided continuity to its system of government, but a Russia that during czarist days exported food cannot today feed its own people. Productivity is low. With absenteeism, corruption, and alcoholism, internal morale is bad and becoming worse. It is no wonder that the Communist party is being eliminated from the country.

Let us look for a moment at the issue of health care by way of a dramatic example of why the Soviet Union is today facing disintegration. Soviet figures tell us that a total of 1.2 million beds are in hospitals with no hot water; every sixth bed is in a hospital with no running water; 30 percent of Soviet hospitals do not have indoor toilets; one-half of Soviet elementary schools have no central heating, running water, or sewage systems. The Rand Graduate School of Public Policy recently reported authoritatively that by any reasonable definition of poverty, 79 percent of the elderly in the USSR are in that condition. There are fewer automobiles per capita in the Soviet Union than among the blacks in South Africa. The Soviet Union, which spans eleven time zones and contains nearly 300 million people, has fewer miles of paved roads than California.

The problem is not the character and cultures of the peoples who make up the Soviet Union. The Soviet peoples are proud and talented, with rich histories and cultures. Its citizens desire peace and human dignity as much as any American, but the government that has set policy and their system have caused them problems and us concern over the years. It is that system which is under attack from within and which was fighting to maintain its place of power.

During one of our visits to Moscow, George Shultz told our ambassador, Jack Matlock, that he and his wife would like to free themselves from the negotiations one evening so that he could meet with independent intellectuals from different walks of life. Jack arranged a dinner at a cooperative restaurant, one of the few privately owned restaurants in the city. The group he assembled was impressive, as was their dedication to the idea of liberty. We were in a public restaurant, and all believed the KGB was someplace at an adjoining table listening to what we were saying.

Shultz suggested that each of the Soviets make some brief statement of experiences and aspirations for their country. The responses ran from a historian who said he was ashamed that the only history books he could depend on for accuracy were written and published in the West, to a poet who said he was in the United States in December 1979 when Soviet troops invaded Afghanistan and felt humiliated at what his government had done. The last Soviet participant was an officer in the cinematographers' union. He sat next to me, and in the course of his contribution mentioned a recent visit to Moscow by Sylvester Stallone, the motion picture actor, who was interested in producing a *Rocky* sequel in the Soviet Union. In an effort to sell his idea, he apparently offered to reshoot part of his last *Rocky* film, changing the ending so that the Soviet boxer rather than the American would win the bout. In response to our laughter as we listened to the story, he added: "Mr. Stallone did not realize that our audiences in the Soviet Union were rooting for the American to win!"

In a public statement while still in office, former Soviet Foreign Minister Shevardnadze said: "In what do we, who have the highest infant mortality rate in the world, take pride . . . who are you and who do you wish to be? A country which is feared or a country which is respected? A country of power or a country of kindness?" The new leaders of the Soviet Union are indeed fully aware of its problems. The failure of their system is compounded by the immenseness and diversity of their size. I am reminded that Charles de Gaulle once exclaimed in exasperation about the difficulty of governing a country whose people made and ate more than two hundred kinds of cheese. One can only imagine the difficulties faced by Gorbachev in governing a people with more than two hundred different languages and ethnic cultures. The Soviet leadership, furthermore, is also aware of our strengths, reflecting the vitality of our values and the healthy dynamism of our system.

Here, perhaps, is an explanation of why I have frequently found myself separated from the mainstream of American liberalism as it began to assert itself in the 1960s. While Communism was failing throughout the world and while our own system was proving its economic, social, and political success, I found growing resistance within our "new left" to the realities of Communist failure and disdain about our own system. It is disturbing that as recently as 1984, Harvard Professor John Kenneth Galbraith, a fine scholar and human being and an internationally known liberal spokesman, wrote that "the Soviet system has made great material progress in recent years" and that the system "succeeds because, in contrast with the Western industrial economies, it makes full use of its manpower." I unhappily have found American liberalism becoming more anti-establishment and more adversarial toward national patriotic values. Hostility toward spending for national defense became instinctive. This was a change from the spirit of Roosevelt, Truman, Stevenson, Kennedy, and Humphrey—the leaders I and America had come to identify with the true spirit of American liberalism: pragmatic, nonideologic, and patriotic.

I had begun to leave my pacifist moorings shortly after the end of World War II. The explosion of the nuclear bomb, dropped from extraordinary heights by pilots pushing a button without any physical or visual connection with the destruction and death caused by the bomb, was a vivid demonstration to me that pacifism, or nonviolent resistance to evil, was no longer appropriate in international relations. To this day, I believe in the power of love in interpersonal relations, but love directed toward the missile or the distant anonymous human being pushing the button would be useless. The alternative, therefore, once diplomacy and other steps short of violence fail to destroy or end the evil, is either submission to it or a reluctant use of force and violence to resist it.

In addition, I became persuaded by experience that the existence of military power and the readiness to use it serve to deter aggression and military adventurism—a belief that is anathema to pacifism and pacifists.

Finally, the decision by mainstream pacifist organizations to engage in political action by identifying themselves with what I considered to be irresponsible far-left positions and leaders antagonized and disappointed me. At a time when the ideas and values of Western democracy were gathering force in so many parts of the world, pacifist organizations seemed to be advancing the agenda of anti-democratic forces. That was my impression, even though I know that many pacifists would have been horrified at the thought, being so proudly preoccupied by the nobility of their motives and consciences. At a time when it was clear that the Soviet agenda was failing and its system was rotten to the core, pacifist organizations seemed to be emphasizing American policy as the primary obstacle to peace. There seemed to be no awareness of the reality that the peaceful resolution of disputes in so many parts of the world became possible only when Soviet policy began to change.

The theme of the political pacifist movement became "anti-anti-Communist." This seemed absolutely incomprehensible to me at a time when growing dissident movements in the communist world and challenges to Marxism-Leninism were all part of real and effective and important anti-Communist movements. It is reported that Armando Valladares, a Cuban Christian and Democrat whom Castro imprisoned for twenty-two years, was profoundly dismayed when he found that religious pacifists were not at all embracing him but seemed to be embracing his tormentors.

The identification of increasing numbers of pacifists and church organizations with attempts at "high politics" rather than the higher ground of morality has meant an important loss to society. An alternative to war as a means of securing peace with dignity when it is threatened is sorely needed. It isn't just that the pacifist movement, whose predecessors directed their moral and intellectual energies in that direction, has lost credibility, it is that society has lost the benefit of that higher morality. It remains vital to teach by words and example that love sometimes can overcome; that hatred destroys; that humankind, including the enemy, is one. These are historic pacifist goals, but they were lost in the noise of radical protest politics.

The Democratic party was influenced by the same destructive trends. I remember listening to New York Governor Mario Cuomo's speech at the San Francisco convention of the Democratic party in 1984. The convention crowd and the press were with him and he was indeed a brilliant orator, but I was convinced he had lost a large number of the voters and me. His compassion appealed to me, but the America he described was not an America that I recognized, or that I felt most Americans would recognize. He sought to counteract Ronald Reagan's emphasis on a united and healing America by depicting Ronald Reagan's America as callous and careless, drug-ridden, polluted, violent, declining, homeless, hopeless, insecure, intolerant, with neglected children and neglected aged. At least that was the message that came across to me. Cuomo was applauded by the new American left, but I felt that they and he had America all wrong. Whatever the inadequacies of the Reagan administration and its domestic policy—and I was sensitive and not blind to them—it seemed quite clear that the characterization was a grossly excessive one and our economy had grown stronger under Reagan.

A dramatic and most disturbing illustration of my dissatisfaction with the Democratic Party came in early 1991, when the party's leadership in the House of Representatives filled four of five vacancies on the House Intelligence Committee. One of those four was Representative Ron Dellums of California, who, I learned, had been a vocal champion of the violence-prone Black Panther Party in California; had publicly identified himself with the U.S. Communist Party newspaper, *The People's Daily World;* and had participated in the Moscow organized World Peqace Council, which, according to public Soviet sources, received 90 percent of its funding from the Kremlin. With the American invasion of Grenada, certain papers were captured linking the congressman and his staff with Castro and the Communist movement in Grenada. Dellums himself was quoted in 1980 as telling an audience in California: "We should totally dismantle every intelligence agency in this country piece by piece, nail by nail, brick by brick." To select him for membership on the important and sensitive Intelligence Committee was a clear illustration of why large numbers of Americans have lost confidence in the Democratic Party's qualifications to govern in areas of national security.

The increase in drug addiction and in homelessness is an American disgrace. But how can we ignore the fact that the homeless problem was clearly exacerbated by the "liberal" drive to push people out of mental hospitals where they belonged and where they could be medicated as needed? The *New York Times*, in a perceptive editorial (December 30, 1990) caught the essence of this problem in observing: "Most of the ragged, homeless people who create this sense of menace are not, first of all, homeless; their fundamental problem is mental illness."

A growing number of Americans find it obnoxious to be approached by homeless vagrants sprawling or begging on our streets. I, too, feel victimized by the "liberal" legal reform program that threw mentally ill people into the streets and led courts to outlaw city vagrancy and no-loitering ordinances. A community should be able to prevent people from sleeping on sidewalks, in hallways, or in public places, where they are frequently surrounded by filth and clutter. These homeless should be provided indoor shelters and required to use them rather than sleep in the street. Statutes can be clearly drafted to provide for public health, safety, and morals with sufficient clarity and precision to protect them from constitutional attack. Compassion for the homeless does not require ignoring the sensitivities or safety of the larger community. But there is a real homeless problem that must be directly addressed economically and socially. It is tied directly to the problem of poverty.

There is more poverty in the United States than most of us appreciate. Our society must deal with it decisively through strengthening our economy and our social structure. But we must also identify it properly. We should not ignore the official poverty statistics from the United States Census Bureau.* The report shows 31.5 million persons in "poverty," but other available statistics, according to the Heritage Foundation, fill out the picture with additional relevant data. These data tell us that 38 percent of those poor own their own homes with a median value of $39,200; more than 100,000 own homes with a value in excess of $200,000; some 62 percent of poor households own a car, with 14 percent owning two or more cars; nearly half of all poor households have air conditioning; and 31 percent have microwave ovens.†

Clearly, these figures should not blind us to the misery that affects too many poverty-stricken Americans, but exaggerating or distorting that problem does not help us to deal constructively with it. The fact of the matter is that a large number of our "poor" are better housed, better fed, and own more personal property than did the average American throughout most of this century. For an international comparison, using the same astounding but data-filled Heritage Foundation report, the average "poor" American lives in a larger house or apartment than does the average West European; eats far more meat; is more likely to own a car and a dishwasher; and enjoys more basic modern amenities, such as indoor toilets, than do West Europeans in general.

So much for statistics and averages. In human terms, however, the problems of poverty are appalling. The urban underclass problem,

* The Census Bureau counts as "poor" any household with a "cash income" less than the official poverty threshold in 1989 of $12,675 for a family of four. This income takes no account of assets and does not include welfare payments. The latter are estimated as more than $11,120 for every poor household.

There is great uncertainty as to the number of homeless in our country. For a long time we were told that 3,000,000 Americans are homeless each night. There was never a justification for that figure. One day last year the U.S. Census Bureau counted 250,000 homeless, clearly too low. The Urban Institute in a 1988 study came up with 600,000 as a maximum estimate. A number between 250,000 and 600,000 is probably a defensible estimate, and a disgrace.

† "How Poor Are America's Poor?" *Backgrounder*, September 21, 1990.

particularly as it relates to blacks in our country, creates social pathologies that stand in sharp contrast with the new opportunities that have opened for blacks to enter the mainstream of American life. Jesse Jackson has said that drugs are doing more damage to blacks than the Ku Klux Klan ever did. Glenn C. Loury of Harvard reports that in big-city ghettos, black unemployment often exceeds 40 percent. Large numbers are dropping out of the economy—not in school, not working, not actively seeking work. In the inner cities, far more than half of the black babies are born out of wedlock, and, government reports show, black babies are dying at almost twice the rate of white babies. Loury reports that black girls between the ages of fifteen and nineteen constitute the most fertile population of any group in the industrialized world. Only about one black student in seven scores above the fiftieth percentile in college admission tests due to inadequate early education. Blacks, whose life expectancy keeps declining due to homicides and AIDS, constitute approximately half of the imprisoned felons in the nation, and roughly 40 percent of those murdered in the United States are black men killed by other black men. Homicide is the leading cause of death among blacks between the ages of fifteen and forty-four.

Here is an unmet challenge to the leadership of our nation. There is no developing consensus, even within the black community, on how best to respond to this challenge. Some blame all of this on racism, a continuing disease but only a partial explanation. I am convinced that there must be a greater sense of developing self-reliance within the community itself. The values of responsibility, work, family, and schooling must be emphasized, but this too is only a partial solution.

Too many slogans surround the political argumentation and analysis of this problem. It is obviously important to broaden and strengthen the black middle class. We must, of course, seek new ways to lift people from poverty. Government alone is inadequate, and so is inner self-help and discipline. Our country has always accepted the reality of social support. This has been one of the foundations upon which our society has strengthened itself. J. Kenneth Blackwell, former mayor of Cincinnati, now U.S. ambassador to the UN Human Rights Commission, points out that whether we are talking about "barn raising, field clearing or quilting bees, Americans have banded together to help one another since frontier days."* This has also necessarily come to include government involvement in the process. An agenda for

* "Strengthening the Social Pillars of the Black Community," speech delivered for Black History Month to the Heritage Foundation, Washington, D.C., February 27, 1990.

progress in dealing with the underclass is going to cost money. Plugging the holes of the social net we erected to keep people from becoming unduly victimized by economic and social pressures must be supplemented by an emphasis on business development, business ownership, and home ownership.

In that connection, demographically we are probably on the way to a labor shortage and a shortage of skills in our work force. A broad national consensus is required to develop government and private programs that emphasize self-reliance, remove the crutches of government dependency, and stimulate the values of responsibility and cooperation.

I have been troubled by the continued, albeit declining, racism in the white community, but also by growing racism in the black community. "Black" is no more a justification for entitlement than "white" is a justification for privilege. White racism, ugly as it is, is in general disrepute; black racism is too often unassailed and rarely challenged, with some "experts" ludicrously arguing that, by definition, blacks cannot be racist. Witness Jesse Jackson's frequent flirtations with anti-Semitism and the obsequiousness displayed toward him at the 1988 Democratic party convention. Witness too the growing acceptance among the established black leadership of Louis Farrakhan and his Nation of Islam, who was crowned with respectability with an invitation to speak to the Congressional Black Caucus in spite of his constant virulent anti-Semitism.

The continued existence of an "underclass," accompanied by the drugs that are decimating that segment of our people, threatens the future stability of our society. I am not a bit pleased that our society, in recent years, seems to be impotent in meeting the urgent needs of our people and our country, foreign as well as domestic. Our roads and bridges and waterways need work. We have far to go to protect our environment. We do not adequately help our cities or conduct an effective war against drugs. We do not help Eastern Europe as much as we should. We have an urgent need to improve our education and stimulate our research and development. Our mental hospitals are in terrible shape. We have law observance and law enforcement problems. In many ways, our country is in a state of disrepair.

We are the richest country in the world, but we refuse to mobilize the resources available to us. We have too long been paralyzed by the rash pledge that our leaders would not raise taxes or levy new taxes. To a large extent also, we are simply unable to mobilize our will to begin a necessary national renovation program. We have the capacity to deal effectively with our remaining problems once we have the national will and the national leadership to do so. The American people are inclined and can be motivated to do what is necessary to attain a just society. We have proven we can do so. I, for one, have always agreed with Mr. Justice Holmes, who said: "Taxes are what we pay for civilized society." I believe that is more than a good bargain.

We have every reason to be proud of our America in the international field. In 1950, the world outside the United States was just emerging from postwar rubble. Our allies were poor, and we set about to make them richer. We succeeded. It makes no sense for us to believe that we are poor just because our friends, who were destitute then, are now enjoying prosperity. Their prosperity, and that of Germany and Japan, has helped us.

People all over the world are standing up and unexpectedly and enthusiastically loudly reciting the American Declaration of Independence or erecting replicas of the Statue of Liberty. It seems as if the whole world is working to emulate the free market and the free politics that are the heart of our system. Our influence is decisive all over the world—and is channeled and directed toward democracy and human dignity.

Have we made mistakes? Yes, and we will continue to do so. The United States democracy is now the oldest stable continuing democratic system in the world. Nevertheless, in many ways, we are still a young and developing country. We did not seek the role of world leader, and our people today still tend to shy away from it. Our relative geographic isolation, our pursuit of liberty, our bountiful natural resources, and our productive people made us strong, so that by the end of the Second World War, our strength was evident to all. We were somewhat like a young giant among nations, and being a giant is not easy. It is not easy living with a giant, and our friends learned that. Being strong, the giant can afford to be gentle, and we usually were. But the giant is also, at times, awkward. Good intentions are not always so interpreted by others, and we have learned that. Giants sometimes stumble, and when they do, others feel the vibrations of the fall. We have made mistakes because we are not accustomed to leadership and hesitant about the responsibilities it entails. Too often our policies, at best, have been accompanied by fits and starts that frequently bedevil and confuse both friends and foes.

Today, it is the Middle East that bedevils and taunts us and tests our ability to lead in a post–cold war period. The future is uncertain. But I am convinced that the Middle East cannot escape the forces of history that are moving the world toward greater democracy, liberty, and human dignity. I have little doubt that the Middle East that is emerging out of the current turmoil and war is one that will reflect those aspirations of its people, despite the current religious, social, and political impediments. This will alter the forms of government in the area and change their social order. Today, only Israel is a democracy with full and free elections. This will spread. Tomorrow, more peoples in the Middle East will vote in societies that are more free than they are today.

It will not be easy. The Middle East today seems to represent the seat of resistance to the changes that are enveloping the world. A number of years ago, a British musical was entitled *Stop the World—I Want to Get Off*. I think of that title frequently as I observe the deep pockets of resistance to our evolving world. It is understandable that the Middle East is the center of that resistance today, but the resistance is elsewhere, too. We see it in the Soviet Union and China. The world is moving too fast for many. They are unaccustomed to the speed. They fear the change. What will it do to their children? What is it doing to their religion and their traditions? They are not comfortable with the change. They want to be comfortable. They therefore withdraw to the traditional, the familiar, the tribal. They fight to hold on to those patterns of life with which they are familiar and comfortable. One can try to hold back the sun by putting blinders on one's eyes, but the tomorrow will inevitably appear.

We will have to face this new evolving reality in the Middle East. Royal families will probably go. A Palestinian state is likely to arise in Jordan. Revolutions will topple dictators. Our energies must be directed to produce political competition and greater freedom. Our hope is that this, in turn, will inject greater rationality into the political and international processes in the area.

In the meantime, the major task under way in Eastern Europe is politically to redefine the relationship between the individual and the state and economically to introduce the concept of competition and free markets. Much of Eastern Europe is now in many ways becoming Central Europe in philosophy and thought, and not only in geography. There is a search for new political structures to guarantee civil liberties, curtail and regulate governmental power, assure a free press, and insulate the judiciary and its integrity from political dictatorship. One characteristic of American government that is attracting keen interest is our institutional separation of power—in effect, checks and balances.*

---

* The American Bar Association recently created a special committee on which Justice Sandra O'Connor serves. One of its major tasks is to help the government and lawyers in the emerging democracies of Eastern and Central Europe to develop the institutions and concepts required for a rule of law society. I am a member of that committee. I am also vice chairman of the International Media Fund, designated to

day when a memo was distributed in the State Department announcing that I would be acting secretary of State that day while George Shultz was away and that all outgoing cables to the world would go out over my signature. It was only a symbol, but it measured a milepost on a long journey.

Beyond Pacifism to Peace:
A Memorandum

To: The Reader

From: Max M. Kampelman

Re: The Coda Chapter

I sit down to write this concluding chapter a few hours after receiving a phone call from Simon Michael Bessie, my editor, publisher, and friend. He and I will meet in a few days to review his editorial comments and suggestions. In the meantime, he proposed that I prepare a short summary concluding chapter, putting it all together for myself and the reader—a coda. It's a good idea. Let me get started.

The call came on the eve of my seventieth birthday. Maggie and the children arranged to celebrate it at a Sunday daytime party in our home in Washington, attended by our personal and political friends and neighbors. Reunions are a luxury of longevity, a celebration by-product of surviving another year or another decade. I remember lying in my hospital bed in March 1987, wondering whether I would make it to my seventieth birthday. Mortality intrudes itself after a serious heart attack, never far from one's thoughts. To paraphrase Samuel Johnson, it concentrates the mind wonderfully. Mine has been a varied and fulfilling life that has taken me places and allowed me to do things I never could have imagined in my wildest dreams.

A friend recently talked to me about Henry Stimson, who served three presidents—Taft, Hoover, and Franklin Roosevelt. He was secretary of State and twice secretary of War. Toward the end of his life, he was deeply concerned with arms control. Mr. Stimson wrote: "The man who tries to work for the good, believing in its eventual victory, while he may suffer setback and even disaster, will never know defeat. The only deadly sin I know is cynicism." It is a sin I have tried to avoid.

It is also appropriate that I quote here an unlikely source. Muhammmad Ali is reported to have said: "The man who views the world at fifty the same as he did at twenty has wasted thirty years of his life." That remark has great truth and relevance for me as I pass my seventieth year.

All human beings since the beginning of time have, by definition, been actors in a history, living it, but not necessarily being aware of it. Those of us living today have been fortunate in that we know it. We have seen history change before our eyes every day on television. Every morning's newspaper is a dramatic page in that history book. No period since the beginning of human life, probably including the period in which fire was discovered, has experienced as much change as the period in which we live.

In my early years, there were no vitamin tablets, no refrigerators, no transcontinental telephones, no plastics, no manmade fibers, no pantyhose, no fluorescent lights, no airlines, no airmail, no photocopies, no fax machines, no contact lenses, no air conditioning, no antibiotics, no frozen foods, no television, no transistors, no microchips, no computers. These developments and dozens more are today commonplace and have deeply altered our lives.

During my lifetime, medical knowledge available to physicians has reportedly increased more than tenfold, and that may be a vast understatement. More than 80 percent of all scientists who ever lived are probably alive today. Gene splicing has replaced leeches. More than 100,000 scientific journals annually publish the flood of new knowledge that pours out of the world's laboratories. The average lifespan is now nearly twice as great as it was when my grandparents were born. Indeed, in 1888, the year my mother was born, life expectancy at birth in the United States was about forty-seven years, ten years below the current levels in India. Today, the life expectancy at birth is more than seventy-five years, an increase greater than has occurred in the previous ten thousand years of human history. Advanced computers, new materials, new biotechnological processes are rapidly altering every phase of our lives, deaths, even reproduction. Looking ahead, the dimensions of the changes to come during the lifetime of today's youngsters are probably beyond calculation or imagination. I read only a few weeks ago that a single computer chip just developed can hold more than 64 million bytes of information.

These developments are stretching our minds and our grasp of reality to the outermost dimensions of our capacity to understand them. And we have had only the minutest glimpse of what our universe really is. Our ignorance remains a sea. Our scientific knowledge is indeed a drop.

We are brought up to believe that necessity is the mother of invention. I suggest the corollary is also true: invention is the mother of necessity. The awesome technological and communication changes that we have observed during our lifetime have made the world much smaller. More than $1 trillion a day is instantaneously exchanged in every twenty-four-hour period between one part of the world and the next—a sum nearly as large as the total annual budget of the United States. There is no escaping the fact that the sound of a whisper or a whimper in one part of the world can immediately be heard in all parts of the world. Canada cannot constructively deal with its acid rain problem without assistance from the United States. More than eighteen countries pollute the Mediterranean. A drop in the Tokyo stock exchange has immediate repercussions in London and New York.

Wherever I go to speak, people who are aware of my negotiating experiences with the Soviet Union ask whether I ever predicted the world changes we are now experiencing. I readily admit that prophecy is not one of my gifts. I agree with the alleged Chinese proverb that "prediction is difficult, especially with respect to the future," and I have always rejected the advice that if you can't predict accurately, predict often. On the other hand, there is an explanation.

Technology and science and communication have all experienced immense revolutions that have propelled humanity forward into "the brave new world" of tomorrow. But there was no similar forward movement in the world of politics and social organization. Indeed, when we consider that men and women are still killing each other in wars and are still instilled with hate, our politics remain in many ways back in the Dark Ages. What we have been seeing in the last four or five years, it seems to me, is the world of politics catching up with the world of science and technology.

When I retired from government service to rejoin my law firm on January 20, 1989, I agreed to serve as chairman of Freedom House, an organization founded by Eleanor Roosevelt and Wendell Willkie, designed to champion a bipartisan and nonpartisan approach to the advancement of freedom in our country and all over the world. One of our tasks is to issue an annual survey grading every country in the world, using well-established criteria for freedom. Our latest survey shows that there are more countries and people today who are "free" than there are those governed by societies that are "not free." This is the best human rights report card that the world has ever received. Liberal democracies, even in a fragile or embryonic form, far outnumber any other political system. We are seeing dramatic changes taking place or evolving in Chile and China, Poland and Paraguay, the Soviet Union and the Union of South Africa—different cultures and different parts of the earth. Not all people striving for human dignity have attained it, but the goal is universal because it is an integral part of the human character.

We are, furthermore, moved by the growing realization that democracy seems to work best. Governments and societies everywhere are discovering that keeping up with changes requires openness to new information, new ideas; it requires freedom that enables ingenuity to germinate and flourish. A closed, tightly controlled society cannot compete in a world experiencing an information explosion of technology and science that knows no national boundaries. During the period I was growing up, when one thought of Latin America, one thought of macho military dictators. Today Latin American governments are, in the main, democratic. In the Middle East, although Israel remains for the moment the only democracy in the region, the picture is changing, as elections and competing political parties intrude in Algeria, Tunisia, Egypt, and Jordan. Even in remote Africa, we note recognition of a "hurricane of change [toward democracy] which is now irreversible."*

Nations of the world are becoming inexorably interdependent. We are clearly in a time when no society can isolate itself or its people from new ideas and information any more than one can escape the winds whose currents affect us all. National boundaries can keep out vaccines, but those boundaries cannot keep out germs or ideas or broadcasts.

Until quite recently, the label "Made in the United States" or "Made in Japan" meant something. Today, the global economy evolving from the new world of science and technology means that items of vital importance and high value can be produced essentially in many

* Statement by the executive director of the sixteen-member Economic Community of West African States. *New York Times*, April 14, 1991.

different locations, serving peoples and industries efficiently in all corners of our world. Dr. Robert Reich of Harvard University recently illustrated the change, referring to precision ice hockey equipment. He pointed out they were designed in Sweden, financed in Canada, assembled in Cleveland and in Denmark, for distribution in North America and Europe, respectively, out of alloys whose molecular structure was researched and patented in Delaware and fabricated in Japan.

He continued that when an American buys a Pontiac automobile, which he believes to be American, he automatically engages, knowingly or not, in an extensive international transaction. Of the $10,000 he probably paid his General Motors dealer, about $3,000 goes to South Korea for routine labor and assembly operations; $1,850 to Japan for advanced components, engines, transaxles, and electronics; $700 to Germany for styling and design engineering; $400 to Taiwan, Singapore, and Japan for small components, $250 to Britain for advertising; and about $50 to Ireland and Barbados for data processing. This leaves less than $4,000, which goes to strategists, lawyers, bankers, insurance brokers, healthcare workers, and General Motors shareholders in many countries all over the world.

In response to these realities, nations are by agreement, knowingly or not, curtailing their sovereign powers over many of their own domestic and security affairs. Under the Universal Declaration of Human Rights and the Helsinki Final Act, nations undertake to behave humanely toward their own citizens and to recognize the right of other states to evaluate that internal behavior.

When I began negotiating with the Soviet Union in Madrid, the Soviets protested my intense criticism of their human rights record, saying that the United States was improperly interfering in their internal affairs. Three years later, by the end of 1985, the Soviets were accepting the discussion of human rights as part of the agenda of meetings between President Reagan and President Gorbachev and between George Shultz and Eduard Shevardnadze.* That pattern continues

---

* The dramatic change became vivid for me during one of the early meetings between Shultz and Shevardnadze in Washington. The secretary of State, consistent with his continuing effort to develop a good personal relationship with his counterpart, suggested an informal chat over coffee in his private office before the nine A.M. opening of the formal talks. Our two delegations were mingling and waiting in the beautifully spacious and historic eighth-floor reception rooms. Finally, as host, Shultz said to the Soviet foreign minister: "Well, it's time to get started. They're waiting for us. Now, let's see. What's the first item on our agenda?" Without a moment's hesitation, Shevardnadze responded: "We have an agenda. We always start with human rights!" The significance of the moment was overwhelming as the secretary, Roz Ridgway, and I looked at one another and smiled.

today with George Bush and James Baker in their dealings with the Soviets.

Nothing is more sacred to the more traditional concept of sovereignty than control over one's military forces. Yet today, as a result of the INF Treaty that we negotiated in Geneva, observers and on-site inspectors are given the right to inspect military facilities and maneuvers within each other's boundaries. We are accepting "interference" and "infringement" with vital ingredients of traditional sovereignty. The Soviets are now struggling and anguishing over how to further adjust the doctrine of "sovereignty" to the demands of the Baltic republics and other national groups demanding and receiving independent recognition.

It took a failed coup, but the current Soviet leadership fully appreciates the urgent need for drastic internal changes if the Soviet Union is to be a significant part of the twenty-first century. The Soviet economy is working poorly. Massive military power has provided the Soviets with a presence that has reached all parts of the world, but this military superpower cannot hide the fact that its economic and social weaknesses are deep. The Soviet Union's awesome internal police force provided continuity to its system of government, but a Russia that during czarist days exported food cannot today feed its own people. Productivity is low. With absenteeism, corruption, and alcoholism, internal morale is bad and becoming worse. It is no wonder that the Communist party is being eliminated from the country.

Let us look for a moment at the issue of health care by way of a dramatic example of why the Soviet Union is today facing disintegration. Soviet figures tell us that a total of 1.2 million beds are in hospitals with no hot water; every sixth bed is in a hospital with no running water; 30 percent of Soviet hospitals do not have indoor toilets; one-half of Soviet elementary schools have no central heating, running water, or sewage systems. The Rand Graduate School of Public Policy recently reported authoritatively that by any reasonable definition of poverty, 79 percent of the elderly in the USSR are in that condition. There are fewer automobiles per capita in the Soviet Union than among the blacks in South Africa. The Soviet Union, which spans eleven time zones and contains nearly 300 million people, has fewer miles of paved roads than California.

The problem is not the character and cultures of the peoples who make up the Soviet Union. The Soviet peoples are proud and talented, with rich histories and cultures. Its citizens desire peace and human dignity as much as any American, but the government that has set policy and their system have caused them problems and us concern over the years. It is that system which is under attack from within and which was fighting to maintain its place of power.

During one of our visits to Moscow, George Shultz told our ambassador, Jack Matlock, that he and his wife would like to free themselves from the negotiations one evening so that he could meet with independent intellectuals from different walks of life. Jack arranged a dinner at a cooperative restaurant, one of the few privately owned restaurants in the city. The group he assembled was impressive, as was their dedication to the idea of liberty. We were in a public restaurant, and all believed the KGB was someplace at an adjoining table listening to what we were saying.

Shultz suggested that each of the Soviets make some brief statement of experiences and aspirations for their country. The responses ran from a historian who said he was ashamed that the only history books he could depend on for accuracy were written and published in the West, to a poet who said he was in the United States in December 1979 when Soviet troops invaded Afghanistan and felt humiliated at what his government had done. The last Soviet participant was an officer in the cinematographers' union. He sat next to me, and in the course of his contribution mentioned a recent visit to Moscow by Sylvester Stallone, the motion picture actor, who was interested in producing a *Rocky* sequel in the Soviet Union. In an effort to sell his idea, he apparently offered to reshoot part of his last *Rocky* film, changing the ending so that the Soviet boxer rather than the American would win the bout. In response to our laughter as we listened to the story, he added: "Mr. Stallone did not realize that our audiences in the Soviet Union were rooting for the American to win!"

In a public statement while still in office, former Soviet Foreign Minister Shevardnadze said: "In what do we, who have the highest infant mortality rate in the world, take pride . . . who are you and who do you wish to be? A country which is feared or a country which is respected? A country of power or a country of kindness?" The new leaders of the Soviet Union are indeed fully aware of its problems. The failure of their system is compounded by the immenseness and diversity of their size. I am reminded that Charles de Gaulle once exclaimed in exasperation about the difficulty of governing a country whose people made and ate more than two hundred kinds of cheese. One can only imagine the difficulties faced by Gorbachev in governing a people with more than two hundred different languages and ethnic cultures. The Soviet leadership, furthermore, is also aware of our strengths, reflecting the vitality of our values and the healthy dynamism of our system.

Here, perhaps, is an explanation of why I have frequently found myself separated from the mainstream of American liberalism as it began to assert itself in the 1960s. While Communism was failing throughout the world and while our own system was proving its economic, social, and political success, I found growing resistance within our "new left" to the realities of Communist failure and disdain about our own system. It is disturbing that as recently as 1984, Harvard Professor John Kenneth Galbraith, a fine scholar and human being and an internationally known liberal spokesman, wrote that "the Soviet system has made great material progress in recent years" and that the system "succeeds because, in contrast with the Western industrial economies, it makes full use of its manpower." I unhappily have found American liberalism becoming more anti-establishment and more adversarial toward national patriotic values. Hostility toward spending for national defense became instinctive. This was a change from the spirit of Roosevelt, Truman, Stevenson, Kennedy, and Humphrey—the leaders I and America had come to identify with the true spirit of American liberalism: pragmatic, nonideologic, and patriotic.

I had begun to leave my pacifist moorings shortly after the end of World War II. The explosion of the nuclear bomb, dropped from extraordinary heights by pilots pushing a button without any physical or visual connection with the destruction and death caused by the bomb, was a vivid demonstration to me that pacifism, or nonviolent resistance to evil, was no longer appropriate in international relations. To this day, I believe in the power of love in interpersonal relations, but love directed toward the missile or the distant anonymous human being pushing the button would be useless. The alternative, therefore, once diplomacy and other steps short of violence fail to destroy or end the evil, is either submission to it or a reluctant use of force and violence to resist it.

In addition, I became persuaded by experience that the existence of military power and the readiness to use it serve to deter aggression and military adventurism—a belief that is anathema to pacifism and pacifists.

Finally, the decision by mainstream pacifist organizations to engage in political action by identifying themselves with what I considered to be irresponsible far-left positions and leaders antagonized and disappointed me. At a time when the ideas and values of Western democracy were gathering force in so many parts of the world, pacifist organizations seemed to be advancing the agenda of anti-democratic forces. That was my impression, even though I know that many pacifists would have been horrified at the thought, being so proudly preoccupied by the nobility of their motives and consciences. At a time when it was clear that the Soviet agenda was failing and its system was rotten to the core, pacifist organizations seemed to be emphasizing American policy as the primary obstacle to peace. There seemed to be no awareness of the reality that the peaceful resolution of disputes in so many parts of the world became possible only when Soviet policy began to change.

The theme of the political pacifist movement became "anti-anti-Communist." This seemed absolutely incomprehensible to me at a time when growing dissident movements in the communist world and challenges to Marxism-Leninism were all part of real and effective and important anti-Communist movements. It is reported that Armando Valladares, a Cuban Christian and Democrat whom Castro imprisoned for twenty-two years, was profoundly dismayed when he found that religious pacifists were not at all embracing him but seemed to be embracing his tormentors.

The identification of increasing numbers of pacifists and church organizations with attempts at "high politics" rather than the higher ground of morality has meant an important loss to society. An alternative to war as a means of securing peace with dignity when it is threatened is sorely needed. It isn't just that the pacifist movement, whose predecessors directed their moral and intellectual energies in that direction, has lost credibility, it is that society has lost the benefit of that higher morality. It remains vital to teach by words and example that love sometimes can overcome; that hatred destroys; that humankind, including the enemy, is one. These are historic pacifist goals, but they were lost in the noise of radical protest politics.

The Democratic party was influenced by the same destructive trends. I remember listening to New York Governor Mario Cuomo's speech at the San Francisco convention of the Democratic party in 1984. The convention crowd and the press were with him and he was indeed a brilliant orator, but I was convinced he had lost a large number of the voters and me. His compassion appealed to me, but the America he described was not an America that I recognized, or that I felt most Americans would recognize. He sought to counteract Ronald Reagan's emphasis on a united and healing America by depicting Ronald Reagan's America as callous and careless, drug-ridden, polluted, violent, declining, homeless, hopeless, insecure, intolerant, with neglected children and neglected aged. At least that was the message that came across to me. Cuomo was applauded by the new American left, but I felt that they and he had America all wrong. Whatever the inadequacies of the Reagan administration and its domestic policy—and I was sensitive and not blind to them—it seemed quite clear that the characterization was a grossly excessive one and our economy had grown stronger under Reagan.

A dramatic and most disturbing illustration of my dissatisfaction with the Democratic Party came in early 1991, when the party's leadership in the House of Representatives filled four of five vacancies on the House Intelligence Committee. One of those four was Representative Ron Dellums of California, who, I learned, had been a vocal champion of the violence-prone Black Panther Party in California; had publicly identified himself with the U.S. Communist Party newspaper, *The People's Daily World;* and had participated in the Moscow organized World Peqace Council, which, according to public Soviet sources, received 90 percent of its funding from the Kremlin. With the American invasion of Grenada, certain papers were captured linking the congressman and his staff with Castro and the Communist movement in Grenada. Dellums himself was quoted in 1980 as telling an audience in California: "We should totally dismantle every intelligence agency in this country piece by piece, nail by nail, brick by brick." To select him for membership on the important and sensitive Intelligence Committee was a clear illustration of why large numbers of Americans have lost confidence in the Democratic Party's qualifications to govern in areas of national security.

The increase in drug addiction and in homelessness is an American disgrace. But how can we ignore the fact that the homeless problem was clearly exacerbated by the "liberal" drive to push people out of mental hospitals where they belonged and where they could be medicated as needed? The *New York Times*, in a perceptive editorial (December 30, 1990) caught the essence of this problem in observing: "Most of the ragged, homeless people who create this sense of menace are not, first of all, homeless; their fundamental problem is mental illness."

A growing number of Americans find it obnoxious to be approached by homeless vagrants sprawling or begging on our streets. I, too, feel victimized by the "liberal" legal reform program that threw mentally ill people into the streets and led courts to outlaw city vagrancy and no-loitering ordinances. A community should be able to prevent people from sleeping on sidewalks, in hallways, or in public places, where they are frequently surrounded by filth and clutter. These homeless should be provided indoor shelters and required to use them rather than sleep in the street. Statutes can be clearly drafted to provide for public health, safety, and morals with sufficient clarity and precision to protect them from constitutional attack. Compassion for the homeless does not require ignoring the sensitivities or safety of the larger community. But there is a real homeless problem that must be directly addressed economically and socially. It is tied directly to the problem of poverty.

There is more poverty in the United States than most of us appreciate. Our society must deal with it decisively through strengthening our economy and our social structure. But we must also identify it properly. We should not ignore the official poverty statistics from the United States Census Bureau.* The report shows 31.5 million persons in "poverty," but other available statistics, according to the Heritage Foundation, fill out the picture with additional relevant data. These data tell us that 38 percent of those poor own their own homes with a median value of $39,200; more than 100,000 own homes with a value in excess of $200,000; some 62 percent of poor households own a car, with 14 percent owning two or more cars; nearly half of all poor households have air conditioning; and 31 percent have microwave ovens.†

Clearly, these figures should not blind us to the misery that affects too many poverty-stricken Americans, but exaggerating or distorting that problem does not help us to deal constructively with it. The fact of the matter is that a large number of our "poor" are better housed, better fed, and own more personal property than did the average American throughout most of this century. For an international comparison, using the same astounding but data-filled Heritage Foundation report, the average "poor" American lives in a larger house or apartment than does the average West European; eats far more meat; is more likely to own a car and a dishwasher; and enjoys more basic modern amenities, such as indoor toilets, than do West Europeans in general.

So much for statistics and averages. In human terms, however, the problems of poverty are appalling. The urban underclass problem,

* The Census Bureau counts as "poor" any household with a "cash income" less than the official poverty threshold in 1989 of $12,675 for a family of four. This income takes no account of assets and does not include welfare payments. The latter are estimated as more than $11,120 for every poor household.

There is great uncertainty as to the number of homeless in our country. For a long time we were told that 3,000,000 Americans are homeless each night. There was never a justification for that figure. One day last year the U.S. Census Bureau counted 250,000 homeless, clearly too low. The Urban Institute in a 1988 study came up with 600,000 as a maximum estimate. A number between 250,000 and 600,000 is probably a defensible estimate, and a disgrace.

† "How Poor Are America's Poor?" *Backgrounder*, September 21, 1990.

particularly as it relates to blacks in our country, creates social pathologies that stand in sharp contrast with the new opportunities that have opened for blacks to enter the mainstream of American life. Jesse Jackson has said that drugs are doing more damage to blacks than the Ku Klux Klan ever did. Glenn C. Loury of Harvard reports that in big-city ghettos, black unemployment often exceeds 40 percent. Large numbers are dropping out of the economy—not in school, not working, not actively seeking work. In the inner cities, far more than half of the black babies are born out of wedlock, and, government reports show, black babies are dying at almost twice the rate of white babies. Loury reports that black girls between the ages of fifteen and nineteen constitute the most fertile population of any group in the industrialized world. Only about one black student in seven scores above the fiftieth percentile in college admission tests due to inadequate early education. Blacks, whose life expectancy keeps declining due to homicides and AIDS, constitute approximately half of the imprisoned felons in the nation, and roughly 40 percent of those murdered in the United States are black men killed by other black men. Homicide is the leading cause of death among blacks between the ages of fifteen and forty-four.

Here is an unmet challenge to the leadership of our nation. There is no developing consensus, even within the black community, on how best to respond to this challenge. Some blame all of this on racism, a continuing disease but only a partial explanation. I am convinced that there must be a greater sense of developing self-reliance within the community itself. The values of responsibility, work, family, and schooling must be emphasized, but this too is only a partial solution.

Too many slogans surround the political argumentation and analysis of this problem. It is obviously important to broaden and strengthen the black middle class. We must, of course, seek new ways to lift people from poverty. Government alone is inadequate, and so is inner self-help and discipline. Our country has always accepted the reality of social support. This has been one of the foundations upon which our society has strengthened itself. J. Kenneth Blackwell, former mayor of Cincinnati, now U.S. ambassador to the UN Human Rights Commission, points out that whether we are talking about "barn raising, field clearing or quilting bees, Americans have banded together to help one another since frontier days."* This has also necessarily come to include government involvement in the process. An agenda for

* "Strengthening the Social Pillars of the Black Community," speech delivered for Black History Month to the Heritage Foundation, Washington, D.C., February 27, 1990.

progress in dealing with the underclass is going to cost money. Plugging the holes of the social net we erected to keep people from becoming unduly victimized by economic and social pressures must be supplemented by an emphasis on business development, business ownership, and home ownership.

In that connection, demographically we are probably on the way to a labor shortage and a shortage of skills in our work force. A broad national consensus is required to develop government and private programs that emphasize self-reliance, remove the crutches of government dependency, and stimulate the values of responsibility and cooperation.

I have been troubled by the continued, albeit declining, racism in the white community, but also by growing racism in the black community. "Black" is no more a justification for entitlement than "white" is a justification for privilege. White racism, ugly as it is, is in general disrepute; black racism is too often unassailed and rarely challenged, with some "experts" ludicrously arguing that, by definition, blacks cannot be racist. Witness Jesse Jackson's frequent flirtations with anti-Semitism and the obsequiousness displayed toward him at the 1988 Democratic party convention. Witness too the growing acceptance among the established black leadership of Louis Farrakhan and his Nation of Islam, who was crowned with respectability with an invitation to speak to the Congressional Black Caucus in spite of his constant virulent anti-Semitism.

The continued existence of an "underclass," accompanied by the drugs that are decimating that segment of our people, threatens the future stability of our society. I am not a bit pleased that our society, in recent years, seems to be impotent in meeting the urgent needs of our people and our country, foreign as well as domestic. Our roads and bridges and waterways need work. We have far to go to protect our environment. We do not adequately help our cities or conduct an effective war against drugs. We do not help Eastern Europe as much as we should. We have an urgent need to improve our education and stimulate our research and development. Our mental hospitals are in terrible shape. We have law observance and law enforcement problems. In many ways, our country is in a state of disrepair.

We are the richest country in the world, but we refuse to mobilize the resources available to us. We have too long been paralyzed by the rash pledge that our leaders would not raise taxes or levy new taxes. To a large extent also, we are simply unable to mobilize our will to begin a necessary national renovation program. We have the capacity to deal effectively with our remaining problems once we have the national will and the national leadership to do so. The American people are inclined

I have had the opportunity since 1980 to see the evolution in Europe through the eyes of an active participant in the negotiating and political process. Secretary of State James Baker asked me to further observe and contribute to that evolution. In June 1990, I headed the American delegation to a Conference on the Human Dimension under the Helsinki Final Act, which took place in Copenhagen. It was a thrilling contrast to Madrid. We formulated a code of political behavior designed to perpetuate the concept of democracy and the rule of law throughout Europe. We agreed on specific details of how to assure and encourage an independent judiciary, fair trials, free and fair elections, political pluralism, and the development of political parties.

We agreed on legal principles, making clear that the state was bound by law and that laws were not merely instruments of the ruling group in society. Democracy and the rule of law, all thirty-five countries asserted, were fundamental to security, stability, and peace. All the countries participating in that meeting, including the Soviet Union at the time, agreed that the best way to assure stability, security, and peace among nations was to perpetuate open political competition through political parties and free elections, all of which would function under broad protections of law.* These principles were reaffirmed and

---

administer a congressionally mandated program aimed at strengthening the role of free media in the emerging democracies of Europe.

* On June 29, 1990, President Bush issued the following statement from the White House:

> Last May, in a commencement address at the University of South Carolina, I identified free elections, political pluralism and the rule of law as the cornerstones of freedom and urged that they be enshrined among the principles of the 35-nation Conference on Security and Cooperation in Europe (CSCE). I am pleased to report that this morning, the 35 nations of the CSCE Conference in Copenhagen adopted a document laying precisely that foundation for freedom. I commend the United States delegation under the direction of Ambassador Max M. Kampelman for its major role in that historic achievement.
>
> With the Copenhagen Declaration, the CSCE has sought and reached an historic new consensus. The nations of Europe, along with the United States, Canada and the Soviet Union, have now committed themselves to the path of democracy based on justice, peace, security and cooperation. The promise of the 1975 Helsinki Accords now has become a program of democratic action. This is the most significant step forward that the CSCE has taken since the inception of the Helsinki process.
>
> This program of action has been shaped and embraced by our NATO Allies, the neutral and nonaligned European states, the Soviet Union, and the emerging democracies of Central and Eastern Europe. It brings together nations large and small and opens the house of democracy—the commonwealth of free nations I have spoken about—to all of Europe's peoples. Together, the CSCE signatory nations now stand before their own peoples and before the world community on the solid ground of shared democratic values. Together, we now must put our program of shared democratic action to work, fulfilling the promise of a Europe whole and free.

strengthened at a Geneva CSCE meeting in July 1991, dealing with the problem of national minorities in Europe, which I also had the privilege of participating in as head of the U.S. delegation.

It took a failed military coup for Gorbachev to cease his political meandering between reformers and traditional communists, but he now seems to pursue programs for political pluralism and the rule of law under democratic principles. The society is in turmoil, and an important Soviet legal official told me that he looks on this new legislation as carrying out a principle under which everything would be permitted except that which is specifically prohibited—in sharp contrast to the old order under which all was prohibited except that which was specifically permitted by law. This brought to my mind a statement made by Dr. Sakharov, describing the old order differently: "Previously everything was prohibited, even that which was permitted by law." Let us hope the Soviet Union will not retreat to that method of governance. Its people deserve better—and so does the world.

I am convinced that within every age, the drive for human dignity has been present. In some ages, it has been more dominant than in others, but the struggle is a continuing one. In our day, the drive and the possibilities for attaining human dignity for ever-increasing numbers of people are great, but there is backsliding, and there will be more. It would be a mistake, furthermore, to believe that the end point of humanity's ideological evolution has been reached. Certainly, the universalists were wrong to have that belief at the time of the French Revolution and it would be narrow for us to assert that Western liberal democracy, desirable as it is, is the final form of human government.

My personal religious convictions lead me to believe that human dignity and freedom in government are consistent with the evolutionary struggle to attain godlike dimensions. For me, this is what our ancient scholars and teachers meant when they said that we are made in the image of God. For me, this is a religious truth arising out of the contributions made by the ancient Hebrew tribes when they asserted that there was only one God, for it is this contribution that gives rise to the concept of human brotherhood, the basis for political democracy. Nevertheless, I am convinced that vigilance is continually required.

Aristotle taught us that all forms of government, including democracy, are transitional and vulnerable to the corrosion of time, new problems, and missed opportunities. We are at risk if we remain smug and content about our present strengths and the weakness of our adversaries. For all that, our political objectives are consistent with the drives and direction of our evolving civilization. That should give us strength and confidence as we prepare to enter the new worlds ahead.

When we are growing up, we are taught not to be afraid of the dark. It is my conviction that as our world evolves, in this moment of history so pregnant with hope and the promise of a free and decent tomorrow, we must not be afraid of the light and where it can take us.

FINIS

(to be continued)

Index

Aaron, David, 291–92
ABM Treaty, 310–11, 311n, 319, 320n, 335n, 341n, 345–48, 347n, 358, 364–65, 368
Abrahamson, James, 343–44
Abrams, Elliot, 362
Adelman, Carol, 213–14
Adelman, Kenneth, 213–14, 317n, 327–28, 335, 359
Afghanistan: and the Geneva Summit, 324; and the Geneva talks, 353–54; and the Madrid talks, 232, 235, 236, 239, 244–45, 258, 259, 268, 273–74, 275–76, 280; Soviet peoples' reaction to the invasion of, 376
Akhromeyev, Sergei, 320n, 335–36
Albright, Robert, 148
Aldrich, Betty Mae, 53
Allen, Barney, 67
Allen, Richard, 233, 252–53
Altman, Milton, 125
Altman (Eddie) family, 11, 16
American Civil Liberties Union (ACLU), 55
American Communist party, 34n, 58n, 111–17, 112n. *See also* Communism
American Federation of Labor (AFL), 34n, 71
American Federation of Teachers (AFT), 71

American Historical Association, 262
American Jewish Committee, 181–82, 212
American Jewish Congress, 181–82
American Law Students Association, 37
American Political Science Association, 161–62
Americans for Democratic Action (ADA), 29n, 69–70, 81, 87, 91, 93n, 108, 111, 136, 188
American Student Union (ASU), 29, 37, 122
Amsterdam, Birdie, 19, 19n
Anderson, Ann, 243
Anderson, Eugenie, 53n, 67, 67n, 81, 83–84, 176
Anderson, William (Bill), 72, 74, 74n
Andreas, Dwayne, 137, 164, 167, 173n
Andreotti, Giulio, 313n
Andropov, Igor, 266
Andropov, Yuri, 266, 269, 273n
Angermueller, Hans, 180–81, 182
Anne (Queen of Romania), 283–84
Anti-Defamation League, 181–82, 212
Anti-semitism, 63–65, 93, 174, 183–84, 222n, 230, 236, 261n, 382
Appleton, Shelley, 38, 38n
Arabs, 181–82, 191–92, 205, 209–12
Argov, Chava, 190n
Argov, Shlomo, 190, 190n